THE CALL OF THE MINARET

The Call
of
the Minaret

KENNETH CRAGG

A GALAXY BOOK

NEW YORK   OXFORD UNIVERSITY PRESS   1964

© Oxford University Press, Inc., 1956
First published as a Galaxy Book, with corrections, 1964
Library of Congress Catalogue Card Number: 56-8005
Printed in the United States of America

TO

HENRY HILL

AND

GEORGE FRANCIS GRAHAM-BROWN

IN

GRATITUDE.

OURS, surely, is an age that more than any other multiplies words. In print and speech, press and radio, we use them in great quantity. But perhaps the quality of intention in the words we use was never less. Many of them, at any rate—unlike coins—lose value in the frequency of their currency. By using as we do we impoverish the used. The quantitative more becomes the qualitative less. Perhaps too many of us are too far away from our language origins, from the meanings of our fathers and the classical worlds beyond them. We have become too often insensitive to the feel of the history in words, the history that makes a dictionary so great a fascination when we go to it for more than spelling and pronunciation.

This book, however, has to do with a very few words, whose long reiteration has not dulled their import, the ceremony and sanctity of whose context has saved them from the debasement of a common frequency. They have been hallowed by their proper mission and are as distinctive in their own realm as the minaret from which they sound.

The two-score words of the muezzin are an imperative invitation in which Islam summons itself to its faith and practice. In them the Muslim is confronted with his own vocation, while the listening outsider learns what shapes and makes Islam. For those within and those without, here is the articulation of the meaning of the mosque. The call of the minaret is perhaps the best single

vii

epitome of Muslim belief and action. To seek in it the clue to Islam, and from that clue to learn the form and dimension of Christian relation to what it tells, is the purpose of this book.

The English word "minaret" belongs, like its Arabic original *Manārah*, to the realm of light, not of sound. But firetowers and lighthouses had a prominence and a vantage, as beacons, that readily suited them to become citadels of the beckoning voice of religion. The vocal function has long displaced all aspects of the old, except the name. But the analogies of one realm are easily transferred to the other. What the minaret proclaims truly illuminates the system that produced it. In its most gracious architectural forms, it arrests the spectator and gives sharp, vertical relation to all that, stretching horizontally around it, it commands. The imperiousness of its contour visually is likewise the quality of its occupant. It is the haunt of a voice, the voice of one crying.

Both imaginative and practical reasons thus combine to make the call of the minaret and the expression of Islam synonymous. He best serves the latter who best heeds the former. This book is one man's effort after an interpretative study of what the muezzin says, an effort inspired by the obligations belonging to Christian conviction—obligations, that is, of awareness, witness, and concern. Some will say that such obligations will disqualify objectivity—a point which is further faced in Chapter vi, within. No study, however, can either begin, or end, *in vacuo*. It may be that Christian commitment, with its proper concern for the significance of God and man, is a surer context for the study of Islam than the type of "science" that knows only how to inquire and not how to worship. Whether this is true, not an author's preface, only the reader's epilogue, can say. All that can be recorded here is the ambition for understanding.

These pages owe much to the stimulus of Muslim friendships and associations through some fifteen years, and to such access to contemporary Islam as the apology of numerous Muslim writers, in Arabic and English, could afford. Academic duties in the Islamic field at the Hartford Seminary Foundation, Hartford, Connecticut, have helped to shape and test some of the conclusions or suggestions that follow. More immediate inspiration to

viii

try to set forth the substance of these chapters came from the fellowship of the Seminar for Islam that has been active for many years, in connection with the Near and Middle East Committee of the National Council of the Churches of Christ in the U.S.A., and which has met in New York, Princeton, Hartford, and elsewhere in the East of the United States. Its members are in no way responsible for the form or the argument of this work but they have contributed to its genesis and debated many of its conclusions. My gratitude for all I owe them and for all other debts, tangible and intangible, without which all authorship would be either failure or folly, is here sincerely recorded.

When the muezzin refers to his *Ādhān,* or call to prayer, he often speaks of it as *Hādhihi-l-Daʿwat al-Tāmmah,* "this perfect summons," "this complete call." Because Islam is ultimate and entire, the invitation to it is something that cannot be improved. But the adjective has also to do with achieving and accomplishing. The vocation is at once perfect and to be perfected. The Muslim is challenged, so to speak, to become what he is. It is just this sense of something to be achieved which also strikes the Christian hearer of the minaret. To give shape and definition to this sense is the intention of the third part of this book. For to be aware of the full measure of Islam and to be committed to all the meanings of Christ is to be summoned to a large duty. The call of the minaret to Muslim prayer becomes a call for the Christian to exacting tasks. He must first learn and then attain, by God's grace, an authentically Christian relation to the mosque and its world. This is indeed, as the muezzin says, an inclusive invitation, an engrossing business, that will spare none of the resources of the Spirit. It may almost compel him on occasions into the language of the guards in *Hamlet:*

> Sit down awhile
> And let us once again assail your ears,
> Which are so fortified against our story.

But at length it must bring the Christian on beyond those areas of conscious otherness into an intimacy of attained interpretation, where Christ is made known to the heart of the muezzin's faith. In this area of its purpose this book invites the reader not merely to an exposition, but to an adventure. Only in such terms could it do justice to "this inclusive call."

I have followed what seem to me proper patterns in the transliteration of Arabic words. *'Ain,* final *hamzāh,* and long syllables have been indicated. Where no *waslah* was involved I have indicated a *ta marbūtah* with an English *h.* But where, as in *Zakāt* and *Salāt,* it is preceded by a long syllable, I have preferred a *t.* The spelling of names and terms almost inevitably involves a somewhat arbitrary decision here and there, since one has to decide whether a word is irrecoverably Anglicized like "Mecca," or can be held to an Arabic form, like *Al-Tā'if.* Opinions are bound to differ on such points. To me *Makkah* is tediously pedantic. On the other hand, outside geography, I have tried to be exact, avoiding those unhappy spellings, "Mahomet," "Koran," "Moslem," and the like, which have too long distorted Arabic and confused outsiders. It is surely part of courtesy to describe people and books as they describe themselves, apart from the more pressing reasons of sound scholarship. Words not italicized of Arabic origin, like "shaikh" and " 'ulamā'," "Sunnī," "Shī'ah," and "Sufism," I have considered sufficiently English to warrant this. Italics are employed where terms are considered technical, as *Sharī'ah* and *Ijmā'.* It is hoped that the context makes the sense of such terms sufficiently clear without a glossary. Where the adjective "Muhammadan" occurs, it refers strictly to what concerns the person of the Prophet, as in "Muhammadan revelation." The word has no proper meaning as a synonym for "Muslim." The abstract from it ought not to exist. "Islam" is the proper and sufficient substantive for the faith it describes. Where "Tradition" is capitalized it refers to the total *corpus* as a source of law, in distinction from an individual "tradition." Considerations of cost have made it necessary to eliminate the points indicating heavy consonants in transliteration. I have allowed myself a certain option in transliterating the Arabic letter *ya* by a *y* or an *i* as in *Wahȳ* or *Jāhilī.* If this offends the purists, I am sorry. To venture into print about so searching a theme as ours is to give the critics so wide a field that perhaps a few little cavils will not matter.

For this book is meant as a humble invitation to a great invitation. Its title tells what it would constitute, as well as what it would describe. And the one because of the other. Can we so become aware of Islam as to enter into all its implications for the Christian? Since that ambition and the pages that here serve it must always turn upon the wide compassion of God, they may perhaps be prefaced with the most inclusive of all Muslim invocations: "In the Name of the merciful Lord of mercy."

July 1956   Kenneth Cragg.
Hartford, Connecticut.

CONTENTS

PART I

THE CONTEMPORARY SETTING

i

ISLAM SINCE 1945

NINETEEN FORTY-FIVE may seem altogether too near a date from which to assess the contemporary situation in the Muslim world. Perspective is usually a prerequisite of sound judgment and a decade is nothing in the evolving story of so vast and massive a reality as Islam. But when the date is not too strictly enforced, there is merit in its closeness, if only because it serves to measure the speed and inclusiveness of contemporary change. Since the year of Hiroshima and Nagasaki, the year in which World War II ended and the uncertain "atomic" peace began, manifest changes have occurred within Islam, gradual no doubt in their genesis, but dramatic in their issue. If historians must wait longer to set them into focus, servants and lovers of men must act within them by what light they can discern in advance of history's sober exposition. For the living present passes beyond the range of our opportunity before it is fully known. Our action must be within the perspectives open to us now as men of Christian purpose. This does not absolve us, however, from evaluating as best we may, in the immediate flux of events, those facts which history will identify as the gist of this century.

In the last decade almost the entire world of Islam has come into political self-responsibility. It may be ironical that this independence has been reached at a time when circumstances created by science have made it an anachronism, bringing as they do the

3

new compulsion to interdependence. None the less independence, in so far as it can continue feasible, has arrived almost everywhere, to gratify and consummate the hopes and efforts of more than half a century. How far is 'Abdal-Nāsir's Egypt from Lord Cromer's! Through successive installments it has passed from tutelage to independence, and from independence to final foreign evacuation—1922, 1936, 1946, 1954. Round the corner of the eastern Mediterranean, Lebanon, Syria, and Iraq have several dates that celebrate their independent status, occasions marking the stages of the retreating West, from the outset of the Mandates to their final termination. But the consummation falls within the last decade—the fruition of hopes often deferred and passions long thwarted.

The concurrent emergence of Israel compromises and embitters the Arab sense of achievement and remains a territorial and spiritual frustration to Arab ambition. The entail of the fact of Israel in every realm is the supreme test of Arab nationhood in this century. But the immediate point is that, for all its provocative quality, Israel has not impeded the arrival of Arab Muslim nationalism. Indeed the depth of Arab resentment over Israel is the measure of how far the Arab world of the Versailles Mandates has come since it languished under the heel of Sultan 'Abdul-Hamīd II. It has grown to independence in interaction with its bitterest problem. But it has grown: and the evolution finds Baghdad and Damascus, old seats of empire, capitals, with Amman, of new Muslim national expressions. Northward Turkey has transformed herself from an overgrown and unwieldy empire into a vigorous, modern, secular state, with a virile nationhood and a new perspective.

Even more arresting changes await the observer when he moves eastward and southward to Karachi and beyond, where over 60 per cent of world Islam is located. Here the two most populous Islamic nations, Pakistan and Indonesia, have come into existence since 1947. Partition on the basis of religious predominance proved to be the solution of the dilemma created by the recession of British power. The finally determinant factor in that solution, it is clear, was the insistence of Muslims that it should be so. Pakistan, therefore, is the most eloquent and compelling witness to the Muslim sense of separate identity and of the validity of Islamic nationalism as the contemporary form of its expression. The seventy million Muslims who followed Muhammad 'Alī Jinnah in the enterprise of Pakistan had traveled far from the days of Sayyid Ahmad Khān and his Anglophile attitudes of the eighteen-seventies. They were also a far cry from the Jinnah of the nineteen-twenties with his insistence on a united India. When the evacuation of the British Raj was no longer a distant aspiration but an impending reality, Islam in India took urgent counsel of its own genius and elected for Pakistan, despite the necessity of excluding from itself what remains the largest "minority" in the world—the thirty-five million Muslims of Nehru's India.

In the even more populous Dutch East Indies the same decade has seen the same phenomenon—emergence to nationhood of a new and growing Muslim expression. Divergencies in its Muslim parts continue to harass its orderly development, as they do also in Pakistan, where a constitution was long unagreed. But these are the growing pains of new life. They are the travail of the present that intends a future. No one mistakes the finality of the Dutch departure. Governmentally, educationally, linguistically, the new self-responsible status is absorbing or shedding the Dutch past.

Elsewhere throughout the household of Islam the same pattern is apparent. Libya became an independent power at the end of 1951, likewise the Gold Coast, arguing further recessions of colonialism in West Africa. Nigeria anticipates self-government in 1956 and the Anglo-Egyptian Sudan awaits the climax of a transition period leading into complete responsibility. If we except a few scattered and relatively small territories like Aden, and the large half-known segment of Islam in Soviet Russia, almost the entire community of Islam in the world has arrived at independence. Of the three territories of French North Africa, Tunisia and Morocco are moving to varying degrees of political self-expression. It can hardly be that Algeria will remain permanently exempt from a pattern of change which everywhere else is discernible.

5

II

A decade, then, may be a short time in human history but it is long enough to witness self-responsibility as the great new political fact of almost all Islam. With that fact go many important consequences, both intellectual and material. The situation seems to many minds like a recovery of the positive values of the Islamic past and a reversal of the reversals of the eighteenth and nineteenth centuries. When the statue of Queen Victoria was removed from a public thoroughfare in the new Karachi and assigned to a corner of the city museum, the citizens assuredly did not intend any calculated scorn. Indeed, as Professor Toynbee testified in *The World and the West,* relations, personal and institutional, between the people of the sub-continent and the British have been steadily improving since they became equals. What the Pakistanis meant was that history had come through an aberration and recovered the main highway of a proper Islamic course. For the community of the final and ultimate religious faith for mankind must necessarily also provide the truest political order and demonstrate how human existence should be organized and controlled. Such a people can only conceivably be subjected to alien authority by a temporary coincidence of events, by some accident of historical forces making an interlude of deviation. Just as the Qur'ān reader continues to recite an abrogated verse of the Qur'ān to remind himself of the mercy of God in the change, so the new present may keep in mind the immediate past in its gratitude for the living resumption of the essential self-sufficiency of Islam.

We do well as observers to recognize this deep sense of vindication, as well as of new opportunity, in the Muslim attitude toward recent changes. But in one important particular the new Muslim world is in marked institutional discontinuity with the old. The Caliphate is no more. Suppressed in 1924 by the new Turkey, efforts to resuscitate it have been fitful and inconclusive and the decade we have in immediate view has done nothing to renew or inspire them. No serious Muslim opinion appears to expect the revival of the Caliphate, not only for lack of agreement on an individual candidate, but for the more important

6

reason of its seeming impracticability in today's world. Yet for thirteen centuries, the Caliphate was considered indispensable to the existence and continuity of a valid Islam.

Some observers, like Muhammad Iqbāl, the Pakistanī poet-philosopher,[1] have loosely compared the changes implicit in the termination of the Caliphate to the Western European Reformation on its political side. The comparison is a tempting one though it needs all the caution due to such generalizations. It is, however, clear that Islam has been moving in the last decade through further stages of a twentieth-century experience which does resemble some of the features of European history four centuries earlier, except that the pace of change is vastly more bewildering. To estimate these changes against their longer background may be our best path into an understanding of the world of today's muezzins. Their total significance involves a variety of new dimensions, new problems, and new attitudes which must be briefly reviewed. In each case we can discern a similarity to the slower moving experience of Europe without attempting to do justice to all the differences. If we consider these elements in the context of one decade, no reader will forget that the waters of the river have come from far upstream.

III

When the nation-states of Western Europe broke out of the imperial, papal world—a process which can be noted as early as Joan of Arc with her doctrine of France for the French—this political change proved coincident with many other changes widening the horizon of man and so transforming his mental environment. There was Columbus as well as Henry VIII, Copernicus as well as Luther—pioneers of new dimensions of human life. Steadily the "nations" discovered themselves in unfamiliar ways. Inventiveness, arising both from new propensities and new ambitions, slowly undermined the static features of the feudal world. The development of gunpowder transformed the arts of war and diminished the value of feudal forms of security. The urge to wider voyages in new directions caused men to stumble upon new America on their way to the old India, an accident of purpose—if the phrase may be permitted—due in the

7

negative sense to the great Muslim land barrier on the eastern route. Great new horizons thus opened before the spirit of man and he equipped himself steadily with a great new range of instruments wherewith to investigate and possess those regions. The horizons themselves receded in front of his advance until they opened into the vast, awesome perspectives of this atomic age.

Muslims of the same contemporary context have come into its process of change at a greatly accelerated pace. The opportunity to digest newness which the sixteenth- and seventeenth-century European enjoyed has been far less gradual for the twentieth-century Asian. The newness, more concentrated in its nature, is also more urgent in its impact. The accumulated results of processes of industrialization and technology, stemming from modern science, have pressed upon older societies so as, in some cases, to link Abraham with Henry Ford. Societies, already preoccupied with national "growing pains," are also summoned to grapple with issues of law, custom, and security resulting from vast economic and technical changes parallel to the political. Just as the spirit of Columbus transformed the vast ocean from a forbidding limit into the promise of a highway, and as Copernicus shattered the old earth-centered astronomy with its comfortable suppositions, so the twentieth century, spilling its manifold legacies over the older world, confronts its multitudes with totally new vistas of life and of meaning.

Consider the phenomenon of the Arabian-American Oil Company set down in the world of Eastern Arabia, and grown into a vast enterprise of oil exploitation since the end of World War II. Formerly the region had changed little in the continuity of an immemorial past. Sparse tribal populations, governed and ordered according to ancient custom, eked out a precarious semi-nomadic existence in the area, while pearl-diving and coastal trade with Aden and Zanzibar constituted the only connection with the world outside Arabia. Such central authority as existed in the whole peninsula represented the most conservative, Wahhābī ideas of Muslim continuity. When that authority re-established itself in the first decade of this century in the spectacular capture of Riyad by the late King Ibn Saʿūd, few could have

8

dreamed that the new leader would meet in Egypt two score years later with the two protagonists of Western civilization, Roosevelt and Churchill, as himself a figure of world significance, or that his long reign would leave the old hearth-land of Islam fabulously wealthy in oil revenues. Yet such is the saga of the house of Saʿūd.

The story writes itself not only in the names of the great but also in the lives of the humble. Bedouin and townsmen in considerable numbers have entered the employ of the Company or have found steady livelihood in subsidiary enterprises arising from its presence or its initiative. New projects are being developed—roads, railways, irrigation, preventive medicine, and commerce. New skills are learned accordingly and practiced for high and constant wages, replacing an economic form of life which was hitherto precarious and primitive. New attitudes are discovered as the new wage earners encounter the cinema and the radio, with novel methods of leisure-recreation and a new dignity, or dimension, in personal living. These accelerating changes influence more than they yet include and penetrate in repute where they do not yet penetrate in fact. The present generation has moved further than a whole score of its predecessors. One of the largest groups of Americans resident on non-American soil can hardly be set down in so static a territory without pointing many parables of technology and opening new vistas to watchful, wistful minds. These are the new horizons of the contemporary scene. An Aramco employee familiarizes himself and his context with new and incisive notions about man and his technical potentiality to make his habitat serve his needs; about a money economy and its advantages; about a society in which women and marriage are governed by other concepts, where leisure, literacy, comfort, and security replace the old perpetual struggle and the old uncertain life.

If other examples lack something of this spectacular quality, it is not because they are less inclusive or less radical. There is a steady and perceptible change in the lot of the fallāhīn. Peasant poverty, disease, and ignorance are still massive. But some state lands have been distributed among the landless in Iran and a

9

start has been made on the long and arduous road toward the liquidation of Egypt's extreme social inequalities. The peasant in Iran, the Arab states, Egypt, and the Sudan is the clue to the deepest questions. And the peasant of today is not the peasant of fifty years ago. His expectation of life is somewhat longer; the suffrage may have come his way, in some cases almost too often; a governmental village center may have entered, if still tentatively, into his agricultural and personal problems. Modest at best and still pathetically insufficient, these measures of social concern for all their paucity are the promise of what can be. Without them the peasant's existence is one unhappy treadmill of "todays" in which the capacity to think of a future beyond the next meal is all but non-existent. The dimension of existence, a little here, more there, is beginning to widen. Like the inhabitants beside the moving frontier of American history, the oppressed populations in many parts of the world are coming to be sensitive of a new summons waiting to be answered, new possibilities calling to be tried. The people who were formerly ignored by pashas or forgotten by governments now have revolutions accomplished in their name. Justice and equality may be hardly less remote. But it is something that they are evoked as goals. The village may be still largely what it was, but the city is much nearer and the world much more intrusive. Where illiteracy still insulates the mind, mass radio undertakes to inform it. What is generally called "the cold war" might better be described as "the shadow war." For everywhere in Asia and in Africa there is a struggle in the shadows about what external order and inward spirit can most surely actualize the aspirations of the multitudes. If there is appeal in Communism, then there must be meaning in its criticism of the old and expectancy toward its offer of the new. It is well, therefore, not to minimize or misread the outlines of hope in the shadows of discontent. For when discontent succeeds apathy, there is a new dimension.

It will be our duty below to turn to specific forms of Christian ministry within this discontent. The argument here is its existence as, in intensity and range, a new phenomenon in the Muslim world. In recent Muslim literature, both Arabic and

Urdu, there are poems, essays, and novels vigorously expressing this social discontent. The old Quranic saying that God does not help a people until they help themselves is assuming new importance as a call to transcend the apathetic. Fatalism was never characteristic of Islam at its best, but, to judge from the strictures of its reformers, attitudes that might be so described have too often blunted its initiative and atrophied its will to change. But those days are proclaimed ended. The creation of Pakistan as the condition of an Islamic social ideal; the revolution in Egypt with its philosophy of work and discipline; the Ataturk legacy in Turkey as an example of drastic and successful surgery—all these and many less spectacular efforts vindicate in contemporary Islam the obedience of a new dimension and response to dynamic impulses.

> My ringing cry has urged along the road
> The throng that lost their way upon the plain . . .

wrote the poet Iqbāl.

> The soul of Persia [he went on] moves at my song
> The caravan moves on, my call is strong:
> Out of my restless spirit the flames start.
> In the East's bosom I have stirred a heart.[2]

If it is not always easy, especially in translation, to know precisely what the poet meant, and if the reconciliation of his meaning with historic Islam must remain dubious, the enthusiasm of Pakistan for his memory and the volume of comment on his ideas make it clear beyond doubt that he has become the spokesman of something deep within the contemporary soul. His self-imposed vocation as a pioneer is confirmed by his posthumous authority. The age then must have felt its need of him. If the Arab Muslim world has not hitherto produced an Arab counterpart, that fact need only be understood as indicating Iqbāl's uniqueness in a role for which the Arab mind makes different provision. It would be wrong, in any event, to equate a single poet with a great faith. There are areas of Islam where Iqbāl is entirely unintelligible. Yet he is witness, as surely as were Columbus or Francis Bacon, that times change.

11

IV

New possibilities then, resulting from economic development and intensive Western technology bring new aspirations in the population and these in turn mean a new participation and involvement in affairs. Muslim nations share in the shaping of international politics. They helped to inaugurate the United Nations at San Francisco and compose a sizable and distinctive "bloc" at the U.N. in New York. All this is in strong contrast with the scant influence of Muslim delegations at Versailles in 1919-20. The widely respected Foreign Minister of Pakistan was recently appointed to the World Court at the Hague. Muslims have been represented, with other Asians, in positions of key importance in world organizations.

More important still is the new dimension of individual life as it reveals itself in Muslim literature and life. Assumptions of a more static time no longer keep men in familiar roles. The social sources of national leadership are changing—witness, for example, the revolutionary Junta in Egypt entirely replacing the former pasha-politicians, whose class once enjoyed almost complete monopoly of "parliamentary" politics. Former schoolmasters find themselves cabinet ministers and private soldiers of two decades ago may become present heads of state. This is not to say that leaders like Sa'd Zaghlūl have not risen to eminence in the past. But the fluidity of today is more remarkable. In his autobiography, the late Dr. Ahmad Amīn, a notable literary figure in Egypt, recalled the circumscribed social patterns of his father's generation. The elder Amīn was a shaikh and a lover of Arabic calligraphy. His life revolved exclusively around mosque and school. He lived in the strict disciplines of his religion. A newspaper he rarely read: politics played no part in his thoughts or actions. The British in Egypt, when he thought of them at all, he regarded as part of the will of God, and as such beyond his questioning. He ruled his household with a strict and patriarchal law, prohibiting his wife from leaving the house without his authority and never seeing his children except to give them studies or hear their Quranic recitation. His only concession to "modernity" was that he believed in the education of his daughters. He died in 1925. Three decades later it would be rare to find in Cairo a similar figure maintaining with like severity the familiar patterns of the old Islamic world. The generations before him had been full of such.

How contrasted is the politically conscious student generation of the present day! The student in politics had grown to be—until the very recent advent of military regimes—an often crucial factor in Arab politics. Perhaps the student was all the more vocal because the influence of wealth in politics thwarted more constructive pathways to a political career. But the attitude that regarded the Western "imperialism" as a Divine providence has long since disappeared. Though the organs of political consciousness are far from finally established in the Muslim world, there can be little doubt about the growth of the thing itself. As in the Western "renaissance," men are less inclined to accept as sacrosanct the old allotment of status and place. Leadership in many walks of life is liable to pass into unlikely hands. The leading scholar is no longer necessarily the Azharite, nor the influential lawyer the learned in the *Sharī'ah,* or religious law. In all fields of education and scholarship there has been an emergence of lay leadership and the prestige of the religious custodians of authority is proportionately diminished. A Pakistanī writer of repute, Kemāl A. Fārūkī, has lately made a plea for a change in the qualifications traditionally required in a *mujtahid,* or one fitted to exercise intellectual initiative in framing Muslim public opinion. He regards status in the community, reputation for integrity in commercial relations, honorable success in life as a whole, as better criteria than abstruse learning in theology and a meticulous knowledge of the minutiae of Arabic grammar and legal lore.[3] His ideas are significant. The prolonged nature of Pakistanī constitution-making may be explained by the fact that so many interests demanded a part in it. This development may complicate affairs, but it argues a new participation for many whose counterparts in an earlier time would have been inarticulate and passive.

V

Nowhere is this so evident and so far-reaching as it is in respect of the women of the Muslim world. When Mrs. Doria Shafīq and other feminist leaders with a thousand followers besieged the Egyptian parliament, complaining that its representation ignored half the nation, they were voicing a notion which would have seemed to most of their parents, of both sexes, and to all of their grandparents preposterous and absurd. Few indeed were the champions of women's rights in Muslim countries when Qāsim Amīn in Egypt at the very beginning of this century wrote his *Emancipation of Woman* and *The Egyptian Woman*. His ideas are now widely recognized and applauded. Though some elements are still fighting a rear-guard action in the name of the old concepts of woman in Muslim society, the main victories seem to be assured. Pakistan, Indonesia, and Syria, among Muslim states, have already granted women's suffrage and the first has appointed women as ambassadors.

The electoral and political aspects of this change are not, however, the most consequential. Changing ideas of marriage are reflected in new developments in the sphere of the home. The often young, always illiterate, brides and mothers of former generations, whose orbit was the inside of a house, are giving way to the more educated and mentally vigorous wives and mothers of today. They tend to marry somewhat later and to enjoy their husbands more exclusively. It becomes increasingly general to interpret the Qur'ān's allowance of four wives on condition of equal treatment as a virtual prohibition of more than one. Whatever may be thought of the exegesis, the result is highly desirable. What a popular Egyptian Muslim author called "the unused lung" is more and more coming into action, to the benefit of the body social and national.[4] For the home is in the end the nursery of the state and the school of the race. In enlarging the dimension of her own world, the Muslim woman is widening the potential of her own society for the better.

It has become the practice of late in many city mosques to install amplifiers on the minarets, which carry the muezzin's recorded voice more widely than of yore. There may be aspects of the change that argue cause for regret. But at least it is certain that the world below the minaret is now a world of larger dimensions and the voice for prayer has further to penetrate. The generation of today is more distracted, more preoccupied, than those of yesterday, thanks to science, industry, and education, to new remedies and new aspirations, to new bewilderments, habits, and demands. Perhaps the new medium may be seen then as a symbol of the new dimensions.

VI

That the external changes introducing the modern age in the West posed immense problems is familiar enough. Many of these found no immediate solution. Historians have noted interesting delays and diversities in the progress of basic ideas in different realms. Many of the features of Islam at mid-century may likewise be regarded as various stages of incompleteness in the patterns of change. The paragraphs that follow have no hope of being exhaustive even as a catalogue, still less as an exposition of these problems.

There is first the political problem. The Caliphate, as we have seen, is terminated, and separate national expressions have replaced it. But nationalism may exist under a variety of institutional forms. What is the true form of the Islamic state? Should it be avowedly Islamic so that non-Muslim minorities do not share altogether equal citizenship? Are democratic forms to be followed irrespective of their practical results? Should representation of the people result in legislative assemblies with absolute lawmaking powers? Or should there be some tribunal to pass upon the Islamic validity of legislation? If so, how is that tribunal to be constituted and reconciled with the representative principle? Should there be necessary religious qualifications, like mosque-attendance and almsgiving, as prerequisites for the right of suffrage? How are constitutions to be squared with the divinely given in revelation? All these questions have been vigorously debated in Pakistan during the six years' existence of the Constituent Assembly. They have also inspired much Muslim Brotherhood activity and writing in Egypt and Syria.

Then there are the questions relating to the actual working

of political systems. Experience since the nineteen-thirties indicates that the party system, so successful in the Anglo-Saxon world, lacks important conditions for effectiveness and vigor in the East. The economic realities justify the fear that democratic processes may not be productive of stable and honest government. While there is no doubt that Islam is "democratic" in that it proclaims that earthly power stands under law—Divine law—and is instrumental to a purpose greater than itself, there is much in Islam to call in question the assumption that it is "democratic" in the sense that it believes in the people as the final arbiters of that purpose. "Government of the people, by the people" is hardly the political philosophy of the Qur'ān where the science of government is in some sense "theocratic." Thus indecision, experimentation, and a search for the answers are everywhere apparent from Indonesia to Damascus.

Alongside these issues of a political nature are questions of law and jurisprudence. Almost all the countries of the Middle East have completed far-reaching changes in their civil and criminal law in the last two decades. Only in the realm of personal status—family, marriage, divorce, inheritance, and wardship—has the old legal order of the *Sharī'ah* maintained itself. Even here modifications have been made which in Egypt are quite revolutionary. Beginning with Turkey in 1924, Muslim countries have in varying degrees rewritten their Islamic law on the model of Western codes, French, Swiss, Italian, and British. The early antecedents of these changes may be found in the Ottoman Mejelle of 1869, which codified some areas of law, and in the example and influence of the Consular (later the Mixed) Courts, which supplied the pattern for a reorganization in 1883 of the national courts in Egypt. But these nineteenth-century measures were limited in comparison to the major legal changes in all the successor states to the Ottoman Empire after 1920, as well as in Iran. The greater range and clarity of the Western codes have served to bring judicial procedures to a sharper precision and a more ready efficiency.

It is not only the substance but also the basis of these adopted codes that is significant. The Muslim *Sharī'ah* was followed because it was divinely legislated. Now it finds itself accommodated to, superseded by, or at best co-existent with, provisions and precepts of wholly alien origin. In the eyes of the old conservatism to erect the man-made and the extraneous into law as binding as the Divine is to commit *Shirk*, or association, since the human is exalted to the status of the Divine. The sanction of law is no longer the decree of God but the will of the state.

In the case of Turkey, of course, these scruples were of no weight. Ataturk intended to be brusque with the past. When the preamble to the Swiss Code, which he was borrowing, referred to "approved doctrines and tradition" as a proper area of appeal if the judge found the Code or customary law silent, Ataturk feared the phrase might leave a loophole for reactionaries. He, therefore, substituted "scholarly investigations and judicial decisions." In Egypt, however, the new civil Code finally promulgated in 1949, provided that in the case of silence or obscurity in the articles, the judge should have recourse to Muslim law, and in default of that to "principles of equity." This provision is in marked contrast to the Turkish deletion. In either case, however, there are far-reaching innovations in both content and spirit. The various codes differ in their selectivity vis-à-vis their Western sources. But this only means differing degrees of the displacement of the old *Shari'ah*. The justification of these measures, according to modern opinion, is that they are necessary because changing times have made changes imperative, and that Islam is a progressive allegiance in "the spirit," not a slavish bondage to the letter.

The argument from necessity is more convincing than the argument from freedom. For there can be little doubt that the conservative is theoretically right in resisting what is un-Islamic in its origin. On the understanding of a thousand and more years that it derived from revelation, Muslim law cannot suddenly and blandly affirm that its true basis is pragmatic, prudential and worldly-wise. Nevertheless time compels modification, adaptation, and enlargement. The modern mind is right in its instinctive awareness that Islam must either baptize change into its spirit or renounce its own relevance to life. Since it cannot do the latter it must somehow do the former. But the problem goes very deep and the debate is, therefore, sharp. What is the valid form of the *Sharī'ah* today and how is its validity identified?

VII

Many of the changes which pose this legal question belong to the economic realm. Here also Islam is confronted with far-reaching problems to which the answers are being sought in new expressions of the old doctrines. Self-government means obviously national pride. Nationalism generates the resolve to demonstrate self-sufficiency. Islam must show itself capable for the solution of twentieth-century problems. New commerce, modern finance, joint stock banking, capital investments, and foreign trade send the Muslim economist back to the Quranic meaning of usury, profit, and property for direction.

There is the pressing problem of population, since numbers are growing in almost every state and are seriously taxing existing, or prospective, resources in several, notably Egypt and Pakistan. A sharp struggle between quantity and quality exists in Egypt where the pressure of numbers is overtaking the increase of crop acreage and general productivity. Some observers see little prospect of success in maintaining even existing standards of living for a population estimated at thirty-three million by 1975. According to official figures of the Egyptian Ministry of Agriculture, the population increased by 121 per cent between 1867 and 1952, while crop acreage from the same date to 1947 increased only 35 per cent and only 1 per cent between 1947 and 1952. It is increasingly apparent to many Egyptians that solutions have to be sought in limitation, in the conscious preference of quality of living, to quantity, in the family. In Pakistan likewise there are not a few minds seeking the answer to poverty and social distress in the same direction. The optimistic may urge against them a sanguine—or perhaps heedless—philosophy. But meanwhile the pressures grow.

There can be little doubt that the consciousness of this situation poses far-reaching religious questions for serious minds. There is the haunting fear that family limitation may be an unwarranted interference with the Divine will—an attitude which could, of course, disqualify inoculation and even surgery in sickness and plague. There is the traditional Muslim conviction that to marry is to fulfill half of one's religion and that the family ought to be large, since marriage fulfills itself in offspring. It may be that the growing emancipation of women will lead to new attitudes in this respect, as women acquire other social roles beyond childbearing and as monogamous marriage becomes normal. Yet it is doubtful whether the effect of such silent changes will be either prompt enough, or large enough, for the problem as it is. When the muezzin in the minaret calls his hearers to their true welfare—*Hayya 'alā-l-falāh*—there may well be searching of heart as to what the good of society demands of the Muslim in this vital area of conduct. The resources of Islam in its teaching on the social order, as well as the duty of Christian ministry in this context, will be taken up below. The Muslim world as a geographical expression may be full of empty places, but they are not where or what they need to be to provide a solution for areas of population pressure. It is from the inner travail of self-responsibility, serving the new nationalism, that this contemporary problem must be met—unless the solution be to leave it with God. And even then, there will be the question of what He intends in returning it to us.

VIII

Those resources of social teaching reflected in the muezzin's appeal are put on their mettle also by a further new issue, about which some Western commentators on the Muslim world are so glib that they are able to speak of nothing else. The problem of Communism has become a matter of supreme political preoccupation since 1945—the year the Soviet Union emerged from war with vastly extended territories and a new authority in world affairs, the year Japan was defeated and the stage was set for the Communist triumph in China. A glance at the map indicates that the Soviet and Muslim worlds are everywhere contiguous, from the Balkans to Afghanistan, and where they are not Islam is a large factor in the struggle over Communism—not least in Indonesia. Astride the frontier of the two worlds are several minority groups, Kurds, Azerbayjanis, and the like, while within the Soviet Union itself are twenty or thirty million Muslims.

Beyond these obvious points of physical or racial adjacence to Communist Russia are deeper facts: the intellectual appeal of Communist philosophy, the economic and social challenge of Communist doctrine and practice. It may be safely said that Islam under the test of Communist pressures in all realms is an Islam facing a totally new summons. In that sense Muslims of this generation are in a position unique in their history. None of their predecessors since the rise of the faith have had to contend with so vigorous a challenge on so many fronts. The quality of response which Communism evokes, and the doctrinal resources of Islam out of which the response must be made, will concern us below, together with the forms that apology, active and written, has so far taken. We content ourselves here with the recognition of Communism as a great new factor in the Muslim obligation to Islam. For Communism refuses to be ignored and avenges itself on those who fail to take its real measure.

We need to beware of vulgarizing our estimates of its significance in the contemporary Muslim scene by assessing it solely in terms of whether or not this or that country can be brought into the orbit of alliances for our security. What matters ultimately is not bases, defensive or otherwise, in others' territories, but truth and righteousness in their hearts. Cultures in the end can only be defended inwardly and of themselves. Their frontiers may perhaps be held by dint of alien force—alien force which may ward off Communist force but is no barrier against Communist thought. We need, then, to see Communism as an inward summons to the Muslim mind and will and to concern ourselves therewith. This means more than estimating Communist party membership above or under ground. It means more than labeling every restless stirring as Communist intrigue. Selfishness, especially when it is afraid, is a poor hand at diagnosis.

What, so considered, are some of the basic problems that Communism poses for the Muslim spirit? The need for a new alertness to the evils of capitalism, a rediscovery of Muslim teaching as to the validity and obligation of property, an assessment of the appropriate Muslim forms of social justice, an investigation

20

of its own history for guidance from the past, are some of the issues. Underlying these are questions of human nature and its attitude to the community and to the good. Communism, with its brutal insistence on the necessity of class warfare prior to the dispossession of the possessed, and its doctrine of the inevitability of violence in social revolution, compels the honest mind to question whether it is enough to say: "X—a religious culture—has what is needed, if only it is followed." For Communism is amused, not satisfied, with exhortation. When we begin to pursue the question and turn serious attention to why it is that the perfect law—whose provisions make a state of affairs where Communist strictures can find no targets—does not actualize the perfect society, indeed never has actualized such a society throughout its historical existence as a revealed law, then it is that the Communist compels us into attention to the mystery of human nature and human recalcitrance.

How do we actualize the good society or obey the good law? How in other words do we come by good men? We cannot face Communism with any evasion in our hearts about this issue. The role of human nature in politics, in economics, in society at large, as the crucial factor in social justice and cultural health, is more and more engaging the attention of Muslim thought. "The good that I would I do not, and the evil that I would not that I do . . . O wretched man that I am who shall deliver me?" St. Paul's impassioned cry is the final term of this problem when it is transferred from the general to the personal. Precisely because of its cynicism about any "good" not physically and politically compelled, and its superficiality in supposing that the "evil" is inherently economic and not human, Communism forces this whole tremendous issue upon our hearts.

It is no injustice to great Muslim thinkers on man's sin and the psychology of temptation, like Al-Ghazālī, to say that the cruciality and urgency of this problem is new in Islam. It is a familiar notion that Islam is optimistic and sanguine in its estimate of human nature—that it is far less radical and incisive than Christianity. Man's sin is weakness and forgetfulness, rather than defiance and rebellion. Today, however, the criticisms by

21

Communism of the social order and its ridicule of "religious" solutions force the Muslim mind to more searching thought about man and his remaking.

In some quarters a passionate nationalism would seem to be the answer to personal selfishness. But, aside from the danger that a national selfishness is a worse, because a bigger, menace, there is the doubt as to whether patriotism alone can always and adequately discipline the "egos." In his illuminating *The Philosophy of the Revolution,* Egypt's leader 'Abdal-Nāsir describes the disappointment experienced by the Junta after they had, as a vanguard, fulfilled their mission and dethroned Fārūq.

> Endless crowds showed up, but how different is the reality from the vision . . . If I were asked then what I required most, my instant answer would have been "To hear but one Egyptian uttering one word of justice about another, to see but one Egyptian not devoting his time to criticising wilfully the ideas of another, to feel that there was but one Egyptian ready to open his heart for forgiveness, indulgence and loving his brother Egyptians."

Personal and persistent selfishness was the rule of the day. "The word 'I' was on every tongue." [5] Out of this sense of undoneness and chaos the Army officers felt compelled to remain in power, insisting that otherwise they would gladly have returned to their staff colleges. That decision was one form of reaction to the need. It is the recognition of its existence which is here important. The remedy must necessarily go beyond any leadership, for leadership itself can so readily succumb to the temptations it bewails. It must go also beyond politics, even beyond ideology as such, into those regions where men and nations are made and remade. All societies in the world are wrestling in some form with this problem. All that might usefully be said about the loss of old values, the rediscovery of new ones, the stirrings and aspirations, the hopes and fears of contemporary Muslims, is somehow comprehended in the mystery of this old saying from the minaret: "Come ye unto the good?" But how?

IX

The twentieth century as it is distilled into the last decade is rife with new attitudes. They are implicit in all that has been noted already. The Pathan tribesman in the Khyber Pass region who begins to enjoy the convenience of electricity in his remote homeland, where lamp and firelight have reigned for centuries, is clearly involved in several. Likewise is the citizen of Jiddah who could pick up from his newsstand after April 1954 the first weekly illustrated magazine in the history of his country. The writer browsed in an Ankara bookshop in July of that year among the Arabic texts of the classical authors. Outside were multicolored printed posters advertising air trips to Mecca for the pilgrimage. To cross the threshold on leaving was to step across half a millennium. New attitudes, then, are legion. But there is point here in trying to assess a few of the more significant.

Among the familiar features of the European Renaissance were the growth of independence of authority in law and letters, the diminution of the "clerical" influence in state and education, the emergence of novel claims to cultural independence of dogma. These tendencies were sometimes dramatic but also always gradual. Many similar novelties can be observed in Islam in our time. The educational monopoly of ancient institutions like Al Azhar in Cairo, Al Zaitūnah in Tunis, the Qairawiyyah in Fez, and centers like Deoband in India has been curtailed if not terminated. The process, of course, stretches far back to Ahmad Khān in India and Muhammad 'Abduh, among others, in the Arab world. Western institutions, Catholic and Protestant and secular, have also played their part. The modern universities of Cairo (two), Alexandria, Damascus, Ankara, Teheran, Karachi, Dacca, Hyderabad, and elsewhere, with many others in embryo development, represent the apex of great new state educational systems which reach down in varying degrees into the whole population, rural and urban. Thus the old mosque dominance over education, with its grammatical and theological emphasis, is almost everywhere broken. New studies, scientific and technical, have become familiar to scores of thousands of stu-

23

dents. With the new scholarship go new attitudes of mind and new preoccupations, as well as new skills—the former loosening the grip of religious concepts on the mind, the latter giving the graduate a more remunerative and often more desirable role in the community. The religious graduate, learned in the older disciplines of exegesis and the law, is liable to find himself a less esteemed, perhaps less significant, member of the community. The old is, therefore, on the defensive against the new, and this fear of its own partial redundancy is itself a new, or relatively new, trial.

Kindred changes can be seen in the attitudes to authority and tradition generated by scientific education. These are not everywhere militantly secular as they were so noticeably in Turkey. Drift, indifference, bewilderment, or just preoccupation characterize the secular Muslim, rather than hostility. Many Muslim writers have criticized the mosque personnel and have noted the tendency of shaikhs and 'ulamā' to be unaware of, or unsympathetic to, the spirit of the age, and their incapacity, in many instances, to meet, with ease and equanimity, the challenge of the cross-currents of thought and opinion.

The old allegiances have lost for many their sacrosanct authority. There are senses in which religion tends to become a cultural expression rather than a theological conviction. This does not argue any diminution—but only a change—in the authority of Islam. Consciousness of history, of community, of political and social distinctiveness, continues to be vigorous. It is alert in its self-defense, without always fulfilling, or even respecting, the obligations inseparable from the old piety. To speak of liberalism perhaps confuses more than it illuminates since the term can have so many meanings. But there can be no mistaking the leavening of new attitudes to life, to authority, to creed, and to outward forms. Old institutions like the pilgrimage and Zakāt receive new interpretations. The quality of this generation's Islam differs subtly from that of its predecessors. In terms of freedom and openness it may be a difference for the better; in terms of piety and discipline, for the worse.

Evaluation, however, is not our purpose, but only description. The new sense of the right of scholarly criticism has produced a few—but only a few—incursions into areas of dogmatic sensitivity. A few authors have suggested new lines of Quranic interpretation or new accounts of matters *de fide*. But theology in Islam is far behind all other academic disciplines in hospitality to new attitudes. None the less there is discernible, for example, a tendency to understand the Qur'ān in terms of religious genius in Muhammad, making him the conscious literary architect of its contents, hitherto understood as wholly God's revelation. Where theological sensitivities are not involved, Muslim scholarship is busily engaged in the critical understanding of Islam's long history.

Perhaps one feature of this newer outlook may be singled out here for reasons which will be obvious. It is the increasing readiness of some Muslim leaders of thought to engage in friendly and equal debate with other religions, especially Christianity. There have been significant occasions of late where Muslims and Christians have met together for discussion. The Muslim impulse is connected with the belief that Islam epitomizes the best in all religions. The more willingness there is to hold this belief seriously and with due reference to its tasks of research and study, the nearer will Muslims come to understanding those other faiths from within. While it would be foolish to ignore the strong tendencies to isolation of mind in some Muslim quarters, there are these contrasted attitudes of new interest and colloquy. They are a striking departure from the long traditions of prejudgment and rejection in respect of Christianity.

Another aspect of the changing temper derives from the impact of scientific procedures everywhere in the world. Applied technology is liable to create a profound sense of the apparent omnicompetence of men. Drainage clears swamps and eliminates mosquitoes and malaria; aerial surveys may forestall locust plagues and with them famine and disease; inoculation banishes smallpox and new techniques produce better crops and serve public nutrition. Wells can be sunk to transform the desert and steps taken to prevent erosion. Space is annihilated by speed and the lot of man transformed by medical skill. The modern hospital becomes a perpetual wonder of human potentiality in the understanding, the treatment, and the conquest of physical foes and ills.

All these, and a hundred other, tendencies of scientific mastery make their happy, yet often disconcerting, way into the minds and lives of man—as the village clinic opens, a mobile cinema visits, or an airplane flies overhead. These revelations are profoundly new to people habituated to disease as inevitable and inured to hardship, bereavement, and poverty as part of the very stuff of life. Unsophisticated Islam is accustomed to a sense of the immediacy of Divine will bearing directly upon all the events and vicissitudes of life—a baby's blindness, a child's dysentery, a cow's death in calving. Then it appears that these disasters are preventable, that trachoma need not happen or tuberculosis prevail. Much that was regarded as the Divine order comes to be seen as human ignorance. There happens a slow recession of the sense of God, imperceptible perhaps, but real. It is a dangerous time. The omnicompetence of men is illusory since it arises only from submission to the secrets of nature. It is as servant that man is succeeding. A new understanding of the relationship of the Divine will to human affairs has to arise—a relationship which leaves room for the valid operation of other wills in genuine, if limited, freedom. Such understanding cannot be attained overnight. But meanwhile, the mentality that relied on charms, taboos, superstitions, and ritual securities has been transformed. Always we have to reckon not simply with the material works of the scientific age, but with the presuppositions that underlie them and the mentality they generate.

Reference to this phenomenon should not, however, obscure from any reader the fact that vast stretches of Muslim humanity are only slightly affected by technology. It would be folly to suppose that the rural world in Asia and Africa is anywhere but at the beginning of what scientific solutions can do for its needs. Any illusion on that score can be dissipated, for example, by a perusal of *Anatolian Village* by Mahmut Makal—a remarkable description of poverty in rural Turkey.[6] Nevertheless, as those solutions do widen, travel, and multiply, experience should teach us to look for the familiar pattern of their impact on religious belief.

26

X

All the foregoing does not exhaust the new attitudes in Islam today. Arising out of them are two contrasted reactions, both of which are in certain senses new. Professor Arnold Toynbee, in *Civilization on Trial* has familiarized us with the idea of "Herodian" and "Zealot" attitudes to alien pressures.[7] There is the instinct to absorb and find compatibles: there is the instinct to reject and affirm distinction. Applying the contrast to Islam we find there are tendencies that reconcile Islam with the new, welcoming it, with some discrimination, as "Islam," and tendencies which express loyalty in antagonism. The two have to be pursued into the understanding of the past, where they both claim to find their justification. There is no space in this context to illustrate either outlook fully or to indicate the varieties that exist within each of them. What matters here is the newness in both of them. The "progressive" feels himself grappling pioneer-like with a new destiny. The "defensive" is conscious of a critical duty new in history. Islam has been in danger before, he knows, but never quite so searchingly. He feels a vocation to serve continuity, just as his opposite number does. They differ in their understanding of what continuity involves.

We hear many voices affirming the Qur'ān's interest in science. Nature, said Muhammad the preacher, is to be contemplated and wondered at. This means empirical science, with its investigating curiosity. Knowledge, whether it be of prophetic lore or academic learning, is to be pursued, even though the seeking take the student as far as China. Science and true religion have no conflict since the Islamic doctrine of *Tauhīd* (unity) proclaims the unity of truth. The two disciplines, science and religion, differ only as to method. A notable Rector of Al Azhar, Shaikh Mustafā al-Marāghī, when asked about the Qur'ān and science, answered:

> True religion cannot possibly be in conflict with true science: and when we are positive of the truth of some scientific proposition which seems to be in conflict with Islam, it is because we do not properly understand the Qur'ān and tradition. We have a universal doctrine of

27

our religion which states that when an apodictic proof is in conflict with a revealed text we must interpret the text allegorically. Besides the Qur'ān was revealed in the Arabic tongue which as you know is quite elastic.[8]

Thus the faith is regarded as entirely compatible with modern learning and Islam can very properly be at home therewith, since it was itself the matrix of medieval science and has long traditions of tolerance.

But this concept still does not reconcile the liberal and conservative attitudes. For the practice of liberal scholarship may lead into conflict with established dogma. The former then demands that there must be no limits to its range of enquiry; the latter requires that certain areas are *de fide* where innovation is heresy and intrusion unwarranted. Such a collision happened in the case of the doyen of Egyptian letters, Dr. Taha Husain, in his discussions of pre-Islamic poetry in 1927.[9] Though he now affirms his conviction that the battles of academic freedom have all been won, there has been a marked tendency to refrain from asserting it in certain sensitive areas, such as the literary study of Quranic sources.

Yet whether defensively meant, or conceived as progressive, the new attitudes are there—new in their sense of the bigness of issues and the fluidity of the times. Nothing since its origin has faced Islam, as the twentieth century has, with exacting obligations for the shape of its future. Variety, debate, and controversy are to be expected within a living entity set in the swift flow of events and charged with a rich heritage. New attitudes toward authority and new interpretations of past legacies are bound to generate, to evoke resistance and so to shape change and continuity alike. It is a sign of the vitality of the world over which the call of the minaret is heard that there should be so many voices sharing in its interpretation and claiming to formulate the appropriate response.

XI

There is one final consideration about contemporary Islam into which we are now led. The pressure of all that is new, within and

28

without, raises in the last resort the question of the definition of Islam. Change is the context and continuity is the theme of the story. But when at any time in history we bring together these two, continuity through change and change with continuity, we are faced with how the one is validated and the other controlled. How is essential continuity recognizable as such? What are the limits of valid change? Who is to define and who enforce them? At what point must we say that change has become destructive of continuity with the old, that the old, in becoming new, has ceased to be itself? This problem which Newman, in his day and situation, called the problem of development belongs to all faiths. It amounts to the question of self-definition. Islam is involved profoundly in such a question at the present time.

It may be retorted that historic Islam is readily recognizable and that there is no problem of identity—belief in the One God and Muhammad as His Apostle. Yet a revered Muslim expounds Islam without a single reference to the Prophet.[10] One writer devalidates what another asserts, both in the name of Islam. A doughty champion of Islam in Pakistan, Abū-l-'Alā Maudūdī, is in prison following street riots over his demand that a sect of "Muslims" be declared heretical—a group which itself prohibits intermarriage with, or the use of the same mosques as, the orthodox.[11] A Muslim Prime Minister visiting the United States equates Islam with democracy and decency in a sense which would make valid Muslims of those who had never learned how to perform the prayers.[12] Examples need not be multiplied. There is nothing unique to Islam in this situation. All traditions know it if their history is long. But its application elsewhere does not make it any less a Muslim phenomenon.

Finally, then, "Islam," as a term and as an entity, is capable of receiving and does receive new meanings. In the diversity of the modern world "Muslim" may be a variable description. Some features of this fact will be taken up later in Chapter VII, "The Call to Understanding." For understanding and sympathy are certainly required. There is much in the situation which resembles for some minds the oft-quoted comment of John Donne on the seventeenth-century scientific destruction of the "universe" of medieval thought:

> *The new philosophy calls all in doubt. . . .*
> *'Tis all in pieces, all coherence gone.*

There speaks the voice of apprehension, which fears for its familiar beliefs and conjectures the loss of all, the voice which, as in the Muslim Brotherhood,[13] calls out for renewed assertion and strives again to organize the present in the form and likeness of the past. It is a glib misunderstanding to dub such attitudes "terrorist" and "fanatic" despite the methods they may be tempted to employ. They are fundamental protests against change seen as peril and adaptation felt as disloyalty. They are the attitude of mind which cannot find the old reality any longer in the new meanings.

But the new meanings persist and develop. The ancient faith somehow disciplines them in its own way and rebukes the fears of its loyal devotees, though perhaps not till the generation has passed that knew the fears. In the strange but inextricable interaction of the faith and the faithful, the ethos and the participant, Islam and the Muslim, the valid changes are digested and the essential continuity maintained. If the course of the process is sometimes obscure, the fact of it must be known and understood. To miss it would be to disqualify oneself from the assessment of what Islam is both continuing and coming to mean for Muslims in the twentieth century.

And so let us follow a typical muezzin in his ascent of a typical mosque in the audience of typical Muslims—if such a combination can be found. To what is it that he is calling the faithful, as with his fellows across five continents he reiterates through the five prayer hours of every day the ancient summons to Islam? At least in the words he uses there is unbroken continuity since first the pattern was formed. Whence come they and whither return? What do they proclaim and accomplish in their going out and their coming in? Here, with slight variations in the number of repetitions are the familiar sentences:

> God is most great, God is most great, I bear witness that there is no god except God: I bear witness that Muhammad is the Apostle of God. Come ye unto prayer. Come ye unto good. Prayer is a better thing than sleep.

Come ye to the best deed. [This phrase among Shī'ahs only] God is most great. God is most great. There is no god except God.

NOTES *to Chapter I*

1

The adjective "Pakistanī" is, of course, historically inexact. But "Indian" is now misleading and "Indo-Pakistanī" cumbersome. The relation of Pakistan to Iqbāl certainly warrants his being described as a Pakistanī, though he died nine years before its formation.

2

Iqbāl, Muhammad, "Payam-i-Mashriq," stanzas 141, 142, translation of Arthur J. Arberry, *The Tulip of Sinai*, London, 1947.

3

Fārūkī, Kemāl A., *Ijmā' and the Gate of Ijtihād*, Karachi, 1954.

4

Khālid, Khālid Muhammad, *Min Hunā Nabda'*, Cairo, 1950. The phrase is the title of the fourth chapter.

5

'Abd-al-Nāsir, Jamāl, *Falsafat al-Thaurah*, Cairo, 1954, translated for Public Affairs Press, New York, under the title *Egypt's Liberation: The Philosophy of the Revolution*, 1955, pp. 33-6.

6

Translated by Sir Wyndham Deedes, under the title *Anatolian Village*, London, 1954, being two Turkish works, *Bizim Köy* and *Köyumden*, Istanbul, 1950 and 1952. Mahmut Makal is a young schoolteacher whose writings have made an unusual impression. See below, Chapter VIII, pp. 219-20.

7

Toynbee, Arnold J., *Civilization on Trial*, New York, 1948, Chapter 10.

8

Quoted from Habīb I. Kātibah, *New Spirit in Arab Lands*, New York, 1940, p. 186. The author recorded these views in a conversation with Shaikh al-Marāghī, who subsequently approved the version here quoted.

9

His original work, *Fī-al-Shi'ar al-Jāhili* (Pre-Islamic Poetry), Cairo, 1926, was re-issued under the title *Fī-al-Adab al-Jāhili* (Pre-Islamic Literature), Cairo, 1927, with some of the more controversial passages omitted or modified. The main points involved were the historicity of the link between Abraham and the *Ka'bah* and the validity of the traditions concerning poetry usually regarded as antedating the rise of Islam, but considered by the author as post-Islamic. This second "deviation," though emphasizing the originality of Islam—and indeed doing better justice to it in many respects—called in question sacrosanct attitudes and affected hallowed arguments as to the matchlessness of the Qur'ān.

10

'Alī, 'Abdallāh Yūsuf, author of a noted English verse translation (Lahore, 1937) of the Qur'ān. The pamphlet referred to had the title *Fundamentals of Islam* and was published in Geneva, 1929.

11

The Qadiānī Ahmadiyyah Community, more fully discussed in Chapter IX (see note 2 to that chapter). On the riots of March 1953, see *The Report of the Court of Inquiry . . . into the Disturbances of 1953*, Lahore, 1954.

12

'Alī Khān, Liaquat, *Pakistan, the Heart of Asia,* Cambridge, Mass., 1951, pp. 11-12, 32-3 *et al.*

13

Founded in Ismā'īliyyah, Egypt, in 1928, by Hasan al-Bannā. See Al-Husainī, Ishāq Mūsā, *Al Ikhwān al Muslimūn*, Beirut, 1952; and Heyworth-Dunne, J., *Religious and Political Trends in Modern Egypt,* Washington, 1950.

PART II

MINARET AND MUSLIM

THE USE OF THE PHRASES *of the Call to Prayer as a basis for a simple presentation of Islam has much to commend it. For prayer, in whatever sense the term may be used, is the recognition and expression of a relationship, and such a relationship between God and man Islam emphatically is. The* Adhān, *as Muslims name the Call—from the same verbal root, which gives us our Anglicized "muezzin"—contains the basic creed of Islam. "There is no god except God and Muhammad is the Apostle of God." It uses the all important word "I bear witness" upon which the issue—Muslim or non-Muslim—turns for every man. To confess this confession, with intention, is to be a Muslim. And further in the inclusive word* Falāh *to which, in and through the prayer, the Muslim is invited lies an epitome of the essence of Islam as a communal allegiance, a social order, and a religious experience. Variously translated as "salvation," "well-being," "good," "welfare," and "cult," it stands, not for an experience of redemption from sin, but for a state of spiritual and social "prosperity"* brought about by pardon and obedience to God's revealed law in the state of Islām, or submission. It, therefore, serves as a comprehensive concept within which we may describe the Islamic order for human society. In this way all the central doctrinal and practical aspects of Muslim religion can be suitably considered under the muezzin's guidance.

There are other considerations also. The Adhān supplies a welcome principle of inclusion and exclusion. In so rich and diverse a theme as Islam, the would-be expositor may easily be bewildered by the quantity of his material and be tempted to perhaps unsound criteria of what he should treat and omit. Moreover, the subject is beset with prejudices and can so easily be provocative of unproductive controversy. It may perhaps be possible to demonstrate at least the will to positive relationships with Muslims if a Christian writer keeps close to the pattern of the mosque's own summary. There is also the fact that seemingly this path of exposition has not frequently been followed in the many manuals, small and great, which have been published about Islam. The most useful of these, listed in the notes and bibliography, must be consulted by the reader who intends a more comprehensive history or analysis than these pages can offer.

But the final reason is what Pascal might have called "a reason of the heart" and is calculated to appeal to the imagination—that source and spring of the active understanding. We do not merely aim at a résumé of Muslim belief and practice. We take it in its own most intimate and inward imperative because we seek to know it, as far as may be, from within. We wish to hear at the minaret what it is which greets every rising sun and salutes every declining day for millions of contemporary men, and thus to enter with them across the threshold of the mosque into their world of meaning. For it is a world which deserves to be penetrated with understanding and for which, as we believe, there is endless significance in another world of faith, whose trustees we are and whose interpreters we would become.

What then does the minaret say to the Muslim?

ii

GOD—THERE IS NONE SAVE HE

لا اله الا اللّه

IN THE Muslim confession of God there are seven syllables and six occurrences of the *l* consonant. LĀ-ILĀHA-ILLĀ-ALLĀH. The first three of the *l*s are what the phonetics writers call "clear" dentals. The second three are "dark" alveolars for which, as Gairdner says, "The tip of the tongue comes back and touches the teethridge, and at the same time the back of the tongue is raised towards the back of the soft palate or velum." A heavy sound is then produced which, if not unique to the Divine Name, occurs there most notably.

If the reader is alarmed at this linguistic beginning he will relent on recalling that the muezzin is our theme. There is a quality about the authentic pronunciation of the first clause of the Muslim creed, which impresses itself upon every sensitive hearer. The "clear" consonants run into the emphatic final syllables of the word *Allāh:* the latter cast their force forward into the consonant of the particle "except" (*illā*), and the result is a kind of powerful climax which matches the emphasis of the sense. It is true, of course, that the diction of many muezzins is raucous and strained and that the Divine Name often loses its forcefulness in certain grammatical or other situations. But there can be no mistaking the insistent and incontrovertible character of the affirmation within the utterance. No English rendering

35

quite captures the Arabic enunciation of the Muslim witness to God. "Lā ilāha illā Allāh."

It is for this very reason that we avoid in all that follows the use of the Anglicized *Allāh*. It is so far from its Arabic original, when pronounced with a thin English consonant and feeble vowels, that many an Arab Muslim would find it unrecognizable. But more important, there have grown up associations with the English usage of *Allāh* that are sentimental, having to do more with melodrama than theology. These should be shunned. There may also be the idea in the user's mind that in referring to God in Islam as *Allāh* he is distinguishing that Deity from the God Whom Christian English denotes. When the word *Allāh* is intentionally used in this way it raises a serious implication we wish here to reject.

Since both Christian and Muslim faiths believe in One supreme sovereign Creator-God, they are obviously referring when they speak of Him, under whatever terms, to the same Being. To suppose otherwise would be confusing. It is important to keep in mind that though the apprehensions differ, their theme is the same. The differences, which undoubtedly exist, between the Muslim and the Christian understanding of God are far-reaching and must be patiently studied. But it would be fatal to all our mutual tasks to doubt that One and the same God over all was the reality in both. Those who say that *Allāh* is not "the God and Father of our Lord Jesus Christ" are right if they mean that He is not so described by Muslims. They are wrong if they mean that He is other than the One Christians so understand. The source of the confusion of thought encountered here is that to say who God is necessarily goes beyond saying that He is. If men agree on the second what they say relates to the same theme or subject, even though they differ markedly as to the first. No faith or believer, of course, can say *that* God is without being involved to some degree in *what* He is. But unless there is radical inconsistency within the very concept of existence itself as applied to God—the sort of difference which does not obtain between Muslim and Christian—they are speaking of the same subject. Perhaps we put the matter concisely if we say that predicates about God may differ widely but that God as the subject of differing predicates is the same subject.

Before, however, leaving the Arabic term *Allāh* in order to keep to the English equivalent God, we must investigate its precise literal meaning. The Arabic form *ilāhun* meaning "a god" is similar to the Hebrew and Aramaic words for deity. When used with the definite article *Al-Ilāhu* meaning "The God" the *l* consonant of the article coalesces with the same letter in the first syllable of the word eliding the *i* sound to make *Al-lāh*. If we take the word to be of genuine Arabic form this is the obvious origin. If, as some scholars believe, the word does not have this origin but is historically derived from a sister language, its significance is the same. *Allāh* means "God" with the connotation English achieves by dismissing even the definite article and using the capital letter—a device which Arabic lacks.

It is clear from the negative form of the Muslim creed, "There is no god except God," that the existence and lordship of *Allāh* were known and recognized in pre-Islamic Arabia. The Prophet's mission was not to proclaim God's existence but to deny the existence of all lesser deities. The fact that Muhammad's own father bore the name 'Abd-Allāh, slave of God, demonstrates that God was known by that name prior to Islam. The Qur'ān in many passages refers to Muhammad's adversaries in Mecca, swearing by God, invoking Him, and recognizing His sovereignty as Creator. The name *Allāh* is also evident in archaeological and literary remains of pre-Islamic Arabic. But the people of Mecca did not understand or allow that God alone should be worshipped. Indeed they contended against Muhammad that if God had willed it they would have refrained from believing in other deities (Surah vi. 148), clearly implying that God approved of their concurrent idolatry. When, however, Muhammad came bringing precisely that Divine claim to exclusive worship they refused the Messenger.

There can be no doubt then that the Prophet's contemporaries knew of a Supreme Being, but He did not dominate their minds. Rather they thought more directly and frequently of the lesser gods, the daughters, perhaps even the sons, of *Allāh* who were far more intimately related to their daily lives, their wars, their harvests, and their fertility. They were also much concerned with a multiplicity of demons and jinns who inhabited natural phenomena, especially winds, hills, and wells. The fascinating theme of Muhammad's inner revolt against these notions and the pattern of his crusading controversy with the Meccans in the name of the Divine Unity must concern us in the chapter to follow, on the second clause of the muezzin's witness.

Here in the context of God and His Oneness we are faced with the supreme sin in the Muslim reckoning, itself the corollary of its great negation. This is the sin of associating with God. The Arabic term is *Shirk*. Its significance must be clearly understood if we are to enter validly into the meaning of the confession. Associating is the belief that God has co-existents or partners. There must be no alienation of His Godhead, or God-ness. It is not merely that He has no co-equals. He has no associates of any kind or rank. This was the gist of the Prophet's contention against the Meccans. God and idolatry were incompatible. It was not enough to confess that God was; He must be recognized as God alone. All the partners whom the pagan Arabs associated with Him were truly nonentities. They did not exist and they had no right to recognition. Muhammad, it is true, continued to believe in the existence of angels and jinns, but he repudiated any notion that these were deities. This tremendous breaking of the idols, dramatized by the physical cleansing of the central sanctuary in Mecca after its conquest by Muhammad, was the supreme achievement of Islam. It was an iconoclasm which came tragically to include in its great negation also the Christian faith about Christ. In abolishing the daughters and sons of Mecca's *Allāh,* Muhammad failed to distinguish the wholly different meaning of the Christian Sonship. To this day the Muslim principle of Unity stubbornly refuses to accept any understanding of unity which it thinks at error by the criteria needed to purge Mecca of multiplied divinities. It has not distinguished between pagan men alienating God's prerogatives and God in His own undivided glory working according to them. But the Christian problem of Muslim attitudes in this realm is to be faced below.

So it came that Muhammad, son of 'Abdallāh, Messenger of

God, proclaimed the Divine Unity and disqualified all other worships, annihilating in word and in action the partners whom the pagan Arabs associated with God. The word *Allāh* itself is grammatically incapable of a plural. It is a proper name. Repeatedly the Qur'ān refers to God as *Al-Wāhid*—the One. The Surah of Unity (Surah cxii) declares:

> *He is God alone, God the Eternal [undivided]*
> *He does not beget and He is not begotten*
> *There is none co-equal with Him.*

It may be that this brief Surah is a reply to a question from Jewish or Christian doctors as to the Muslim doctrine of God, though tradition regards it as a very early utterance before such questions could have been formulated. It is held to be worth a third of the whole Qur'ān and the seven heavens and the seven earths are founded upon it. To confess this verse, a tradition affirms, is to shed one's sins as a man might strip a tree in autumn of its leaves.

This doctrine of the Divine Unity, of the inalienable quality of God's Divinity, was a tremendous passion in Muhammad's heart. By virtue of His remoteness beyond His intermediaries, God was half unreal to the pagans. To Muhammad He was the only real. The Meccans might acknowledge and yet ignore Him saving their intimate worship for familiar substitutes. Did not God Himself say (Surah l. 16): "We know what man's soul whispers and are nearer than his neck artery." The Messenger was dominated by the Divine Reality and spoke of Him and for Him in the burning language of conviction. The strictly theological problems were all postponed, to be taken up in the centuries after Islam's expansion by thinkers of other races than the Arab with more inquiring minds and less intensity of purpose. Indeed "postponed" is perhaps an inexact word. The problems were not consciously deferred. They were not even felt. They had no place to develop in a mind that was fully possessed with its single mission. There is no valid understanding of Muslim theology that does not first strive to enter into this vivid awareness where it had its genesis.

II

"There is no god except God." Except God. The negation was the form in which Mecca could most arrestingly be given the affirmation. Muhammad proclaimed God to them in a sequence of descriptives which have been called, on Quranic ground, the Beautiful Names, *Al-Asmā' al-Husnā*. These number ninety-nine though the collections are not always quite identical. Most of them are found in the Qur'ān itself, the remainder being traditional. Their variety is explained in part by the poetic style of the Qur'ān, which tended to the use of rhyming endings, derived from a much smaller number of original roots with nuances or shades of adjectival meaning. The Names have been variously classified and interpreted by theologians. Edwin Arnold's *Pearls of Faith* is one familiar English rendering. The well-known Muslim "rosary" (*subhah*) or chain of beads, in thrice thirty-three arrangement, is a means of recollecting serially the Ninety-nine Names of God. They may also be seen in the Arabic numerals 81 and 18, adding up to 99, which can easily be read in the left- and right-hand palms.

The most important of the Divine Names in Islam are the twin titles, *Al-Rahmān al-Rahīm*, usually rendered into English "The Compassionate, the Merciful." They derive from the same verbal root, meaning mercy or compassion, but the first should probably be regarded rather as a noun than an adjective, with the second qualifying it: "the Merciful Mercier" or "the Compassionate Compassionator." The sequence is not mere repetition. The *Rahmān* is the One Who is in His character merciful. The *Rahīm* is He in merciful action. He Who is merciful behaves mercifully. His mercy is of His essence, and also of His deed. This double title is used as an invocation at the head of all the 114 Surahs of the Qur'ān, with the exception of Surah ix. The *Basmalah*: "In the Name of God, the Compassionate, the Merciful," is, after the *Shahādah*, the most familiar epitome of Muslim devotion. It is used in the recognition of God in all the ventures and vicissitudes of life even more widely than the confession itself.

Before pondering further the quality of the Divine mercy, it is necessary to study the more significant of the Beautiful Names. The next most familiar are the contrasted pairs: "The First and the Last: the Outward and the Inward"—sometimes called "the mothers of the attributes" since they comprehend all else. They suggest God's eternity, omniscience, and self-sufficiency. The same attributes are affirmed in: "the Living," the "Comprehending," "the Self-sufficing," "the Abiding," "the High," "the Mighty," "the All-Powerful," "the Exalted," "the Great," "the Praiseworthy," "the All-Compelling," "the Guardian," "the Victorious." Another title used only twice in the Qur'ān, *Al Qayyūm*, may be translated as "the Self-subsisting," though Al-Baidāwī, the most famous Muslim exegete, suggests the physical sense of "the always Erect"—"the Standing." The term graphically conveys the idea of God in alert relationship to the world.

This eternal and all-encompassing God is described as "the Creator," "the Fashioner," "the Life-Giver," "the Provider," "the Opener," "the Bestower," "the Prevailer." He brings to life and He brings to death. He is "the Reckoner" and "the Recorder," He is "the King of Kingship" and "the Lord of the worlds." It is repeatedly declared in the Qur'ān that there is no strength and no power save in Him. "He is over all things supreme." His also is the final knowledge. For the Muslim who has entered into this understanding, all problems end in, or are lost in, the phrase: "God is the Knowing One." He is the One Who is always "Aware." He hears, sees, and discerns. Nothing escapes His watchfulness or eludes His gaze.

The actions appropriate to these names, most of which are participial or adjectival forms, are frequently noted in the events and situations of the Quranic story. The relation of God to His Prophet, to His believing community, and to His adversaries is depicted in the active sense of these attributes. The Names are far, then, from being mere attributes to be listed in a theology: they are awesome realities of daily life. For God is *Al-Haqq*— "the Real," "the Veritable." He is the Supreme Reality of all existence, Whose nearness, judgment, and will are the great facts of human life.

The relative frequency with which the different names occur is a matter of deep interest. The terms, or their corresponding verbs, that have to do with strength, majesty, and greatness are most prominent. There are also certain nouns used occasionally, such as "Peace" (Surah lix. 23) with the sense, probably, of self-perfection, "Justice" (in the tradition only), and "Light." The last occurs in the oft-quoted passage from the Surah (xxiv. 35) which bears the title "Light."

> God is the Light of the heavens and the earth. The likeness of His Light is a niche wherein is a lamp. The lamp is in a glass. The glass is like a brilliant star lit from a blessed tree, an olive neither of the East nor of the West, whose oil would almost give light though no fire touched it. Light upon light.

The Prophet, it is said, was once asked about seeing God. "Can one see light?" was his reply.

There are a few passages, outside the very frequent usage of *Al-Rahmān al-Rahīm*, which refer to God's mercy. The word *Quddūs*, or "Holy," is used in the Qur'ān of God on two occasions. It is also applied to the Spirit, to Gabriel the archangel, to the angels, and to places of revelation. Its precise connotation is not readily apprehended. God is described as "the Forgiver" in several passages using three different derivatives from the same verbal root. He is also described as the "One Who repents and relents," "the Kindly," and "the Clement." Two passages only use the word *Wadūd* meaning "Loving," the second adding: "The Lord of the Throne, the Glorious, the Doer of what He intends" (Surah lxxxv. 14-16). That final phrase is indeed the perpetual condition of all the attributes. They are to be understood finally as characteristics of the Divine will rather than laws of His nature. Action, that is, arising from such descriptives may be expected, but not as a matter of necessity. What gives unity to all God's dealings is that He wills them all. He as Willer may be recognized from time to time by means of the descriptions given. But He does not essentially conform to any. The action of His will may be identified in this or that quality: His will of itself is inscrutable. One may not, therefore, say that God is necessarily loving, holy, righteous, clement, or relenting, in every and all relations.

It is this fact which explains the antithesis in certain of the Names. Such antithesis would not be theologically predicable if either element within it were essential to God's nature. Seeing they are not His action may demonstrate each element in differing relation. The antithesis is dogmatically resolved in the realm of will, in that God wills both—in every other sense and realm, it remains. But the problem has no anguish and is, indeed, inscrutable, given the conviction of the Divine will as an ultimate beyond which neither reason nor revelation go. So God is "the One Who leads astray," as well as "the One Who guides." He is "the One Who brings damage," as also does Satan. He is described also by terms like "the Bringer-down," "the Compeller" or "Tyrant," "the Haughty"—all of which, when used of men, have an evil sense. In the Unity of the single will, however, these descriptions co-exist with those that relate to mercy, compassion, and glory. While we are concerned with Muhammad's own awareness of God we must leave the pressing intellectual questions, as to the relation of this unity of Divine will to the ultimate Unity of Divine Being which Islam confesses. It is the first unity which is perhaps most fully expressed in the single word *Al-Rabb,* "the Lord," by which Muhammad proclaimed God, especially in the period of greatest preaching.

One final observation on the Beautiful Names will introduce another important aspect of the Muslim understanding of God. There are other adjectives among the *Asmā' al Husnā* which are also used of men, so that they stand for both the Godward and manward sides of the same transaction. *Shakūr,* for example, means the grateful when applied to man, "the Cognizant of gratitude" when applied to God. God acknowledges the thankfulness man renders. One epithet suggests both postures. Similarly, *Al-Mu'min* used of God means "the Trustworthy," of man it means "the trusting." God is the object and man the locus of faith. Perhaps most interesting of all, because nearest to the Christian teaching as to the Comforter, is the word *Al-Walī,* sometimes translated "the Friend" or "Patron." The root is very widely diversified. It means in its simplest sense "one who is near." So Surah x. 62 refers to "the wālīs of God"—a phrase on which much mystical devotion to the saints of Islam has been built. Men may stand in nearness to God, even as Abraham was the *Khalīl*, or Friend of God. But God Himself is also *Al-Walī*—"the One alongside"—in Whose protection and succor man may find strength. So we have in the same term the idea of the human dependent on God and the Divine Patron of man. It may be added here that the Qur'ān does not contain any articulated conception of God as Holy Spirit, though the terms "Spirit" and "Holy Spirit" are variously used in connection with the mediation of revelation.

III

Mention of these dual terms leads into the large and crucial theme of Divine-human relationships. For in so far as any doctrine of God is meaningful it is an account of such relationships. No theology could exist on the assumption that its theme meant nothing and mattered nothing. Certainly a monotheism so tremendous as that of Muhammad and Islam is through and through a Divine-human encounter. As such we must strive to know it. Whenever we study or confess doctrines of God we proceed upon parallel affirmations about man. So inseparable are the two realms that every theology is inevitably also an account of man. By what he means when he says "I bear witness that there is no god save God," the muezzin is involved in an equally compelling faith about the men who walk the streets and come to worship in the court beneath him.

God's relation to man begins in and with creation. The created universe takes its rise from God's fiat. He says "Be and it is." The initiative in creation is itself inscrutable. We need not relate the motive to the nature of God. He wills it. And all the sequences and generations of life are likewise willed. Nothing exists save by His providence, and there is nothing except Himself and His creation. All arises directly from Him and through Him. Man is His dependent creature.

As far as the Qur'ān is concerned there is an unresolved duality about the Divine and the human wills, though the reconciliation is not recognized as necessary. Many passages refer to the will of God as the immediate source of all events. He has created both men and their actions. There is no other Originator than

44

He. His is the *Qadar,* or "determination," of all things and His *taqdīr,* or "subjection," covers all mankind and all history. Nature, whether animate or inanimate, is subject to His command and all that comes into existence—a summer flower or a murderer's deed, a newborn child or a sinner's disbelief—is from Him and of Him. Had God so willed, there need have been no creation, there need have been no idolatry, there need have been no Hell, there need have been no escape from Hell.

This complete and stringent sovereignty of the Divine will is, however, counterbalanced by corresponding truths. The Qur'ān proceeds upon them and leaves the tension of duality to the subsequent theologians. Clearly neither life nor religion can subsist on the inclusive hypothesis that God is *immediately* involved, involved, that is, without any human intervention, in all that is and all that happens. The Holy Book assumes that men are responsible creatures. Muhammad repeatedly exhorted his hearers to repent and believe. He treated them as capable of response and as responsible for their states of mind. He harangued them as creatures of will. The creation itself, though in origin inscrutable, results nevertheless in a universe whose signs may be read for those who will to understand. The world is a witness to God's goodness and a means to His worship. Surah iv. 79 remarks: "Whatever of good happens to thee is from God: whatever evil happens to thee is from thyself." And there is the familiar passage, frequently cited in modern discussions of this theme: "God does not change what has to do with a people until they change what has to do with their own souls," arguing clearly that there are necessary human conditions upon which what God will, or will not, do is made to turn. The passage adds, however, that if God has willed evil to a people then none can turn it away (Surah xiii. 11).

That quotation epitomizes the Quranic situation. God is the direct source of all existence and all occurrence, but man is treated as a responsible and, therefore, in some sense also a free, creature. The most characteristic descriptive of the human status before God is *'abd,* "servant" or "slave," a term that is so frequent an element in Muslim names. Man the creature stands under the Divine authority in all realms. He masters the natural

45

world, in so far as he is allowed to, only by stooping to obey the conditions it imposes. The span and course of his days are ordered by God. Man is the creature of the Divine purpose and responds to it in worship and in submission. He is a creature also in that, when he falls short of that law, the offense is seen as lapse rather than as defiance. In its discussion of Adam as the archetypal man, the Qur'ān does not see him as rebellious. For that would be to enlarge his stature over against God. It sees him rather as weak and forgetful, or lacking in firmness and resolve. Though still his responsibility and sternly requited if God so wills, his sins are nevertheless rather his weakness than his revolt. Quranic man in other words is not Promethean or Shakespearean. When the stubborn recalcitrance of the unbelievers appears like a calculated defiance of God, it is understood rather as a delusion possible only by the Divine permission and as the prelude to their condemnation. Man is not able spontaneously to flout the Divine revelation. If he appears to do so it is because God has ordained this way to his destruction. For the rest, the sins of the believers, the delinquencies of the faithful, are lapses, over which there is hope that God may be lenient and merciful.

The status of *'abd* makes the meaning of *Islām,* or submission, the only appropriate relationship with God. But to enter it consciously, to accept it for what it is, is itself by God's permission. The belief, or unbelief, by which men are distinguished into Muslims and non-Muslims is itself the determination here of God. Within the relationship of surrender, man recognizes the entire sovereignty of God in worship and behavior, in the two great concepts of the Call to Prayer—*Salāt* and *Falāh*—which will be studied in later chapters. The postures of the Muslim in the one and the dispositions of his conduct and possessions in the other are alike expressive of the single state of submission.

In its finest form as exemplified by the Prophet himself, and by such successors as 'Umar, this relation of the *'abd* to his Lord means a constant quality of consciousness and will unique to Islam. It produces a sense of totality in religion evident in the familiar refusal of the classical Muslim mind to differentiate between sacred and secular. Though many of the attitudes of the Muslim within religion may seem to outsiders to be in tension with his *'abd* relationship, they are, as the Muslim sees it, nevertheless controlled and tempered by it. It is so because God Himself is inescapable. Therefore relationship to Him in everything is likewise inescapable.

> There is not a private conference of three, but He is their fourth, nor of five but He is their sixth, nor of a lower or a higher number but He is with them wherever they may be. Then on the day of resurrection He will tell them what they have done. God knoweth all (Surah lviii. 7).

It was this realization which gave to Muhammad's Islam that overwhelming sense of "the face of God" everywhere constraining the submission of His servants.

IV

But surrender implies the revelation of the will to which obedience is rendered. The Quranic account of the relation between God and man hinges upon the fact of revelation. The Holy Book is the climax of a long sequence of volumes of revelation with which it is continuous, vouchsafed to a long succession of "prophets" of whom Adam was the first and Muhammad the last. Belief in God, therefore, for the Muslim involves also belief in His prophets, His angels, and His books. For these are the agencies of His making known His law to mankind. The revelation is conceived of, not as a communication of the Divine Being, but only of the Divine will. It is a revelation, that is, of law not of personality. God the Revealer remains Himself unrevealed. The Qur'ān is a guidance for mankind. It brings that which men need to know in order to relate themselves to God as His slaves.

Revelation is not a personal self-disclosure of the Divine. It is for this reason, apart from its fear also of compromising unity, that the Qur'ān does not use the term "Father" of God nor "son" of the believer. It allows only *Rabb* and *'abd*. In either case, the terms require each other. If God is not addressed as Father, neither is it as sons that men come to Him. There remains beyond the revelation the impenetrable mystery of the Divine.

47

What the revelation does is to give men to know how God wills that men should live. It has a practical intent. It is true that intellectual curiosity has apprehended the Qur'ān in many more senses than the practical. Revelation, too, whatever its intent, is necessarily involved in implications beyond law. The Qur'ān has itself been understood as proclaiming this larger relevance. A crucial verse in Surah iii. 7 distinguishes between the unambiguous and the ambiguous, the clear and the allegorical. A succession of mystics found endless scope for their reverent minds in the manifoldness of the Qur'ān. Nonetheless it remains broadly true that the substance of what God reveals is His will rather than His nature, and that the end of revelation is obedience rather than perfect knowledge. God sends rather than comes. Though He makes plain, He remains above. Revelation is by *tanzīl,* as the phrase goes, by causing to come down. God Himself is withdrawn in *tanzīh,* or transcendence.

Though there has been a vigorous, if intermittent, Muslim theological expression in history, the crux of Islam was law not metaphysics. Muhammad certainly was concerned only with what God demanded. His conviction was that God, in proclaiming His Oneness, proclaimed His sole sovereignty. In revealing His "Names" He revealed His relation to men. In sending His prophets and books, He communicated His intention for man in his affairs. Response and submission were the sole necessities. These beliefs were their own justification.

So the Qur'ān was the speech of God, breathed instrumentally into the ear of the un-read Prophet and so transmitted into human ears by preaching and into the human mind by the record. Problems implicit in the precise relation of that speech to God Himself were left to develop in later ages. God was simply uttering through Muhammad the words that would proclaim His Unity, warn "the associators" or idolaters, and guide the faithful. It was auricular revelation in that it came to the Prophet's ear, as he understood it, in independence of conscious mental processes. It was oracular, also, in the sense that Muhammad uttered it without other argument than its own content, claiming implicit acceptance on the sole ground of its status as revealed, and his status as its messenger. The revelation did not envisage or

48

establish the kind of situation in which men may speak to God, as to each other, and yet in the expression of those thoughts become truly instruments of a Divine revelation to all generations of the world. We cannot fully appreciate the Quranic doctrine of God apart from an understanding of its concept of revelation as something in which God uses agents but teaches them by word, rather than by travail, by ear rather than by thought, by audition rather than by anguish.

A counterpart of the Quranic truth of God as revealer is the reality of God as judge. Indeed the imminence of the Divine judgment was a most compelling note in the original Muhammadan preaching. The day of judgment was not some distant event, but terrible and close at hand. It is proclaimed in some of the most eloquent passages of the Qur'ān. It was the day of the encircling wall closing inexorably upon the wicked: the day of the reckoning: the day of the separation. Surah ci. on this theme is almost untranslatable. "The *Qāri'ah,* who shall teach you what is the *Qāri'ah?*" it begins. The word has been rendered "the Clatterer" (Arberry); "the Calamity" (Pickthall and Muhammad 'Alī); "the Striking" (Bell); "the Smiting" (Palmer); "the Blow" (Rodwell). All of them fail. It might almost be called "the Knocking" if one keeps in mind the Hell's gate of the porter in *Macbeth.* It is a fearful summons striking terror into the hearts of all and ushering in the dread assize, the day of the retribution of God upon men. He whose deeds weigh heavy in the balance will lead a pleasant life. But he whose deeds are light in the balance will be thrown into the mother Pit. "And who shall teach thee what is the Pit?—a raging fire."

That day is in the absolute disposal of God alone. It is a day, as Surah lxxxii. 19 declares, on which "no soul hath any power at all for any other soul." The terrors of punishment and the blessings of Paradise are graphically portrayed, with vivid detail. The judgment turns mainly on belief or unbelief, with the idolaters and "associators" or polytheists in certain and condign damnation. There is some ambiguity on the point as to whether the confessed Muslim will enter the Fire. Though there are passages, and many more traditions, to suggest he will not, there is

49

no ground for presumptive assurance. Only at the end will the end be known.

There are many aspects of the doctrine of Divine judgment into which we cannot enter in this context. The doctrine itself completes for present purposes that understanding of God—One, Sovereign, Omniscient, Revealing, and Judging—which Muhammad proclaimed. Wherever the Qur'ān is read, pondered, and experienced this is the sense of God it conveys. When the muezzin in his witness links together God and His Apostle he bears witness to the identity, for multitudes of men, of the God they worship and the God Muhammad preached.

V

The fullness of the *Shahādah*, however, is not appreciated by limiting ourselves only to the Prophet's word and time. A preacher's silences, in retrospect, are sometimes as meaningful as his words. It might be possible to expound the Muslim doctrine of God, in a further stage, not so much for what it says, but for what it forbears to say. It will be well, however, to attempt to hearken to the silences by means of subsequent Muslim thinking which did something to explore them. By these means also we shall be listening, as Emerson once said, to the centuries over against the hours. The almost fourteen centuries of Islam's existence, or some of them, must be consulted, if we mean to penetrate into the meaning of God in Islam.

It should not be supposed that the "silences" of Muhammad were culpable. His purpose, as we have insisted, was not theological debate. He was a preacher not a systematizer: a prophet not a theologian. His vocation was to confront men with the Living God, His law, His claim, and His judgment. But, precisely for this reason, the doctrine needed to be related by philosophic minds to its own assumptions and to other men's creeds. Islam in expansion through the first two centuries after the Prophet's death came into contact beyond Arabia with Christian, Persian, and other influences which contributed considerably to its classical form. The entire Umayyad (Damascus) Caliphate (*c.* A.D. 661-750) was occupied with physical expansion and the Arabization and Islamization of the territories absorbed. Then began to develop under the 'Abbasids (from A.D. 750) the articulation of Muslim theological problems in the minds, for the most part, of non-Arabs. There is no intention here to attempt even the outlines of that story. The desire is to sketch the main themes of intellectual concern, without losing sight of the fact that our purpose is not a history of theology but the Muslim apprehension of God. We must be confined to those questions which serve to illuminate further what Muslims understand God to be and to will.

VI

All the questions were in some way aspects of the meaning of Divine Unity. *Tauhīd* was the term used to describe that theological principle by which there was only God and God was One. And all the points were somehow involved in the silences of the Prophet, the issues he had not recognized or raised.

The earliest questions were, characteristically, practical. In the time of the Umayyads, Muslims, even exalted ones, became careless and worldly. Many were content to confess the faith, but unwilling to live austerely in its obedience. Were they then true Muslims? And if rulers, had they the right to be obeyed by Muslims who were? A group known as the Khārijites thought they had not and refused allegiance on the ground that the ruler's Islam was invalid. Here was the problem of faith and works. Did confession alone make a Muslim, or was performance indispensable? This problem merged into larger ones. Who should decide? The community, the "puritan" groups, the worldlings, or God? How was God's will to be known in this matter? For indubitably He had a will and, moreover, nothing but this will could be done. How, then, explain the quarrel? If the will of God was being done in the actuality, the complaints were baseless, not to say blasphemous. If it was not being done, as the Khārijites insisted, then in this respect the will of God was being overborne? How came it that men could behave with such recalcitrance?

These questions, fed by other perplexities, shaped themselves into the most characteristic of Muslim theological inquiries: the relation between the human and the Divine will. The reader may be assured, or warned—as mood requires—that we intend no exhausting investigation of predestination, Muslim or Western. The question was simply an aspect of *Tauhīd*. Was God all in all? Was there no other god than He? If not, why was not His will necessarily done? Could there be any successful alternative to the Divine will? If not, why were men ever involved in disobedience? The course of thought oscillated for two centuries over this question. But despite some "liberal" tendencies, perhaps overesteemed in Western orientalism, the Muslim mind was rarely ready to accept any view that left a real freedom, even unto lawlessness, to man within the permissive sovereignty of God. In the early tenth century the discussion reached its term in the classical solution associated with Al-Ash'arī. It was a solution that gave the questions back in the form of an answer. The Muslim mind was not prepared to compromise its belief that God was the sole Creator. Therefore He was the final source of every event and every deed. But it saw the need to recognize the role that man played in life and the reality of moral choice. To hold the two together it fixed upon the concept of "acquisition" (*kasb*). By this man "acquired" the action, which was created in him by God. God willed evil in the act of the sinner and good in the behavior of the well-doer. God remained the sole source of creativity; man remained responsible. The power and choice by which the individual performs his action are God's: man "acquires" the action which is consequently his. Though this theory may serve to explain the illusion of freedom, if such it be, it hardly succeeds in reconciling moral responsibility with Divine sovereignty. But it pointedly illustrates one facet of what orthodox Islam means by the confession "There is none other than He."

The belief in the Unity led into an even more searching question. Was God Himself morally accountable? How were the different aspects of God, His Beautiful Names, reconciled where they were morally antithetical? Could God be both "loving" and "the best of deceivers"? If we answer: Yes! because He is One will and both the attributes describe that One will at different points, then what of the moral sense which disposes men to say, even of God, "This ought not to be"? Can we in other words forbid attitudes to God which, when found in men, are morally reprehensible? The instinct was always to answer "No!" since no limits could be placed on God's action and no criteria placed upon His choices. His will was His law. Yet there were sensitive thinkers in the ninth century who felt that if there were to be valid moral distinctions applicable to men, they must have their ground in the Divine character. God Himself must be motivated by them. Otherwise they would lose also their human authority. These thinkers, therefore, preferred to think of "justice" rather than "will," as the ultimate term of reference to God, so that what God willed was always just and He could not be conceived as willing the unjust. But the majority of thinkers feared that this meant somehow a limitation of God. It left them also with the problem of how to account for evil, if the thesis of an only good will in God were accepted. Moreover, they were reluctant to believe that God was under any necessities, not even moral ones. So they fell back upon the belief that God was open to good and evil as He pleased and that His will was finally inscrutable. This was the measure both of the price they were ready to pay for the idea of Unity, and of the way they understood it.

VII

There are other clues to this understanding of God's Unity which must be considered in order to estimate it further. "There is no god save God" says the witness. How were human minds to understand the relation to God of the realities that issued from Him? These were chiefly two: the created world and the revealed law. Clearly God was in relation to men and the world. Man, as we have seen, was the "slave" of God. From God other existences took their rise. But were they necessary to God? Orthodox Islam has always inclined to the answer: No! For God is Self-subsistent. Had He willed otherwise no worlds would have been. Yet to believe that the world is not necessary to God is a poor basis for religion, since it is liable to make unreal the faith that man has meaning for God. If prayer and worship are to be meaningful to man, he surely needs to believe that they are meaningful to God. Much mysticism in Islam has solved this problem devotionally by bringing God and the world closer together, and explaining

Unity in pantheistic terms. But, though built upon possible Quranic exegesis, this attitude has remained suspect among orthodox theologians. Yet if God is One in a religiously meaningful sense the Oneness must leave room for the world as somehow within its range and yet maintain the Self-sufficiency of God. This was the problem of creation.

It had ramifications in other areas of life, notably in relation to physical causality. When leaves fall and the seasons change, when fire burns and wounds fester, are these physical events to be accounted for by causal connections in the chemical or physical environment? If so, are they an area distinguishable from the Divine will? Are they independent of God? In what sense are they attributable to Him? In more recent times this question has been sharpened by man's increasing ability to manipulate natural causality for his own ends. The modern Muslim tends to understand this as an aspect of the authority given to man in the Qur'ān. But many in an earlier time were required, by their understanding of the principle of Unity, to believe that all these multifarious events issued directly from the action of God.

The problem involved in revelation, however, is even more controversial in Muslim intellectual history. The Qur'ān was God's word, God's speech. It was what God Himself said. When, however, you use an apostrophe after God, and refer to "God's speech," or even "God's will," or "God's face," you may appear to speak of a second thing besides God. The word is clearly not the speaker. Yet it cannot be a second God. Nonetheless, if it is truly God's speech, it must be as eternal as He. From musings of this kind rose the bitter controversy, which reached its climax in the ninth century, on the status of the Qur'ān. Was it created or eternal? The final orthodox view was that it was uncreated. For to think otherwise surely would be to render dubious its Divine origin. The more adventurous thinkers, who were finally overcome, were impressed with the problem of regarding as eternal that which was involved in temporal issues, in the fortunes of specific battles and the domestic relationships of particular families. If these occasions in time were themes or points of revelation, were they somehow eternal also?

This question merged into an equally puzzling issue where the

Muslim mind found decision difficult. It related to the sense in which men should understand the Divine Names or attributes. When adjectives like "kind," "gracious," "wise," and the rest were used of God, did the meanings hold which the terms carried when used of men? To answer with an unqualified "Yes!" seemed to bring God and men too close together and so compromise His transcendence and otherness. This might amount to a violation of *Tauhīd* and an indirect form of *Shirk,* since human descriptives were "associated" with God. But to answer with an unqualified "No!" threatened all theology with meaninglessness. In any event such terms were used in the Holy Qur'ān and the Tradition. Their use must, accordingly, be valid.

Classical Muslim theology developed a form of compromise solution in effect inclining to the negative answer. There developed the idea of *Al-Mukhālafah,* "The Difference." Terms taken from human meanings—and there are of course no others—were said to be used of God with a difference. They did not convey the human connotation but were used in those senses feasible of God. When the further question was pressed: What then do they convey as applied to God? no precise answer was capable of being formulated. Islam here falls back upon a final agnosticism. Terms must be used if there is to be religion at all. But only God knows what they signify. Muslim theology coined the related phrases *Bilā kaif* and *Bilā Tashbīh.* We use these names "without knowing how" they apply and without implying any human similarity.

In a real sense the Muslim awareness of God is an awareness of the unknown. The revelation communicated God's Law. It does not reveal God Himself. He remains inscrutable and inaccessible to knowledge. Sometimes described as the negative theology, this faith that only God knows the sense of the terms in which we speak of Him has characterized Muslim attitudes far beyond the range of those who could understand its intellectual grounds. If some readers find the point under discussion abstruse, they can be assured that it attaches to the Muslim sense of God in everyday life. Only God knows. The problem of meaning in language exists for all religions and is not unique to Islam. It can only be solved within the conviction that the Divine and the human are truly meaningful to each other: only in the confidence that the relationships God has with man are really indicative of His Nature. We only put these convictions more shortly—and sublimely—when we say: "God is Love." Islam has never felt able to say that. The pressure of these problems is the measure of its reluctance.

VIII

This brief attempt to convey something of the historical travail of Islam over its belief in the One God must face one other issue —and seek forgiveness for the torturing brevity into which it is compelled. This formal problem, like all the foregoing, arises out of the doctrine of Unity. As a religion of revelation Islam believes that God has communicated His will and has caused the faithful to use, if not fully to apprehend, His Names. This realm of revelation, however, is not the sole source of human knowledge. There is the natural reason of man operating from sense experience to study and know the external world. In the Qur'ān there are fervent appeals to man to recognize the splendor of God in nature and the sureness of His ways.

A ready example can be found in Surah lv, with its repeated refrain: "Which of the favors of your Lord will ye deny?" and its eloquent celebration of the punctual sun and moon, the pearls of the sea, and the fruitful oases. "Lord of the daybreak" is one of the titles of God. It is He Who has set in the heavens the lamps of the stars and bounded the everlasting hills. "Praise the Name of Thy Lord most High Who creates and makes complete. He determines the ends (of things) then guides them. He brings forth pasture and turns it into tawny stubble" (Surah lxxxvii. 1-5). "Wilt thou not regard . . . the heaven, how it was raised . . . and the earth how it was spread forth?" (Surah lxxxviii. 18-20). These passages are also understood as injunctions to the scientific spirit. From this natural scientific area of human knowledge, certain ideas of God and man, of duty and meaning, may be constructed by rational processes. There comes, then, the problem of reason and revelation in their inter-relationship—again a large issue, not unique to Islam.

The Muslim doctrine of the Unity of God includes the unity

of truth. Truth is not inconsistent with itself. Though it may be known by different methods, it is one essential truth. Accordingly, traditional Muslim thought has tended to explain the difference between reason and revelation primarily as a difference in method or means. It has two words *'aql* and *naql* to describe reason and revelation. There is what man investigates and what God delivers.[1] There is a tendency evident in some Muslim thinking to leave aside the task of reconciling what reason thinks and revelation says, on the ground that they are simply different methods. This may generate an insensitivity in some theologians to the full impact of scientific criticism. It tends to immunize dogma from critical exposure and to leave science mistrustful of faith.

Some of the greatest Muslim thinkers, however, have erred in the other direction. Writers of great eminence inclined to the view that religion and faith were the form in which the vulgar throng of ordinary men in the mosque could grasp spiritual truth. These men needed the help of symbol. The philosopher, however, with his educated mind, could dispense with external forms and hold loosely to established dogma. Such thinking was hard to detect under outward conformity. Founded on an aristocracy of reason, these attitudes were by no means common. But they represent another form of the tension in the Muslim mind between *'aql* and *naql,* and an original account of their relationship.[2] There are some in contemporary Islam who accept religious dogmas as a political or communal necessity without giving their minds to them. Moreover, the obligation to concerted theological thinking is not stimulated by the underlying feeling that only God knows. Conviction about the oneness of truth sometimes excuses the mind from the task of understanding its unity.

It is for these reasons that the Islamic faith that God is God alone is not always adequately articulate in the intellectual sense. As Professor Gibb remarks, the genius of Islam is finally law and not theology.[3] In the last analysis the sense of God is a sense of Divine command. In the will of God there is none of the mystery that surrounds His being. His demands are known and the believer's task is not so much exploratory, still less fellowship, but rather obedience and allegiance.

57

The foregoing venture into some of the characteristic issues of Muslim thought on God is in no sense an adequate analysis. It does scant justice to its vast theme. It is intended only as illustrating what faith in God has meant to Muslims, in so far as that meaning can be gauged in external debate. We can perhaps understand more fully the all-embracing principle of Unity if we take note of what it has meant to some who have essayed its exposition. We turn now to some of the significance of the confession of the One God for the moral life of the believer.

IX

The first duty of the Muslim is belief; belief in God, His Unity, His revelation, His prophets, His books and angels, and the Last Day. This *Imān,* or Faith, must issue in *Dīn,* or Religion. The latter has its five pillars, Confession, Prayer, Almsgiving, Fasting, and Pilgrimage. These will be discussed in later chapters on religious and social life in Islam. They are the particular focus of the inclusive sovereignty of God which is held to pervade the whole of life. Islam does not accept the interpretation of religion which allows it to be understood as a branch of human life, a piece of personal privacy, or the area of existence that relates to God. All things relate to God and the God-relationship of man involves all his affairs. This inclusive interpretation is under some criticism from within in view of the factors demanding the separation of politics from religion. But it remains the classic Muslim concept—a God-relatedness in all things.

The ideal does not, in its Muslim form, take note of the human capacity for insubordination. It knows, of course, that man, in all realms, political, social, and personal, does not fully do the Divine will. But it does not take that knowledge seriously into account in its doctrinal estimate of the situation. It believes that human life is a realm in which the Divine will can be done simply by its being known—as known it is in the Muslim law. All is, therefore, in the classic view, an aspect of *'Ibādah,* or worship. *'Ibādah* is the abstract noun defining the attitude of the *'abd,* or servant.

This does not mean, however, an extravagant saintliness or abstraction. On the contrary, the law, when those demands which

58

might in some contexts be called the "religious" ones are fulfilled, leaves men and society a wide freedom. The customary division of ethical categories in Islam is fivefold. There are those
actions the performance of which is obligatory and their omis-
sion forbidden. Conversely there are actions which must be
shunned absolutely and whose commission is forbidden. In the
center are a great number of actions which are matters of indifference, where there is an entire option. On either side of these,
but not as far as the two absolute extremes of "must" and "must
not," are actions not commended but tolerated, and not forbidden but disapproved. Among the worst of the latter, incidentally,
is divorce. Since our purpose is to understand the sense of God,
there is no occasion to pursue this analysis further as an ethical
study. Though the demands of God are thought of as paramount everywhere there are many areas where they neither enjoin nor prohibit. These areas of complete human option are
evidence of the largess of God. But even where no specific injunction controls an act the sovereignty of God is to be recognized in the attitude that enjoys the freedom.

These issues implicit in the Muslim understanding of God occupied the minds of successive generations of Muslim theologians and philosophers especially from the ninth to the eleventh
Christian centuries. A close study of the course of their debate
would be a most effective commentary on the theme of this chapter. It would then, however, cease to be a chapter and become a
tome. Some scant justice may be done to its history by means
of three representatives. The first two belong to the "classical"
age, the third is possibly the most adventurous of Muslim philosophers in the twentieth century. There will remain one vital
task when these three authorities have been heard.

x

Since three out of many scores is drastic selection, it may be well
to explain why Al-Nasafī is first chosen. Of no great distinction
in his own right, he was the author of a creed in the second
quarter of the twelfth century which had prolonged currency as
a textbook and manual. It became the basis of later commen-
taries. Al-Nasafī himself was a disciple of Al-Māturīdī, whose

school of teaching, along with that of Al-Ash'arī, formed the main orthodoxy of Islam after the controversies of the earlier centuries. With little to choose between them, the two schools fashioned and dominated the mind of Sunnī Islam. To quote the main paragraphs of Al-Nasafī's creed in relation to God is to have in convenient form a concise statement of how orthodoxy understood its own confession. The translation is by Duncan Black Macdonald.

> The Originator of the world is God Most High, the One, the Eternal, the Decreeing, the Knowing, the Hearing, the Seeing, the Willing. He is not an attribute, nor a body, nor an essence, nor a thing formed, nor a thing bounded, nor a thing numbered, nor a thing divided, nor a thing compounded, nor a thing limited: He is not described by quiddity, *Māhiyah,* nor by modality, *Kaifiyyah,* and He does not exist in place or time. There is nothing that resembles Him and nothing that is beyond His Knowledge and Power.
>
> He has qualities from all eternity existing in His essence. They are not He, nor are they any other than He. They are Knowledge and Power, and Life and Strength, and Hearing and Seeing and Doing and Creating and Sustaining and Speech.
>
> And He Whose Majesty is majestic speaks with a Word. This Word is a quality from all eternity, not belonging to the genus of letters and sounds, a quality that is incompatible with coming to silence and that has a weakness.
>
> God Most High speaks with this Word, commanding and prohibiting and narrating. And the Quran is the uncreated Word of God, repeated by our tongues, heard by our ears, written in our copies, memorised in our hearts, yet not simply a transient state in these. And creating is a quality of God Most High from all eternity. . . . and Willing is a quality of God Most High from all eternity, existing in His essence. . . .
>
> And God Most High is the Creator of all actions of

His creatures whether of unbelief or belief, of obedience
or of rebellion: all of them are by the Will of God and
His sentence and His conclusion and His decreeing.

After discussing man's ability to do actions of choice within
this decreeing, the creed adds: "God leadeth astray whom He
wills and guideth aright whom He wills, and it is not incumbent
upon God Most High to do that which may be best for His
creatures." [4]

XI

An older contemporary of Al-Nasafī and a far more significant
figure was Al-Ghazālī (A.D. 1059-1111). A formal creed is one
thing but a deep personal travail of conviction is another. There
is no more eloquent document of religious experience in Islam,
outside the Qur'ān itself, than the autobiography of Al-Ghazālī,
known as "The Deliverer from Error." Though responsible in
part for an unhappy anti-intellectualism in subsequent Muslim
theology, Al-Ghazālī illuminates, as no other writer does, the
meaning of faith. Beginning as a successful teacher in the Ash-
arite tradition, he experienced in his late thirties an intense
crisis, in which rational confidence forsook him. He was overcome by a deep religious skepticism and a sense of self-reproach
from which he was finally delivered by reliance on the path of
moral discipline and intuitive insight. Herein he was greatly influenced by Al-Muhāsibī, and others of the Sufi, or mystical,
school, who taught that the knowledge of God turned upon
purity of soul, to be sought by sustained asceticism and spiritual
renunciation.

Al-Ghazālī himself renounced his role as an academician and
became for some years a pilgrim and a wanderer. Out of the fullness of his inner experience he found certainty of a different
quality from that which he had known within scholastic theology. Something of his legacy might loosely be expressed in the
idea that he altered the "person" in the Muslim confession
from: "There is no god save He," to: "There is no god save
Thou." The use of "He," only, serves to convey the sense of in-
adequacy in the formal relations of orthodoxy in the soul of Al-

Ghazālī. He saw the importance, as he said, of experiences rather than definitions, and recognized his lack, not of instruction, but of ecstasy and initiation. In "The Deliverer from Error," he examined the theological limitations of reason and defended *kashf,* or discovery through illumination, as the sure way to the knowledge of God. Yet he was careful to recognize credal theology and he saw in the Qur'ān and the Prophet the supreme example of revelation through and to the pure in heart.[5]

In this understanding he was aided by a remarkable sense of the psychological in worship and religious practice. His greatest work, known as *The Revival of the Religious Sciences,* discussed such themes as the psychology of temptation, the relation between ritual and belief, the disciplines of the soul and its intricacies. It contained forty books divided into two parts: (a) external acts of religious devotion, both Godward and manward and (b) the heart and its workings, including both the destructive and the redeeming elements in human life. The whole was an eloquent compendium of living religion, more deeply self-aware, more alert to its duties and dangers, more vibrant and intense, than anything in the history of Islam after Muhammad. Here many of the earlier "silences" were treated with a painstaking devotion.

A prolific author, Al-Ghazālī reproduced many of the arguments of his *magnum opus* in short manuals for believers. He also expounded his view of the theological limitations of reason in a famous work: *The Disintegration of the Philosophers.* Elsewhere he expounded the stages of the mystic's way through the degrees of the Divine unveiling.

No summary can do justice to him. There were many commentators on his works. But thanks, in part, to the suspicion of reason he helped to generate, Muslim theological activity became more and more a matter of Quranic exegesis and traditional commentary. The celebrated names after him are those of Quranic commentators and historians of past theology.

Nevertheless, no attempt to understand the meaning of *Lā Ilāha illā Allāh* is complete without a deep reckoning with Al-Ghazālī. He lived to express that conviction on its inward side as an experience and a way of life. He sought a psychology that would subdue every subtle challenge in the recesses of the will and spirit to the sole mastery of God. He practiced a loving submission that went far beyond the bare requirements of the pillars as traditionally understood. He taught men to realize that the Beautiful Names of God were not for description merely, but for imitation. Men were to strive after a Divine likeness, even when they confessed His credal unlikeness. The emphasis was not on the ways in which God could be meaningfully defined but on the attitudes in which He was to be devoutly obeyed. If God was called "the Repenter," man must know the meaning of repentance. Something of the starkness of transcendence was corrected and man's knowledge of God became a ground of communion with God. For: "If it assuredly be that God is beautiful, He must certainly be beloved by him to whom His beauty is revealed." The creature might remain the *'abd*. But he was also a lover and this was the clue to the meaning and the health of his *'Ibādah*. It is not without significance that the subtitle of "The Deliverer from Error" is *Al-Muwāsil*, "the bringer unto" the Lord of might and majesty. For he was concerned not only to escape falsehood but to enter into truth and peace. Perhaps we may say that, for Al-Ghazālī, the Muslim confession: "There is no god save God" had come near to meaning: "Whom have I in heaven but Thee? there is none upon earth that I desire beside Thee" (Psalm lxxiii. 25).

XII

There is a pregnant Islamic phrase which may serve as a bridge from Al-Ghazālī to Muhammad Iqbāl, from a great medieval figure in Islam to a twentieth-century thinker. It is the command: "Be fashioned after the fashion of God," or "Seek the character which God has." For this conception, which summarizes much of the message of Al-Ghazālī, is also often cited by Iqbāl. Born in 1876 in the Punjab, Iqbāl became famous as a philosopher and poet. He has been remembered, since his death in 1938, with great fervor and admiration. It would not be improper to regard him as the patron saint of Pakistan where Iqbāl Day is a national festival. In his poems, and in a series entitled *Lectures on the Reconstruction of Religious Thought in Islam,* he set forth a dynamic theism which, though not everywhere accepted, or even understood, in Islam, represents an attempt to express anew the fundamentals of Islamic faith in terms of modern thought.

For this reason, though without analysis and only the scantiest exposition, he may be taken here as expressing the meaning the *Shahādah* has come to hold for some modern Muslims. Iqbāl had studied Nietzsche, Bergson, and Bernard Shaw, among others, and sought in part to interpret the God of the Qur'ān along the same lines. Crusading against apathy and decadence, he proclaimed the cultivation of the Self, or Ego. The universe was itself growing and maturing in dynamic creation, ever moving toward an unrealized perfection. Iqbāl tended to see in the Quranic deity this continuous flow of creative energy and in the prophets the special agents of creative life in which a dynamism was at work, to overcome inertia in the on-going surge of the life-force.

As a poet he availed himself of the privilege of suggestiveness, allusion, and even inconsistency. He was more concerned to galvanize believers than to define belief. He summoned the Muslim to exalt his Ego so high that God Himself would consult him before determining his destiny. He did not stay to explain how so daring a sentiment was to be reconciled with the traditional Muslim understanding of the sovereignty of God. His *Lectures* were of necessity more integrated than his poems. Nevertheless they left unfaced many questions involved in the "reconstruction."

For himself, and for numbers of his subsequent expositors, he found the secret of Islam in creative dynamism. "God is most great" meant that God is the inclusive Ego. Muslim history became for him a unique example of dynamism at work. The worship of "the Lord of the Worlds" was the Ego affirming itself. Iqbāl addressed God in the words: "How farest Thou without me, O my whole?" The God Whom Islam proclaimed was also "the not-yet," the still-to-be realized unfolding of infinite possibilities. Creation was not a deed which made the world something "other" than God. It was, and is, the self-revelation of the great "I Am." The Islamic doctrine of the Divine Oneness meant that there is no reality outside Him. Nature is to the Divine Self as character is to the human self.[6]

A critical evaluation of the form Iqbāl gives to classical Islamic meanings cannot be undertaken here. This brief reference does justice neither to the daring range of his intellectual flights nor to their often tenuous connection with what is historically Islamic. But their boldness and the reputation of their author are sufficient indication that, for all its authoritative simplicity, the Muslim creed is capable of widely diverse interpretations. Without staying to ask what was the sense of Quranic passages to Muhammad himself and his immediate hearers, modern interpreters proceed to borrow and claim them for beliefs that may well owe more to current philosophy than to traditional faith. Such spirits are, no doubt, part of the valid fullness of any wide religious system, however disconcerting they may be to the orthodox. Even the most emphatic dogma stands finally in the meaning believers give to it. The faith that "there is no god save God," is terse enough, inclusive enough, vast enough, to mean tremendous, and not always recognizably compatible, things to different Muslims.

XIII

If we have concentrated on the classical, historic meanings in this chapter that is no more than our duty to the consensus of the Muslim centuries. But it is with the fourteenth in the series that we are also concerned. Iqbāl, who, for all his provocative quality, deserves fuller study, is here no more than a witness to the inexhaustible meanings which Muslims may yet find and proclaim, within their ancient creed of the Oneness of God. Though the muezzin and his colleagues in the mosque are among the last to yield to the possibility of these modern interpretations of their familiar words, the sense of God is evidently more fluid, less clearly definable, among many of their listeners.

It is into this realm of the awareness of God in the Muslim community that we finally attempt to pass. Leaving behind the traditional issues of theology and representative leaders of interpretation, there is need to face the question: What does the fact of God mean in the life of the individual? Theology always issues in doxology when it is true to its theme. It is the worshipper, in the fullest Muslim sense of the word, who really demonstrates what faith in the Unity means. The temper it fashions in the people who hold it is the final clue to the nature of a religious faith.

Yet how formidable a task rightly to identify and to describe the elemental truths about this Muslim sense of God! Multitudes of humble believers have given no tongue to their experience. The sultans and viziers do not always speak for them. There are competing voices and discordant sounds. Shall we take Hārūn al-Rashīd and his splendid autocracy in Baghdad as an index to the faith, or its gilded travesty? The stories of *The Thousand and One Nights,* though, for all their diversity of origin and content, unmistakably Islamic, give the lie to as many Muslim virtues as they depict. That unpredictable tyranny, the cheapness of life, the successful villainy, and the unabashed casuistry —are these to be taken as the consequence, in some sense, of the enthronement of celestial will? The *Assemblies of Al-Harīrī,* among the most famous of Arabic literary works, breathe a dubious piety and make a hero of a charlatan. Should their moral then be the ethical discredit of excessive transcendence in popular theology? And that old familiar charge of fatalism, as dogging perpetually the average Muslim believer, with his apathetic conclusion that what is, had to be, and what will be, will be—should these be the text of a critic's sermon on the *Lā ilāha illā Allāh?*

Hardly. These are elements in the total picture. But they, and much more from all the centuries, could as well be attributed to the enervation of faith as to its vitality. Though the kind of compromise that happens to a faith is sometimes a clue to its nature, it is not in compromise that faiths should be finally judged. The student must acquaint himself with all that Muslim literature and history have to tell him about what God came to mean to Muslims. But it will be soundest in the end if he assesses the lights more than the shadows.

He will find a consciousness of God which has produced a recognizably Muslim character, sometimes even of face, always of conduct. Pressures of secularity may have gone far to transform it in this century. But in history it is there. It is a temper that is grave, perhaps even a little joyless, but marked by probity and discipline. The sense of God's Oneness, at its purest, has emancipated men from all other fears and so fostered imperturbability and strength of soul. Legality and communal consciousness may have their demerits, but they generate a dignity and loyalty that are characteristic Muslim virtues. Islam's faith in God has taught the oneness of believers and class consciousness, though it may be economically real, is religiously repudiated. The relative ranks of men diminish alongside the sole sovereignty of the Divine. Then there is hospitality, that identifying quality of Muslim society. There are attitudes of responsibility—to family, to community, to God—which mark the believing Muslim, as a moral consequence of the recognition of God.

But the task of assessing fully the bearing of the *Shahādah* on the making of the characteristically Muslim temper and attitude is in the end too large and intangible. Nor are the necessary criteria all agreed. Our duty is rather to invite the student to keep always in view the reciprocity between the idea of God and the idea of life as it abides through the Muslim story, and to trace its workings as he can.

No doubt his surest clue will be the Prophet himself. For the meaning of God to Islam is told and retold in the biography of the Prophet in its inward compulsion and its outward success. We come back in the end to that eloquent "and" that links the Unity of God with the Apostleship of Muhammad in the muezzin's witness. It is in what Islam came to believe about the Prophet of God that the community found and learned its awareness of the nature of God and His relation to men. As Muhammad was the final instrument of revelation, so his story in all its aspects provides the framework in which we may understand the God revealed.

NOTES *to Chapter II*

1

There is also *kashf*, or disclosure, by which Sufi systems describe an insight into truth, not open to intellect and not dependent, in an external manner, on dogma. See p. 60.

2

Ibn Rushd (1126-98), known in the West as Averroes, may be cited as an outstanding example of this tendency. Any conflict between rational truth and revealed dogma was to be resolved by interpreting the latter allegorically. The primary functions of religion are popular in character and pragmatic in purpose. Its "truths" are the form under which ordinary people, in their non-philosophical way, can apprehend and venerate the mysteries which the intelligent few investigate. Since religion is for law, not learning, philosophy wisely avoids fruitless conflicts with it.

3

Gibb, Sir Hamilton, in *Mohammedanism*, London, 2nd ed., 1953, p. 88.

4

Macdonald, Duncan B., *Development of Muslim Theology, Jurisprudence and Constitutional Theory*, New York, 1903, Appendix i, pp. 309-10.

5

See Watt, W. Montgomery, *The Faith and Practice of Al-Ghazali*, London, 1953.

6

On Iqbāl, see Singh, Iqbal, *The Ardent Pilgrim: An Introduction to the Life and Work of Muhammad Iqbal*, London, 1951; also Iqbāl's own *Lectures on the Reconstruction of Religious Thought in Islam*, Lahore, 1934; *Aspects of Iqbal*, by various authors, Lahore, 1938; *Iqbal as a Thinker*, by various authors, Lahore, 1945.

iii

MUHAMMAD HIS APOSTLE

و محمّد رسول الله

I BEAR witness that Muhammad is the Apostle of God." So the muezzin and so every Muslim, in the indispensable second clause of the *Shahādah*, with its inseparable relationship to the first. Though there is no doctrine of divinity as to Muhammad in Islam, but rather sustained insistence to the contrary, the Prophet of Arabia's is the human name most closely associated with that of God. In many a mosque, great and small, the name *Allāh* appears on the right, that of Muhammad on the left, on either side the *mihrāb*, or above where the dome springs from its supporting arches. The two names are the double motif of calligraphic design and are uttered in close succession on the lips of multitudes of the faithful. "I bear witness that there is no god save God and that Muhammad is His Apostle." Small conjunctions often carry profound significance. There is none more tremendous than that which links the One God with the human instrument of His revelation and His will, in the creed and the devotion of Islam.

A few sentences from a familiar manual of adoration in one of the orders of Muslim mystics, or Sufis, will serve to illustrate and introduce this theme. After the proper acknowledgment of God Himself, there follows the traditional petition: "Let blessing and peace, O God, be upon the noblest of all creatures, among men and jinns, the master of glorious illumination. O God, let blessing and peace be upon him, his people, his children, his wives, his seed, the members of his household, his brethren among the prophets and faithful ones and also upon whoever believes on him and follows him, from the first to the last—our master and guardian—Muhammad." The manual continues: "O God, make him unto us a spirit, and to our worship a secret (of well-pleasing). O God, cause his love to be our nourishment, whereof I seek help in magnifying him. O God, make the celebration of him life in our hearts. I perform it seeking help from it for his remembrance, and the remembrance of his Lord."

There, in the same intimate association, is the recollection of God and of His Prophet. This mystical ardor may exceed in degree and expression, but not essentially in kind, the consciousness of Muhammad which pervades Islam. The more strictly orthodox disqualify some of the terms of Sufi fervor. Yet these only give a warmth of personal intensity to the general attitudes toward Muhammad in the community that confesses his apostleship and lives by the confession. In the spate of new publication in Islam there have been more Muslim biographies of the Prophet in recent decades than in the same number of centuries past. Most of them dwell enthusiastically on the same features of excellence and uniqueness. That by 'Abbās Mahmūd al-'Aqqād, a noted Egyptian author, may be taken as typical. Entitled *The Genius (or Excellence) of Muhammad*, it proclaims that his greatness is evident in all fields.[1] He entered a world which had lost faith, and with it the secret of inward peace and outward order, a world which, accordingly, was waiting for the liberating voice of Islam. Muhammad was the paragon of both the preacher's and the soldier's virtues. He had eloquence, conviction, and intensity as the one; courage, chivalry, and success as the other. Superb in his gifts and character, he dominated his time as he dominates all succeeding history. No event that has since happened, writes the biographer (the date is 1942), has been what it would have been had Muhammad never appeared. Before him history is one thing and after him another.

In similar vein writes another biographer, Muhammad Husain Haykal, former President of the Egyptian Senate and author of the longest and most scholarly of Muslim studies of the Prophet in Arabic.[2] At the close of an intimate discussion of the pilgrimage in *Fī Manzil al-Waḥy* (*In the Home of Revelation*), Haykal writes of Muhammad:

> His is a power which can lift mankind to the heights of the spirit where life will be brotherhood and love and care for the knowledge of all that is in the world of existence, so that knowledge may illumine brotherly concord and love, and that both may grow in human worth and excellence and bring us by their protection into the fullest peace.[3]

Comparable expressions of the surpassing merit and influence of Muhammad could readily be quoted from scores of Muslim pens in this generation. Our duty is to study how Muhammad is for these multitudes the supremely significant figure in history and what their conviction means in their experience. What is this Muslim meaning of Muhammad? The attempt to answer will be the aim of what follows rather than an analytical biography. The latter can be found in several competent studies in English. Our purpose may be served by adopting a division used in a popular account published in 1954 by Fathy Radwān, Minister of State in the first revolutionary Cabinet in Egypt following the 1952 changes, and entitled *Muhammad: the Greatest Revolutionary*. On his title page are the celebrated words of Abū Bakr, the close friend, father-in-law, and first successor of the Prophet, who, summoned to his daughter's apartment after Muhammad's death, turned back the coverlet and addressed the departed leader: "Thou art my father and my mother, O Apostle of God, most sweet in life, most sweet in death." Muhammad in life, then, and Muhammad in death, or rather, in history.

II

There is a passage in a later Surah of the Qur'ān (Surah lviii. 12) enjoining an alms on all who seek an interview with the Prophet, though it is added that this is not to deter them if they lack the means. The Prophet was always accessible, though in later years, because of greater pressures or wider veneration, almsgiving became an appropriate prelude. To come into spiritual colloquy with the life of Muhammad is an aspiration that exacts a claim on imagination and painstaking. The student must be ready to pay in diligence the price of understanding. The Qur'ān, although its biographical data is limited, is our prior source. The traditions are most unlimited. Both are alike demanding in their character—the former with its almost untranslatable "feeling" as well as its discouraging repetitions, its lack of order and its intricacy; the latter with their strange meticulousness, bewildering variety, and tedious fullness. Then there are the difficulties deriving from times and places contrasting so completely with our own, not to mention the formidable relations between dogma and history belonging to this field. All conspire to make a challenging task for any who would adequately face the question: "What manner of man is this?"

It is not that the general outline of Muhammad's biography is not clear. The hard part is understanding the full import of the facts. The latter can be readily set down. The historical fulcrum of Islam is the *Hijrah,* or Emigration, of Muhammad and his small community of believers from Mecca to Medina. This event, marking the beginning of the Muslim chronology in A.D. 622, makes the story of Islam a tale of two towns. The transition also marks an evident development in the function of the Prophet, implicit in the emergence of the preacher into the ruler, the "warner" into the warrior. Dates in the earlier life of the Prophet have to be reckoned backwards from the *Hijrah* at which time he had been teaching and preaching from some twelve or thirteen years. This sets the original call to prophecy at A.D. 609-610, when he was about the age of forty years, the date of Muhammad's birth being A.D. 569 or 570. Few figures of such significance in history have begun their active careers at so late an age as the Prophet of Islam.

Mecca was the first of the two towns in the story of primitive Islam. Though often surpassed in later history by imperial centers, Damascus, Baghdad, Cordoba, Istanbul, it has always remained the focal religious point in Islam, its name a synonym for a magnet of the faithful. Such was Mecca at the time of Muhammad's birth. The pilgrims who then came to it from widely scattered areas in the Arabian peninsula were pagans. The *Ka'bah* or shrine, in the heart of Mecca, contained the famous Black Stone, an object of immense veneration, as well as numerous idols, the most familiar among them being *Al-'Izzat,* goddess of power, *Manāt,* goddess of fate and *Allāt,* goddess of fertility. These deities were far from being the only objects of worship. Arabian paganism at that time is best described as polydaemonism, the worship of a multiplicity of divine powers or agencies, associated with particular natural phenomena or events or places. There is overwhelming evidence, from inscriptions and from pre-Islamic poetry and nomenclature (Muhammad's own father being named 'Abd-Allāh), that there was knowledge of a supreme deity, already called *Allāh*—the God. The essence of Muhammad's message was not the enunciation of His existence, but of His *sole* existence and of the criminal folly of all worship outside His worship.

Another notable feature of contemporary Arabian society was belief in jinn possession, often evidenced in ejaculation, divination, and the utterance of rhyming prose. One of the first and most persistent accusations against Muhammad was that he was demon-possessed. It seems likely that he feared this himself before he grew into a firm conviction as to the heavenly origin of his revelations. There were dark features about this pre-Islamic Arabian society, this *Jāhiliyyah,* or Time of Ignorance, prior to the coming of Islam. Pressure of poverty led to the practice of infanticide among the bedouin tribes and outside the month of truce there was widespread feuding and inter-tribal warfare. Attempts had been made earlier in the sixth century to bring about some political order and unity, but they had failed for lack of a compelling moral and religious force, such as Islam was shortly to supply.

The picture, however, is not wholly dark, even on the religious side. The Qur'ān speaks of men, known as *Hanīfs,* whose anti-idolatrous sentiment was an important factor in the background of Muhammad's experience. The extent and precise form of the *Hanīf* attitude are somewhat obscure, though the subject has great fascination. But Islam is later described as fulfilling the religion of the *Hanīfs,* whose great ancestral prototype is Abraham, the hero of ancient iconoclasm in the name of the single sovereign Lord. It seems reasonably certain that Muhammad was, in some sense, the spiritual kinsman of these disclaimers of idolatry and that they planted in his searching spirit the seeds of ardor against idol-worship which blossomed into the experience that made him the Prophet of Unity.

III

The other, and apparently greater, factor in the formation of Muhammad's mission was the presence of "the People of the Book"—the Quranic phrase for Jews and Christians—greater because they symbolized the germinal idea of prophecy and of peoples unified around a "scriptural" center. Scholars have differed widely both as to the details of Arabian Jewry and Arabian Christianity in the sixth century and as to the circumstances and quality of Muhammad's personal contact with these sources. Traditions as to his acquaintance with Christian monks and priests on caravan journeys have to be treated with reserve. If we take the contents of the Qur'ān as the decisive area for discussion of this problem, it would seem conclusive that Muhammad had no personal contact with the written Scriptures of either antecedent faith. The Biblical narratives reproduced in the Qur'ān differ considerably and suggest oral, not direct, acquaintance. There is an almost complete absence of what could be claimed as direct quotation from either Testament.[4]

The matter hinges in part on the vexed question of Muhammad's literacy. The well-known phrase *al-nabī al-ummī*, "the unlettered Prophet," could signify: "The Prophet to the people without a Book," to those who are as yet scriptureless. Certainly a great part of Muhammad's vocation lay in the conviction that his fellow Arabs should also have their Divine Book, an Arabic Qur'ān, a purpose which awaited an Arab Prophet, in the same tradition as Moses, David, and Jesus. Because non-Jews are referred to in the Qur'ān as *ummī*, the word is sometimes taken as meaning "without Scriptures of their own," rather than "illiterate," though this argument is weakened by the fact that Jews are occasionally referred to also as *ummī*. In their case it can only mean "illiterate." When the Qur'ān states explicitly that Muhammad did not write the Qur'ān, it may mean that he did

74

not compose it—as orthodox Islam firmly insists he did not—
rather than that he could not actually pen any word.

Be the historical verdict on this question what it may, two
facts are clear. Traditional Islam believes Muhammad to have
been actually illiterate, so that the Qur'ān is indubitably and entirely God's Word. Muhammad can hardly in fact have been a
reader of any older Scriptures. What then of his oral sources of
knowledge? Here, too, there is a tantalizing divergence of opinion. Some hold that the predominant influence was Jewish, others that it was Christian. The most confident theory on the Jewish side is that which actually gives Muhammad a Jewish rabbi
for tutor in Mecca, assuming that he sought out such a person
when his religious yearning was first aroused.[5] All that can be
said with certainty is that Muhammad knew of Jews and Christians and something of their history; that the former were numerous around Medina and present in Mecca; that the latter
were strong across the Red Sea in Ethiopia and had a checkered,
declining role in Southern Arabia and in the border areas of
such princedoms as the Ghassanids in the north, where Byzantium merged into the peninsula. It was not, by and large, a
Christianity calculated to present Muhammad with a fully authentic picture of Christ and the Church. Some of the urgent
issues of early Church history, docetism and monophysitism, are
mirrored in the Quranic account of Jesus as non-crucified
Prophet-Messiah. But it gave to Muhammad, under what precise
circumstances may never be known, the most fundamental concepts in his vocation and in subsequent Islam, a sure monotheism and a prophetic mission in which a Divine relationship of
revelation, through a Scripture, created a community of faith.
It was a tremendous step when Muhammad became assured of
himself as a new and final term in prophetic continuity, making
a new book, and thence a new faith.

IV

If this be the creative background of Muhammad the Prophet,
what of the circumstantial setting of Muhammad the man? Mecca
was "no mean city," with its pilgrim prestige and its wide rang-
ing caravan commerce. For Islam was not of desert origin, despite

the persisting illusion which calls its rigid monotheism a reflection of desert vastness and the majestic sun. In its genesis it was an urban entity. Its founder was not one of the *badū*, but a citizen and reputedly a merchant. He was a posthumous child and became in early boyhood a complete orphan, protected first by his grandfather 'Abd al-Muttalib and later by his uncle Abū Tālib. His parents were 'Abdallāh, grandson of Hāshim, and Āminah. The young child thus knew the privations of poverty and yet also the dignity of a family line. For his parents belonged to a branch of the powerful Quraish, custodians of the sacred *Ka'bah* and the leading tribe of Mecca.

History has little to record, though tradition is fertile, about those early years. Muhammad rose to manhood with a reputation for reliability and at twenty-five was married to Khadījah, a widow his senior in years, in whose service he is said to have been employed. The marriage gave Muhammad security and domestic happiness though not—unhappily—any male issue surviving. Four daughters of the union grew to adult life. Two sons died in early infancy. Muhammad remained in sole wedlock to Khadījah until her death, which occurred at a very low ebb in his fortunes just before the scene moves to Medina. His plural marriages belong entirely to the period following Khadījah's death. She played an important role in the formative years of Muhammad's vocation and he was steadfastly devoted to her memory. Her death is probably reflected in some of the changes which later supervened.

Little is known about the Prophet's personal and commercial life in the decade and a half between his marriage and his prophetic call. But undoubtedly two formative ideas were working deeply in his soul—the oppressive folly of idolatry and the role of prophethood, through Scriptures, in the life of great religious communities, both corroborated by the strong, if rare, example of the *Hanīfs,* with their repudiation of idols and their wistfulness for larger truth.

Brooding in the gaunt foothills of Mount Hirā' in the region of his native Mecca, Muhammad came into the strong conviction that idolatry was criminal folly and that God the One commanded utterance against it. "Let the word be spoken." "Cry in the name of the Lord." God Who taught man the use of the pen and from Whom flowed all the scholar's wisdom was about to teach a more urgent and more potent truth, a word of mouth, an oral affirmation. Steadily the mission to be the mouthpiece apprehended Muhammad until it drove him into preaching and transformed the Meccan citizen into the "warner" from the Lord.

Such was the ground and meaning of Muhammad's call, in a brooding "wilderness" experience, where facts of conscious observation in the contemporary scene became articulate in a personal calling to utterance and warning in the city. Though Muslims in general hold that Muhammad's call did not derive from the conscious processes of his mind, but came wholly from without, so that what he felt and said was entirely God's and not the product of genius, of travail, or even of intelligence, that are the Prophet's own, it seems impossible to do justice to his stature without reference to the personal context.

Let us, then, accompany Muhammad on the decisive journey into Mount Hirā' when the first revelation came. It was the forerunner of many and the climax of a deepening experience. The earliest accounts vary in lesser details but describe Muhammad as within, and then without, a cave. He became aware of a voice and of a figure which stood compellingly on every line of vision wherever he turned or walked. The figure was the angel Gabriel bearing the message of God. His command, if the traditional identification of the first revelation is correct, was to recite, cry, speak, in the name of the Lord.

> *Recite in the name of thy Lord Who created*
> *Created man from a clot*
> *Recite! for thy Lord is most gracious*
> *Who taught with the pen*
> *Taught man what he knows not* (Surah xcvi. 1-4).

The commanding voice assured the wondering listener that he was the Apostle of God. Referring later to the same experience, Muhammad is made to say:

> It is none other than a revelation revealed. One mighty in power taught it to him, One endued with strength

77

and he stood erect on the highest horizon. He drew near and came nearer still, until he was within two bows' length or nearer and He revealed unto his servant that which he revealed (Surah liii. 4-10).

The injunction was to "Read," or "Recite." The word means the making vocal of that which is already written. The revelation, here in its initiation and throughout, is understood as the coming down of a pre-existent Book, a transaction that extended over some twenty-three years during which the contents of the original Book ("The Mother of the Book") preserved in Heaven with God were uttered, recorded, and then perpetually recited in devotion, on earth. The instrumentality of this process known as *Tanzīl*, "sending down" is usually that of Gabriel or of a Divine Spirit. The recipience on the earthly side is Muhammad's alone, standing as the last in the long series of prophets each of whom had received earlier "Books."

It was in the nature of Muhammad's initial experience that it should be successively repeated, from that first occasion in the month of *Ramadān* until death terminated the then perfect Book and took away the point of its earthly impact. It was well that the experience renewed itself, for Muhammad's first reaction was dubiety and apprehension. He feared lest he had been beset with malicious jinns or was the victim of a destroying illusion sent to mock him. Reassurance, however, slowly displaced misgiving, thanks in part to the tenacious confidence and discerning kindness of Khadījah, who solaced and supported her husband. He had great need of her faith and friendship. The revelations were accompanied by intense emotional stress, physical limpness and perspiration, and a state of trance. Though the onset of the experiences subsequently came to occur without the same intensity of degree in these phenomena, they seem always to have been present in some form as the qualifying accompaniment of the "Quranic" state, as distinct from the other, personal deliverances of the Prophet incorporated into the later traditions. In some accounts the state of Quranic revelation had further physical symptoms, so that a camel, for example, sank down under the sudden weight when the Prophet was riding. It would appear that the coming of the experiences was unpredictable. In the Medinan years they bear more appearance of conscious relation to particular, legal or administrative situations for which directives were necessary. There is no time or place here to seek to penetrate into the deep inward mystery of Muhammad's revelatory experience. It is perhaps too distant and too charged an area of historical significance for any purely scientific analysis to be either feasible or sound. What is of vastly greater importance is how these experiences shaped Muhammad's life-story and what they came to mean for him in terms of character and destiny and for his followers as a God-given reality.

v

As his assurance of the validity of his call increased, Muhammad began slowly to fulfill the preacher's commission and the revelations came in greater frequency. The style and form of his message is reflected in the earliest Meccan Surahs of the Qur'ān, with their ecstatic quality—short, staccato sentences, proclaiming the majesty of nature, the evil folly of idol-worship, and the impending judgment. Though the style later became more argumentative and hortatory, with lengthy passages developing the themes of patriarchal history, the earliest deliverances are fervid and trumpet-like. Muhammad's reception in Mecca was at first dubious. His hearers were uncertain how to take him. Was he unbalanced, jinn-possessed, or eccentric? As he persisted, however, and became more defiantly assertive, within his small, mainly domestic, circle of early adherents, bemused interest passed into scorn and contumely. These, in turn, grew into active hostility as the people of Mecca came increasingly to sense in Muhammad's doctrines a threat to their dearest vested interests. They could not have known that Mecca's Ka'bah, purified of its idols, would remain as the integral center of Muhammad's monotheism, its pilgrimage prestige unimpaired. Had they known this in advance, their championing of idolatry might have been less insistent. But in prospect a threat to idols looked unmistakably a threat to the Ka'bah and thus a threat to the hegemony and income of the Quraish.

Despite this intensifying antagonism, Muhammad was person-

79

ally secure in the constancy of his powerful uncle Abū Tālib, who without accepting Islam refused to bow to intimidation or subterfuge and surrender his nephew. Others in the small group of believers, being more exposed, suffered considerably. In the sixth year of the revelations Muhammad encouraged a party to seek refuge in Ethiopia, whither a second emigration followed shortly afterwards. The earliest of Muhammad's prominent disciples after Khadījah was Abū Bakr, *Al-Siddīq,* two years Muhammad's junior and a staunch comrade. 'Umar, another close associate often thought of as the Saul of Islam, by reason of his dramatic conversion, acceded after the Ethiopian emigration. Both were to become fathers-in-law to Muhammad.

The fewness of these converts and the resistant quality of Meccan heathenism perplexed and tried the Prophet.[6] Was the new movement to remain perpetually in jeopardy, a despised minority with no Arabian foothold, compelled to seek sanctuary across the Red Sea and denied victory in the central citadel of the idolatry against which it was set? Muhammad slowly ripened into a decision that shaped the whole future of Islam. The faith must find expression in a community which would insure it external force and the opportunity to prevail against the opposition. The Qur'ān, in this middle Meccan period, lays increasing stress on the historical parallels of earlier prophets, all of whom are pictured as manifestly victorious over their foes. Noah's denigrators are drowned in the flood; those of Moses in the Red Sea. Abraham and Joseph, teachers of the Divine Unity, come into their own. Just as it had been with those generations so it would be with the scornful fellow citizens of the Meccan Prophet.

Little is clearly known about the internal organization and worship of the Muslim group inside Mecca during these early years. Institutional Islam is more readily studied in the second city of its genesis—Medina. Meanwhile, however, that city had not come within the conscious hopes of Muhammad. Only the decision was shaping within him that if Mecca did not respond, the faith of Islam must root itself elsewhere and find some civic cradle where it might one day grow into a purging conqueror of Mecca. The eleventh and twelfth years after Muhammad's call moved imperceptibly in the direction of such thoughts, with the future center beginning to present itself. The developments came only just in time to save Islam from the possible Meccan consequences of the deaths, in 619, of both Khadījah and Abū Tālib, the devoted wife and the loyal protector.

Though their passing exposed and saddened the Prophet, it also sharpened the decision facing the Meccans. Should they slay Muhammad, their own kin? Putting him under a ban had been tried without success. There seemed no hope of silencing him. Nor was he to be cajoled into retreat. On the other hand, since 'Umar, he had won no conspicuous allegiance. Even while they were debating he had returned from a preaching mission to Al Tā'if, southeast of Mecca, chastened, scorned, and upbraided, with nothing save scars and defeat. There seemed little likelihood that any other center would receive him. Though Abū Tālib no longer remained to deter their threats, they perhaps need not take the irrevocable step. Islam might peter out in the frustrations of an odd enthusiast.

If they did reason thus, the Meccans reckoned without Yathrib, the important city to the north, soon to be renamed *Madīnat-al-Nabi*, "the City of the Prophet." A few of its pilgrim people encountered Muhammad in Mecca after his return from Al Tā'if. They showed a welcome interest in his message and took back in their hearts the seeds of potential discipleship. Jewish influence in Medina was greater than in the Meccan region and may have disposed the citizens towards Muhammad's message. There were also family ties. Muhammad's great-grandfather Hāshim had married a Medinan lady. Internally, the situation in Medina awaited a master-hand which might curb dissension and unite the factions. In 621 the Medinan group returned on pilgrimage and to Muhammad's great joy demonstrated their continued affinity with his teaching. In the First Pledge of Al 'Aqabah, they bound themselves to abandon idolatry, theft, adultery, fornication, and infanticide and to obey the Prophet in all that was right. They returned to their city and subsequently called for a teacher who had marked success in widening the Muslim allegiance.

Muhammad's hopes grew. "Northward, look!" he might have said, "the land is bright." He bided his time, concealing from

81

the Meccans his Medinan links. He knew they could be relied on to appreciate that Muhammad at large would be far more serious a danger than a restive and frustrated Muhammad in Mecca. In 622, the Medinan Muslims returned, reporting a larger adherence to Islam and entered the Second Pledge of Al 'Aqabah, this time binding themselves to defend the Prophet. This undertaking was all that he needed. It was an implicit invitation to seek a new base of activities in the northern city. Muhammad ordered his disciples to emigrate to Medina where the Medinan Muslims were ready to receive them. The famous *Hijrah* happened with most timely expedition. The suspicions of the Quraish had been aroused and they had been anxious at all costs to forestall such a departure. But they were the victims, in part, of their own indecision and had not reckoned that the whole Muslim band would forsake all their immovable property. When at length they did take action, Muhammad and Abū Bakr, following in the wake of the main emigration, succeeded in eluding pursuit and made good their escape.

VI

The emigrating party was probably less than seven score strong but it made one of the most successful voluntary exiles in human history. The step brought clearly into the open the logic of Muhammad's inner decision. The faith was built into a community. The city of the lawgiver and ruler made possible the ultimate reconquest of the city of the preacher. The tale of the two towns passed into its second period and both Muhammad the man and the Qur'ān the Book reflect the inclusive meaning of the transition. Muhammad had passed upwards of twelve years proclaiming the message in which his mission was generated. The following ten years were to see him establishing the empire in which his mission was embodied and enforced.

Henceforward, the biographer finds the increasing amalgam of faith and rule, of creed and organization, in the Prophet's story. Those parts of the Qur'ān belonging to the Medinan years are predominately legal and political. Their concern is with campaigns, confiscations, customs, and behavior, rather than with patriarchs and preaching. There are corresponding changes

in the role and quality of the central leader himself. Those unmistakable elements of greatness in the suffering preacher-
prophet, bearing obloquy and calumny with tenacious fidelity to
the truth he had been given to see, loom greater in retrospect
than the qualities demonstrated in the mingled magnanimity
and opportunism that mark the post-*Hijrah* leader.

When Muhammad arrived in Medina the position was fraught
with peril. The allegiance in which Muhammad had read an
invitation to immigration there was far from unanimous. The
non-Muslim Medinans, at worst resentful, at best uncommitted,
needed to be brought into unequivocal allegiance. Even the Muslim Medinans were committed only to a defensive pledge. Islam
now had two component groups, in a situation potential of much
strife and misunderstanding unless a sagacious mind controlled
them. For the Meccan fugitives were without homes and possessions, helpless guests of their Medinan co-religionists. Yet they
had been longer in the Prophet's obedience and had suffered
more. Tact and statesmanship were manifestly required. That
Muhammad lacked neither was symbolized when he rode into
the city and, throwing the reins on the neck of his camel, vowed
that the camel should decide where his headquarters and the first
mosque should be located—thus saving himself from the invidious consequences of any personal choice.

Though he succeeded resoundingly in riding out these initial
difficulties, there was one area of his expectation where Muhammad suffered acute disappointment. Throughout his preaching
he had looked confidently toward the Jews and Christians, as
"People of the Book," to welcome and accept his prophetic
claims. In Medina this hope had occasion to be tested, at least in
respect of the Jews, far more extensively than was possible in
Mecca. The result was bitterly contrasted with the Prophet's
hopes. Closer proximity to larger numbers of Jews soon revealed
to Muhammad that, far from acknowledgment, Jewry treated
him with amused disdain. His claims they flatly rejected as pretentious. The inevitable consequence was that Muhammad became increasingly hostile to the Jews and interpreted their non-
acceptance as disloyalty to their own inheritance. Islam became,
from this point, much more distinctive and consciously self-suf-

ficient. The Quranic passages, exhorting to friendly relations
with the "People of the Book" and confirmatory study of their
Scriptures, give way to flat disavowal and explicit condemnation.
"God fight them, what liars they are" (Surah ix. 30). Most sig-
nificantly of all the *qiblah,* or direction of Muslim prayer, was
changed at this time from Jerusalem to Mecca, evidently to the
initial consternation of some of the Prophet's own followers.[7]
At this time Mecca, though associated with traditions of Abraham, was still idolatrous. The change of *qiblah* surely implies
the intention to repossess it. Jerusalem's monotheism was a per-
ennial symbol, which was none the less abandoned in the name
of Islam's independence and distinctiveness.

Apparently in the same context are the larger emphases concerning Abraham at this time. In the early preaching he had
been cited as a preacher of God's Unity and as a champion
against idols. Ishmael now comes into great prominence in association with Abraham and both are linked with Mecca and the
building of the *Ka'bah.* Islam is proclaimed as the faith of Abraham, going back beyond the Mosaic law, whose Jewish legatees
had been unfaithful. Similarly we find in the years after the
Hijrah a growth of distinctive Muslim rituals and practices,
some of which will be our concern in the chapter that follows.

Meanwhile the Jews, having failed to fulfill Muhammad's expectations, came increasingly into the line of Muslim hostility.
But they were not alone in this experience. A kind of triangular
situation developed in which the "corners" are Muhammad, the
Meccans, and the Jews—excluding the non-Jewish, non-Muslim
elements in Medina itself, whose steady approximation to Muhammad's cause was brought about largely by their involvement
with him in the other struggles. It proved difficult to live in the
same city as Muhammad and not become physically implicated
in his purpose. War, deliberate if intermittent, is what followed.

VII

To set forth this period in the Prophet's career objectively, without offending modern Muslim susceptibilities, is difficult in the
extreme. His departure from Mecca and Meccan hostility to the
prosecutor of their idols certainly made for a situation of poten-

tial conflict. It should be noted that some of Muhammad's allegiance and circle, remaining in Mecca after his departure, were
unmolested. The Muslim thesis, however, is that the campaigns
which followed were essentially defensive. They were necessary
to the survival of Islam. The position of the Qur'ān itself is that
war, not least in the month of truce, is essentially an evil, but
the threatened extinction of Islam is a far greater evil (Surah
ii. 217). Peace, therefore, is not to be preferred to war, until
Islam is inviolable and secure. Muhammad is to be the judge
of the extent and persistence of the danger which justifies fighting. Some observers interpret this necessity to fight as arising
from the need to provide, through booty, for the unhoused
Muhājirūn, or immigrants, to consolidate all Medina by implication in Muhammad's cause, and to accumulate the means of
warfare for the final conquest of Mecca. But taking the basic
thesis of Muslim apology that the wars were defensive, another
basic decision is evidently involved, namely, that religious survival should be served and guaranteed by force. Muhammad's
policy, as recognized by the highest Muslim evaluation of the
events now to be summarized, was to answer the situation as
the soldier does.

Medina under the Prophet's rulership thus found itself increasingly implicated in hostilities with the Meccans. They began
over the Meccan caravans whose route to the north passed precariously within Medinan range. The Muslims participating in
these activities became steadily more bold and more numerous
until the Battle of Badr closed the first chapter of the Medinan
period with a clear victory to which the Qur'ān refers as "the
day of the Furqān," or criterion—a day of putting to the test and
of the emergence of Islam as the signally favored, and so distinctive, cause (Surah viii. 41). The Battle might well be described as an encounter since by later standards the numbers involved were slight. But even skirmishes can be historically decisive. Having tidings of a Muslim venture, a returning Meccan
caravan from the north sent for protective reinforcements from
the city and it was with these that the Muslim band engaged.
Under the Prophet's own skillful military leadership some three
hundred Muslims dispersed a thousand Meccans, losing only

fourteen slain to some fifty of the Meccans, not to mention a large number of captives. Muslim history regards the Battle of Badr as crucial. Certainly the sword was unleashed and the scabbard cast away. The *Jihād,* or appeal to battle, had been irrevocably invoked.

Before the Muslims faced the inevitable Meccan reaction to this reverse, the opportunity was taken to bring increasing pressure upon the Jews, several of whom were put to death or dispossessed. Within a month after the return from Badr there were individual acts of intimidation, culminating in the expulsion of the Banŭ Qainuqā'a. Almost a year after Badr, came the Meccan advance to revenge. On this second occasion the issue was less favorable. Apparently in overconfidence the Muslims lost discipline and were in danger of being routed. They were only rallied in a desperate effort by the Prophet himself. The Quranic passage relating to the Battle (Surah iii. 120 seq.) rebuked the Muslim presumption and interpreted the reverse as a test of faith and a deserved chastisement. Over seventy Muslims were slain to some twenty of the Quraish. Muhammad had need of all his resourcefulness to survive the serious loss of prestige, though the Meccans on their side do not seem to have realized or utilized the full extent of their victory. They withdrew after mutilating the dead and Muhammad, after a delayed show of pursuit, returned to Medina.

Perhaps enheartened by this set-back, perhaps fearful of further Muslim acts of hostility, the Jews of the Medinan region began to make closer cause with the Quraish. Their economically superior position exposed them to dangers of expulsion such as had already been indicated. The increasing menace from the Muslims suggested common action with Mecca, with which, however, there were few other ties. It was the familiar story of the common enemy bringing together unwilling allies. While it seems clear that Jewish elements were implicated in Meccan enmity to Muhammad, it is also clear that both elements in the uneasy alliance were blundering and vacillating. Any situation like that confronting them, and relating to an adversary of Muhammad's resolve and resource, calls for comparable resolution and tenacity. These the Jews and Meccans lacked—as is only too evident from the ill-starred and inept "siege" of Medina known in Muslim history as "the Battle of the Ditch." Like people acting inadvisably out of fear and bewilderment, they only succeeded in fulfilling their worst dread.

The siege was raised after the besiegers found the weather too cold for them and the irresolute Quraish, lacking energetic leadership, withdrew, leaving their Jewish partners to face the accumulated wrath of Muhammad. There followed the massacre of the Banū Quraizah which marks the darkest depth of Muslim policy, a depth which the palliatives suggested by some modern Muslim historians quite fail to measure. The whole tribe was dispossessed and after suing for clemency, the women and children were enslaved, while the men, traditionally numbered at seven hundred, were executed beside long trench graves in a day of signal terror. The fearful fate of the Banū Quraizah far outweighed their deserts and contrasted darkly with the magnanimity of Muhammad when subsequently he faced their Meccan allies in the "siege" after his reconquest of the Holy City.

But the circumstances were different. Muhammad, by canons of soldierly wisdom, could hardly yet afford to be magnanimous. Not all the *Muhājirūn* Muslims were yet re-propertied, nor was the situation at all secure in the region. In approving, and later eulogizing in a funeral speech, the judge who had decided the sentence on the Banū Quraizah, Muhammad was no doubt following the behests of a stern policy. Certainly the step succeeded. Disaffection, both religious and political, was cowed into paralysis, if not submission, throughout Medina. The next main confiscatory enterprise took the Muslims some hundred miles north of the city to the Jews of rich Khaibar, who could have been only remotely related to Medinan affairs but who none the less were made to forfeit all their possessions.

This immense plunder greatly consolidated and enlarged Muhammad's potential. Meanwhile his decision to revisit Mecca in A.D. 628 six years after the *Hijrah* revealed the direction in which his policy was moving and for which the potential was required. The Meccans, having word of his coming, refused to admit him as a pilgrim, fearing the consequences, but entered into an agreement whereby he would be free to make the pilgrimage

87

peacefully the following year, when the Meccans themselves would evacuate the city for three days. As part of this compact, known as the Treaty of Al-Hudaibiyyah, Muhammad agreed to a ten years' truce between the Muslims and the Quraish, during which either side would be free to federate with any tribes. He also allowed a Meccan right to extradite all fugitive Meccans coming over to Islam, while conceding that any fugitive Muslims returning to Mecca should not be handed back by the Meccans. This seemed to some of Muhammad's followers a concession of weakness and he was much criticized also for deferring to a Meccan demand that he should not sign the treaty document as Apostle of God, but as Muhammad, son of 'Abdallāh.

But the Prophet was playing his hand shrewdly and overrode the querulous Muslims. He had established a kind of equality with the Meccans, by having negotiated with them. The pilgrimage permission was important. He calculated that there would be few, if any, Muslim fugitives to Mecca, while would-be converts sent back to Mecca would be rescued by Islam in the final conquest. The truce would give valuable time for preparations and tribal accessions. When Muhammad returned to Medina, the logic of events leading to their consummation in Mecca's reconquest unfolded itself steadily. Within two years the Prophet returned not to debate with the Quraish but to accept their capitulation. The story of the two cities was moving to a dramatic climax in which they would both become Islam's.

There was first, however, the intervening pilgrimage duly performed in 629, under the terms of the treaty, which the Meccans strictly observed, evacuating their city while Muhammad and the Muslims performed the rites, but refusing, when requested, to prolong their absence more than three days. The visit brought Muhammad a few notable accessions, including the custodian of the *Ka'bah* and a future leader Khālid, destined for great military exploits.[8] The star of Islam was moving into the ascendant; that of the Quraish was waning.

Muhammad's plans for the final settlement with his Meccan adversaries were carefully laid and boldly carried through. Despite clearly growing aspirations for the expansion of the faith into northern regions, indicated in letters summoning several potentates in the Christian world to Islamize, and in expeditions into Ghassanid territory, he concentrated on the prior Meccan objective. When a tribe in treaty-bonds with the Quraish attacked another tribe in alliance with Medina, he denounced the truce and refused to heed the pleas of Abū Safyān, personally made in Medina, for its restoration. The head of the Quraish returned to Mecca with no assurances and much misgiving. But even with this premonition, the Meccans were completely surprised by the speed and thoroughness of the Prophet's moves. He gathered a formidable force and set out early in the ninth year after the *Hijrah*, not revealing his destination until secrecy had become unnecessary. As he drew near to Mecca, Al-'Abbās, his uncle, came out and joined him and was followed later by Abū Safyān. The Quraish resistance evaporated before it could be mobilized. Four Muslim columns entered the city and occupied it in the name of Islam. The Prophet's triumph was complete. The tale of the struggle of the two towns had ended: the tale of their new empire was about to begin.

VIII

Muhammad, conqueror of Mecca, proved a magnanimous victor. The Meccans were required to abandon and destroy their idols and seem to have done so with far less compunction than later characterized the heathen of Al Tā'if. There was almost no bloodshed. The Meccans were assured that their city was the dearest place on earth to the Prophet's heart. Its citizens as Muslims underwent no confiscations—even the returning *Muhājirūn* foregoing their old properties. Muhammad was anxious to pacify the religious capital of Arabia as rapidly as possible and to incorporate the purged *Ka'bah* into Islamic pilgrimage, thus preserving for the new faith the cohesive power of Meccan prestige.

The subsequent year was spent in extending the sway of Islam over an increasing number of tribes beyond Mecca until at the pilgrimage of the tenth year after the *Hijrah* Muhammad, who was not present, caused the "Immunity," or "Release," to be read as an edict by 'Alī. This document, preserved in Surah ix, served notice on all pagans that none such could participate in any later pilgrimage. It gave the tribes four months in which to return to their homes and, thereafter, declared them lawfully immune from protection and exposed to any Muslim attack as long as they failed to Islamize—saving only those having treaty arrangements with the Prophet. When these had run their course, such groups might also be attacked. In the same Surah, though not in the "Release" itself, is the command to fight Jews and Christians until they also become subject peoples. Thus was enunciated the basic principle of *Jihād,* or martial endeavor, on behalf of Islam, going beyond the earlier provision which enjoined fighting only after the enemy had first attacked. It thus became a ruling precept in Islam that all areas of non-Islam were areas whose conquest the true Muslim was enjoined to seek until the inhabitants either submitted or were reduced to subject status, the second alternative obtaining only in respect of the tolerated minorities, "the Peoples of the Book." It will be seen that this principle was the extension in permanent, legal form of the plan of action developed by Muhammad in the early years of the *Hijrah.* That pattern which had been brought to conspicuous success in the case of Mecca was to become the precedent for all other victories, far and wide, over territories yet to be brought under the political suzerainty of Medina and into religious allegiance to Mecca, now cleansed of idolatry.

The Prophet himself survived to see only the beginnings of the *Jihād* that, within a decade of his death, was to add Egypt, the Levant, the valley of the twin rivers, and Western Persia to Islam in one of the swiftest conquests of history. Symbolically, at the onset of his last illness, an expedition was ready to set out into the border lands of Arabia and Byzantium. He completed the Farewell Pilgrimage to Mecca, one year after the "Release." In a moving address he proclaimed the perfecting of the religion, *Al-Islām,* as the culmination of the Divine Mercy to men. He was sixty-three years of age. Worn by two and a half decades of intense, emotional and spiritual stress, as recipient of the Qur'ān, as leader, ruler, legislator and nerve-center of a new and vibrant politico-religious entity, he seems to have sensed the approaching end. But the climax of his last illness was dramatic. When death took him, it seemed to some of his stunned and grief-stricken disciples that it could not be. It was A.D. 632. When finally Abū Bakr, his long companion and immediate successor in authority, prevailed upon the distracted assembly gathered in the mosque to realize the truth of the incredible, it was with the reminder that the Prophet, who had now breathed his last, was no more than the servant of the ever-living God. Abū Bakr's speech beside the death precincts linked together, as the call to prayer has never ceased to do, the One God and His Apostle, the first faith of Islam that belongs with the second: "There is no god save God and Muhammad is His Messenger."

To the numbed and distraught faithful in Medina and beyond, to the new and sometimes dubious adherents throughout the peninsula, some of whom were ready to withdraw in pagan reassertion, it was as if some giant oak that filled the landscape had been felled, making a great void that left the very scheme of things shorn and unfamiliar. How Abū Bakr, and 'Umar after him, succeeded in rallying the whole cause and launching it upon the vast career, for which the Prophet had shaped and destined it, is part of Islamic history. What faith, devotion, and religious awe have done with the vacuum left by the Prophet's death, filling it with the possessive instincts of communal memory, will concern us shortly in this chapter. It remains to try to take, in some inclusive assessment, the measure of the historical Muhammad.

IX

Of the broad sweep and import of the facts as now summarized, there can be little doubt, though specialists will be always delving afresh to reconsider some particular aspect. Finally it is not so much the facts, but the criteria, which constitute the problem for the biographer of Muhammad. Shall he look backward into Arabian paganism and find the Prophet great and reforming? Shall he look forward into the first Muslim century and beyond to see in this biography one of the rarest potentialities of human history? Or is he to look backward into the great Old Testament prophetic tradition, to Amos, Hosea, and Jeremiah, to find in Muhammad a strange, and yet unmistakable, shift in the whole concept and expression of prophethood? Or backward, less far, to the hills of Galilee and Judaea where there are criteria of almost insupportable contrast? Should the criteria be only local and contemporary, when Muslim faith and practice give to the facts of that place and time a significance of universal range? Perhaps here, as not seldom in human relationships, the task of the outsider is only rightly to formulate the questions. He can never give the answer from within, though he may well be in a better position than the adherent to see what it should include.

Two crucial points are all that can be made. It should be understood, in the first place, that to account for Muhammad in terms of personal genius, though an increasing number of Muslims tend to do so, is to part company with orthodoxy. When Sayyid Amīr 'Alī, for example, in his well-known and often reprinted *The Spirit of Islam,* spoke of "the wisdom of the inspired lawgiver" and referred to Quranic institutions as Muhammad's provision, he was adapting the older belief that the revelation came wholly from God, without involving Muhammad's conscious will or reason. The traditional view insists throughout on the instrumentality of the Prophet, not his initiative; on his being the agent not the originator. Nevertheless, it is impossible to resist the conclusion that historic Islam is decisively shaped by the manner of man Muhammad was.

Here, in the second place, there is need to beware of missing the ultimate in the circumstantial details. The latter have been the theme of much unhappy controversy which has tended to confuse itself. Too much and too little is then made of him. Too much, it may be, of plural marriages and too little of their political, and other, significance and of Muhammad's devotion to Khadījah; too much of the opportunist tactics, too little of the unswerving singleness of mind; too much of the tribal confiscations and repressive measures, too little of the solicitude for orphans and magnanimity to certain foes; too much of his ruthlessness, too little of the hypocrites and false dealers with whom the Qur'ān affirms he was often surrounded. Or it may be that, conversely, too much is made of Muhammad's circumstances and too little of his obligation to the absolutes of every age. If much criticism is too naïve, it shares that quality with much vindication. Muhammad has been condemned, and again justified, in terms that have not taken the measure of their theme. He has proved, both for good and ill, profounder than much criticism and eulogy.

Where, then, shall we seek this ultimate decision? Surely in the supreme crisis of the biography where the faith has located and dated it genesis. As the tale of two towns, the Prophet's biography is finally the story of a crucial choice, no less crucial than that implicit in the contrasted Gospel saying: "The cup that my Father hath given me shall I not drink it?" It is the decision arising from the question: "How should Prophethood succeed?" What is the final relation of the messenger of God to the people to whom he is sent when they forbear to hear? The Muhammadan decision here is formative of all else in Islam. It was a decision for community, for resistance, for external victory, for pacification and rule. The decision for the Cross—no less conscious, no less formative, no less inclusive—was the contrary decision.

It is impossible to say precisely when the choice became final in Muhammad's career. We have suggested that he determined on a new center because he sought a means of prophetic victory. But it may be that finding himself in a new center he resolved to make it an instrument for the submission of the old. Some have argued a marked deterioration in the character of Muhammad in the Medinan years. That is probably too simple, mistaking a symptom for its source. The deeper truth is that at some point Muhammad elected for a religious authority, armed with sinews of war and means of government, and that the decision worked itself out in character, conduct, and destiny. Externally it succeeded. It has become fashionable in vindicating the decision to insist that it was reluctant and uncharacteristic.

> He who never in his life had wielded a weapon, to whom the sight of human suffering caused intense pain and pity, and who against all the canons of Arab manliness, wept bitterly at the loss of his children or disciples . . . this man was now compelled from the necessities of the situation, and against his own inclinations, to repel the attacks of the enemy by force of arms, to

93

> organise his followers for self-defence, and often to send
> out expeditions to anticipate treacherous and sudden
> onslaughts.[9]

The original Muslim historians do not bear out this idealistic
view. But the more out of character the choice, if so it be, the
more evidently chosen. The more fully the modern Muslim interpretation of the choice be accepted, the more decisive its
quality as the way Muhammad took to answer the fundamental
question confronting all religious mission: "How shall, how
should, the truth prevail?" Opposition there was, in Mecca;
vested interest, bigotry, sin, and evil. Bearing the brunt of that
opposition in single-minded devotion, Muhammad the preacher
is a person whose nobility still reaches us through the intervening
years. Is the returning conqueror a greater figure?

x

The meaning of the muezzin's witness to the Apostle of Islam is
not, of course, limited to his biography. The Prophet's passing,
as we saw, left a tremendous vacancy in the lives and emotions
of his followers. But death itself in certain ways closed up the
gap it had created and Muhammad in death became the universal possession of Muslim history, so soon and so far to spread in
the world. It did so, in that the vacuum for practical purposes
demanded to be filled. The institution of the Caliphate was the
answer. Abū Bakr immediately stepped into the administrative
authority of Muhammad and with 'Umar, his next successor,
provided the leadership for which the new day of Muslim expansion called. Whether we regard this as a Divinely willed succession or an empirical solution to an obvious need (the latter view
being very recent), the fact is the same. Muhammad had been so
towering a figure that wherever his mantle fell it necessarily con-
ferred immense prestige and authority. Its first two bearers were
equal to their destiny, and what they inaugurated continued
through all vicissitudes until 1924.

This succession, however, was civil and administrative only.
Muhammad, as Prophet, was unique, final, irrepeatable. Thus
death closed as well as occasioned the prophetic break. It was

true that Muhammad would no longer be there among men to receive the Quranic revelation. But by the same token that volume was now entire and complete. The loss of the Apostle was the final fulfillment of the Book. Those twenty-three or so years had sufficed for its coming down and the point of its earthly impact was in that sense no longer necessary. Muhammad passed into history, in the legacy his death had made final of the book his apostleship had made complete. Any consideration of Muhammad in history takes us at once to the Holy Book of Islam, of which he was the human instrument and which epitomizes so much of his story.

Some brief attempt will be made below under "The Call to Understanding" to appreciate the Muslim significance of the Qur'ān. This Book, among the shortest of Holy Books if allowance is made for much repeated material, shows a marked development of style from the sharp poetic language of the earliest Surahs, to the long prosaic legal form of the latest. The substance also reflects a similar evolution. Muhammad is first the "warner" and Prophet proclaiming judgment on idolatry. He passes into exhortation and preaching, drawing at length on the example of patriarchs and former prophets to enforce his appeal against recalcitrants. Later this historical material gives way to the themes of the legislator and the leader, directing his community in peace and war, amid the gathering issues of its life and struggle. The whole Book is a repository of the Muslim story though it never sets out to be biographical or historical. References to historical events outside Arabia and Islam are rare. But the very stuff of the development, arising from the original call to recite and culminating in the perfecting of the religion, is here in all its inward quality and drama. The Book perpetuates, as it were, the preaching and the leading by which the Prophet both summoned and shaped his people.

The Qur'ān is the ultimate miracle of Islam. It is the final evidence of the Divine origin of the Prophet's mission. Its Arabic eloquence is indicative of its source in God, since its bearer was illiterate. Its literary form, in the orthodox view, is inextricably part of its nature. Its contents alone do not constitute it as the Qur'ān. Inasmuch as translation inevitably destroys the form, however successfully it renders the contents, translation has been regarded until the second quarter of this century as generally inadvisable and impossible. The initiative to Quranic translation has mainly come, until lately, from non-Islamic sources and while orthodoxy has come now to admit the desirability of making it available for non-Muslims, such non-Arabic renderings are technically not the Qur'ān, but only its meaning.[10]

The Qur'ān has a culminating relation to all other Scriptures which it confirms in so far as they are valid and corrects where they have been corrupted. Muhammad is thus the "Seal of the Prophets" with whom Divine revelation reached its climax. This conviction of continuity with previous Scriptures is an important reason why the Muslim is satisfied that Islam is final and that all valid religion tends toward it. The Qur'ān is the determinative source of all dogma and law. Through it the overriding sense of God through the Prophet, of the Prophet on behalf of God, that makes Islam, is continually renewed to the devout soul. The Qur'ān brings Mecca and Medina, as the Prophet addressed them, into the ken of every generation. In these pages, "he being dead yet speaketh." If attention to doctrine compels us to correct ourselves and say "God speaketh," there is perhaps no great point in the distinction. For the whole Muslim status of the Qur'ān is that God here speaking has Muhammad for His voice. Forever wedded together and heard by the pious soul in mosque and wilderness, in home and street, is the cry of the seventh-century Apostle as the speech of the Eternal God. Every memorizer of the Qur'ān, every reciting muezzin or *khaṭīb*, renews in this living perpetuity the words that made Islam. Muhammad in the Qur'ān becomes, so to speak, the great contemporary of them all.

Nor need there be serious doubt that the voice in the Book is authentically the voice of the Prophet. That there are critical problems connected with the Qur'ān no intelligent student will deny—not least among them the chronology and the vocabulary sources. But there is no place for serious misgiving that what is here was substantially what the Prophet said or that what he said under conditions of Quranic inspiration is not here. Though at first recorded on diverse scraps that lay to hand, animal bones,

leaves, skins, and the like, the growing revelations were carefully treasured and devoutly memorized. When the contents were
collected in Zaid's recension, later made the basis of 'Uthmān's
authoritative version, or canon, of the sacred Scriptures, it was
believed that the Prophet's own will in the matter had been
fulfilled. It can hardly have been that the Prophet himself made
any final decision on the order and arrangement of the Holy
Book. Had he done so it would seem impossible for anyone else
to have undertaken the task. Perhaps it was that death overtook
him before this could be taken up. 'Uthmān, it is true, ordered
the destruction of all alternative versions such as had been gathered in different centers like Kūfā, Basrah, and Damascus, thus
making almost impossible any comparative study. None the less
the consensus of view—Shī'ahs excepted—is that the Qur'ān as
it stood in 'Uthmān's recension omits no significant and includes
no extraneous material. The Prophet's death had decisively closed
the Book. Twenty-three years and sole authorship allowed no
time or opportunity for confusion and the canonization was
complete before the original Arabian generation of readers had
finally passed away. All these factors, coupled with the retentive
memory and reverent literalness of the faithful, seem to have
insured an authoritative text, whose puzzles are not of authorship.

XI

Yet despite the authority and sanctity of the volume of revelation, it does not exhaust the historical legacy it enshrines.
Muhammad has a place in history beyond that implicit in his
being the spokesman of the Qur'ān. Given its brevity and its
context of events, the Qur'ān proved an incomplete source of
communal guidance, as the community spread into new lands
and discovered new cultures. The Qur'ān, for example, contains
no single comprehensive code of personal or commercial or
social conduct, though there are several passages which suggest
codes in embryo.[11] It is full and detailed on certain matters,
especially those of personal status. But in other realms it is either
completely silent or strangely brief. Orphans find more legal
space than Caliphs and private heirs than public courts. While

exegesis and interpretation have greatly widened the scope of Quranic brevity, the very existence of alternative, though subordinate, sources of law demonstrates that the Qur'ān alone awaits and requires enlargement consistent with itself. Where, then, should Islam better turn than to the person, the behavior, the *obiter dicta* of the spokesman of God's directive and of the Holy Book? This explains the rise of Tradition, *Hadīth,* on a vast scale, giving to the biography of the Prophet, a kind of implicit, legislative quality and turning the indicative of description into the imperative of law. "Muhammad did this," it runs, "the Muslim ought to do the same."

It should be clear that Muhammad as the source of Tradition stands in a different category from Muhammad as the recipient of the Qur'ān. The latter status is that of *wahȳ* or revelation, accompanied by external signs, in limpness of body, swoon, ecstasy of spirit, which have remained a perpetual and puzzling theme to his biographers. Quranicity is more than Tradition. It is God's speech, which the Prophet hears and relays. But this recipience gave Muhammad such status in the community, such uniqueness in the Divine economy, that everything about him, even outside this Quranic sphere, came to be considered in some sense revelatory. This further role met, and largely satisfied, the extra-Quranic needs of the community, though requiring to be supplemented further by analogy and communal consensus. Tradition thus became the second major source of Islamic law. A term less than *wahȳ* and indicating non-Quranic inspiration is used to designate this exemplary quality attaching to Muhammad's deed and word. Tradition, as a matter of record, is called *Hadīth;* as a matter of obligation it is called *Sunnah.*

Undoubtedly, large areas of customary law in the conquered lands came into Islam in the form of traditions about the Prophet, Muhammad being credited with behavior or preferences or attitudes which reflected newly absorbed practices compatible with Islam. Similarly the main political and local factions and divisions which developed in Muslim history during the decades after his death inevitably expressed themselves in terms of competing traditions about him, each party being anxious to give their position the sanction of his anticipatory favor. The devel-

opment of Tradition thus became a prerequisite of the development of law in Islam and Muhammad became, so to speak, the
posthumous arbiter of his people's destinies and daily lives. His
mind and his example were endlessly, and inconsistently, invoked, until a host of traditions related the Prophet, positively
or negatively, approvingly or disapprovingly, with almost every
conceivable issue of life and society.

The great mass of traditions later required rigorous pruning.
The name of the most famous of the outstanding traditionalists,
Al-Bukhārī, has a tremendous sanctity in Islam. Al-Bukhārī is
said to have been aroused to his life task as editor of traditions
by a vision in which he saw the sleeping Prophet's face pestered
with innumerable flies, which a merciful fan kept at bay. It
certainly was a life task which he and his fellow traditionalists
undertook. For the verification of a tradition depended not
primarily on the substance or *matn* but on the *isnād* or chain of
attestation. The question was not so much: Could the Prophet
have said this? Is it reasonable and in character? but rather:
Who said that he said this? Was that reporter an eye witness?
Was he honest? And who tells us now, that he heard or saw the
Prophet do or say it? Is the chain of attestors unbroken? Did
they all know personally the man in front of them in the sequence going back to the first source? All these technical questions, though they had their importance, almost excluded internal concern with substance. Biographical lore about attestors
and companions become voluminous. Traditionalists traveled
across the continents in search of authentication or in order to
add their own name as the last in the chain, through face-to-face
contact with the immediately preceding reporter. To eliminate
the indirect and the second-hand became more important than
to identify the conjectural.

This fascinating subject might be pursued much further but
we must strive, as the best traditionalists did, to keep close to
the Prophet. Despite the prolixity of invented or unverifiable
traditions, there remains a substratum—variously estimated by
scholars, Muslim and Western—of biographically valid data. But
if we cannot always be sure that we are receiving authentic material about the Prophet, the question of criticism is perhaps un-

99

important. It is not so much whether this or that is validly Muhammad's but that numbers of Muslims thought so. It is the principle rather than the detail that here matters, the fact of belief rather than the bare fact. Muhammad became the universal exemplar. The assumption, theologically unexamined, was that in *this* particular—Muhammad in Arabia A.D. 570-632—the universal made itself manifest. The good, worthy to be the timeless example, was available for recognition and imitation, *in this life at that time.* This meeting of the universal and the particular, the plural and the singular, the eternal and the temporal, is the ultimate mystery of all existence. There is, therefore, nothing unfamiliar in thus conceiving of the universal as having become an inclusive particular, a singular which embodies, in a revelatory way, the eternal. Christianity sees just this fulfilled and realized in the Incarnation of "the Word made flesh," in "God with us." It acknowledges this situation with joy as an act of God in grace and assurance.

The instinctive Muslim acceptance, however, of a universal significance for the person of Muhammad not only lacks, but specifically repudiates, this metaphysical confidence in God made man. Nevertheless, the view of Muhammad implicit in the traditions amounts to some form of the belief that a human particular has become a universal, that all particular men may know God's will. But this attitude to Muhammad has never been expressed in a recognized metaphysical doctrine of his person that would undergird its tremendous ethical and legal role.[12] As often elsewhere, Islam has been content with the practical result. Some effort to think out the implications in the relation of this exemplary Muhammad to God is long overdue.

These considerations, though theological, are inseparable from any adequate discussion of Muhammad in history. For Tradition implies a cosmic relevance in the historical character. It proceeds upon it with great thoroughness and close detail. Even the smallest points about the Prophet become significant. Al-Ghazālī writes in the eleventh century on the *Sunnah* as follows:

> Know that the key of happiness is following the *Sunna*
> and imitating God's Apostle in all his goings out and

comings in, in his movements and times of quiescence, even in the manner of his eating, his deportment, his sleep and his speech. I do not say that concerning his manners in matters of religious observances alone, because there is no reason to neglect the traditions which have come down concerning them: nay, that has to do with all matters of use and wont, for in that way unrestricted following arises. God said: "Say: 'If you love God, follow me and God will love you'" (Surah iii. 29). And He said: "What the Apostle has brought you, receive; and what he has forbidden you, refrain from" (Surah liv. 7). So you must sit while putting on trousers and stand while putting on a turban: You must begin with the right foot when putting on your sandals, and eat with your right hand: When cutting your nails you must begin with the forefinger of the right hand and finish with its thumb: in the foot you must begin with the little toe of the right foot and finish with the little toe of the left. It is the same in all your movements and times of quiescence. Muhammad b. Aslam used not to eat a melon because the manner in which God's Apostle ate it had not been transmitted to him.[13]

To this meticulous degree Muhammad became the norm of true Muslim behavior and the unconscious source of the community's manners and total conduct as far as the pattern could be ascertained. The whole phenomenon, whose detailed illustration might be—as it often was—a life-study, is one of the most remarkable of the Prophet's legacies. There are some traditions that indicate it was an unintended legacy, though many more sustain the contrary. But however, precisely, this outcome is associated with the conscious will of Muhammad, there could be no clearer evidence of his stature and uniqueness in his day and beyond. Only the very few so effectively determine the shape of the world after they have left it, and maintain their authority by their example so far, so deep and so wide. The Muhammad of Tradition belongs to all ages of Islam, inasmuch as each of them returns in some measure to him as its criterion of all that it approves.

It can hardly be doubted, however, that the process is in some sense reciprocal. It is not simply that the historical Muhammad fashions the values and standards of the centuries, but that the centuries in their turn make and define the traditional Muhammad. Almost from the beginning forms of customary law, or policies of special groups, were read back into prophetic conduct or table-talk and in that form found Islamic expression. Down the centuries there has been, in differing degrees, the same tendency to draw the image of the Prophet in harmony with prevailing needs. The tendency is conspicuous enough in our own day. Muhammad is taken out of the seventh century and emerges in some biographies as the protagonist of the welfare state, as the first practical socialist and the prototype of Lincoln or Garibaldi, the spiritual ancestor of John Stuart Mill and Henri Bergson. It may be argued that any great personality who belongs to the ages comes to be reinterpreted in new lights and his "legend" is not always strictly tested by his historical role. But it can also be argued that these posthumous achievements are part of the historical role itself, seen in large perspective. Historians are obliged to take note of what the communal memory affirms to have been, as well as what the chronology contains. There are few personalities where this double duty is more important than in respect of the human founder of Islam. This is true perhaps most of all for those who would be Christian ministrants to his heirs.

There are yet other aspects of Muhammad in history which will become apparent in the two succeeding chapters—the Sufi repossession of the mystical Muhammad; the social reformer's invocation of the iconoclast and the rebel; the contemporary philosopher's appeal to the dynamic Muhammad. There can be no hope here of completeness. Nor is the story itself finished. The process, so to say, is proceeding. But perhaps we have succeeded in doing some justice to the muezzin's total meaning when he reiterates his conviction that Muhammad is the Apostle of God. It is those Arabian years, now thirteen centuries away; it is how the Muslims of those centuries have understood those years and what the sacred Book has made of them as believers and followers.

NOTES *to Chapter III*

1
Al-'Aqqād, 'Abbās Mahmūd, *'Abqariyyat Muhammad,* Cairo, 1942.
2
Haykal, Muhammad Husain, *Hayāt Muhammad,* Cairo, 1935.
3
Haykal, Muhammad Husain, *Fī Manzil al-Wahÿ,* Cairo, 1938, p. 637.
4
This subject is dealt with more fully, especially in relation to the New Testament, in Chapter x.
5
See Torrey, Charles C., *Jewish Foundation of Islam,* New York, 1933.
6
It is at this point that strong Muslim tradition places the story of Muhammad's experience of Satanic disruption into the revelation which stands in its true form in Surah liii. 19 seq. Here the Qur'ān decisively rejects Allāt, Manāt, and Al-'Uzzat, goddesses of Mecca and its vicinity, and does so with a derisive assurance that they are nonentities. But embedded in tradition in a manner that can hardly have been invented is the story that the Prophet allowed that their intercession could be looked for. Subsequently the statement was abrogated as a Satanic interjection and the Prophet was assured that in experiencing this trial he was only enduring what all other prophets had experienced before him (see Surah xxii. 52). It is not clear, however, how much time elapsed between the compromising deliverance and its correction. Some insist that the latter was immediate but the early historians indicate that the words were taken as a basis for a *modus vivendi* with the Quraish, on the ground of which some *émigrés* returned from Ethiopia. If that is so, the "concession" must have lasted some time. Some authorities deny the whole episode, reject the possibility of Muhammad's having been subject to Satan's interference (he being unique among prophets in this regard), and insist that no thought of Meccan accommodation ever arose. But in any event, the final, if not perpetual, attitude of the Prophet was an unwavering monotheism. The only ultimate *modus vivendi* between Islam and Mecca was the latter's surrender.

7

The consternation seems clear from the Quranic passage, Surah ii. 142-5. "Indeed it was a big thing." The implication clearly is that some of the Prophet's followers were seriously dismayed by the abandonment of Jerusalem. The change tested those who were willing to follow him unconditionally and it made Muslims a "middle" (distinctive?) community. The dubious were reassured that God's presence is everywhere and that the former *qiblah,* though valid hitherto, was not perpetual.

8

It would appear that the provisions of the treaty of Al-Hudaibiyyah about Islam returning Meccan converts did not apply to these accessions during the Return Pilgrimage.

9

'Alī, Sayyid Amīr, *The Spirit of Islam,* Christophers, London, 1922, p. 61.

10

This may be illustrated in the title of M. Pickthall's English rendering, *The Meaning of the Glorious Koran,* London, 1930. As a Muslim, the translator sought permission for his work and received it on condition that the English version was not entitled *The Qur'ān* (or *Koran*).

11

See, for example, Surah xvii. 26-39, Surah xvi. 114-16 (both Meccan) and also the wisdom of Luqmān in Surah xxxi. 12-20, also a Meccan Surah. These passages are cited as having a somewhat "codal" appearance. However, the Medinan Surahs ii, iv, and v are predominantly legal in character.

12

"Never" is, of course, a too inclusive word, but the emphasis here is on "recognized" and "metaphysical." There exists, it is true, a permanent and vigorous tendency to hypostacize in Muhammad the Divine light. The religious belief in *Al-Nur al-Muhammadī* has given to much Sufi, and other, devotion a relationship to Muhammad which comes close to deification, in implication, if not in fact. But these attitudes, wherever they occur, and recur, have no status in orthodox theology and all that they imply is roundly repudiated. Islam, however, is not the only faith where there are irreconcilable tensions between theology and religion, or rather, between orthodoxy and devotion.

13

Robson, James, "Al-Ghazālī and the Sunna" in *The Muslim World,* Oct. 1955, Vol. 45, No. 4, pp. 324-33.

iv

PRAYER AND THE RELIGIOUS LIFE IN ISLAM

f ROM the twofold witness now considered, the muezzin
passes to a twofold summons to response, with an interesting imperative or evocative verb that might well be translated:
"Look alive," or, more usually: "Come." It calls the hearer to
Prayer, *Salāt*, and to Good, *Falāh*. These are inclusive concepts
whose significance is the theme of this and the following chapter.
The form used as an imperative is in the singular. For though
the response involves community, it is made by the individual.
Moreover, the word does not differentiate, as other imperatives
do, between masculine and feminine. It is a kind of common
singular, including all who hearken and respond.

Even those who know least about Islam are somewhat familiar
with the place of prayer in its life. If they have traveled, they
may have seen Muslim seamen on shipboard, or stevedores on
the quayside observe the hours of prayer, with a naturalness, an
absence of self-consciousness, surprising to the Westerner. Or
they have seen photographs of serried ranks of prostrate forms
behind a leader, or *imām*, filling the wide mosque spaces, or
pictures of a solitary cameleer spreading his prayer mat on the
desert sands. Islam and Muslim prayer are in truth inseparable.
Just as Muhammad's career revolved around Mecca, the city
of his first prophetic warnings and his final victory, so his community acknowledges the religious centrality of the Meccan

qiblah, or direction of prayer, toward which every praying Muslim turns his face in a gesture which makes him part of one history and one solidarity. "Come ye unto the prayer" says the muezzin. For generations Muslims have actualized their Islam in their response. The ground, meaning, and pattern of the resulting religious life deserve patient and discerning study. For, however true it may be to speak of Islam in our time as a cultural or a political expression, it is only such because it is primarily a religious allegiance. As such it must first be known.

The institution of Muslim prayer rests upon the precept of the Qur'ān and the example of the Prophet. The word itself is perhaps better translated "worship," [1] since it means to supplicate with adoration. The same word is used of God in the familiar invocation upon Muhammad: "May God magnify (or exalt) Muhammad and preserve him in peace." It should be distinguished from spontaneous and intercessory prayer, known as *Du‘ā’*, where the individual may use ejaculatory phrases of his own choice, Quranic or otherwise, without following any necessary pattern or ritual. *Salāt,* however, is strictly ordered. The form must be followed if the prayer is to be valid. "Establish" or "perform" the worship is the usual formula by which the Qur'ān enjoins the practice, often in the context of conversion. There is no doubt that Muslim prayer is meant to be a distinctive rite, the fulfillment of which is a witness to the new allegiance.

Apart from the enjoining of the *qiblah,* the main details of the *Salāt,* including its fivefold daily iteration, rest on extra-Quranic injunctions. In one passage (Surah xi. 114) the Qur'ān directs: "Establish worship at the two ends of the day and in the parts of the night close to them." (See also Surah xxiv. 58.) Tradition, however, has understood the directive to include the five prayers as follows:

> *Salāt al-Fajr*—the dawn prayer, said when the dawn has broken and before the actual sunrise.
>
> *Salāt al-Zuhr*—the noon prayer when the sun passes the meridian.
>
> *Salāt al-‘Asr*—the late afternoon prayer.

Salāt al-Maghrib—prayer immediately after the sun sets.
Salāt al-'Ishā'—prayer after sunset before retiring to sleep
and not later than midnight.

Each occasion of *Salāt* has its stipulated number of ritual movements or *raka'āt* and never less than two. In addition to the five
obligatory prayers there are two optional ones: *Salāt al-Lail,* said
in the night after sleep but before dawn and *Salāt al-Duhā,* which
would fall between the dawn and the noon prayer and perhaps
coincide with breakfast. It can be seen at once that these daily
prayers make a considerable demand upon the faithful. Though
their performance takes a brief time their frequency requires
a readiness to combine prayer with affairs. Many exponents have
seen this as one of their chief lessons—the obligation of the believer to recognize God in the midst of, rather than in escape
from, his distractions and duties. For a similar reason Islam does
not recognize a Sabbath. The daily hours replace the holy day.

The ritual of each *raka'h* (plural: *raka'āt*) is carefully prescribed
and rigorously followed. It consists of seven movements each
having certain accompanying recitations as follows:

> The two hands are raised to the ears, while the pray-er
> stands, facing the *qiblah*. He says the *takbīr:* "God is
> most great."
> The right hand is then placed over the left upon the
> chest or bosom with ascriptions of glory to God and the
> confession of submission, ending with the phrase: "I
> seek refuge with God from the accursed devil." Then
> the opening Surah—*Al Fātihah*—is recited. This position
> is called "The Standing."
> With a new *takbīr,* the worshipper lowers the head
> with the palms of the hands on the knees—a position
> called "The Bending." He repeats ascriptions of praise
> to God.
> A standing position is resumed, followed by the pros-
> tration proper. The toes of both feet, both knees and
> both hands touch the ground as well as the forehead,
> while ascriptions are repeated.

With a *takbir,* the worshipper raises the upper part of his body to the sitting posture with two hands on the knees. A prayer for mercy and protection is offered.

A second prostration, repeating the praises of the first.

The worshipper returns to a standing position, saying a *takbir,* and the *raka'h* is at an end.

There are certain slight divergencies according to whether or not the series of positions known as a *raka'h* is the last in the sequence of the whole prayer. The final one ends with a salutation on all brother Muslims and the angels with the face turned right and left as in greeting. The prescribed phrases must be used in Arabic if that language is known. The worshipper may only add praises of his own when the ritual is complete.

The whole ordinance is intended as indicative of the relationship to God implicit in the Muslim understanding of Him. Though Islam prides itself upon its freedom from sacramentalism and priesthood, in that each worshipper worships for himself, it is evident that in the general sense the *Salāt* postures are profoundly sacramental. Prostration, in particular, proclaims and serves to actualize a totality of surrender. The face, the proudest thing in man, comes into contact with the dust, the lowest thing in nature. The physical thus embodies and expresses the spiritual. The same may be said of the careful washing, or *wudu'* which precedes every *Salāt,* typifying a cleansing of the soul accomplished therein. "Prayer," according to Surah xxix. 45, "preserves from impurity and evil." To remember God in this way is to be restrained from evil. The washing, therefore, both fits the worshipper for prayer and demonstrates what his worship is meant to do for him.

It relates to those parts of the body which are mostly exposed, the hands and arms to the elbow, the mouth and nostrils, the face and the head, and finally the feet to the ankles, beginning with the right foot. Running water is always preferred for Muslim ablution and it is used from, not in, receptacles. Hence the picturesque fountains in mosque courts. If water is not available a less desirable cleansing can be had with the use of sand or clean earth. The familiar prayer mat is linked in the same realm. It protects the worshipper from possible contamination and makes clean the immediate area of his prostration. To pray in a dirty state would be improper and nugatory. The Quranic passage (Surah v. 6) which stipulates the washing, explains that God does not wish to be tedious with His people, but seeks to purify them and fit them for His goodness.

All times of prayer must be prefaced by the *niyyah*, or "intention," just as is the case with the other four pillars of religion, or obligatory ordinances of Islam. The "intention" is the declaration of purpose. It would be possible to go through all the motions and phrases of the ritual without in fact performing the prayer, just as the syllables of the Confession recited, for example, in a grammar lesson, would not constitute a personal witness. The need for the "intention" makes evident that true prayer cannot be perfunctory or mechanical. It is a means of defense against inattentive and external performance. The movements no doubt become habitual, but habituation should not be forgetful.

The place and pattern of the mosque in Muslim religious life is a vital topic to which we will return. But discussion of prayer would not be complete without reference to its public, but in no sense exclusive, place. The English word is a corruption of the Arabic *masjid,* or place of prostration. If a mosque is accessible and convenient it is desirable to use it at all times. Water for washing is available there, if anywhere, and there is the stimulus of association and fellowship. But every man's prayer mat is a portable mosque and wherever he chooses to spread it he can find his *qiblah* and fulfill his worship. He needs no priest or mouthpiece, since the prayers are known. Since prayer has to intermingle with his journeys, his trading, and his conversing he cannot always repair to certain precincts. The physical mosque is dispensable.

Nevertheless the noon prayer on Fridays is to be said as far as possible in the place of corporate prayer. When so said its four *raka'āt* are reduced to two. Occasion is taken for a discourse from the mosque pulpit and the worshipper shares the unison prostrations as led by the *imām* standing toward the niche, or *mihrāb* which indicates the direction of Mecca. The Friday, however, in contradistinction to the Jewish Sabbath and the Christian Sunday, is not a day of rest. Business precedes and follows the noon prayer (see Surah lxii. 9 and 10). For the *Adhān,* or Call to Prayer, the mosque is, of course, indispensable. But the duty to which it calls may be answered without as well as within.

II

Prayer in Islam is by no means confined to the ritual form now described. There is the whole realm of petition and adoration in which the Muslim soul relates itself to God in the various crises of existence and in the lesser occasions of daily life. Even here, however, the worshipper tends to rely on familiar phrases or forms of an ejaculatory kind many of them being derived from the Qur'ān or Tradition. A new-born infant is greeted with the phrases of the muezzin's call recited in the ear. At death there are prayers over the dead body in the mosque or dwelling or at the graveside, after the corpse has first been thoroughly washed, beginning with those parts which are customarily cleansed in the *wudu'* before prayer. The *imām* and those present recite the *takbīr* and the *dhikr* of the Prophet with variant forms of intercession in which there will be phrases like the following:

> Forgive O God our dead and our living. Cause him who is alive amongst us to live in Islam, and he whom Thou takest to Thyself let him die in the faith. Do not forbid him his reward: make gracious his reception and spacious his coming in. Cleanse him with water, with snow and with ice and purge him of sins as Thou cleansest a white cloth of its stain.

At marriage there are exhortations setting forth the duties of the parties and recitation of the *Shahādah,* as well as various optional prayers for the welfare of the couple and the prosperity of all families. Many of the routine events of daily life are occasions of ejaculatory petition—entering and leaving the house, entering and leaving a lavatory, retiring and rising, or visiting the sick, passing a graveyard, embarking and disembarking, before and after meals, in front of a mirror, after a bath, on first partaking of any item in the yearly harvest, in distress, and in trial. In many cases the words have come down from traditional practices or phrases of the Prophet himself. The purpose of such devotional recognition of God in the minutiae of the everyday is to make one's *Islām,* or submission, comprehensive and alert and to evoke the spirit of gratitude and humility. Bodily functions which may so easily go awry and which in their wholeness are so wonderful should be the occasion of ejaculatory worship.

The characteristic phrases of these acts of devotion deserve study. The keynote is surrender and trust. "O God I have given my soul, my journey, my objective, into Thy charge." The idea of submission is usually linked to that of refuge and the re-iterated phrase is "I seek refuge with Thee," from the accursed one, from wandering and error, from danger and mischief, from fear and calamity. This seeking argues reliance, expressed in the words *Alaika Tawakkaltu:* "In Thee have I trusted," often to be seen inscribed on trucks and buses, and elsewhere. These attitudes are no doubt comprehended in the most familiar of all phrases: "*Bismillāh,*" "In God's Name," which when used with attentive sincerity confesses the God-relatedness of all things. Other petitions make the occasion a parable of larger need: a bath may denote spiritual purity, entering a house serve to recollect the entering of heaven, and a mirror's reflection remind one of the call to be virtuous as well as comely. The Muslim's principle of *Tauhīd* or Unity runs through all these prayers. God alone is a sure protector, or right guide. There is no other arbiter, no other enricher, no other Lord. Hence the blessing of God is indispensable. Its enjoyment or its denial makes the entire difference. May we, then, as the opening Surah has it, be among those upon whom God shows favor, not among those who stand under His wrath. The awesome distinction felt and feared here is an ever-present element in the form and quality of these prayers.

A glance at a selection of other prayers used in the Qur'ān shows that the devout Muslim in his incidental petitions is close to the temper of his Holy Book. Many of these Quranic phrases are recited voluntarily after the *Fātihah* on any occasion when the latter is used. They express a strong sense of life's precarious nature and the decisive role of faith. "O our Lord grant us good in this world and in the world to come and save us from the pain of the fire." "O our Lord do not let our hearts stray after Thou hast guided us and grant us mercy." "O our Lord forgive us our transgressions and our excesses." "Let us die with the righteous and bring unto us what Thou hast promised by the apostles and let us not be confounded on the day of resurrection." Throughout, there is this sense of the confrontation of the believing and the unbelieving and the confidence that the former are the gainers and the latter are the losers. Yet there is no presumptuous assurance. The categories are clear and fixed but membership is not. "If Thou forgive us not and dost not have mercy upon us then are we verily among the losers." "O Lord indeed I am a poor man in need of all the good Thou bringest down unto me."

All these prayers are associated, in some sense, with the character and attributes of God. The Ninety-nine Names are used, with varying frequency, as the ground of the petition or the point of the aspiration, as well as in adoration. The Christian notices at once the entire absence of anything resembling the traditional Christian phrases of commendation: "for the sake of . . ." or "in the name of . . ." For the offering of prayer depends altogether for its acceptability upon the Divine will and all that can rightly be said is to associate some known descriptive of God with the relevant petition. In one respect the pattern is the same. For the Christian use of the Name of Christ is the invocation of that inclusive sense of God, upon which all prayer depends, as it is made plain and sure in Jesus Christ. The Christian's standing in Christ is not external to God as if it were a persuasion from without. It is rather his recognition of the place where God has made His grace actual and His accessibility indubitable. Muslim prayer links itself to the attributes of God without believing that they are anywhere finally pledged or necessarily operative.

As for the question of the intercession, *Shafā'ah,* of prophets and saints in Islam, there is some uncertainty as to how the Qur'ān should be understood. There are several passages like

Surah lxxiv. 48 which affirms: "The intercession of those who make *Shafā'ah* will not avail them." Surah ii. 48 depicts the day of judgment as a day on which no intercession will be allowed. These verses, however, can be understood, in a less than absolute sense, as disqualifying certain groups from intercessory power or efficacy. Such an interpretation is confirmed by other verses which attribute intercession to the angels or speak of it as occurring by God's permission. Surah ii. 255, it is true, asks: "Who should intercede with Him (God) even by His permission?" But Tradition has given an affirmative answer and has expressed itself fully as to those capable of intercession by Divine consent. There are prophets, martyrs, saints, and apostles, as well as angels. But traditional belief is insistent that Muhammad is the truest intercessor, where he is not also the sole one. A repeated tradition describes the day of judgment when all the prophets from Adam to Jesus transfer, each to the next, the role of intercessor, all disclaiming the privilege. Finally Muhammad takes it up and intercedes with God, by God's permission, until there are left in Hell only those for whom no intercessor can avail.

Intercession is much more widely believed in Shī'ah Islam, and belief in the saintly efficacy of holy founders is one of the main factors in the cohesion of Sufi orders. There are also strong traditions of Muhammad's own practice during life in visiting the cemeteries, often by night, to seek from God the forgiveness and the welfare of the dead.

III

Two other pillars of religion fall within this chapter, namely fasting and pilgrimage.

The ordinance of *Saum,* fasting, in the month of *Ramadān,* in which the Qur'ān began to be revealed, is at once a product of, and a reaction against, Jewish-Christian practices. Though *Ramadān* seems to have been a holy month among the Arabs prior to Islam, its designation as a month of fasting derives from the example of ascetic discipline among the "People of the Book," and the fast of the Day of Atonement. In the Meccan days the early community appears to have followed something of this pattern and Surah ii. 183 declares: "Fasting is enjoined for you

113

even as it was enjoined for those before you." But in the sequel to this passage is the record of the duty prescribed for and by Muhammad when his experience with the Jews in Medina provoked him into studied disconnection. The Day of Atonement fast in *Muharram* was abandoned, except as a voluntary act, for one of a month's duration in *Ramadān*. Moreover, a still later revelation transferred the fast from the period between sunset and sunrise to that between sunrise and sunset. "Eat and drink until it appears that a white thread may be distinguished from a black, then keep the fast strictly until nightfall" (Surah ii. 187). The same passage indicates that abstention from sexual intercourse by night is not incumbent as part of the fast.

The observance of *Ramadān* is binding upon all adult Muslims of both sexes, save for the aged, the sick, pregnant women, nursing mothers, and travelers. When the exempting circumstances are changed the equivalent period of consecutive fast is to be observed. The month of fasting is a rigorous exercise and is probably more widely practiced than the daily prayers. Muslims who may sometimes omit the latter keep the former. No food or drink is to pass down the throat, from the break of dawn to sunset. Food is partaken during the hours of darkness. The fast closes with the *'Id al Fitr,* the Feast of the breaking of the Fast, which is the Little Festival of the Muslim year. It is begun when the new moon appears, and is celebrated with even greater éclat than the Great Festival, or *'Id al Adhā,* which coincides with the offering of pilgrimage sacrifice at Minā, near Mecca. *Bairām,* an alternative name generally but not solely used for the feast that ends *Ramadān,* is derived from the practice of giving and receiving gifts of sugar sweets. Greeting cards also are exchanged.

Indeed there are some aspects of the *'Id al Fitr* which resemble certain features of the Western Christmas season. It is a time of general desire after better things. Presents symbolize mutual affection and there is a surge of satisfaction and aspiration which, for Muslims, terminates an exacting discipline. Evil is somehow temporarily allayed. Shakespeare, in *Hamlet,* found the nights of the Christmas season joyously wholesome.

> *The bird of dawning singeth all night long*
> *. . . no planets strike*
> *No fairy takes, nor witch hath power to charm,*
> *So hallowed and so gracious is the time.*

The Qur'ān observes that on the night in *Ramadān* of the Book's first descent: "Angels and the Spirit descend to earth. . . . and it is peace until the rising of the dawn" (Surah xcvii. 4 and 5).

Through the fast there is also an emphasis on deepened devotion and more frequent mosque attendance. "Be at your devotions in the mosque" says the passage enjoining *Ramadān* (Surah ii. 187). The need for the "intention," daily repeated, emphasizes the conscious discipline the soul requires, and into which it enters intelligently. The traditions and Muslim theologians concur in this understanding of the fast. Though, doubtless, multitudes in Muslim history observed it as a *fiat* of their own faith, as an ordinance which required no justification, the perceptive modern exponents recognize that in itself the transference of eating and drinking to hours of darkness has nothing intrinsically to commend it. What is significant is the assertion that man has larger needs than bread, that his body is to be his servant not his master, and that ordered voluntary privation is a fine school of patience and endurance. There is no doubt of the value of the fast as a witness to these truths, though, when the revolving Muslim calendar brings *Ramadān* into the trying summer heat, it may be questioned whether exasperation and strain are not also a consequence. These, it will be said, are part of the price of a necessary institution. There is no general tendency to permit symbolic interpretation of the fast to weaken the actual observance. *Ramadān* may stand for spiritual discipline but such interpreters cannot claim their own freedom to override it. Islam, by and large, is as tenacious of its times and seasons as any other faith, including those more commonly described as sacramental. Fasting is good. But to fast in *Ramadān* is traditionally thirty times better than at any other time.

Such other fasts are possible as a means of expiating manslaughter, or a broken oath, or the killing of game while on pilgrimage. Though traditions emphasize the meritoriousness of fasting in general there is a strong insistence, throughout the Qur'ān and in Muslim practice, upon the error of asceticism. *Ramadān* sufficiently demonstrates the soul's priority. This truth must always be kept in mind. But the stipulated fast suffices. The good things of nature and of appetite are to be taken in moderation and not refused. It is unwise and unbecoming to reject the gifts of God. Whatever may be said of Muhammad's debt to hermits and monks as examples of solitary devotion, the Qur'ān in the Medinan period, repeatedly urges that the reasonable desires and needs of the bodily life—food, drink, sex, and sleep—be properly and thankfully satisfied. Islam disavows "monkery." There is nevertheless a strong, though limited, temper that seeks the ascetic way, thus dissociating itself from the general teaching. Al-Ghazālī insists that a fast which means only a consequent hunger and thirst is not a finally meaningful fast. For if only hunger results the fast is only physically felt. It should be an occasion of that remembrance of God which is not a temporary, negative abstinence, but a positive preoccupation with God. So understood, there are fasts for the eyes, from impure seeing; for the ears, from unsavory listening; for the mouth, from scandal and gossip. Such purposeful asceticism as the pathway to the Divine knowledge is admittedly a special vocation. As a deep and important area of Muslim religious life we shall take note of it later. Its existence only serves to throw into contrast the more general attitude to natural satisfactions and to the *Ramadān* fast as a yearly reminder that the gracious God, Who gives for our enjoyment, also requires that we observe a month of special endurance as an education in submission. Christianity is often reproached by Muslim writers for its alleged renunciation of this world. It errs in asking too much of the natural man and so remains either an unsound, or an unfulfilled, ideal.

IV

By means of the *qiblah,* Islam made Mecca the center of day-to-day devotion. The pilgrimage or *Hajj,* the fifth "pillar" of religion, makes it the focal point of a yearly homage that often represents the aspiration of a lifetime. The pilgrimage is, so to

speak, the annual expression of the constant centrality of the
Ka'bah and its environs in the practice and faith of Islam.

The Qur'ān, in Surah iii. 97, lays upon the loyal Muslim, who
is capable of travel to Mecca, the obligation of pilgrimage once
during his life. "Whoever is able to make his way thither"
should repair before he dies to the holy city, the navel of the
earth, and to the haunts of Abraham and Ishmael where the
Holy Prophet was born. 'Arafāt and Minā in the Meccan vicinity are included in the pilgrim rites but Medina, city of the
Prophet's death and burial, is not, though many pilgrims include
Medina in their travels before leaving the Hijāz.

What constitutes ability to be a pilgrim has been much discussed within the schools of law and by individual Muslims de-
ciding whether and when to make the journey. Lack of means,
slavery, feebleness of mind, lack of escort (in the case of women)
are traditionally recognized as proper incapacity. The first has
often been extended to excuse neglect on the ground of preoccupation with necessary affairs, insecurity on the road, hazards
to health, and the like. With others strength of will has made up
for arguable deficiency of means. In the long history of Islam
there have been many, Caliphs and Shaikhs, the mighty and the
erudite, as well as the lowly, who never sought the sacred precincts. There have been others like Hārūn al-Rashīd and his
predecessor Al-Mansūr, who made repeated pilgrimages to the
Holy City. It would be impossible, as well as idle, to attempt a
statistical assessment of the incidence of pilgrimage in any single
generation. Some inveterate travelers in the heyday of Muslim
tradition-building and of science wandered almost incessantly
over the wide areas of the Muslim world, taking in Mecca at pilgrimage time as they went. There have been communities which,
over long decades, through circumstances, local or Meccan,
through schism or indifference, sent scarcely a trickle of visitors
to the sanctuaries. Into these vicissitudes we cannot enter. A full
and detailed history of the pilgrimage in Islam is yet to be written. It should be remembered also that the glory of Mecca has
been borrowed or usurped by other centers. For pilgrimage is a
powerful factor in the cohesion of empires. Thus Shī'ah Islam
has its Karbala and Najaf and Persian Muslims have Meshed

and Qum.[2] These rivals apart, the holiest city in Islam has been at times besieged by rebel Muslims. Nevertheless the age-long sanctity remains and the pilgrimage today is a powerful unifying factor in the life of Islam.

In recent years official returns place the annual number of pilgrims at around 170,000. A sizable proportion are now air-borne. The air line agent is more and more replacing the old *muqawwim* into whose care a caravan would entrust itself when setting out from Cairo or Damascus. Pilgrim ships to Jiddah are also more commodious than of yore. There have also been great improvements of late in the facilities for the health and security of the pilgrims on Arabian soil. Several leading Muslim states have opened national hostels in Mecca for their citizens. The deterrents which formerly intimidated the intellectual or the cultured have now been greatly mitigated. Currency control is more the stumbling block now to some would-be pilgrims than the lack of health control that daunted earlier generations.[3]

There are many intriguing issues connected with the contemporary pilgrimage but the temptation to discuss them must be resisted. Our purpose here is with an understanding of its general role in Muslim life. No discussions of numbers and conditions, however, would be complete without the observation that the pilgrimage in Islam involves and affects more people than physically perform it. It becomes in a sense a vicarious experience. The village, the small mosque community, or the city quarter greets the returning pilgrim with possessive pride. It dubs him now a *Hājj* and relives in his tales the emotions he has known. His impact provides, so to speak, a participation by proxy. In this way the real defaulter, if not stimulated into action, at least knows what he has neglected. The believer who is genuinely incapable of pilgrimage enters in part into an awareness of Mecca that compensates for his inability to go there. Attendance thus mediates the meaning of Mecca to all the local levels of Muslim society. How many there are who are impervious to this secondary influence it is impossible to say. More important to discover is what the pilgrimage experience constitutes for those who are directly or vicariously part of it.

It should be clear that pilgrimage like any other pillar of

Islam can be physically performed without being spiritually fulfilled. It is possible and desirable to visit Mecca at any time but
the proper pilgrimage is that which takes place, with intention,
in the stipulated month of *Dhū-al-Hijjah.* This, like all Muslim
months, rotates round the seasons: the summer pilgrimages are
the most exacting. There is a lesser pilgrimage, known as the
'Umrah, which is not fixed to any particular month. The rites
are restricted to Muslims. No non-Muslim has in fact entered
Mecca except in disguise or by subterfuge.[4]

The confession of the pilgrimage is symbolized by the ceremonial state of consecration, or *Ihrām,* into which the pilgrim
must enter at some point between his departure and his arrival
in the Hijāz. This state is symbolized by the wearing of a white,
unsewn robe thrown across the body leaving the right arm and
shoulder bare. The robes should be simple, silk being forbidden.
While in the state of *Ihrām* the pilgrim neither shaves nor
washes, apart from the ceremonial ablutions at the various stations of the pilgrimage. Women are traditionally clad in a long
robe reaching from head to foot. The veil is held off from the
face in some way, so that the skin is technically uncovered. Sexual relations and other infringements of the *Ihrām* render the
pilgrimage null and void.

The stages of the pilgrimage, in brief, are as follows. After
arrival in Mecca the pilgrim makes seven circuits of the *Ka'bah*
in the Great Mosque, during which he touches, or if possible
kisses, the sacred Black Stone in the wall of the shrine. The circuits are performed barefoot. Leaving the mosque by another
door from that used for entry the pilgrim makes the ceremonial
running between two points in a wide Meccan street. This pro-
cession may be a recollection of Hagar's search hither and thither
for water for Ishmael and is also connected with Abraham's
eluding Satan. On the eighth day of the pilgrim month, these
ceremonies being completed, the pilgrimage proper begins.
After a mosque discourse the pilgrims set out for Minā and
'Arafāt some five and thirteen miles respectively from Mecca.
The former is a narrow defile and the latter an open area, below
the Mount of Mercy. Here the pilgrims stand from noon to sunset and sermons are delivered. This is the ninth day of the

month and the climax of pilgrimage. The night is spent in the open at Muzdalīfah, on the route back to Minā. The following day comes "the stoning" in which each pilgrim casts seven small stones upon a large stone heap. Abraham is believed to have dismissed Satan by this means. The stoning brings to an end the pilgrimage proper and the pilgrim prepares to withdraw from the state of consecration. He sacrifices a sheep, a goat, and a camel and has his head shaved. He returns to Mecca where again he does a *Ka'bah* circuit and bathes in the water of the holy well of Zamzam, or sprinkles himself with it. There follows on the eleventh, twelfth, and thirteenth days of the month the so-called *tashrīq*, or relaxation and pleasure. The consecrated state is terminated though stone-throwing ceremonies continue. Before leaving Mecca the pilgrim briefly resumes the *Ihrām* for a farewell visit to the Great Mosque.

Precise details of the ceremonies differ from time to time and from school to school. The lesser pilgrimage makes circumambulation the central ceremony and desacrilizing follows at once. Simultaneously with the sacrifice at Minā and the *tashrīq* of the pilgrims at Mecca the whole Muslim world celebrates its Great Festival, the *'Īd-al-Adhā*, when besides exchanging presents the devout Muslim may offer sacrifice. This association of the Great Festival with the pilgrim rites serves to bind into one celebrating community the whole household of Islam within and beyond its religious center. After the completion of his farewell the pilgrim, in the state of *Ihlāl*, or "secularity," makes his way home, visiting en route as he wills.

Some aspects of the pilgrimage have passed into Islam from pagan Arabian practice. Other elements of that origin, like circuits at 'Arafāt and the state of nakedness during the *Ka'bah* circuits, were eliminated by Muhammad. The "standing" at 'Arafāt is probably a pre-Islamic survival, as is also the sacrifice at Minā. But Islam gave new meaning to the surviving practices and baptized them into its strict monotheism. The incorporation of the pagan pilgrimage into Muslim ritual may be seen as the ceremonial counterpart of the political importance of Mecca already studied.

No discussion is possible here of the topography of Mecca and the historical affinities of the pilgrimage. The writings of Burton, Rutter, and Hurgrönje abound in descriptions of the Meccan terrain and the pilgrimage rites as they appeared to these observers.[5] More significant here is the *Labbaika* cry with which the pilgrim punctuates his devotion from his first entry into the consecrated state to the completion of the stoning at Minā. The cry of the *takbīr*, "God is most great," is, of course, characteristic also of all the pilgrim stages. But *Labbaika* takes us even more expressively into the heart of this experience at its best. "Doubly at Thy service, O God" is perhaps the best English rendering of the word. It is twice repeated, each time in the dual form to indicate emphasis. Arabic grammar describes it as an absolute complement of its original verb. It thus means that the pilgrim presents himself wholeheartedly before God with no other thought than this Divine encounter. His physical coming to Mecca is a kind of parable of his spiritual response to the revelation and law of God which he believes were historically communicated at this focal point. His cry of recognition of God and of what God has sent down pledges him to a sustained and ever-renewed devotion. He is gathering the rest of his life in the protest of unfailing allegiance: "Thee it is before Whom I stand."

A description of the pilgrim rites and the observations of travelers, Muslim and Western, suggest to some outsiders a feeling of strangeness, if not revulsion. What can be the significance of thousands of flying pebbles and of animal carcasses strewn on the ground after a devotional "massacre," or of seething multitudes of humanity in the hot discomfort of unwashed garments and unshaven faces? Abuses, too, of pilgrim devotion there have sometimes been, and other unhappy features incidental to the whole. These are diminishing in face of a stricter system and more developed organization. But in any event it is well for the outside observer to look with understanding, even where he quite fails to penetrate the secret. Diverse and sincere participants have expressed in Muslim literature, old and new, their sense of elevation and insight during the pilgrim days. The pilgrimage, known from within, appears as a potent sacrament of Muslim unity and conveys a sense of inspiring solidarity. It is a yearly renewal of Meccan, or rather of Muhammad's, history in the Muslim soul. It is a geographical expression of the religious heritage.

Perhaps the surest way to enter into this experience is to study the pilgrim prayers. Various manuals of pilgrim devotion, known as *Manāsik al Hajj*, are supplied to Muslims bound for Mecca. A few extracts follow from one of them. On first beholding the buildings at Mecca, the pilgrim says:

> In the name of God, the compassionate, the merciful, O God, let this become to me an abode and grant me herein a valid profit.

On entering the precincts of the sacred *Ka'bah* he cries:

> O God, this sanctuary is Thine, the country is Thine, the safekeeping is Thine and the worshipper is Thine. I have come unto Thee from a distant country with many transgressions and evil deeds. I beseech Thee, as one who has deep need of Thee, seeking the merciful relenting of Thy punishment, to receive me in Thy pure pardon and to bring me into Thy spacious paradise, that gracious abode. O God, this is Thy sanctuary and the sanctuary of Thy apostle. So keep me, flesh and blood and bone, inviolate from the fire. O God, preserve me from Thy condemnation in the Day when Thou dost raise up Thy servants. I beseech Thee, for Thou art God, there is none other save Thee, the beneficent, the merciful. Blessing and peace be upon our Lord Muhammad, upon his household and his companions. Let it be a great, eternal peace.

The prayer at the seventh circuit of the *Ka'bah* runs:

> O God, I ask of Thee a perfect faith, a sincere assurance, a reverent heart, a remembering tongue, a good conduct of commendation and a true repentance, repentance before death, rest at death and forgiveness and mercy after death, clemency at the reckoning, victory in paradise and escape from the fire, by Thy mercy, O

mighty One, O Forgiver. Lord increase me in knowledge and join me unto the good.

At the "standing" of Abraham, the pilgrim prays:

> O God, Thou knowest my secret and my open things. Receive my plea. Thou knowest my need, grant me my petition. Thou knowest what is in my spirit. Forgive me my trespasses. O God, I ask Thee for a faith which will occupy my heart and a sincere assurance so that I may know that nothing will befall me except what Thou hast written for me. Thou art my guardian in this world and that to come. Let me die a Muslim and join me to the good. O God, do not let there be in this standing any guilt, save what Thou hast forgiven: no grief save what Thou hast assuaged: no need save what Thou hast satisfied and hast made easy. Render our affairs prosperous and enlarge our bosoms and illumine our hearts and seal our deeds with good things. O God, let us die Muslims and raise us to life as Muslims and join us to the good, not as those who are ashamed, nor as those who are seduced.[6]

V

The prayers of the pilgrim at Mecca bring us back to the Meccan direction of all prayer, and so to the mosque, the local focus of Muslim devotion. Imaginative and observant study in the mosque may more truly apprehend the nature of the Muslim's religion than many a treatise in Islamics. Each mosque is in some sense an epitome of Muslim life and the Muslim story. Some of them are former churches recognizable still, yet unmistakably transformed. Others are vast, original monuments of Muslim architecture and vitality. Not least appealing are the unpretentious and modest ones which in their very ordinariness seem to embody more intimately the life of believing generations. Nor are they all out of the far past and laden with years. The traveler in Algeria, for example, will come upon many new mosque structures, gleaming in their whiteness, an index to the vigor of the Society of the 'Ulamā' responsible for their erection.

Whether old or new, majestic or unobtrusive, the mosque is full of clues to the nature of religious life. It expresses in structural form the pattern of the Muslim faith. Its most conspicuous features are the minaret, the *mihrāb,* and the *minbar.* These serve respectively the call to prayer, its direction and unity, and its interpretation. They are identical with three roles belonging to the mosque personnel—that of muezzin, *imām,* and *khatīb.* In large and well-endowed mosques these are usually different individuals. They may also be assisted by others such as the *muwaqqit,* who keeps the hours for the muezzin, the *qāss,* who relates stories for instruction and devotion to the faithful, the *qāri',* or reader, who chants the Qur'ān and, perhaps, a *muhtasib* to supervise the morals of the community. In the more modest mosques these offices may be performed by the same individual at different times.

The duty of the muezzin, in this context, needs no further description. The earliest call to prayer seems to have been given from the roof-tops of the Prophet's quarters in Medina or of other near-by houses. Traditionally, the first muezzin was Bilāl, an Ethiopian. The minaret, though admirably suited to the call to prayer and itself, in some forms, a kind of stabbing summons to the upward relation of life, may not have evolved only for this religious function. It no doubt incorporated features of the Christian architecture absorbed through conquest. Its name, place of light or fire, suggests that it may have had strictly utilitarian origins, as a watchtower for fire signals. Christian history reminds us, too, that towers had their attraction for ascetics and devotees. There is record of at least one outstanding Muslim theologian who owed much to the seclusion of a minaret.[7]

But whatever the diverse factors, architectural and otherwise, contributing to its evolution, the minaret is the muezzin's world. It is the vantage point of a devotional appeal. The artist may find in it an excuse for an exquisite theme. But the man with a mission in words is finally his master. When the minarets began to go up one by one, in the fifteenth century, around the ancient Church of Saint Sophia in Istanbul they marked the edifice as indubitably Islamic. The minaret everywhere serves to identify on the landscape the community of the faith of Muhammad. Its form is a silent embodiment of the oral summons which it houses.

The *imām*, however, within the mosque, is a more important official since he leads that to which the muezzin only calls. The word *imām*, in Sunnī Islam, means simply the leader who stands in front of the assembled believers, to insure unison in the movements of the prayers. The congregation follows him in the recitals and prostrations. The *mihrāb*, or niche, toward which he stands, marks the *qiblah* toward Mecca. It is always empty, though its walls may be exquisitely adorned with tiles and texts. The recess serves as a focal point that sets the faces of the faithful on the line to Mecca where they find spiritual rendezvous with the rest of their brethren. By the *mihrāb* the congregation is consciously set on one of the radii from the gravitational center of Islam.

Like the minaret, the *mihrāb* may also have derived from non-Islamic factors similarly subdued. The earliest traditions suggest that a spear, thrust into the ground, sufficed to mark the direction. But when churches were taken into Islam, the numerous niches in familiar use for statuary or episcopal thrones, seemed to suit the need. Emptiness was all that was required to baptize the old into the new and to proclaim the iconoclasm and equality of Muslim devotion. Similarly the *minbar*, or pulpit, gave the mosque a rostrum for exhortation and preaching, in which earlier forms were readily adapted. The characteristic Muslim pulpit is a projection at right angles to the main wall, often adjacent to the *mihrāb*, with steps leading upward through a screen or curtain surmounted by a lintel. The preacher faces down the steps from the platform at the top, and addresses the people without a reading stand. His words are usually extempore, though carefully prepared. The spacious areas on both sides of the *minbar* give ample scope to the artist in calligraphy and design. Sometimes the *minbar* is retractable, being provided with wheels in order to be pushed into a recess when not in use. For the sermon by the *khatīb* is a weekly institution at the time of the noon-prayer on Fridays. At other times the shaikhs and readers recite or catechize from lower, less pretentious, desks or platforms, on which they squat in closer audience among smaller groups. Several such low rostrums may be seen in any sizable mosque. In populous cities the visitor will often find such instruction in progress.

The place and function of the mosque sermon in Muslim religious life needs to be more fully investigated. The discourse is generally hortatory rather than discursive. It does not so much defend the faith as commend it: it encourages to practice rather than to apology. The underlying assumption seems generally to be that the believers know what they believe but may be forgetful in the fulfillment of their duties. The non-believer is never present to listen so that the sermon is never directed toward an outsider. This fact has deeply influenced the form and temper of the average preacher. His discourse is usually divided into two parts, the first and much longer section beginning with certain conventional openings and containing the substance of the theme, the second following as a brief peroration, after a pause.

Many mosque preachers follow a calendar sequence and fit their themes to the significance of the season or approaching festival. They may also comment widely on current political and social affairs, though the liberty to do this has been strictly curtailed in certain areas of late because of the delicate nature of mosque-state relationships.[8] Nevertheless, the close connection between the preacher's duty and social life is traditional. The *minbar* was in early Islam the place of Caliphal pronouncements and sometimes of judicial and other judgments. The sermon has often been an instrument of public education in particular points, even in emergencies of public health. It has also been a means of ruling indoctrination or propaganda. This was natural in a society when the mosque was the chief place of assembly amid a population that was largely illiterate and where there was no sense of any incompatibility between worship and affairs.

Much contemporary criticism of the mosque-preaching in the past concentrates on this point of its subservience to ruling authority and its function as a means to state control. Other critics deplore the lack of originality displayed by many preachers and trace the neglect of the mosque by some sections of the population to the stereotyped form and content of the sermon.

There is impatience when the preacher repeats pious platitudes and demonstrates that he is incapable of any adequate intellectual or spiritual wrestling with the realities of the world as some at least of his hearers know it. The need for the improvement of the mosque sermon is widely felt in responsible circles and there have been a number of manuals in the recent past seeking to grapple with it.[9] The ultimate future of the preacher in the life of Islam would seem likely to turn upon the adequacy of theological education.

The following sermon from the Dīwān, or published collection of 'Abdallāh al-Marāghỹ of Cairo, may serve to illustrate the manner and content of a mosque discourse. The theme is "Faith in God."

> Praise be to God, Who guides the hearts of His chosen ones by faith, and makes tranquil the hearts of His elect in confidence. I bear witness that there is no god except God. In His dominion nothing occurs save by His willing it. I bear witness that our Lord Muhammad is the Apostle of God, whose resolution was not weakened by adversities.
>
> O God, bless and preserve and be gracious unto our Lord Muhammad, his people, his companions and those who follow him.
>
> God most High has said in His glorious Book: "He who believes in God, his heart is guided, and God is in all things most knowing."
>
> Ye who worship God: Faith is the devoting of the heart unto God by man and his acceptance of what God has revealed to His Prophets, his belief in His determination and His will. It is a breath from the spirit of God, by which He confirms those who sincerely believe among His worshippers, in trials. It is a torch lighted from the light of God, irradiating in the hearts of the chosen ones among those who love Him. Faith has signs which point the way to it, and conviction has indications that guide (men) towards it. God Most High said: "Those believers whose hearts glow at the men-

tion of God, and whose faith is increased when his verses (signs) are read to them, those who rely upon their Lord and perform the prayers and give generously of that which we have bestowed upon them, these are the true believers indeed, they have honour with their Lord and forgiveness and gracious benefits."

These are the indications of the true faith: the fear of God which impels a man to magnify Him and extol Him, meditation on His signs which stimulates him to trust in His promise, reliance upon God leading him to conformity to His decree, so that he reverences Him in his prayers and is obedient in his almsgiving. God will increase him in rank and forgive him his evil deeds and bestow upon him gracious blessings and guide him in the path of the upright.

Ye worshippers of God: how wondrous it is that everything belonging to the believer is good. It is only so for the believer. If some good fortune befalls him, he gives thanks and it becomes a blessing to him. If some misfortune, he is patient and it becomes a blessing. A gift does not make him negligent, nor does catastrophe anger him. That is how Muhammad was. God tried him with blessings and he received them with great gratitude. He tested him with calamity and he met it with splendid patience. He went one day to the people of Al-Ṭā'if to preach to them the message of his Lord. They stoned him until the blood flowed. He took refuge in a vineyard and sought shade there. Then he turned unto God and said: "O God I plead before Thee for the feebleness of my strength which has been patient with men. O Thou Most Merciful Thou art the Lord of those who acknowledge weakness. Thou art my Lord. It is not Thy anger that is upon me. I will not care anything of it."

Such also was the life of his companions, the believers. They did not weary of the animosity of the unbelievers and did not despair at their seeming victory. They drew out of failure the means to success, and out of disaster a road to victory, taking refuge with their Lord in loyal resolve, and entire confidence. They it was who hearkened to God and to the Apostle after wounds befell them. They it was to whom people said: "Verily men have gathered together against you so fear them." But that only increased their faith and they said: "We have considered God and the grace of the One we trust." So they overcame by grace and favour from God and no evil touched them. They followed a course well-pleasing to God Who is the Lord of great goodness.

O ye worshippers of God. Faith guides believers, both as individuals and communities, to bear hardships, however great they may be, and to clear open the way to a happy life, however difficult be its attainment, and to the performance of religious obligations however arduous. Hardships reward the believer with rest and quiet and confidence. Difficulties repay him with strength and courage. Acts of worship make him grow in faith. Fasting is half of patience. Patience is half of faith. How great is our need in this life of a disposition which will implant fasting in men's souls. It will nourish the feeling of mercy and train the power of the will and the purpose and lift man to the loftiest character. Prayer is a link between the servant and his Lord and between the believer and his fellow believers. Pilgrimage means mutual awareness and mutual goodwill, sacrifice, patience and fortitude. *Zakāt* is goodness, liberality, righteousness and the payment of debt.

Then fear God, O ye worshippers of God and lay hold of the bond of faith for that is the strong tie of God, gathering believers into one mind. Take pleasure in his blessings and find your beauty in His glories. May God cause quietness to descend upon you and bring your hearts unto unity.

Tradition records that the Apostle of God said to his companions: "Ask me anything you wish." A man cried:

"O Apostle of God: What is faith?" He said: "Sincerity." "And what is conviction?" and he said: "Honest dealing." [10]

Despite the criticisms directed against him from several sides in Islam the preacher still has an influential role in the community. On his lips the religion becomes articulate and something of its daily meaning is expressed. Though there are powerful factors working in the direction of secularity and irreligion the mosques are frequently crowded and listeners overflow on to the sidewalks where loud-speakers relay the discourse. Even in Turkey where the pressure of a laic state has been strong for three decades, there are marked signs of a revival of mosque attendances, not least in Ankara itself. If then the *khatīb* is far from enjoying the prestige he once wielded, he and his art maintain a vigorous continuity with the great past and have still to be reckoned with in the understanding of Muslim religious life.

Certain other features of the mosque as an index to Islam deserve attention. The notable lack of seats strikes the Western visitor—though it is by no means so strange to the Eastern Christian. More significant still is the total absence of a special sanctuary or altar. Two large candlesticks may flank the *mihrāb* but their meaning does not hold a central place. Long lines of pillars support the flat roofs, or wide expanses of carpeted space stretch beneath a soaring dome. The Qur'ān is everywhere the theme of decoration. A clock will often be found in a prominent position. Small folding stools that serve to support the reader's Qur'ān are about the only movable furniture. In some mosques a balcony or gallery runs along one side or even around the structure. Outside the mosque proper is a wide *sahn*, or court, unless the mosque is small. Here stand the fountains in open cisterns or under cupolas with columns. If the mosque is famous it may boast some celebrated tomb of patriarch, traditionalist, exegete or ruler, where, behind a grille or under an ornate canopy, a sarcophagus will be found. Around these shrines the visitor may see candles, ribbons, and other decorations, placed there by the faithful at times of remembrance or invocation. In small local mosques the memory of some saint or *marabūt* may dominate. Signs of special veneration then become more evident. For popular Muslim devotion has not seldom broken out of the strict rigidities of orthodox theology to find satisfying popular forms by which to express and arouse itself.

For all its wide variety, however, the mosque has a clear unity of function pervading and constraining all its architectural diversity. This unity arises in the last analysis from Islam itself and has been deepened by the fact of pilgrimage. In the great ages of mosque-building, travel was frequent and extensive. Masons, designers, craftsmen, and ceramicists traveled from center to center, on their long way to or from Mecca, studying the edifices they saw, noting details, and comparing skills. They learned in this way how to combine their artistic tastes with the requirements of the faith. Such luxury as they might allow themselves was transmuted into forms at least basically subdued to the dictates of dogma. Carpets on which men prayed could be richly dyed and patterned; lamps by which they recited the sacred text could be lavishly inlaid with gold and silver; domes that symbolized the over-arching unity could be elaborately adorned with color or gold. These were compensations for the prohibition of statuary, ikons, and pictorial art. The mosque, then, can be seen as the majestic synthesis of prevailing religious dogma and a worshipful art that accepted its limitations creatively. Nowhere can the soul of Islam be so movingly read and pondered as in its hallowed precincts.

VI

A study of the religious reality which the mosque expresses would not be complete without some reference to its principal historical division. Early in its career, Islam suffered a serious schism, dividing it into two major groupings described as Sunnī and Shī'ah. There is no space here for a detailed exposition of the factors involved, nor of the other subdivisions into which both, but Shī'ah Islam in particular, are divided. The context of devotional life seems to be the most appropriate area in which to set a brief explanation of this duality in Islam, though originating factors were political as well as theological.

Sunnī Islam follows the rule of the orthodox *Sunnah,* or Path, of the Qur'ān and the (Sunnī) Tradition. It believes in the validity of the historic Caliphate and in the utter finality of the Prophethood of Muhammad. Shī'ah Islam holds that 'Alī, fourth Caliph, cousin and son-in-law of the Prophet, should have been his immediate successor and, therefore, disallows the first three Caliphs and the *de jure* status of the subsequent Umayyads and their successors. The dark family tragedies of the house of 'Alī, culminating in the massacre of Husain and his retinue at Karbala in A.D., 680, gave to Shī'ah Islam a background of martyrdom that shaped its whole theology. Devotion to the tragic three, 'Alī, Hasan, and Husain, evoked religious attitudes to which Sunnī Islam has remained for the most part a stranger.

In its main areas in Iraq, Iran, Afghanistan, the Yaman, and India, Shī'ah Islam is devoted to the memory of the Prophet's family and sees in its story of death and defeat a drama of redemptive sacrifice. The celebration culminates in the *Muharram* rites when the tragedy of Husain is re-enacted with intense emotion. Here, more than anywhere in Sunnī Islam, the Shī'ah Muslim comes to grips with the mystery of suffering and grapples with areas of meaning the average Sunnī ignores. Descriptions of Shī'ah devotion in its supreme festival are readily accessible.[11]

What is of importance here is to appreciate the underlying reasons for the deep contrasts in Shī'ah devotional life. The crux lies in the contrasted Shī'ah concept of the relation of the Divine revelation to men in time. Shī'ah Islam believes in Muhammad as the culmination of prophethood. But whereas the Sunnī believes that the succeeding centuries enter into the Muhammadan revelation through the Qur'ān and the orthodoxy of the possessing community, Shī'ahs believe that it is mediated to the generations through *Imāms*, without whom its relevance cannot be known. These *Imāms* do not replace the Prophet or impugn his finality. Rather they are the indispensable media of the understanding of the truth the Prophet proclaimed. It is through them, and them alone, that he is made contemporary. The truth is not possessed in an orthodox continuity of retrospective education. The community is not the repository or the guarantee of valid understanding in reliance upon the prior documentary sources. The guarantee lies in the *Imām* who is thought of as an emanation of the Divine light and of the wisdom of God in the time of his life.

Whereas the term *imām* in Sunnī Islam simply signifies the leader of the mosque prayers, habitual or actual, in Shī'ah Islam the *Imām* signifies the agent of the Divine illumination of the age. The succession begins with the Prophet and 'Alī and his sons and passes down to the number of seven (in some Shī'ah thought), or to twelve (in other sects). By virtue of its more immediate sense of Divine revelation, Shī'ah Islam has shown much greater tendency to sectarianism and schism. It is subdivided into many forms, one of the most notable being Ismailism. Its doctrine of the Hidden *Imām* gives rise to speculative excesses far more readily than the disciplined orthodoxy of Sunnis. Shī'ahs have their own traditions and separate schools of law. Many racial and cultural tensions can be read into this central schism and the cleavage goes very deep. New sects like Babism and Bahaism arose in the nineteenth century from Shī'ah Islam, carrying some of its ideas into wider disparity.

The issue between Sunnī and Shī'ah ultimately concerns the relation of dogma to devotion and of the eternal universal to the temporal particular. Is the individual believer related to Muhammad as the place of final revelation, backward through the generations? Or does that essential truth break upon him freshly in more contemporary occasions of new radiance and articulation? Shī'ahs have affirmed the latter. What they have lost in schismatic divisiveness when compared with Sunnis, they may have gained in devotional immediacy and the sense of urgency. Though devious and proliferating in many of its forms Shī'ah Islam has often greater spontaneity and intensity. It has escaped the aridity and formalism which have periodically afflicted the Sunnī segment. It has shown more hospitality, or been more exposed, to esoteric confusion. Under its influence many non-Arab elements have come to coalesce with original Muslim forms. Because of their doctrine of the sinlessness of the *Imāms* Shī'ahs look much more largely for intercession and mediation.

Relations between Sunnī and Shī'ah have varied through the

centuries. The extremer sects, carrying their doctrines of emanation to a point where the supremacy of Muhammad is denied and
he comes to be merely one in a series, have naturally aroused
the strongest antagonism. Shī'ahs in general have much ground
for hatred when they relive the agonies of Husain or remember
such episodes as the defeat of their own Fātimid Caliphate by
that earnest Sunnī Saladin or the bitter zeal of the last great
Mughal, Aurangzīb. On the other hand, there have been many
efforts to draw the household of Islam together and to develop
its underlying common heritage. But devotionally it would seem
that an irreconcilable difference of mood, emphasis, and emotion
divides the two.

VII

If Shī'ah Muslims represent a plea for greater immediacy of the
soul to truth than Sunnī Islam provides, the same is true of the
long and deep tradition of mysticism, the Muslim forms of which
are known as Sufism. It is in this area that the devotional achievements of Islam as religion are greatest. Sufism has a long and
chequered history. There were times in the later centuries when
it did more to conserve and perpetuate Islam than did orthodoxy
itself. Its beginnings go back to the Prophet who is claimed and
possessed by some Sufis as the supreme exponent of disciplined
mystical ecstasy. The Qur'ān, in this view, is then the greatest
product of the Sufi approach. This understanding, sustained by
many texts capable of such interpretation, justifies the Sufis in
asserting a direct intimacy with the truth such as outrages or
dismays the orthodox custodians of the faith.

The strong development of Sufism, associated with such teachers as the Brethren of Purity and Al-Muhāsibī in the ninth and
tenth centuries of the Christian era, largely came in protest
against the increasing formalism of Muslim theology. Whatever
elements in primitive Islam served to give it positive generation,
it drew strength from the failure of the orthodox to satisfy the
demands of the devotional spirit. The mystic, being always suspect to the custodians of dogma, seeks the attainment of Divine
knowledge by a contrasted attitude to the deeds or documents
of the historic faith. He believes in an alternative way to truth,

beyond reason and revelation dogmatically defined. He discounts what Muslim theology calls 'aql, intellect, and naql, or transmitted truth, and concentrates on kashf, or discovery, in which the meaning of faith and truth is given in experimental immediacy to the seeking soul. The insight is the reward of a path to knowledge which involves moral discipline and ascetic life. This Sufi way, or tarīqah, is understood to consist of stages, the three main grades of which are the murīd, or novice, the sā'ir, or traveler, and the wāsil, or attainer.

The conditions of knowledge are, for the Sufi, primarily spiritual, not intellectual. Muhammad is the exemplar of the path. He exemplifies faith as an attitude rather than dictates it as a dogma. The Qur'ān likewise is a textbook in the method. The findings to be valid must be the Sufi's own. But because they are experimentally known they cannot be readily defined in intellectual terms. "Come where I am; I can show you the way" is the mystic's call to man, not: "Believe what I teach, I can tell you the orthodox truth." As such the Sufi represents at once a protest, an aspiration, and a goal. His very lack of rational concern and some of the forms of his technique are liable to lead him into aberration and bring his purpose into disrepute. Some Sufi doctrines of passivity and the Sufi veneration of saints have occasioned no little apathy and crude superstition. Sufism has suffered from its own excesses and is reproached by many modern reformers. Yet even these critics, Muhammad 'Abduh, for example, and Iqbāl, have themselves owed not a little to Sufi influence in their upbringing.

In its finest forms Islamic mysticism has inspired the greatest devotional literature in Islam. There is the celebrated poetess Rābi'ah (died A.D. 801); Al-Hallāj, the Persian writer (crucified in A.D. 922); Al-Ghazālī, himself; Ibn al-'Arabī "the greatest mystical genius of the Arabs" (died in Damascus in A.D. 1240); his contemporary the famous Jalāl al-Dīn Rūmī, author of the immortal Mathnavī. The writings of these and lesser leaders are becoming increasingly available in translations and anthologies for Western readers.[12] They are living testimony to the vitality of the tradition to which they belonged. Here the student may find in their most eloquent expression the characteristic Sufi intensities: the yearning after the knowledge which is absorption; the joy of penetration beyond the shell of selfish selfhood into wholeness; the price of discipline and the meaning of temptation; the purity and poverty of the ardent spirit; the disinterestedness of valid love; the stations and states of the progress of the soul; the anticipations of illumination and the climax of *fanā'* where the soul transcends itself and its search in passing into love.

The most notable external feature of Sufism is its organization into orders for the better fulfillment of its purposes. These orders became a profound factor in the whole life of Islam. They resembled economic guilds or fraternities and gave a cohesion to Muslim social life that often outweighed the mosque and orthodoxy in local importance. The orders gathered around first the person and then the reputation of some great founder, whose devotions they used. The most famous of the orders were the Qādiriyyah founded by 'Abd al-Qādir al-Jīlānī (1078-1166); the Suhrawardiyyah, named after Shihāb al-Dīn al-Suhrawardī (1144-1234); the Shādhiliyyah, deriving from Nūr al-Dīn al-Shādhilī (1196-1258); and the Maulawiyyah, from the title of Maulawī, given to the author of the *Mathnavī*. Numerous other orders and innumerable offshoots developed throughout the world of Islam. Their rituals differed considerably but all in some sense used the technique of the *dhikr*. The dervish is no doubt the most familiar image to the Western mind in this connection. The *dhikr* is the use of rhythmic recitation and rhythmic movements of the body to induce that sense of abstraction from the physical world which the Sufi seeks. Repeated ejaculations of *Allāh* or *Subhān Allāh* or the words of the *Fātihah* serve to sever attention from the senses and concentrate it on the thought of God. That the practices of the mystics have encouraged charlatans and rogues is a familiar denunciation. But the scandalous excesses of some should not blind the critic to the force and fervor of restrained and disciplined mysticism. For all the tensions they have set up in Islam the Sufis have not seldom been its salvation. Among their humblest devotees one may still find a rare quality of spiritual desire and a sensitivity of soul to God, life, and eternity.

Here from a Sufi manual, or rather, scroll, of devotion carried in the long robe of what unknown artisan or in the camel holster of an unnamed cameleer, undated and yet timeless, is a translated extract.

It breathes an unmistakable, religious self-awareness, that knows both repentance and confidence, entreaty and adoration.

> O Lord, open to us Thy mercy and clothe us, O Lord, in the most excellent robe of guidance and prayer. Be glad, O God, at Thy greatness . . . and let the sighing of our tears flow, O God, into Thine awful worship. Correct, O God, in me the allurements of evil for the sake of my entreaty. O my God, if Thy mercy had not shown me the good way then who would have led me unto Thee in a plain path? . . . If Thine aid had forsaken me when self and Satan struggled with me, then verily Thy forsaking would have left me in misery and loss.
>
> O my God, I knocked at the door of Thy mercy with the hand of my hope. I fled unto Thee, seeking refuge from my multiplied sins and I hung upon the borders of Thy garments with the fingers of my trust. So pardon, O God, the wrongs I have done, the evils and the sins, and rid me, O God, of my evil state, for Thou art my Lord and Sovereign, my reliance and my hope, the goal of my desire in my calamity and distress.
>
> O my God, how wilt Thou reject a worthless one who takes refuge with Thee, fleeing from his sins: or how wilt Thou disappoint one who implores guidance of Thy excellence with entreaty: or how wilt Thou cast off one who longs to drink of Thy waters? No! Thou wilt not . . . for Thy door is open to the seekers and the homeless. Thou art the end of our search and the goal of hope, O my God.

This is the Sufi's *Alaika tawakkaltu,* "Lord in Thee have I trusted"—one of the most familiar phrases in the religious life of all Islam.

NOTES *to Chapter IV*

1

As in Calverley, Edwin E., *Worship in Islam*, Madras, 1925, q.v., being a translation of Book IV of Al-Ghazālī's *Ihyā' Ulūm al-Dīn*, one of the greatest works of Muslim theology.

2

Professor Arnold Toynbee has developed this theme of the role of pilgrimage in culture-renaissance in *A Study of History*, Volume IX, New York, 1954, pp. 96-114.

3

Vigorous protests over financial restrictions on pilgrims were voiced in 1953 and 1954. See *The Muslim World*, Oct. 1953, Vol. 43, No. 4, p. 308, and Oct. 1954, Vol. 44, No. 4, p. 280. For earlier deterrents in the insanitary conditions and for a typical, sophisticated disinclination to pilgrimage, later overcome, see Haykal, Muhammad Husain, *Fī Manzil al-Waḥy*, op. cit. pp. 35-8.

4

The redoubtable Charles M. Doughty never visited Mecca, though he traveled courageously as a Christian in Arabia. Among those who visited Mecca *incognito Christiano* were Ludwig Burckhardt, Richard Burton, and Christian Snouck Hurgrönje. See note below.

5

Burckhardt, L. J., *Travels in Arabia*, 2 vols., 1829; Burton, Richard F., *Personal Narrative of a Pilgrimage to Al-Madineh and Meccah*, 2 vols., London, 1893; Rutter, E., *The Holy Cities of Arabia*, 2 vols., London, 1928; Hurgrönje, C. Snouck, *Mekka*, 2 vols., in German, the second translated into English as *Mekka in the Latter Part of the Nineteenth Century*, Leiden, 1931 (the translator was J. H. Monahan).

6

Quoted from *The Muslim World*, July 1955, Vol. 45, No. 3, "Manāsik al-Hajj," pp. 269-80 (translation by the author).

7

Al-Ghazālī (1058-1111) writes that he used to lead a solitary life in the mosque at Damascus, spending his days on the minaret, having first closed the door behind him. He adds that later in Jerusalem he shut himself up in the Sanctuary of the Rock for study and devotion.

8

Sermons, for example, in Egypt are controlled by the Ministry for Religious Affairs. Action to bring this about was taken in 1954 as a sequel to the use of the pulpit by foes of the regime.

9

Dīwān al-Khutab li-l-Juma'i wa-l-A'yād, Damascus, 1948. This manual was produced by a Committee of 'Ulamā' at the behest of the

Ministry of Waqfs; Al-Khaulī, Muhammad, 'Abd al-'Azīz, *Islāh al-Wa'z al-Dīni*, Cairo, 3rd ed., 1952; Rifā'i, 'Alī, *Kaifa takūnu Khatīban*, Cairo, 3rd ed., 1953, *et al.*

10

Translated by the author from Al-Marāghȳ, 'Abdallāh, *Diwān al-Khutab al-Hadīthah fi-l-Wa'z wa-l-Irshād*, Cairo, n.d. "Faith in God" —a typical sermon—is found on pp. 10-12 of the 2nd ed., n.d.

11

For example, Hollister, John N., *The Shi'a of India*, London, 1953, pp. 164-80, and Stark, Freya, *Baghdad Sketches*, London, 1937, pp. 221-7. In *The Road to Mecca*, New York, 1954, Muhammad As'ad has some interesting comments on Shī'ah lamentation for 'Alī, Hasan, and Husain, which he describes as "extravagant."

12

Interpretative studies in which there are numerous excerpts and references to an even wider field are: Nicholson, Reynold A., *The Mystics of Islam*, London, 1914; Smith, Margaret, *Readings from the Mystics of Islam*, London, 1950, and *The Sufi Path of Love, An Anthology of Sufism*, London, 1954; Arberry, Arthur J., *Sufism, an Account of the Mystics of Islam*, London, 1954.

v

THE ISLAMIC ORDER FOR HUMAN SOCIETY

حيّ على الفلاح

THE SECOND clause of the double summons which the minaret lays upon the Muslim because of his confession of God and the Prophet employs one of the most inclusive concepts in the Arabic language. With the imperative *Hayya,* noted in the previous chapter, it demands an alert response to what it calls *Al-Falāh.* "Come ye unto the Good" it cries—the Good, implicit in the revelation already acknowledged. It is the Good to which worship leads and for which the Muslim is enlisted in the ranks of the believing. *Falāh* is not, then, some pietistic abstraction, nor the indulgence of a private sanctity. It is the true state of welfare, the proper prosperity, of the people of God, fulfilled in communal existence and realized in social life. "Come ye unto the good life." "Alert yourselves in mind and will to the authentic well-being of Muslim humanity, achieved within the Islamic order." Such is *Falāh* as the muezzin proclaims and defines it.

It is a term to set the mind strenuously to work and well calculated to serve as the ruling idea in any careful exposition of Islam in its external meaning for human society. What, as the Muslim sees it, does Islam mean for the political, economic, and social areas of human life and relationship? What is the *Falāh* to which men under Islam are bidden? How is it conceived as to its content? How is it to be expected as an actuality? To these

140

questions and some, at least, of their answers in historic Islam
we must now turn.

As familiar as the prayer mat to the traveler among Muslims
is the doctrine that religion pervades all life to the student of
Islam. Repeatedly in classical dogma and in current apology the
reader comes upon the fact that Islam is totalitarian. It does
not separate between duty as a believer and duty as a citizen;
between what is owing to God and what is owing to society. All
man's social responsibilities are religious in character and his
religion is fulfilled not only in what ensues in the mosque but
also in the market. There has been a constant tendency to interpret Islam as unique in this respect, though these attitudes often
derive either from a misunderstanding of the distinction between
religious and secular elsewhere or from incomplete scrutiny of
their "identity" in Islam. But the fact remains that Islam sets
out to be an inclusive system in which the relation of the person
to God pervades also his relation to his fellows.

Falāh, then, exists for the muezzin as a concept. The ideal
revelation is in hand. In its light men see light. God has sent
the knowledge of His will and in its obedience and fulfillment
the good life for mankind is to be attained. Those attitudes of
mind and soul which relate uniquely to God in worship and
have been described under "Prayer" have their counterparts in
attitudes toward the world of fellowmen within Islam. *Īmān,* or
belief, has as its corollary *Dīn,* or deed, including manward as
well as Godward obligations. The true Muslim is he who "performs," because, and as, he believes. Such "performing" covers
not only the ritual prayer, fasting, and pilgrimage but almsgiving
and all that it implies. It symbolizes responsibility toward one's
fellowman. Islam, as proclaimed from the minaret, is *Falāh* as
well as *Salāt,* the *laborare* of goodness as well as the *orare* of worship. Just as in Christian terms the word "service" may mean a
good deed or an occasion of worship, so in Islam the obligation
of religion means behavior as well as belief. "The pillars of
religion" in Islam involve not only credal confession but the
recognition of God in all realms of human conduct. *Falāh,* as
a word, seems to have obvious kinship with Hebrew and Syriac

terms for "cult" or "prayer," though its immediate Arabic sense is "good" or "success." [1]

This comprehensive quality of Islam is epitomized in the historical form of its genesis. From the moment people and tribes became physically, as well as spiritually, tributary to Muhammad in Medina, Islam was an external as well as an internal loyalty. This post-*Hijrah* amalgam was repeated and intensified in the subsequent expansion of Islam. The new faith did not extend as a religious understanding enjoining submission to "the powers that be." Rather it came superseding those powers with impressive rapidity and finality. To become a Muslim was to become a subject; while those who remained non-Muslims were the more subjected. When Islam conquered, everyone exchanged rulers. Heraclius or the heirs of Khosroes went; 'Umar, Mu'āwiya, Al-Mansūr came.

This pattern of external dominance was only the outward form of the inward fact. Islam was not an account of human relationship with God that could co-exist with a variety of political expressions. Rather those political expressions gave way to the Islamic. The Caliphate became the symbol of a trusteeship of Muhammad's once for all prophethood and of a perpetuation of his model rulership. Both were permanently fused together and remained ideologically intact until this twentieth century. It is in community, in political expression and political sovereignty, that Islam is realizable. The true law in the custody of the true community is the condition of the true society. The ideal state of affairs, the muezzin's *Falāh*, demands the proper ideology under the proper conditions. The law which defines the one also establishes the other. We may perhaps go so far as to say that within the Muslim concept the religious ideology, not simply requires but *is* a communal order realizable by political sovereignty within the life of this world. This is the ultimate meaning of law in Islam and of Islam as law. Even the phrase "Islam as law" is ambiguous, however, since it may imply that Islam could also be, in a parallel sense, something else. It is just that something else which the term "Islam as law" is here meant to rule out. Properly conceived, the historic religion is a total way of life, known and learned from Divine disclosure and attainable in political, social, and economic existence, by men on earth.

II

Though this definition would not coincide with some expressions of the contemporary Muslim mind, these should not take priority here over the exposition of the classical meanings. Turning to an attempt at a summary of them, it seems reasonable to divide the study of *Falāh* into two parts: definition and actualization, the "What?" and the "How?" of the ideology which is Islam.

The underlying incentive of Islam has always been to *do* what God willed. The ultimate status of man before God, that of the *'abd,* or slave-servant, points to deed rather than to contemplation. The definition of man before God is an active relationship. Though this does not obviate theology, it means that Islam is finally, and characteristically, concerned with what the Lord requires.

The ground and form of the requirement is revelatory. The Qur'ān is interpreted as validating human reason as an instrument for tracing the majesty of the Divine mind in the universe of nature. But reason is not an appropriate means for the discovery of the Divine will, except in a confirmatory sense. God Himself is the Author of the law by which we acknowledge His sovereignty. He Himself shows us the way wherein we should walk. Rational ethics or political science or economic theory— as the product of human logic, argumentation, dialectic or pondered experience—do not theoretically exist in Islam. The basis of human conduct and organization is revelation. Only in writing the lesser points or the "by-laws" into the fundamental "constitution" for human life, given in revelation, have these human systems any validity. The true form of the family, the state, the economy, are discoverable in the Divine will. Man is not meant to argue for democracy on the ground of inalienable rights; nor for *laissez faire* on the greatest-happiness principle; nor for mutual help as proper to the human mind; nor for beliefs because they work; nor for any one of the multifarious *pros* and *cons* of utilitarianism, pragmatism, libertarianism, egalitarianism, and all the other forms of political or ethical theory. The right for man in society has been revealed in the Divine law in the trust of the Islamic community. Some in recent times might let in the theorists on the grounds that some points of human organization are too detailed and insignificant to be worthy of revelatory action on the part of God.[2] But this tendency to confine revelation to big principles and elevate it beyond the level of the meticulous is foreign to the historic mind of Islam and is a modern innovation.

Law, then, as the secret of *Falāh* comes in revelation from God. But it still requires definition in the manifold of human activity. Revelation as a process is consummated once and for all in Muhammad. This completion of revelation is the Qur'ān where the Divine law is recorded and known. The Qur'ān, as the first and ruling source of law, is the definitive court of appeal as to the meaning of the good. But Tradition interpreted and enlarged the meanings of the Qur'ān and so became the second element in the structure of Muslim ideology.

But Tradition tended to proliferate under the double impetus of external need and interior veneration. Much came into the Muslim heritage of obedience in this way from the customs and cultures of the conquered territories. Muhammad became the posthumous repository of many ideas and practices which Islam had neither will nor power to eradicate from the behavior of its new devotees. But there is little evidence that elements incompatible with crucial Muslim teachings found any such entry. For the rest, Islam sought to give sanction to new ways and patterns of behavior in the positive form of traditions about its supreme human leader. If the expanding community was in a real sense legislating in an expanding manner for itself, it did so in the name of its great earthly architect. The fact that things must be believed to turn upon prophetic precedent is no more than a measure of the veneration in which revelation and its agent were regarded.

When such communal "legislation" outran its validities, however, and distorted its posthumous memory it confronted itself with a problem of correction undertaken by the great traditionalists. When the mind of Islam was uncertain about the legal validity in many areas of its traditions, the authority of the great schools of law was the practical answer. How far their editing succeeded it is almost impossible to determine precisely. Perhaps it is unimportant. What matters is the general validity of this second "Muhammadan" source of access to the mind of God.

For all its multiplicity of traditional sources, law was still incomplete. The Qur'ān and the valid traditions alike did not suffice for the regulation of the behavior of the community. Since that behavior required revelatory criteria and directives there had to be evolved other sources of ideology continuous with the first and second. The structure of Islamic law is generally regarded as complete with the establishment of two other regulative sources, namely Qiyās and Ijmā', or analogy and consensus. Intricate and sometimes bitter controversies raged around these concepts, their limits and their operations. These, however, are the task of the historian rather than the expositor.

III

The first—analogy—is more readily understood. It was a principle of extension of Islamic law on the basis of a likeness in two situations one of which was specifically provided for in the Qur'ān or Tradition. The inclusion of the other, and analogous, situation might then be reasonably inferred from the first. Thus, if the Qur'ān prohibited the use of wine, the prohibition might be understood to include other intoxicants, not actually wine, which had similar deleterious effects, the avoidance of these being presumably the intention of the prohibition. The schools required careful definitions of what was properly analogous within the terms of the point being argued and differed somewhat as to whether the intention had to be explicit or simply inferred. The dangers involved in analogy made it suspect in the eyes of some who disallowed it altogether.

Of much wider range and subtlety was the idea of Ijmā'. Reliance on consensus goes back to the Qur'ān and to traditions— some of them disputed—underlying the notion that truth is safe with the community. Individualism is heresy. The private person it is who goes into untruth. The whole is not likely—according to some statements is not able—to stray universally. Put in its most daring form, consensus means that Islam is what Muslims define it to be. In the more modest and circumspect view, it means that there is a source of security in the communal mind. The Muslim community is not likely to go long, or far, into a position which is not validly Islamic. In some such form, though its organs of expression may differ, reliance on the community is characteristic of, indeed necessary to, all religions.

Consensus is not conceivable or proper except in a complementary relation to the documentary sources. It affords a principle of development in Islam whereby a new attitude, or a new requirement, can gather the force of law and so a sanction of "revelatory" status, through its acceptance in general by those who believe. After God and the Prophet, the Community. They, in whose custody of worship and conduct the truths of the religion are, may be reasonably accepted as a frame of reference, a court of appeal, for the validation, or otherwise, of what is truly and authentically Islamic. This, it should be clear, is not democracy as such. It is not majority opinion statistically ascertained. It is the attainment of a common mind on a particular point, the legal recognition of an existing state of affairs—or of opinion—which has come to be in the community, in an area of former silence and present compatibility vis-à-vis the Qur'ān. The schools again have differed profoundly on problems associated with consensus but most minds of good will have been ready to accept its sanctity. There has been no general reluctance to allow *Ijmā'* because its operation resulted in law just as binding as the law that came down from heaven. Of late some have suggested that consensus may be a hidden form of the sin of association since it results in a product which becomes a part of the *Sharī'ah,* or Holy Law, equal with what God spake. The exaltation of the humanly originated to the level of the Divinely originated might be *Shirk,* or idolatry. But these fears have been largely disallowed, a fact which indicates the importance understood to belong in law to the community.[3]

Consensus, however, does not arrive without stimulus and direction. The community is a large and somewhat indefinite entity. Its mind, especially in what is novel or problematic—obvious areas for *Ijmā'*—only comes through pioneers, through individuals who propagate creative thoughts. Most consensus starts with minorities: it may even start with heretics. It is a process of becoming, or of thinking, which someone must originate. And when it is originated it is manifestly not consensus. Yet if only consensus validates, how can a pioneer opinion ever be launched? How can a consensus ever legitimately arise, since it cannot be, without coming to be, and cannot come to be legitimately, without being?

To confront this dilemma, Islam developed the much more controversial notion of *Ijtihād*, the means to *Ijmā'*. *Ijtihād* means, in its technical sense, enterprise or initiative. It involves diligence and implies great effort, either to understand or to discriminate the right action in any general issue. It is usually held that a *mujtahid,* one judged capable of *Ijtihād,* qualifies only on the ground of prolonged grammatical, legal, and theological training. The *mujtahid* was not an administrator of law in a court, but a scholar learned in all its niceties and so capable of reaching conclusions that might commend themselves to a general consensus in the course of time. In this way the *lacunae* in Islamic ideology or the *Sharī'ah* might gradually be filled and the documentary sources made complete.

Ijtihād as a means to an ultimate consensus was only valid when it did so eventuate in a public approval. Just how wide such approval had to be, or when it could be understood to exist, were matters on which definition varied. The ways in which the *mujtahid* could operate were also a theme of long controversy. Some allowed a relatively wide freedom to what was called *Ra'ȳ,* or expert private opinion. Others held that this could only be practiced under certain limits. There was the idea of *Istihsān,* whereby the legist considered a certain course of action good, somewhat after the manner of Western equity. There was *Istislāh,* by which a position could be validated for its soundness, not in general, but in respect of public welfare. There was also *Istishāb,* in which the argument went back toward analogy and found validity for a course of action by associating it with a provision in the Qur'ān or Tradition. But these nice technical points of detail cannot be treated adequately here. Their variety is only a measure of the desire to insure that even the competent experts should only reach conclusions on new rulings under strict safeguards.

Some authorities denied *Ra'y* and *Ijtihād* altogether, asserting that the documentary sources were sufficient or preferring to make them so by crude invention of traditions. In any event, *Ijtihād* was understood as limited to the realm of law and had no competence over dogma. There was much discussion as to whether *Ijtihād* was a permanent function, whether "the door of *Ijtihād*," as the phrase was, remained open. Or was *Ijtihād* a kind of self-curtailing process less and less needed as the *Sharī'ah* was steadily completed by its exercise? The steady parallel emergence of ever new demands, especially in modern times, tended to render the latter view untenable. But many held it with great tenacity, claiming that *Ijtihād*, having fulfilled its entire duties and enabled through *Ijmā'* the completion of the perfect law, was no longer an available function in the Islamic community. This controversy still continues while the complexities of life make ever more necessary the new judgments the old mind so much fears.

On a conservative hypothesis, those fears are perhaps justified. The idea behind *Ijtihād* and *Ijmā'* clearly has very wide potentialities. It can be developed into an inclusive principle of change on the ground of the majority mind and extended to many areas of inconsistency with the traditional meanings of the *Sharī'ah*. It is, in fact, being so used, tacitly more often than avowedly, in the present scene. Most Muslim nations have considerably modified their civil and criminal laws, in the name of the popular will, expressed in representative parliaments or otherwise. Such changes are claimed by their champions as Islamic in a spiritual sense. They are valid because the community attests them as desirable. When appeal in this way is made to the spirit, as contrasted with the letter of Islam, it is evident that the criterion of what is authentic becomes much freer. The community, therefore, assumes a much more crucial role, which is often definitive rather than complementary. Such reinterpretation of what Islam means and requires may be seen as the modern form of *Ijtihād* and a new concept of the *mujtahid* role, even though those who make the changes do not invoke it.

In the classical past, however, *Ijmā' via Ijtihād* was only a fourth and subordinate source of ideological definition. And it was not valid on the democratic principle of the majority but in the assumption that the community mind was a right clue to the voice of God, where that voice had not otherwise spoken. This, then, is the structure of Islam—the Qur'ān, Tradition, *Qiyās,* and *Ijmā',* shaping the Holy Law that makes the conduct and measures the responsibilities of true Islam. That law was totalitarian in the sense that it pervaded all life and had authority over all realms. Admittedly there were many areas of behavior where it was indifferent and left many options, not reprehending or commending possible lines of action. It did not seek to be inquisitorial or burdensome. It recognized the natural desires and frailties of men. In some realms it spoke absolutely: in others permissively. But nothing was exempt from it that it saw fit to include.

Before we turn to the actualization of the Islamic law so defined it should be noted that historic Sunnī Islam relies upon four great schools of law which grew up in the second and third Muslim centuries and gathered to themselves an authority that has insured their perpetuity. Other schools flourished only fitfully and fell away. The Shī'ah Muslims follow their own schools. The first and largest of the Sunnī schools is that of Abū Hanīfah, centering in Baghdad. One of his chief pupils was Abū Yūsuf the famous casuist of *The Arabian Nights.* Mālik ibn Anas founded the Mālikite school in Medina and established its authority on the central role of Medina in the tradition and government of Islam. Muhammad al-Shāfi'ī, personally the greatest and most gifted of the founders, built the Shāfi'ite school with Cairo and Baghdad as its main centers. He was a skillful mediator between competing positions. The fourth and least of the schools, the Hanbalites of Ibn Hanbal, was a conservative extremism such as Al-Shāfi'ī failed to reassure. It was the latter who most contributed to the establishment of *Ijmā'* as a valid, formal source of Muslim law. He was one of the most remarkable figures in the whole history of jurisprudence. The diffusion of the leading schools varied considerably from time to time and from dynasty to dynasty. Their historical vicissitudes are not here our concern. In many centers of jurisprudence and legal lore they co-existed in varying strength. The individual Muslim, as well as the individual judge and lawyer, belongs to one or other of the schools. Opinions are divided as to the limits of movement from one to another. Intriguing as the details are, the point of relevance here is that the schools represent the historic form of Muslim law or communal ideology as it is interpreted, taught, and defined by authority. Areas of diversity are many but small. What is common is great and serious. The schools are, so to speak, the focal points of the communal recognition by Islam of the Divine guidance for the life of man. They are organs for the definition of what that guidance means for the Muslim, wherever time and circumstance have needed its restraint and constraint. They are the lexicographers, we may say, of applied law; the grammarians of the Divine mind or word or will.

Such definition is, in a sense, an on-going process, since new situations are constantly requiring new relevance from the ancient law. But these aspects call for discussion below, under the theme of actualization. It is in the realm of practical attainment that problems of re-definition most plainly arise. It is in facing the question: How? that men are often sent back to the question: What? for new scrutiny. For historic purposes, this exposition of the organs of definition and of the sources of ideology must suffice. How the Muslim law is realized in community must now be studied. It will be clear that we are concerned with the social and the political. The Godward areas of Muslim duty, worship, fasting, and pilgrimage have already been considered. These have, it is true, their social import and this will be implicit in what follows. "Come ye unto the Good." The law defines it. What does obedience entail?

IV

We shall be following the order of presentation in many a recent Muslim author if we turn at once to the third of the pillars of religion, *Zakāt*, or the obligation to almsgiving. For here one of the basic principles of the ideology is embodied. It is the principle of social responsibility by which the possession of wealth obligates the possessor to concern himself about those who lack what he enjoys. It distinguishes ideally between essential possession and actual possession. The former is the right and stake of the community in what any man owns; the latter is his actual ownership. It teaches that what is mine in point of fact is the community's in the ultimate reckoning. I, as a possessor, must remember the "not mine" aspect of what I call "mine," and give this recollection practical shape by donating a proportion for the public use. Only so do I validate what I retain. Private property is recognized on the condition of private benevolence. This is *Zakāt*, as interpreted in Muslim social thought.

The institution takes its honored place with witness, worship, fasting, and pilgrimage among the five Pillars of Islam. It has clear Quranic force. *Zakāt* is frequently linked with *salāt* as one of the first, confirming obligations of the new Muslim. "Perform the prayer and do the poor-rate" was the formula of submission (Surah ii. 43, 83, 110, 177, 277, *et al.*). Those who withhold the poor-rate are a class synonymous with the idolaters (Surah xii. 7). *Zakāt*, as serving to identify the Muslim as such, is noted in Surah lviii. 12, 13.

The root idea of the word *Zakāt* may be purification. But whatever may be the etymological truth there is no doubt of the understanding of the institution. Property is not purely held which recognizes no obligation, in and beyond possession. The Qur'ān uses an alternative word for alms, *Sadaqāt*, which is nearly synonymous and introduces the idea of rightness and friendship. *Sadaqāt* are wholly voluntary. On the basis of Quranic injunction and traditional exhortation the practice of almsgiving became a basic social institution in Islam. It figured in the life of the community from pre-*Hijrah* days. Meccan Surahs enjoin and describe it. After the *Hijrah* the emigrants had great need of the charity of the Medinan Muslims. The pattern for the integration of more and more non-Muslim Medinans and their tribal neighbors into Islam is given in Surah ix. 103. "Take alms of their wealth wherewith thou mayest purify them and mayest make them to grow and pray for them." There is no doubt that giving seals believing: it dramatizes effectively a

new allegiance. It may also express an otherwise inarticulate repentance.

The use of *Zakāt* when received in the early community was
varied. It was distributed for the relief of the poor and needy,
for parents, widows, slaves, and orphans, and was also utilized
in military ways, for the furtherance of the *Jihād* and, in certain circumstances, for the inducement of allegiance. It is meant
to provide the means for progress "in the way of God." [4] By
and large, however, it was the internal soundness, rather than
the external expansion, of the Muslim community for which
Zakāt was meant, though the former is often a most important
condition of the latter.

There is no space here to outline the intricacies of detail into
which this subject divides. The proportion of the payment of
one's possessions varied widely from time to time and also in
respect of different forms of property—land and its produce,
wealth in gold and money, merchandise and the rest. Some
taught that *Zakāt* should comprise everything above a stipulated
maximum retainable for legitimate self-support. Abū Dharr, for
example, a notable Muslim teacher, invoked by exponents of
the welfare state today, is said to have required that a man
should give up everything he did not need. But the generally
prevailing view fixed a limited percentage, 10, 5, or 2½ per
cent, for example, beyond which the believer was not required
to go.

The agencies for the collection and distribution of *Zakāt* payments also varied from time to time. In early days the state
played a large role. Mosque personnel frequently provided an
obvious agency for this purpose. It was sometimes claimed that
Zakāt could be paid directly from the rich to the poor. But general considerations made it preferable that the transaction should
be publicly supervised and administered. When *Zakāt* was officially levied as a tax, it still hinged to a great degree on individual declaration of property. Just as the will to pay was its
final sanction so the will to avoid payment, if it existed, could
discover numerous means to evasion and could offset much laud-
able exhortation.

Though incumbent or required (as distinct from *Sadaqāt*

which were voluntary and which could be used for needy non-Muslims) *Zakāt* was, nevertheless, not always physically compulsory. In modern times with far-reaching fiscal changes supervening in all Muslim nations and with the rise of state schemes of social welfare, there has been an insistence on the fact that such taxation is not technically *Zakāt*. Taxation is not confined to Muslims but falls on all citizens, whereas *Zakāt* is a Muslim ordinance. The Muslim, therefore, who pays taxes today which are used in part for social welfare must not suppose that he is absolved thereby from his *Zakāt* duty. The Government of Pakistan so ruled recently when it agreed to foster the payment of *Zakāt* by the sale of *Zakāt* stamps in Government Post Offices. Pleas from some quarters that taxation by the state in the interests of the poor of itself constituted *Zakāt* were disallowed.[5]

Technicalities apart, *Zakāt* is understood by almost all apologists as the basis of an ideology of social responsibility. It is the institutional witness to the duty implicit in ownership. Thus when fiscal policy in the modern state undertakes to bring about economic equality through graded taxation, poor-relief, and related measures, it is fulfilling the ideal to which *Zakāt* bears witness. Though the Muslim believer may still be obligated to pay his poor-rate, he has the satisfaction of knowing that the witness of its continuity has shaped the concept of all taxation and made the state actively cognizant of poverty.

This third pillar of religion is, likewise, a main support in the Islamic case against the evils of both capitalism and communism. It renders the first innocuous and the second unnecessary. It draws the sting of both by depriving Marxism of any legitimate argument against property and property of any scandalous features. The owner who truly recognizes, in an active sharing, the debt his very property imposes on him vis-à-vis the human whole obviates the criticisms which exploiting capitalism evoked. Thus the *raison d'être* of communism is destroyed at the root and capitalism, by the same token, is disciplined into validity. Some exponents of the meaning of *Zakāt* have gone so far as to say that communism is sufficiently disproved on the sole ground that if it prevailed payment of *Zakāt* would be impossible. Capital cannot be destroyed without the elimination of the institution which humanizes it. The further point is frequently made that *Zakāt,* when practiced, reverses the vicious spiral that Marx identified as the inner contradiction in capitalism. *Zakāt* transforms it into a happy spiral. For distribution of alms stimulates popular purchasing power and thus quickens the market, sharpens production, boosts profits, and so finally rewards the payer of *Zakāt* and gives him a still greater income out of which to disburse again.

A crucial assumption about human nature is implicit in this understanding of *Zakāt.* As Muslims see it, the institution of alms solves what is at issue between the great rival philosophies of this century. Islam, it is believed, has always had the secret. But there remains the question whether it has taken the real measure of the communist critique. It answers, with charity, the communist denial of the right to possess. It solves the problem of poverty by leave of the rich, where Marx proposes to solve it by their liquidation. His insistence on the necessity of violence, it counters with the efficiency of exhortation and religious obligation. The Qur'ān makes it perfectly clear that hoarding is hateful with God. Monopolists and cornerers of the market will be condignly punished in Hell. Islam demands economic justice and social neighborliness. *Zakāt* proclaims for all to understand the sovereign principle: "To have is to share." Only giving cleanses keeping. Property is a trust. The community is the context of value. As these precepts are followed the Islamic good is actualized. Mankind is rescued from the militant robbery of communism and from the cynical robbery of unalerted and untempered capitalism.

V

Two other factors in the actualization of Islamic ideology should be noted as a postscript to *Zakāt.* The law of inheritance in Islam, though of great intricacy and diversity in its details as interpreted within the various schools, makes, in general, for division and impedes the concentration of large capital wealth in individual hands. The Qur'ān and the *Sunnah* give specific directions for the division of personal estate after death and no bequests the testator made could override or disturb these proportions. Any transference of property the testator wished outside the provisions of the law had to be made during life and actually vested in the recipient before death. No will could be made settling property on legatees beyond the allowable proportions or by the deprivation of legitimate recipients.

This was so in conformity to basic Quranic legislation on inheritance in Surah iv. 12 *seq.* But an earlier verse in Surah ii. 176, enjoining on a man the equitable bequeathing of his property to his parents and kindred—a verse sometimes held to have been abrogated by Surah iv. 12—has been used of late to justify new legislation that makes possible testamentary gifts without the consent of legal heirs, in partial liberation from the earlier stipulations. These new interpretations of what is in the public interest, however, only serve to emphasize the long-standing practice, still hailed by apologists, by which inheritance becomes a means of distributing wealth, and so, in turn, a part of Islam's crusade against excessive capitalism.

The definitive Quranic passage gives males two-thirds, to females one-third—this being an advance on pre-Islamic Arabian practice. Heirs on the paternal side take precedence over heirs on the maternal side. There is no primogeniture. Sons are equally treated. It is this fact, together with the recognition of numerous secondary heirs who might have been ignored in a free bequeathing, that has given Muslim inheritance its significance as a deterrent to excessive concentration of capital. When this has been regarded as unfortunate there have been attempts made to surmount it by constituting estates as religious *waqf* or endowment, the administration of which could be more readily—and freely—determined.

Alongside inheritance is the familiar Muslim prohibition of usury. In Surahs ii and iii, the Qur'ān strongly condemns *ribā'*, or—in the generally accepted sense—the making of gain without due return or compensation. A careful distinction is made between usury and legitimate profit. One of the passages concerned, that in Surah ii, is in fact a spirited reply to those who tried to get away with usury under the plea of fair profit. Muslim economists have discussed and defined the distinction with great pains and ingenuity. It is suggested that the only legitimate

form of return for wealth is where the investor is personally involved in the enterprise and seeks no guaranteed return for his
investment. It is asserted that even in the modern world, banking, commerce, and capital development are perfectly feasible on
this basis. Instead of the present system of stock market transactions, where investors are entirely out of relation with the enterprises that use their capital and from which they demand to
receive assured gains, Islam envisages a direct relation of capital
to enterprise in such a way as to make gains not usurious but
legitimate. If a road or a bridge is to be built, for example, the
Government or the company should invite specific participation
from those with money to invest. They must be consciously
linked with the work in hand and be rewarded from the fruits
of that particular scheme. When the bridge or road is complete
the profits from tolls and the like are distributed proportionately
when all demands of construction and maintenance have been
met.[6]

Whether this concept of economic "involvement," as the only
valid condition of financial profit, is feasible under modern conditions is for economists to say. The idea of "zero interest" is
the Muslim form of valid investment profit. Banking also should
be made to conform to the same pattern. For interest to be
legitimate it must be dissociated from the idea of usury and
linked only to the valid meanings of profit. The ramifications,
not to say the viability, of this approach cannot be estimated
here. What matters now is the ideology—the demand that all
the operations of finance shall be uncompromised profit only.
The ideal is the form in which Muslim economics seeks to shape
in practice its conviction that there should not be exploitation
and that the will to work, not the will to make money work
for you (presumably to somebody else's detriment somewhere),
is the true economy. "Come ye unto the Good," whatever it
finally means, does not mean the hardly concealed gambling of
the Stock Exchanges.

Zakāt and the forms of inheritance and usury-prohibition together constitute the main elements of Islamic economic teaching as both an ideal from which direction can be found and
an active means for realizing the right. It is hardly necessary

to add that these three are corroborated by many Quranic and traditional passages calling for probity, honesty, and integrity in social and commercial relationships. The Qur'ān is understood to teach the main bases of economic planning in what one writer calls "four postulates"—economic trusteeship, economic co-operation, limited private property, and state enterprise. Islam learns in the Qur'ān that God is against the covetous and that trade should be always in fairness and good will. The over-arching truth of God's sovereignty means that man, properly understood, has no right of exploitation. "Not one of God's created servants" says Sayyid Qutb, "has the power to cut off any man's provision, or to withhold from him any part of that provision." The fear of God is the final assurance of reverence for law. In honoring God, man fulfills what such honor demands in his human relationships. "The basic principle," says the same writer, is "that there is an all-embracing identity of purpose between the individual and society, and that life in its fulness is inter-related." [7] The invitation: "Come ye unto the Good" has in some way a force in itself that facilitates the response.

VI

Nevertheless, it is clear both within Islam and outside it, that the actualization of the muezzin's *Falāh* is not possible only through economic provisions and moral exhortation in the Holy Law. That law may be meticulously and validly defined so that ignorance, as the arch-enemy of the Good, is eliminated. Yet full obedience tarries or falters. The principle that no man has right to exploit his neighbor does not of itself suffice, if some man should willfully assert such a right. He may possess no valid power to do so: he may exert a real actual power. There may be an all-embracing identity between the individual and society. But that identity, if axiomatic, is not automatic. Men in their recalcitrance can refuse to recognize its ideal existence and proceed actively on the contrary hypothesis. The question, therefore, of the actualization of the good necessarily leads us into the realm of the political. Islam has thought long on the relation of the order of the state to the *Falāh* of the minaret's call.

The urgency and inclusiveness of this issue is, of course, implicit in the very concept of law as the instrument of good. For law always involves enforcement or sanction in some sense. How does law get itself fulfilled? It cannot be indifferent to the question. For if its will is seriously thwarted or its directives flouted, its inherent authority will sooner or later be undermined. A law which remains permanently unobeyed becomes a dead letter. The very vitality of law as law depends on active obedience. Should the law then be equipped with means whereby defection can be punished, insubordination checked, and conformity insured?

There is a tendency in some modern circles in Islam to answer this question, in the last resort, with a reluctant No! It is felt, if not always very clearly expressed, that somehow a moral, religious law cannot be served by force. Obviously in some respects every society will and must punish its disturbers and every system its criminal rebels. Such punishment is necessary for the protection of basic rights and securities. But beyond this, the high moral desiderata of a fully religious ethic cannot be suitably compelled, says the view we are expounding. The nature of obedience is so often inward; its compromises subtle and inaccessible to evidential scrutiny and court procedure. Moreover, the quality of an obedience that is not morally spontaneous and free is called in question. The good, in other words, that can properly or feasibly be compelled, is of a limited and often rather negative kind. The full law of Islamic ideology can only appropriately proceed by religious sanctions and by the force of purely moral persuasion.

There is much to be said for this view and it underlies in part some recent pleading for the separation of religion and the state. It comes near to the distinction, made in some faiths outside Islam, between two orders or levels of human life—that of the political realm where feasible, enforceable standards of behavior can be legally defended and applied, and that of the spiritual order where goodness must arise through moral and religious forces, to which law may bear witness but which law cannot actualize. This is not to argue two standards of equal validity, but two standards of accountability—a lesser one which courts can apply and a higher one over which conscience and God must preside. On this basis, some in Islam today desire to distinguish between feasible, "secular" criteria of a citizen's accountability, on the one hand, and the full free vocation of the true "religious" Muslim on the other. The first need not be thought of, on this view, as un-Islamic. It may partake of the spirit of Muslim culture. But it will not pretend to be achieving the full meaning of Islam, since the latter is the law of a goodness which cannot be compelled and remain itself.

Despite its force, however, this line of thought, though it may prevail one day, is clearly uncongenial to the historic Muslim mind. Its account of Islam is not one which would commend itself instinctively to the Muslim centuries. The emphasis has rather been to refuse the distinction upon which this view proceeds. There ought not to be two realms of the good. Islam, as a law unto good, should be attainable within the political order. This has been instinctive and characteristic from the beginning.

But such a decision only sends the mind back to the problem of the external condition of the good which the law enjoins. The historic answer, at least in theory, was the Caliphate. Islam originated as a politico-religious expression and by the Caliphate intended to remain so. Muhammad founded a state. He did not merely launch a religion. Perhaps even that distinction is unsound. We should perhaps say he launched a religion in founding a state. Through the Caliph the non-prophetic functions of the founder were perpetuated, the prophetic ones being already completed. The Caliph was the acclaimed guardian of the *Sharī'ah* and though he stood under it and was its creature he insured the conditions under which its application was possible. The Caliphate stood for the headship of an ideal empire in which the perfect amalgam of faith and society which the Prophet had attained would be perpetuated for all time.

Unfortunately the Caliphate fell early on evil days. After near-perfection under Abū Bakr and 'Umar, it suffered the misfortune of the aged 'Uthmān and later of the Umayyads. These suppressed the true elective principle and introduced features of disloyalty to the Prophet's example which made inevitable a distinction between *de facto* and *de jure* authority. The necessity of this distinction in itself made clear that the external ideal was not being maintained. In subsequent centuries the Caliphate became the center of unhappy and often inglorious controversies and by the eighteenth century important stretches of Islam found themselves under the rule of non-Muslim powers in a complete reversal of what Islam had always envisaged.

Only slowly and with great travail has the alternative political answer to that situation emerged, and a great debate, as indicated in Chapter I, still continues. The alien authority has now for the most part been terminated and Islam has digested the new principle of nationalism. Some of its writers, however, protest that nationalism is ultimately incompatible with Islam and that its acceptance is only a temporary stage designed to insure freedom from interference within which the new form of Islamic politico-religious expression will be evolved.[8]

VII

This leads at once into the consideration of current ideas of the Islamic state, as the external means to the Islamic ideology. For some, in line with the alternative considered above, the Islamic state is no more, no less, than a cultural expression. The Islam it safeguards and embodies is simply the recognition of the values of Islam through institutions and laws which reflect its spirit. Religion is then understood in a way that could readily admit of a multi-religious state, did circumstance require it. Islam, on its Godward side, becomes an individual's religious relationship, generally informing the national heritage but creating no dogmatic requirements for the state itself. Laws will not have to satisfy any considerations other than the sovereign will of elected assemblies. The right to elect and be elected will not turn upon any religious criteria. The Muslim as such will be an equal citizen with any non-Muslim who is also a citizen. The Islamicity of the state is cultural, general, spiritual: not militant or divisive. This reading of the state takes us back to the position on law and the good earlier outlined. If the future is, possibly, on its side, certainly the past, predominantly, is not.

Champions of that past understanding, on the other hand,

seek to give it a viable present form. They look to the kind of state in which there will be some degree of identity between the historic *Sharī'ah* and the forms of conduct in all realms. They are looking for a new expression of the sovereignty of the *Sharī'ah*, in the name of the sovereignty of the God Who gave it. This leads in turn to the ideal of theocracy—a term about which there is much confusion of thought. Since it incorporates within itself so many of the issues at stake it is well to explore the Muslim sense of the term carefully.

In the bare literal sense of the word, there never has been and never can be a theocracy in human affairs. For God is a Spirit, eternal and Divine. He does not sit immediately in any national senate or upon any political throne to rule. His reign is necessarily involved in the viceregency of man. Islam has always recognized this truth. God is in heaven; government proceeds on earth. Theocracy, then, in any feasible sense, must mean Divine authority in and through human institutions. In its barest sense, it could mean a perfunctory acknowledgment of God by rulers and men who did substantially as they liked. But such an interpretation is neither sensible nor Islamic. It does not warrant such a term to describe it since the relation to God is so nebulous.

Does theocracy mean, then, a form of Divine sovereignty applied by those who speak for God? If so, who are these? There are times when some Muslim accounts seem to suggest this. In one sense Muhammad's own authority was such a sovereignty. So was that of his worthy successors. But later successors disqualified themselves and left the location of the theocratic rule still to seek. Moreover, even while the true successors ruled, they were themselves subject to the Holy Law whose servants and creatures they were.

A more suitable answer would then be that the theocracy is really the sovereignty of law Divinely revealed. The community stands under God because it stands under God's law. This is the Muslim confidence. But still the theocracy, in practice, remains incompletely defined. For the law needs interpretation. Are the interpreters agents of the theocracy? If so, then how are they constituted and attested? Does authoritative interpreta-

tion make them somehow lords over God's heritage? This is
what some have feared and others have claimed in the long controversies. Does theocracy really mean shaikhocracy? Or should
it mean nomocracy—the rule of an inviolate legal tradition? Or
is the Divine sovereignty self-renewing and dynamic in a sense
that makes it ill-served by a static law? In which event, perhaps
the community of obedience is the true organ or repository of
the Divine mind which alone is worthy to rule? When this view
is taken, opinion may still differ as to the forms through which
the obeying community truly functions as referee of the Divine
will.

All the current debate on actualizing the Islamic ideology in
the Islamic society revolves around these questions. What is clear
to most who attempt to answer can be stated in this way. Islamic polity must be based on Islam. The ideals of the Qur'ān
and the Prophet are sufficient to it. The business of the Islamic
state is to serve these Islamic concepts. Islam demands the entire allegiance of the believer and the state should insure as
best it may that those demands are satisfied.

Beyond that, there is division. Some would have the organs
of state as free as possible, developing a creative obedience to
Islam with an over-all court, somewhat like the Supreme Court
in the United States, to determine whether particular legislation
was inconsistent with the *Sharī'ah*. Others would tie the state
very firmly, in both constitution and life, to the traditionally
interpreted *Sharī'ah* in the hands of the 'Ulamā'. For some, the
Islamic state is a matter of long definition and plain adherence:
to others a realm of valid experimentation and reconstruction.
The issue of this fascinating debate on how to understand theocracy cannot be here foreseen. It is all the time proceeding.
The whole discussion is indeed a running commentary on the
muezzin's invitation. How are we to come?

The answer thus far is: By adherence to the economic institutions of Islam and the principles they teach: by the aid of the
Islamic state as the political form of a true theocracy, however
determined. Deep thinking Muslims, however, realize that there
remains a question beyond these answers. Just as the economic
realm led into the political, so both lead into the spiritual. The

demands of this realm have been with us already in discussing true political forms. But they need some further thought at this point if all the muezzin's implications are to be clear.

VIII

Zakāt teaches responsibility. The Islamic state seeks to provide the framework for obedience to the *Sharī'ah*. What of human response? "Come ye." If the good is made plain and made possible, what else delays it? Here any realist social order encounters the problem of human nature. Much Muslim thought is aroused at this point. Numerous writers criticize the existing Islam in the name of the Islam that ought to be. Or better, they incriminate unworthy Muslims in the name of a proper Islam. They are aware of Muslim un-Islamicity, if the phrase may be permitted.

Some are persuaded that the solution is a more vigorous state compulsion. The falling short of the actual when compared to the ideal is due to external circumstances. These can be identified throughout history. For some writers the true Islamic society has never actually existed since the Prophet's death, or since the Caliph 'Umar. External reasons, varied and unfortunate, have always obviated the true achievement of Islamic ideology. In proportion as these factors are dealt with that ideology will come into its own.

Others seem content with a potential perfection, or prefer to state the ideal in neglect of the actual. Thus Sayyid Qutb, already quoted, writes that the duty of alms habituates the Muslim until such payments become "a natural part of the will of the wealthy." [9] He writes thus in a land where, seven years after this sentence was penned, a strong internal revolution broke forth to abolish long-standing and grievous extremes of wealth and poverty.

But such neglect of the realistic does not obtain everywhere or with the same authors all the time. True to its ultimate concept of law as the means to good, Islam finally leaves the problem to conscience within and exhortation without. "When reverence for God," writes Sayyid Qutb again, "is not in conscience, then there is no safeguard: for the law can always be deceived or evaded, and the ruler, the judge or the people cheated." [10] Man in the end must respond to obligation: he must recognize and accept responsibility. For otherwise even the law itself will be somehow imprisoned in non-fulfillment. Here is a clue which should be taken further still—further, that is, into a radical explory of human recalcitrance. But writing on the Islamic social order usually turns from this region back toward a new confidence in the conformity that ought to be and new efforts to serve and stimulate it, in every way possible.

Much emphasis in this connection is naturally laid on education. The means to the good in Muslim ethical thought has always been closely linked with sound habits and an amenable disposition. Ibn Maskawaihī, for example, one of the most noted of the ethical writers in Islam, insisted on the necessity of wise habituation. Like the Greeks whose ethics in the pre-Stoic periods Muslim moral philosophy so much resembles, Ibn Maskawaihī sought to inculcate the good life on the condition of proper environment, native inclination, and educative discipline. In all three respects he modeled himself largely on Aristotle. The basic conviction that ignorance is the root of evil and that, therefore, knowledge is virtue was the common ground. When such a point of view encounters the problem of insubordination and rebellion in man it is inclined either to minimize its essential seriousness or to find a way through in still more vigorous education, concentrating on the human material that is most promising in the circumstances that are most hopeful.

This is the reason that explains the frequent citation of traditions, not only in mosque sermons but in the many manuals of political and economic theory, in the pamphlets of the *Ikhwān al Muslimūn* and the writings of such teachers of today as Abū-l-'Alā Maudūdī. It is not simply that the passages quoted embody the right doctrine. It is also that the example is stirring and evocative of obedience. At times in this literature the outsider senses in the writers an apparent unawareness of the wide disparity between the situations covered in the tradition and those in which the contemporary Muslim finds himself. A tradition that the Prophet proclaimed communal rights in water, pasture, and fire is understood as enshrining in principle the idea of state ownership and nationalization. Practices of self-discipline or gracious largess in the Caliph 'Umar adumbrate modern forms of social conscience. This exhortation from history is an important element in the Muslim response to the burden of actualization. For, as one writer puts it, Islamic idealism is not merely an "ethereal minstrel." "It is a concrete plan for Islam, not merely Aristotle's philosophizing, that good citizens of a state ought to be good men too. Each member of society, embued with the right spirit of righteousness (cf. Surah ii. 177) is intended to develop a dynamic personality." "The Islamic blend of rich subjectivity and powerful objective urge will guarantee not only the use of man as an end, but the reaching of the goal of ideal civilisation. But before that, much leeway has to be made up towards salvaging the guiding subjectivity from the morass of disuse and unmeaning use, and establishing convincing records of objective welfare." [11]

There we must leave the matter of man, his recalcitrance and his obedience. The road from ideology to reality, from law to life, from knowing to doing, passes inevitably through the narrow portals of the human heart. The good in general goes no further than we are willing to come into it in particular. Whether the God behind the good has anything more to do in this situation than He does in law we cannot ask in this context. The minaret calls: *Falāh* invites.

IX

As a postscript to this discussion of the Islamic order for human society it is appropriate to summarize briefly the main features of marriage and the family in Islam. For the family is the first context of the individual, the earliest school of his habits and, therefore, a crucial factor in the struggle for the good. The clearest enunciation in the Qur'ān of the status of man and wife is the passage in Surah xxx. 20. "And one of His signs is that He created mates for you from yourselves that ye may find rest in them, and He established between you love and compassion. Verily therein are signs for a people who reflect."

The reader is here invited to contemplate the relation between the sexes in marriage as a clear evidence of a gracious providence: a clue to the mystery being found in worship. But Islam has never gone to the point of understanding marriage in such a sense as to make monogamy essential to its nature. "They twain shall be one flesh" is not taught. Rather the possibility of a plural marriage relationship is evident from the oft-quoted passage in Surah iv. 3.

This reads: "If ye fear that ye cannot do justice with the orphans, then marry as pleases you, two, three or four women: and if ye fear that ye cannot be equitable, then only one, or that your right hands possess (i.e. female slaves). That will be more suitable to prevent you from doing injustice." Though this passage was for centuries—and in places still is—taken as a clear allowance of up to four wives, much modern exegesis considers that it is a virtual prohibition, in that it puts a condition on plural marriage which is ideally unattainable, viz. equality of treatment between plural wives. Opinions differ as to what is meant by equality—equality of financial and temporal provision or precise and constant equality in emotional regard. The first would be perfectly feasible: the second manifestly not. Those who take the second view consider that, an impossible proviso being attached, the passage in effect forbids more than one wife. "The mere suspicion," writes Mahmūd Hoballāh, formerly Director of the Islamic Center in Washington, "that the husband may not be absolutely just in his feeling and in his treatment of his wives makes it illegal for him to marry more than one wife." [12]

But this interpretation, if it be the sound one, still leaves the matter open to experiment. There is nothing in the passage to check a husband who believes he can attain equality of treatment. He is left as the sole judge. If he fails it will be a *post facto* failure and then the marriages exist. There is nothing in the passage to suggest that it would be a violation of obligation to an existing wife for a husband even to think that he might duplicate her. This would be total, not virtual, prohibition, founded on the belief that the gift of the self in marriage is by nature inalienable and incapable of being concurrent. This Islam does not teach. Though the plurality of Muhammad's wives to almost thrice the maximum mentioned in Surah iv. 3 has inevitably affected Muslim concepts, it is explicitly stated in the Qur'ān that it is not exemplary. Most exegetes and biographers insist that there were peculiar reasons in the Prophet's situation—the need to provide for widows of fallen warriors, the multiplication of desirable examples, the political aspects inseparable from a ruler's matches. They also point out that Muhammad was loyal to Khadījah alone, throughout their marriage and that his subsequent wives, except 'Ā'ishah and Mary the Copt, were not virgins.

Though it is customary, and perhaps sound, to think of plural marriages as necessarily intranquil, it should not be overlooked that many Muslim homes, where they were practiced, were often close units of loyalty and honor. The evils of plurality and feminine seclusion are many: but some husbands have built their relation on the Muhammad-Khadījah pattern and have practiced tolerance and benevolence. It is in this sense that the best minds understand Surah ii. 228 "And men are a degree above them." The male is superior in physical powers and has protective duties. The same verse says that women have equal rights to men in kindness. There are numerous passages that enjoin modesty in both sexes and gentleness in relationships, though corporal punishment is noted in the Qur'ān as permissible in wife-discipline when all else has failed. Marriage needs headship and this is the man's. "Men are the protectors and maintainers of women because God has given the one more strength than the other" (Surah iv. 34). The woman for her part is to appreciate that realm in which men are weak and she is strong and not flaunt or display physical attractiveness beyond the limited circle of the immediate family (Surah xxiv. 30-31).

The marriage contract in Islam is public and requires the maturity and marriageability of the parties, though they need not necessarily be the contractors. It is not intended then to be limited in time, but the form of contract does not refer to death as its only terminus. One passage in Surah ix. 28 has been understood to approve *Muta'*, or temporary marriage, on the part of strangers temporarily away from home in commerce, war, and the like. But the exegesis is varied. The purposes of marriage are generally defined as procreation, unification of families, mutual cherishing, and purity of life. The new relationship is not less, not more, important than that of blood relationship.

The marital bond is dissoluble at will by the husband. But divorce is the most hateful to God of all the things that He permits: so it should not be determined rashly. When the marriage relationship for any reason has become undesirable it may be terminated. No other cause need be shown than that the desire has lapsed. The reason why the initiative in Quranic law lies with man has been stated as follows by the President of the Muslim Board of Elders, Jerusalem: "Since the man is sounder in judgment, and more capable of self-control and the one who has to pay the alimony, Islam has given him the right to dissolve marriage. Yet he is admonished not to divorce unless it is absolutely necessary, for that is hateful to Allāh, and a good Muslim would not want to displease Him. The woman is liable to abuse such a right since she is temperamental and emotionally unstable. . . . Yet Islam has permitted the woman, on concluding wedlock, to ask that the matter of divorce be the same for her as for the man. Furthermore the woman is permitted to seek a *qādī* to help her divorce, if the man has mistreated her or been too miserly." [13]

While an increasing number, both men and women, would dispute this analysis of reasons, the inequalities in divorce are being diminished by new legislation in many directions. Moreover, even in respect of the old masculine freedom there are several Quranic exhortations or provisions that check its worst excesses. Couples are encouraged to think again and the divorced woman is to be treated fairly and not hindered from remarriage, after due time. There are also provisions about the custody of the children of such broken unions. Some quarters argue that divorce is a necessary evil and that the Muslim view of reasonably ready dissolubility is realistic. Certainly its incidence is widespread in the Muslim world. Because of the view of dissolubility inherent in marriage the relation between the sexes is much more fluid, within law, than where Christian concepts have some sway. Plural marriage is steadily diminishing due in part to economic and social factors. But consecutive marriage still falls short

of the best in monogamy. Islam by and large enthusiastically rejected "the dreariest and the longest journey" of Shelley's lines—
the unhappy marriage on

> *. . . the beaten road*
> *Which those poor slaves with weary footsteps tread*
> *With one chained friend—perhaps a jealous foe.*

It has all too little known the contrasted benediction which
Robert Burns described but never attained:

> *John Anderson my Jo, when we were first acquaint*
> *Your locks were like the raven, your bonnie brow was*
> * brent*
> *But now your brow is bald, John, your locks are like*
> * the snow . . .*
> *John Anderson, my Jo, John, we clamb the hill together*
> *And many a canty day, John, we've had with one anither*
> *Now we maun totter down, John, but hand in hand*
> * we'll go*
> *And sleep together at the foot, John Anderson, my Jo.*

This is not the context to discuss further the Muslim view of
the place of women in society. Vigorous feminist movements bear
witness to the struggle that is being waged to establish equal
rights and opportunities in every realm. They have evoked a
variety of counter statements from conservative minds, sometimes
in tactical retreat, sometimes in unqualified opposition. As noted
in Chapter 1, the whole theme is a continuing debate. The relative obligations of woman to home and to society and the appropriate opportunities for each are areas of the good to which
the muezzin invites and which await contemporary definition
from those he addresses. The realm of womankind is perhaps the
most formative of current issues and one that is certainly fruitful
of irresistible controversy.

It has been a deliberate purpose here to refrain from discussion
of the darker sides of polygamy and the harem in history. Our
study has been Islamic ideology rather than the Muslim situation at any given time. We have been at pains to understand the
good of the minaret's call, *Falāh,* in this final area of human

relationship—the area that begins the determination of all others. What that relationship has been at its best and what it may still mean in changed times should be sufficiently clear from the fundamental interpretation, out of which all its other aspects flow.

So in all the realms of its relevance Islam calls the Muslim unto good, as husband, father, son, as merchant, citizen, friend, as believer, confessor, worshipper. It enjoins on him an ideal of human inter-relationship built on a Divine. What the minaret utters puts the world into its own perspective. When the perspective is understood and followed the world is in harmony with the muezzin. And where, because of secularity, preoccupation, or carelessness, this does not happen, the minaret still stands on the landscape. The culture it begat remains as formative in life as its symbol is conspicuous. In all circumstances of the relation of its people to its message, active or passive, eager or reluctant, Islam through its muezzins continues to invite: "Come ye to Prayer, come to your true well-being. God is most great, Muhammad is His Apostle. There is none save God." Our other task in this book is to discover what its invitation to the Muslim should mean for the Christian.

NOTES *to Chapter V*

1

In nineteenth-century Christian writing on Islam, the rendering "success" was often taken for granted, and that in its barest material sense. While it must be admitted that Muslim attitudes and explanations frequently justified that view, there is no doubt that the term *Al-Falāh* both deserves and supports a much more comprehensive and spiritual interpretation.

2

For example, 'Alī 'Abd-al-Rāziq in *Usūl al-Hukm fi-l-Islām* (*Principles of Government in Islam*), Cairo, 1925, insists that God's revelation concerns the essentials, not the minutiae, of Islamic life.

3

Kemāl A. Fārūkī, in *Ijmā' and the Gate of Ijtihād*, op. cit. raises in sharp terms the question whether the derivation of some elements of law from popular sources—if these have then the same status as other, and revealed, law—does not involve *Shirk*. He received a clear dismissal of such fears from a group of 'ulamā' whom he consulted and whose dicta he quotes, pp. 11-17.

4
The Quranic phrase is *fī sabīl-Illāh*. It connotes whatever carries forward the cause of Islam, whether fiscal, social, military, or general.

5
See *The Muslim World*, April 1955, Vol. 45, No. 2, p. 205.

6
Compare Ahmad, Shaikh Mahmūd, *The Economics of Islam*, Lahore, 1947, Chapter VII.

7
Qutb, Sayyid, *Al-'Adālat al-Ijtimā'iyyah fī-l-Islām (Social Justice in Islam)*, Cairo, 1945, translated by John B. Hardie, Washington, 1953, p. 36 and p. 68.

8
Iqbāl, Muhammad, *Lectures on the Reconstruction . . .* , op. cit. p. 159.

9
Qutb, Sayyid, op. cit. p. 73.

10
Ibid. p. 99. Quoted, as are the extracts noted in 7 and 9, by permission of the American Council of Learned Societies, Washington.

11
Sharīf, M. Reihān, *Islamic Social Framework*, Orientalia, Lahore, 1954, pp. 22-3.

12
Hoballāh, Mahmūd, in *The Moslem World and the U.S.A.*, Jan. 1955, Vol. 1, No. 1, p. 9.

13
Ghosheh, 'Abdallāh, in a paper prepared for the Colloquium on Islamic Culture, Princeton, September 1953, entitled *The Philosophy of Freedoms in Islam*. Quoted by permission of the author, who is President of the Muslim Board of Elders, Jerusalem.

PART III

MINARET AND CHRISTIAN

THE READER *has thus far followed the meanings of the call to prayer, as they address those who belong, with the muezzin, in Islam. Unless the foregoing pages have entirely failed of their purpose, he has entered in some measure into the inner fullness of the Muslim summons.*

What follows is based on the conviction that there is a call in the call which the non-Muslim ought also to heed. The muezzin certainly intends it so. The witness of God and His Apostle is clearly not meant only for believing ears. Islam addresses all men. It is out of our comprehension of its import for ourselves that our answer must be constrained.

It is, of course, possible to relate ourselves to the Muslim call to prayer wholly in the realm of the academic. Islamics is that branch of study which takes its subject matter from the vast historical reality called Islam, even as ornithology occupies itself with birds and forestry with trees. Within Islamics there are fascinating realms of specialization offering a lifetime's satisfac-

tion for the philologist, the architect, the historian, the theologian, the lawyer. The impulse to such scholarship about Islam is plainly increasing. Its history is long. There have been many who in response to it have looked out upon the world of the minarets and, falling under its spell, have become travelers, scholars, grammarians, writers, at its behest.

But for all its painstaking service to the understanding of Islam, scholarship in Islamics is not a final response to the muezzin. The mosque does not exist to be admired: nor the minaret to dominate a landscape. Nor does the Holy Book expect the devotion only of calligraphers. A purely artistic or academic interest in historical religion fails to do it justice. If Islam speaks of God and for God imperiously, God cannot be greeted with a mere agreement to study Him. This truth does not invalidate the scholarly duty to understand, to analyze, to explore Islam. It does affirm that such a duty remains partial even when it is perfectly discharged.

Many in recent years have been prepared to go further than this academic relation to an enduring phenomenon in human affairs. Their impulse has been a sense of the cruciality of the times and the potential relevance of Muslim beliefs to their own apprehensions and aspirations. Islam has come to seem for them an obvious factor of importance in cold wars. Association with Muslim states and diplomats of the United Nations brings home the place and potency of Muslim millions and Muslim meanings in today's world. So a growing interest in the muezzin is apparent, in his message, his reception, his background, and his outlook. This topical concern seldom goes so deep as that of the scholar, though it seeks a relationship that is more than knowledge. It moves in the direction of association—anti-Communist, pro-democratic, mutual-monotheist, and the rest.

Understandable as this attitude is, it still falls short of a satisfactory response to the fact of Islam. It rests finally on incomplete criteria. It does not strive to penetrate Islam with genuine objectivity. It is motivated too largely by utilitarian attitudes. It is looking for allies rather than inwardness. Its standpoint is the significance of Islam for the West, rather than the meaning of Islam for Muslims. The self-preoccupation of this attitude is

174

liable to preclude its coming to a valid relation. It does not face the demands the minaret makes upon the Muslim nor relate itself to his response to those demands. It needs to take with a more objective seriousness the concepts within the summons, to go deeper than interest, prudence, or policy into areas of spiritual communication.

But when we reach that realm we are beyond Islamics only and beyond external common interests into true mutuality. The Muslim has become for us more than a mode of religion, more than a potential ally. And we, for our part, have become more than students, more than observers, more than tacticians in internationalism. As such, we must bring, in all honest openness, the faith by which we ourselves live and understand. It is the relationship thus ensuing which this third part has in view, in bringing together Minaret and Christian. The shape of this religious, Christian relationship to contemporary Islam must first be briefly set down, before the duties to which it calls can be made plain.

vi

MOSQUE AND MEETING

RABIC-SPEAKING Muslims refer to the mosque not only as a *masjid,* or place of worship, but as a *jāmi'a,* or, literally, a gatherer. It is a place of assembly and the day of the week when, at noon, this assembling is imperative is called *yaum al-jumu'ah,* the day of assembly. These verbal significances serve to remind the reader that Islam is meeting and that, as such, the mosque is its most characteristic ground. The muezzin, it may be said, is a herald of encounter.

The mosque is exclusively the meeting place of the faithful. The non-Muslim may admire its architectural glories and study its meaning at any time other than the weekly assembling. In some countries, it is true, prevailing conditions make it impolitic to visit mosques even for this purpose. At the Friday noon hour the outsider is only present on very rare occasions and under unusual circumstances. Nevertheless, the mosque remains a gatherer: the minaret proclaims an invitation that has no limits of race or background. If one cannot become an habitué of the mosque without being first a Muslim, the latter is a possibility which is always open. The muezzin means to be taken seriously when he calls to worship and the good. If his summons is primarily an interior exhortation and not an exterior evangel, the whole impact of the faith and culture he symbolizes is certainly open to adherence. Mosques, then, are for meeting in the ulti-

176

mate, as well as the immediate, sense. One of the first acts of the Prophet in Medina was to build one, and through it in the years that followed numerous accessions, Medinan and tribal, "met" Islam.

The Christian who seeks to meet Islam in the fullest sense and to do justice to its content in the realms which, as we have insisted, go deeper than academic comparison or orientalism, finds himself confronting an exacting task. As he follows the cadences of the muezzin he hears terms—God, apostle, witness, prayer, good, sovereignty, unity—already familiar to him in a Christian context. Here are words already full of associations bound up with Christ, in Whom, for the Christian, they find the fullness of their significance. As he listens earnestly to a call he must regard as more than merely "interesting," he can hardly fail to relate the good in Christ, salvation and God's saving health, the transforming forgiveness and newness of life, to the good of the call to prayer. He cannot escape the relation of his own coming to God through Christ to the Muslim call to surrender. His convictions about the Apostles of the New Testament must bear upon his attitudes to the Apostle of Islam. Prophethood as he has known it in Isaiah and Jeremiah must shape him as a reader when he comes to the Qur'ān. The degree of his sincerity in his Muslim relationships will be the measure of his loyalty inwardly to the insights by which he himself religiously proceeds. One cannot have a religious relationship which begins by neglecting religious criteria. If the Christian is to meet the full meaning of the mosque with the hospitality it deserves, he cannot begin by behaving as if there were no church. Inevitably sincerity of conviction means that the insights of faith become the norms by which the contents of other faiths must be judged.

It is precisely here that the supreme difficulties of our present exposition lie. In bringing together minaret and Christian in this whole discussion it is assumed that there is a mutuality of significance between them. In proposing the mosque as a place of meeting, of Christian meeting, it is believed that they cannot remain in mutual exclusion, if either is to be loyal to its essential nature. What such meeting involves on the Muslim side cannot be inwardly set down by any but a Muslim. Though the traditions of mutual alienation are long and persistent there are elements, Quranic and otherwise, which point decisively in the direction of openness and concern. Nor are signs wanting that sincere Muslims are susceptible to the appeal of items of Christian faith to which there has been a traditional hostility. Moreover, the Muslim conviction of finality and ultimacy, involves, as it does for all who hold such claims, a reverent awareness of all that is so consummated. It ill becomes the final faith to spurn the insights or neglect the assurances to which it claims to have done the most entire justice. There can be little doubt that, within such general duties Islam has to its own claims, the areas of Christian belief are the most serious and the most searching.

But it is only the reverse side of the situation about which these pages can properly aspire to deal. Muslim attitudes to Christianity are the inward responsibility of the contemporary Muslim. What follows here is rather an attempt to see and to express the form of a Christian meeting with or at the mosque, to reflect upon what is implicit when the Christian comes within spiritual earshot of the minaret. His first, perhaps inarticulate, reaction may well be to wish that he had never done so. For the more he penetrates into the world of meaning that waits for him there, the more he realizes the exactingness to mind and spirit of what he confronts. But that point of realization is also the point of no return. Once the measure of the involvement of things Christian in things Islamic has been taken, there is no evading its demands. The Christian remains haunted with the obligations to interpreting fidelity and patient expression. He may at times feel almost where the friend of Hamlet found himself in the sequel to the words:

> If thou hast ever held me in thy heart
> Absent thee from felicity awhile,
> And in this harsh world, draw thy breath in pain
> To tell my story.

For here indeed in Islam is a harsh world, harsh to some of the Christian's tenderest convictions, a world that disallows the Cross and strips the Christian's Master of His most tremendous meanings. Yet the harshness has to be transcended, for much of it is well intentioned. And in any event the story to be told is only safe in the custody of those for whom every antagonism is an opportunity. For that, precisely, is the heart of the story itself.

So we must proceed by holding resolutely together the springs of our duty and its demands. For they arise in the same context. Not to care about Islam would be not to care about Christ. To hold back from the fullest meeting with Muslims would be to refrain from the fullest discipleship to Christ. For the valid Christianity is the interpretative Christianity. Wherever there is contrariety there is obligation and, likely, there are clues. Nor is the Muslim situation, for the Christian, contrariety alone. There are wide areas of positive mutuality which it is a joy to explore and enlarge. There are tremendous questions inseparable from a glad acceptance of what Islam in measure portends, questions of the how and the whence within the good the minaret declares. How do men come to the good? Is its being identified for them the sum of their need in relation to it? How are we to conceive the sovereignty in God which we proclaim? Is worship the obligation of servants only, or is it also the relation of sons? When we recognize the mighty prerogatives of God must we not the more explore how they are active most Divinely? It is these, and many other, themes which make the intelligent, reverent confrontation of Islam and Christianity so profound an exercise in religion. The only condition of its authentic fullness is that it should be deep and honest, and uncompromised by vitiating motives.

But lest the whole enterprise of Christian-mosque meeting should be dismissed as a sentimental indulgence for theologians, it may be well to recollect its deep practical significance for the present day. For the Christian mission and all its intellectual and spiritual corollaries are no idle pursuit, isolated from the realities of contemporary life. Urgent practical issues impinge upon it: to these it relates itself vigorously. In being concerned for a world-wide expression of Christ, the Christian mind is involved inextricably in the major issues attaching to one-worldness in our day.

II

In his definitive fashion, the great lexicographer, Samuel John-son, once remarked that outside Islam and Christianity all else was barbarism. One need not subscribe to this outrageous dictum in recognizing the immense role in human affairs played by these two great monotheisms of the Near East. Both stand heir in part to the earlier traditions of Judaism but each has far surpassed the latter in the extent and variety of their diffusion. Both have shown a consistent capacity to transcend racial and provincial boundaries and to root themselves in a diversity of lands and communities. Together they embody the religious terms of ref-erence by which vast numbers of contemporary humanity and crucial areas of human relationships are shaped and informed. There can be no doubting the urgency to affairs of their mutual attitudes and their separate quality both of belief and action. For they constitute two predominant households of faith in a world increasingly alive to the dangers of its disunity.

Neither mosque nor church, then, can properly disregard the religious bearings of the present predicament of states and na-tions. They stand, witnessing to their faith in the true dimensions of life, in a world that is afraid to make war and unable to make peace. The pains and perplexities of co-existence lie upon all nations, a co-existence that has been dictated as a necessity by science, but has not yet been defined by politics or safeguarded by the moral will. In this precarious context no self-respecting religious expression can evade its duty to demonstrate the mean-ings of its conviction about God and men and nations in the dilemma humanity confronts. For religions themselves appear to some observers as part of the very divisiveness which must be changed. Does the co-existence of peoples require the co-exist-ence of religions? Does the latter, in turn, mean an entire abeyance of missionary expression? Would that, again, involve a radical reassessment of the concept of witness as inseparable from valid faith? How do expressive religions metamorphose themselves into tacit religions? Stars become planets when they are cool enough no longer to shine by any light of their own. Must religions, somehow, do the same? Will they still thereafter be religions? Will their transfiguration into incommunicative and introverted entities effectively serve the guidance of bewildered mankind? Assuming it to be feasible, may we not in fact be retrogressing thereby to something resembling the old household deities, where men worshipped their own tribal preservers and made no effort to believe in the commonness, either of their gods or their societies? Shall we truly serve supranationalism, transnationalism, or whatever it is that we know not yet how to describe, by abandoning the will to universality which underlies the sense of obligation to witness? The diversities of religions may have in fact contributed to the disunity of men. It is true that there are ways of religious relationship that provoke or exacerbate human resentments. But will a divided world truly be served by self-preoccupied religious faiths that continue to deal with the same themes but do so in timid isolation?

The present context is not the one in which to pursue these issues with the fullness they deserve. The immediate point is only to urge that the obligation of religious systems to the contemporary malaise is inevitably an obligation toward each other. They can no longer remain physically sheltered in an alienation bridged only by the curious or the aggressive. Indeed, technology has compelled both them and their worlds into adjacence and mutual involvement. It is a commonplace that science is transforming the world into an uneasy neighborhood. Neither habitat nor heart can escape the increasing physical oneness of a globe where distances are less and less and intrusivenesses more and more. But the physical interpenetrations of human diversity are far from being the only compulsion to mutuality. The meeting of faiths is not to be seen as a prudent conformity to external necessity. It is rather the obligation of their nature and their ancient sense of the metaphysical oneness of humanity. For the latter must be the spring of guidance when physical forces impose an externally common predicament but do not of themselves illuminate its nature or undertake its burdens.

In this vocation there can be no doubt that Christianity and Islam have each a crucial place. Their territorial and cultural seclusions are largely at an end. Transcending as they already do the barriers of race, language, and geography, they must take up the spiritual seclusions that still persist within their widely spreading households. Their duty in the total situation of today must in large measure hinge upon their duty to each other. If the mosque is truly to be a "gatherer" for its people it must reach out into the realms of Christ within the Church, into the travail and the confession of Christian humanity, of Christ's disciples through nineteen centuries. If they, in their contemporary allegiance, are to be worthy of their Master and Lord, they must go out in reverent and fervent expressiveness to the place of Muslim assembly, to the home of the Muslim soul.

III

The chapters that follow are concerned with aspects of that task. Some attempt will be made in them to define and argue the shape of the Christian obligation. But out of what fundamental convictions does that obligation arise? Having justified the impulse to meeting by reflections drawn from our present point in history, it will be well to set it also in the more ultimate context of the faith that feels it. For ultimately the nature of the Christian mission takes its rise from the nature of the Gospel. The Church is sent because Christ came. The Gospel as such has no native country. Its historical "beginning" as the evangelists affirm was truly in Palestine, where "Jesus came preaching." But if the events so initiated are seen as the activity of a Divine redemptive purpose at work in the world, then the fruits of that redemption belong indifferently to all humanity. There are no Palestinian or Western monopolies in Christ. The eternal Gospel of a world-inclusive love can never be treated as a piece of Anglo-Saxon privacy. The description of mission as religious egoism may have some validity in relation to some of its disloyalties. But it is finally the abeyance of mission which would be the supremely damnable egoism for it would argue a proprietary right in that which is too big to belong to a few and too inclusive to be arrogated to some alone. The Christian Gospel in its world-wide expressiveness proceeds upon convictions about the nature of God and of man which by their quality cannot be localized.

To attempt, therefore, to finalize its significance in ourselves is to disqualify our allegiance. To believe in Christ at all is to acknowledge Him a universal Christ. Because He is requisite for all, He is perquisite to none. The Christian mission is simply an active recognition of the dimensions of the love of God. Christ only belongs to us because He belongs to all. He is ours only by virtue of His universality. To think otherwise would be unpardonable presumption.

This sense of an obligation as wide as one's sense of relevance confirms itself when it is obeyed. One discovers that all other religious faiths are diversely and variously concerned with just those areas and issues of life and death, of time and mystery, with which the Christian faith is dealing. Parallels are plentiful in the interrogative aspects of religions. They are present also, fruitfully, in the indicative aspects. And if these grammatical similes may be extended, points of meeting also offer themselves in the imperatives of religion. The uniqueness of what the Christian finds in Christ does not mean or argue the exclusiveness of everything Christian. On the contrary, the ruling concepts of Christianity, where the human is the vehicle of the Divine and God and man are in living relation, in law and revelation, in compassion and rebellion, necessarily recur, sometimes in articulate, often in inarticulate, form in the religious faiths of the world. He who goes out humbly with Christ into the world of all races will perpetually discover the multiple, but constant, relevance of what he takes. Moreover, the transactions of such expression are mutual. It is the ruling conviction of the ecumenical movement within contemporary Christianity that it takes a whole world to understand a whole Christ. Those who take are not vulgarly universalizing their own culture: they are conveying that by the apprehension of which both they and their hearers learn. If the claims of the Gospel are valid, it could not be otherwise. For those who take only themselves may not expect to do more than teach. They who take Christ are in a state of perpetual discovery. The discoveries they make are through the discoveries they enable.

It is finally this abiding conviction of relevance which makes the Christian mission and also makes possible a truly adequate response to the contents of other faiths. It is for just this reason that the minaret represents a genuine call to the Christian. Away with the thought that it is improper to bring them together. Away with the Muslim suspicion that the Christian could only take cognizance of the mosque like some conspirator spying out the enemy's terrain. Away with the unChristian arrogance that thinks only of that world as something to be conquered by a Western religion. The muezzin from his minaret calls his hearers to come to grips with life. The earnestness of that *Hayya* is also in the Christian Gospel. He invites men to a relationship with God and to an attitude toward his fellows. He stands ideologically upon revelation. His concern is for a world of men in which the reign of God obtains. He acknowledges himself the trustee of what is greater than himself. In all these respects the elements of Christianity also are not only and altogether contrasts. Contrasts there are, sharp and ineluctable, as we must see. But there are terms about the same things and confrontations with the same reality. To go into this world of the mosque in the name of one's duty by Christ is not to be an enemy: no misconceptions, Muslim or Christian, should be allowed to make it seem so. For mission is grounded in relevance and the bearer of relevance is never the alien. If the inward demands upon his hearers of the relevance he brings make the bearer sometimes in appearance a disturber, the disturbance has to do profoundly with what the Muslim faith itself is all about. To embrace and then fulfill the wide dimensions of these disturbing but tremendous relationships is the Christian answer to the summons of the muezzin.

For this man is not a theme for fascinated sentiment. He has not arisen from a museum. He is not merely part of a picture created for a tourist. He is a man in earnest; a voice with an imperative. If we respond to him with his own seriousness we shall not silence or suppress the meanings we have learned in Christ to the very things for which he pleads or for which he speaks. The more fully we do him justice, the more inevitably we involve him, and so ourselves, in the significance of Christ. For us that involvement means expression. Who shall say all that it involves for him?

Here, then, is the Christian summons toward that fellowship which links the centuries in allegiance to Muhammad and proclaims itself from dawn to sunset each returning day. What does this Christian vocation mean in the light of the manifold moods and aspirations around the minaret today? Ascending with the remembrancer of prayer, how do we survey the life that spreads below him? Descending again into the bustle of multitudinous humanity, which through the waking hours the muezzin punctuates with prayer, what shall we be constrained to say? How shall we explain to the worship the minaret enjoins the worship we owe to God in Christ? How shall we take the meanings of Christ into the summons from the mosque?

vii

THE CALL TO UNDERSTANDING

W ITH notable frequency Muslim writers of various schools have joined to salute Thomas Carlyle and to accord him a unique place in their estimate of English literature. The fact might be surprising were it not that he began, in his *Heroes and Hero Worship,* a new chapter in Western interpretation of the Prophet Muhammad. The very limitations of Carlyle's appraisal, when tested by the standards of Muslim dogma, make the Muslim welcome all the more significant.

In "The Hero as Prophet," Carlyle was at pains to vindicate Muhammad from calumny, but this did not mean that he was ready to consider a personal acceptance of Islam.

> We have chosen Mahomet not as the most eminent Prophet: but as the one we are freest to speak of. He is by no means the truest of Prophets: but I do esteem him a true one. Farther, as there is no danger of our becoming, any of us, Mahometans, I mean to say all the good of him I really can.

In doing justice to the Prophet of Arabia and his role in history, Carlyle adopted a manifestly non-Islamic hypothesis. "A man of genius," he saw in Muhammad, "an earnest confused voice from the unknown deep," whose utterances were "the Alpha and Omega of his whole Heroism," in "a bastard kind

186

of Christianity, but a living kind." When he went on to speak
of the Qur'ān, as he knew it in Sale's translation, he found it

> as toilsome reading as I ever undertook. A wearisome
> confused jumble, crude, endless iterations, long winded-
> ness, entanglement . . . insupportable stupidity, in
> short. Nothing but a sense of duty could carry any
> European through the Koran. We read in it unreadable
> masses of lumber, that perhaps we may get some glimpses
> of a remarkable man.

Carlyle's vindication is clearly far from being admissible to
orthodoxy. "The confused ferment of a great rude human soul"
is hardly a Muslim account of the Holy Qur'ān; while the thesis
that Muhammad was great by the standards of his day and race
is dubious praise for one whom Tradition makes an exemplar
for all time and all mankind.

The eagerness that approves Carlyle becomes more comprehensible, however, when his views are seen against the background of animosity and innuendo he repudiated. For he initiated
a transformation long overdue. "Our current hypothesis about
Mahomet," he wrote "that he was a scheming impostor, a Falsehood Incarnate, that his religion is a mere mass of quackery and
fatuity, begins really to be now untenable to any one." If Carlyle's
account reads more passionately than would now seem necessary
after a hundred years, his strictures on the ignorant and malicious
critics, his generous recognition of earnestness and sincerity in
the origins of Islam, were unusual enough in the generation for
which he wrote.

Lingering memories of the ultimate frustration of the Crusades
and implacable hostility to the Ottoman Turk in a later day
had bequeathed to Christendom a temper of bitterness in which
the wildest calumnies were circulated. While Dante had made
Muhammad a heresiarch, later writers dubbed him a sensual impostor. He appeared in the guise of a frustrated cardinal, who
revenged himself on the Christian world, when disappointed of
the Papacy, by inventing a rival religion. He was a fabricator
and a devil, who swindled many women and was finally eaten
at his death by swine. Mammets were images of Muhammad al-

legedly worshipped in Mammetry by Turks and that in the most anti-idolatrous system known to history! This is not to say that generations of simple Muslims were innocent of all un-Islamic superstitions, nor yet that everybody in Western Europe was ignorant of the historical character of Islam. But informed honesty was rare. A preacher in the reign of James I characterized Muhammad as "that cozening Arabian whose religion, if it deserves that name, stands upon nothing but rude ignorance and palpable imposture . . . a subtle devil in a gross religion . . . a monster of many seeds, and all accursed." [1]

The satisfaction of Muslims over the efforts of Carlyle may be taken here as a symbol of their hunger to be understood and recognized. But to examine what such understanding involves is to be prepared for deep-rooted and abiding suspicions. When Muslims approve of Carlyle they do not abandon mistrust and resentment. Rather the interest in citing him is often to justify their retention. The depth of this suspicion in many quarters has to be realistically appreciated, if it is to be finally abated. It can only be dissolved by positive attitudes that make reparation and win understanding by displaying it.

No Christian thought about Islam, then, can properly start with a querulous complaining over suspicion and ill-will. It must resolve to surmount prejudice wherever found and brace itself to correct error, restrain bitterness, and dissipate antagonism. We begin simply with the will to understanding, divested of the susceptibilities that would compromise its purpose and alert to its own duty of inward integrity. Foregoing the impulse either to excuse or upbraid, we must seek an openness of soul and sensitivity to all that is deepest in our fellows.

What is it to be a Muslim in today's world? Part of the answer has been attempted in the chapters under the theme Minaret and Muslim. Such was their purpose. But the Christian concern must go beyond the effort of understanding represented by the most careful study of books and documents, into that which these can only serve. For the Christian is the ambassador of a person-to-person relationship. He is an individual debtor to his fellow man. He must surpass the limits of merely academic knowledge. More than the student, he must learn to be in some measure the participant. As the bearer of "the Word made flesh," he must strive to enter into the daily existence of the Muslims, as believers, adherents, and men. This is the prerequisite of being understood and the first element in his response to the minaret's significance.

II

We begin with those aspects of being a Muslim which are most to the fore in the external scene, before attempting to penetrate into the inner meaning of personal Islam. "Community" may be an inadequate word, inasmuch as Islam, notably in Pakistan, has gone beyond communalism into nationalism. But there is hardly a better word available to express the consciousness of "otherness" deep in the Muslim mind and soul, whatever precise political or cultural form is chosen to implement it. *Dār al Islām* and *Dār al-Harb* is a fundamental distinction running through all humanity: the household of submission to God and the household of non-Islam still to be brought into such submission. The militancy which for long attached to the division has been reinterpreted in many quarters. But the sense of "otherness" abides. The household of Islam is aware of itself as a community which belongs together and does not belong elsewhere. The cleavage is to some degree softened by the necessities of contemporary life, by the common factors in world society and current technology, by the sharing of common ideals of democracy and progress. Contemporary Muslim political leadership speaks often in the language of the West.[2] Moreover, such affinities of thought and outlook only reproduce basic similarities between the Muslim and the Christian patterns of philosophy in the Middle Ages. Even when engaged in bitter polemic Muslim and Christian controversialists in those centuries moved on a similar plane of thought and held many presuppositions in common.[3] It has often been remarked that Islam belongs to the Western side of any East-West division of human history. Its place is with the Hebrew-Greek tradition, not with the faiths of Asia proper.

Nonetheless, despite these aspects of Islamic participation in the stream of Western history, it remains true that Islam conceives of itself as unique, as a community of belief and culture which is essentially different. This sense of "otherness," moreover, is often strong against the Western world, in whose heritage from Abraham to Aristotle Islam intellectually belongs. Nor is it seriously weakened, much less jeopardized, by the obvious diversities that lie within it.

It would, of course, be foolish to forget the manifestly varied quality of the Muslim world from Marrakesh to Djakarta, from Tashkent to Zanzibar. Nor must our poles of contrast be only geographical. There is a far cry from the impoverished peasant of Baluchistan to the affluent citizen of Lahore and from the Nuba Muslims of the Sudan to the erudite scholars of Al-Azhar. Economic, cultural, racial, physical, historical factors divide and subdivide the vast and teeming household of Islam. Even the individual feels often within himself a division of soul to which he is compelled by contemporary change. It is little wonder, then, if Islam is endlessly diversified and if the very definition of Islam itself, or of the Muslim, becomes in some quarters problematical.

Yet for all the elements of variety, there is a peculiarly tenacious quality about the continuity and identity of Islam. The current Egyptian revival of letters may assert, as Taha Husain does, that Egypt belongs to the Mediterranean world and that the task of its educational systems is to produce a good Egyptian citizenry rather than serve the purposes of antiquated Muslim theology.[4] But Egypt remains Muslim. Pakistan asserts its Islam in a national form which sunders the household of Islam in India. But it insists, in self-defense, that a division which excluded no Muslims and embraced no non-Muslims was impossible to draw; that Pakistan serves by its existence those whom it does not include; and that only so could the essential otherness of Islam be asserted and expressed. Thus Islam proclaims itself unique even when it resorts to a principle of nationalism which would seem to belie the Islamic universal. Though Pakistan is a principle of exclusion which cuts it off from Muslims, this is the paradoxical price of the principle of inclusion by which it affirms a Pakistanī household of Islam.

The partition of India and the genesis of Pakistan are by no means the only examples of how the principle of nationalism has been appropriated to the expression of Islamic "otherness." The Pakistanī became such, not with the idea of being less like the Egyptian or the Turk considered as Muslims, but with the idea of being forevermore unlike the Hindu considered as a physical neighbor. It is in this sense that Muslims see no inconsistency in the growth of the national expression. It is, they believe, a nationalism devoid of the bitter divisiveness of European nationalism. The fact that the old Caliphal unity of Islam has been destroyed implies no diminution of the essential spiritual oneness of Muslims, however politically they may now be organized.

Cynics and realists may be inclined to question this interpretation. Certainly no concrete scheme of Muslim world-federalism is on the horizon. Whatever may be true ideally, centripetal forces are very potent in actuality. Even within the more homogeneous Arab world the forces of unity are compromised by personal and dynastic rivalries and suspicions, which the common hostility to Israel has some part at least in abating. The political disunity of the Arab world, despite strong Muslim preponderance in the population, except in Lebanon, is the more remarkable in view of the fact that the frontiers of many of these states were drawn as recently as 1919-20 by Western powers, themselves divided, in alleged pursuit of the adage *Divide et impera*. Arab Muslim political behavior since seems to require us to rewrite the adage: "Ceasing to rule is not ceasing to divide."

Nevertheless, in the circumstances of the contemporary world, the failure of the household of Islam to achieve any outward form of unity higher than a fragmentary nationalism need not be interpreted as implying any essential failure in the consciousness of Muslim singularity in the face of the non-Muslim world. Islam may have baptized to itself some of the forms of political order which, in parts of the West, are associated with religious neutralism or indifference. But it has shown a steady capacity to harness those forms to its own world of ideas. Even where nationalism needs to be sensitively aware of the rights and participation of non-Muslim minorities, it makes no compromise of its essential Muslim character. Moreover, even in Turkey, where it may be said that the concept of the laic secular state made the greatest inroads into Muslim ideas of state and religion, in the two decades since Kemal Ataturk, Islam has shown a surprising resilience and power of continuity under change. He would be a rash observer who presumed to deny that Turkish Islam, for all its vicissitudes and upheavals, remains a recognizable, virile, and sustained Muslim thing. There are, indeed, those who see in recent Turkish history, not a disruptive change in Islam, but a conscious experiment which never ceased to be Islamic.

Be that as it may, there can be little doubt that, for all the political diversity of its existence today behind national frontiers, Islam is no less self-conscious and singular than it ever was. *Dār-al-Islām* is still a meaningful concept and an actual reality. And though the political and the national forms of the present day seem to belie much of Islamic history, Islam itself has demonstrated its capacity to survive into the contemporary political order with no essential loss of identity. Perhaps we doubted it could be so only because we conceived of Islamic unity in terms of Empires and Caliphates. If these have departed, the community they once ruled remains.

Though we are accustomed to investigate that capacity to survive as one, in relation to the political order, because that order is so much in our ken and in our daily press, it is equally apparent on the social and tribal frontiers of Islam. African Islam must here provide the obvious example. Writing of the slow assimilation of paganism to Islam in the horn of Africa, J. Spencer Trimingham remarks: "Although at no single point in the process can anyone draw a definite line and set up a boundary stone inscribed: 'Here paganism ends and Islam begins,' there is a stage where one can say thus: 'This man is a Muslim and not a pagan.'"

Though elements in pagan life persist in the new allegiance, its Islamic quality is definitive. Trimingham continues:

> We often find fierce loyalty to Islam combined with utter ignorance of teaching and complete laxity in the performance of even primary religious duties. They may not know how to pray, but they divide mankind into

believers (*mu'minūn*) and unbelievers (*kāfirūn*). We may find it difficult to distinguish between their customs and manner of life and those of pagans if we examine them in isolation, yet if we look at their life as a whole, we shall find that it is Muslim . . . The test is a psychic one. Some subtle factor in their outlook on life has changed. Pagan life sanctions have been changed into Islamic sanctions. Although they may believe in a vast realm of spirits, they now believe in only One God . . . The only possible criterion is *to know whether they themselves claim to be Muslims.*[5]

If and as they do they are inexorably identified with an Islam that slowly re-creates their entire existence.

Whether, then, on the fringelands of its contacts with paganism, or in the strongholds of its history, we find a community of faith, of worship and allegiance recognizably itself—people claiming to be Muslims through an almost endless variety of otherwise diversive factors. It is this "sense of being Muslim" which is the first quality with which our enterprise in understanding must grapple.

III

Its immediate corollary, explaining so much else, is the awareness of what, as Muslims, they are *not*. Identity spells also antipathy. The Egyptian Muslim is not a Copt, the Indonesian Muslim not a Christian, the Sūdānī Muslim not, essentially, a pagan. Cairo is not London, nor Teheran New York. Islam, in a word, is not the West. Nor is Islam Hinduism, nor yet Buddhism.

It is manifestly the Western directions of this antipathy which are most serious and exacting for our purposes here. The ultimate incompatibility of Islam with Hinduism, or "Indianism" as some more passionate writers describe it, we have seen demonstrated in the creation of Pakistan. Islam it was there believed could not validly survive in an all-Indian political unity, despite sincere guarantees and numerous forcible reasons pointing toward such unity. There could be no clearer assertion as to the unique and separate quality of Islam over against the other religious systems of Asia. In Indonesia, the Philippines, and elsewhere in the Far East, Islam maintains, under much variety, this essential distinctiveness. But what may be called its Asiatic religious distinctiveness is intensified in relation to Europe, the West, and Christianity, though to these, Islam is historically much closer.

There has always been a peculiar susceptibility to tension in the relations of the two great monotheistic faiths, for reasons deeply rooted in Muslim origins and expansion. But our concern is with the immediate, present aspects of Muslim "otherness" in relation to the West and to "Christian" nations. It must not be thought that the adaptation of many Western forms of political and social life signified either a passive or a hospitable attitude toward the West itself. Rather the nationalism into which the West has educated the Muslim East means a sharpened quality in the sentiments of the newly independent peoples.

It is this which explains the urge to political neutralism so evident in the Arab world, the desire to be outside the conflicts and the power-blocs, the assertion of non-involvement in the quarrels and legacies of the West. It explains the tendency to negativism and isolation. Only with difficulty do nations pass from the negative attitude of reproaching and evicting the foreigner to the positive and constructive attitudes of mature self-responsibility. Dr. Mossadegh may become symbolic in history of the mentality which transforms legitimate grievances and valid antagonism into hysterical and self-frustrating hatreds. The retrospect of imperialism is so near, memories so long and bitterness so painfully allayed. Criticism is slow to turn from its favorite external targets to an inward cleansing.

IV

For all these manifestations of readjustment, and for the basic aspirations of which they are the surface evidence, the Christian needs and must bring a wide and warm understanding. Not deploring that his task is difficult, he must undertake cheerfully the burden of being on many counts a suspect. Is it to be wondered at if a Christian of British origin encounters obstacles and problems in any ministry in Christ among Egyptians? Would it not be surprising were it otherwise, given the legacies of seven decades? But to enter on such an exacting mission without first entering into the soul of those to be served is worse than futile.

Not only for its assurance and its confidence does this Muslim nationalism need to be patiently understood. Sympathy is demanded for its problems. Its pathway is not all clear and confident. It is beset with many uncertainties and dilemmas. In several countries of the Arab world, as hinted in the introductory chapter, the pattern of parliamentary government applied in the post-Versailles period proved a dubious blessing in all the circumstances. Urgently needed reforms in land tenure and fiscal measures necessary to correct extremes of wealth and poverty were not effectuated in any adequate form, as long as the institutions of democracy were manipulated by wealth in the interests of the *status quo*. Necessary reform only eventuated by the intervention of military leadership and the abeyance, temporary or otherwise, of constitutional forms. The new regimes may represent far more truly the will of the people, but they do so in departure from the recognized forms of constitutional democracy. While the immediate present reaps benefits long overdue, the question of the forms of power is fraught with great future consequence. Thus the exhilaration of newness and confidence is allied with experimentation and venture.

For Arab Muslims, there is the massive problem of Israel. What this means on the physical side concerns us later. As a deep bitterness in the Arab soul, it is an abiding factor in the contemporary situation. It is important that we be able to see and to suffer it in the terms in which the Arab knows it and to pierce through the tangle of historical controversy to the emotional reality as it is among the neighbors of Israel.

Israel from the Arab point of view is an intrusion. The justice it represents for fundamental Jewish aspirations, denied or tormented in the European world, is achieved at Arab expense. The virility of the new state, the circumstances of its establishment, the revelation of Arab disunity and failure, the fundamental insecurity as to the future, combine to make Israel a supreme test for Arab leadership. The justice and the futility of the demand for repatriation; the injustice and the hard finality of the displacement; the Arabs "attacking" as defenders, the Israelis "defending" as invaders, in the war of 1948—these are some of the bitter paradoxes of the struggle. If Israel is not to remain a kind of national ghetto, she must find a means to co-existence with the Arabs. If the Arabs are ever to recover from the Arab tragedy of Israel, they must make terms with it. Otherwise their future will be perpetually mortgaged to their past.

Entangled in these exacting spiritual decisions, to which Israel as a state compels the Arabs, are bitter reactions against other parties in the shaping of events, the British Mandatory and the United States in the United Nations. If the historian who would be impartial finds it difficult to unravel the story of those years, it is little wonder if its victims read it as they find it in their lives, their broken homes, their disrupted souls. History as one knows it in one's own person is always more compelling than history as it may be written in the cold analysis of documentary research. If there have been few issues in our time more charged with emotion, more confused by competing interests than "Palestine," the first duty of the Christian servant must be an imaginative sympathy for those who pay in their persons, with their property and their bewilderment, the human cost of those events. The instinct to recognize resolution, ardor, toil, and tenacity in the creation of Israel only makes more imperative a wise and patient understanding of the Arab sense of loss, of defeat, of humiliation, and of wrong. Sentimental as such understanding may seem in the eyes of cynical politicians or partisans, the assurance of it in the Arab soul, as a debt recognized by the conscience of the world, might well be the necessary prelude to their redemption of their history. If meanwhile, negativism, the search for the scapegoat, blind nostalgia, and sullen resentment persist, the fault will not be wholly Arab. There are peoples in history, it would seem, for whom events are more than usually unjust—the Poles, the Koreans, the Jews themselves in Hitler's Europe. Not to see that the Arabs of Palestine are now among that number is to have failed to recognize what Israel means. Those consequences in the Arab world are a serious element in contemporary Islam.

V

The dilemmas of the modern age, however, are not all of them political. Among the changes noted in Chapter 1, "Islam since 1945," was the educational duality running through the Muslim world. Schools and universities under state supervision and control attempting a general modern education inclusive of new sciences have all too little in common with mosque schools and universities which conceive of education as the means of continuity for a religious heritage through the generations. There is education that seeks the future and education that hails the past. These contrasts reflect themselves not only in institutions but in individuals, and so call for discerning relationships on our part. Our ministry must discriminate wisely between unfaith and secularity, skepticism and the drift to irreligion on the one hand, and on the other the mind that closes itself to defend itself, the faith that is at once insecure and assertive. In the contemporary literature of Islam, where these tensions are reflected, an understanding can best be sought. We must labor to appreciate what Islam means to its people, both as a legacy from the past and a vocation in the present. We must be prepared for interpretations, by Muslims, of the meaning of their Islam, as varied as themselves and for a new alertness of outlook. Much of the old apathy and lethargy had physical causes for which science has remedies. An awakened agricultural population will be a factor of vast import in the years ahead.

In this review of factors in the relation of the Muslim with non-Islam, we are far from exhausting all the items that belong there. The sense of unique community and consequent "otherness," its confidence and its stresses, political and social issues, the Arab meaning of Israel, and accelerating material change—these are the most obvious. They are offered only as a measure of the task of understanding to which the Christian is called, in respect of the Muslim in his external relationships.

VI

We must, however, go beyond external circumstances, if we are to penetrate into contemporary Islam. Being a Muslim, which is what we seek to understand, involves more than these. It is imperative that we strive to think ourselves into the interior life of Islam and to appreciate the inwardness of its external problems. Such a purpose calls for steady effort and imaginative sensitivity.

Such understanding must have its tools. Among the first is a deep acquaintance with language and literature. Early generations of the modern missionary Church possessed not a few men of stature in the field of Arabic study, whose successors in the present day are, it would seem, fewer and feebler. The Arabic Bible itself, the centenary of whose completion is not too far away, remains a monument to the pains and erudition of Drs. Eli Smith, Cornelius Van Dyck, and their associates. It has established itself in the affections of evangelical Arab Christians throughout the Arab East, and such need for revision as it now has derives partly from improvements in Biblical texts since their time, and from a proneness for Arabizing Hebraisms, rather than from serious failure on the part of the translators themselves. From Henry Martyn to Samuel Zwemer, the Christian Church has produced a notable series of missionary Arabists—notable but always too few. The tasks of each generation fall, justly and inevitably, upon the representatives of each. We in ours, have great need of the consecrated scholarship which knows that dictionaries and diction, vocabulary and syntax, have much to do with the faith of "the Word made flesh." Fascinating fields of study and of achievement are open to those who can find their way from the Kingdom of God to a grammar and back again to the Kingdom.

The difficulties of the Arabic language have been often overrated, though it is well not to begin by minimizing them. But a student who does not expect fluency via a phonograph or competence in a year can find ample compensation for the tedium and the troughs of his Arabic adventures. His increasing reward will be steady mastery of a beautiful instrument, a language of fascinating structure, strict phonetics, and consistent behavior. As he extends his range, he will be able to see from within the response of a language to the demands of new times and new themes. Arabic literature of the present day is in process of an interesting revival and adaptation. In proportion as literacy increases, its vigor will no doubt discover new forms. The current debate between the classicist and the modernist will find appropriate solution.

If this seems too remote an enjoyment for the beginner, he may at least allow "the distant scene" to sustain the painful present. Temple Gairdner's *Phonetics of Arabic* may well deter him at first with its frightening illustrations of the Arab mouth, the workshop of the spoken Arabic.[6] He will discover that he needs much more throat energy than English requires. But slowly the sounds and the syntax will yield to him and even if they never become authentically Arabic in the native ear, they will at least insure him entrance into the Arabic mind, both past and present. Stiff enough to be challenging, satisfying and rewarding enough to be enthusing—such is Arabic with its tantalizing invitation to the would-be missionary. Nor need he lack a wealth of aids. Perhaps the perfect Arabic teaching manual will never be written, but there are a growing number of good ones.[7] As for the vagaries and varieties of the colloquial language, he can rely upon keenly co-operative tutors in his own area. The discipline of classical study will pay rich dividends in mastering the dialects—though the reverse is not generally the case. But the common speech will open doors everywhere. The Greek of the New Testament is an excellent precedent for relying on it.

Was it unguarded enthusiasm which prompted the idea that every Christian ministrant to Islam would aspire to be an Arabist? For the theological aspects of our relationship that ideal is imperative. To discover the Qur'ān in its untranslatable character and to feel the pulse of Arabic literature from Al-Mas'ūdī to Taufīq al-Hakīm is an ambition no such missionary should dare to abandon. But it may be allowed that in Pakistan, Iran and Indonesia, in Turkey or Malaya, Arabic for certain types of service may be unnecessary. But in each of these territories there are new and growing national literatures. If old in heritage and wealth, Urdu in Pakistan has an emerging literature in the new day of Pakistanī independence. Persian studies are a vast area in themselves, second only to Arabic in their importance for the understanding of Islam. Turkish in the nine-teen-twenties suffered a rude, but—as many believe—a salutary break with its traditional script, that marks a new chapter in its long history. Everywhere in Islam, literature is alive with new aspirations, new issues, new impressions, as the index of the literate mind. No Christian who means serious communica-tion can absolve himself of the duty to enter and to apprehend this literature. As long as his own expression, whether in preach-ing, in conversation, or in print, remains English and Western, he is that far failing to make articulate a universal Christ.

It should not be thought, however, that English has no place. Indeed, the desire to learn English has often proved, and will no doubt remain, an important point of contact with younger Muslims. There will be many opportunities of ministry for those who are unable to master Arabic or any other Muslim tongue. Those who are born to English should recognize their immense good fortune in having the easiest access to the language in which so much of contemporary science and life are in turn accessible. We have neither wish nor right to withhold or dis-allow what this language might mean to those who seek to know it. There is also a wealth of Christian thought and writing in the English language, properly a part of the universal treasure of Christian experience and truth, to which access should be widely available. We do well to see in the aspiration after Eng-lish fluency a means to larger aspiration after the knowledge that belongs to human right and dignity. To help men to it may, therefore, be a Christian purpose. But any easy reliance upon English on our part, any assumption that the natural in-terest in it of many to whom we go, absolves us from the duty of knowing them in their own tongues, any disinclination for the toils of disengaging ourselves from English for their sakes —these must be forsworn. The bearers of the Word of God must everywhere be students and users of the words of men.

But our duty is not merely with language as the grammar books present it. There is the duty of attention to proverbs, to local lore, to stories and familiar heroes. Dr. Eugene Nida in his *God's Word in Man's Language* has illustrated from many lands the necessity of being able to translate not only the word but the idiom. "Behold I stand at the door and knock" must become "Behold I stand at the door and call," in a speech where knockers knock to insure that the house is empty as a prelude to robbing it, while true friends are glad to betray themselves with the familiar voice.[8] Examples are legion. In the Arab and the Muslim world this sense of meaning is especially urgent. There is a difficult contrast about much of the Arabic of Christianity and the Arabic of Islam. It arises in part from the contrasted concepts upon which the two faiths diversely proceed. The Arabic of the Qur'ān differs widely from the Arabic of the New Testament. Much needs to be done in the field of vocabulary alone, if there is to be effective theological interpretation. It is imperative, therefore, that the Christian strive to enter as fully as he may into the Quranic world, with the painstaking ambition to know it from within. This does not mean that Christian Arabic will ever be recognizably Quranic. It does mean that there must arise a Christian Arabic to which Quranic readers will be more readily drawn. Only Arabs can produce it. But for us of the Western churches is the duty of recognizing, in the implicit strangeness of Christianity and the difference of Islam, the large effort involved in "knowing and being known."

VII

Language, vocabulary, idiom, concept, lead us progressively into specific fields of Christian study in Islam. The relation of the individual Muslim to the Prophet Muhammad is the first. In his person and his story meet the ideals and aspirations of Muslim peoples. His posthumous role in shaping Muslim society and fashioning Muslim ethical ideals is only second to his living role in transmitting from God to man the Book of Divine disclosure. He is the point of final, culminating Divine contact with humanity, represented in the Arabs. He is the focal human point at which the Divine will is translated into religious law, for the blessing and guidance of mankind. From his devotion to vocation arises the asceticism of the Sufis, or mystics, in Islam. Muhammad and his people (*āluhu*) are bound together inseparably. Through him the world of Islam finds the crux of its credal and moral relationship with God. What the Prophet means in the convictions of innumerable Muslims must be apprehended with discerning sympathy, if we are to mediate the Christian meaning of Christ to the Muslim sense of Muhammad.

Effort is no less imperative when we turn to the Qur'ān. Essentially the Qur'ān is prior to the Prophet, though historically it comes to earth through him. As the speech of God it shares God's eternity. But its place in the interior life of Islam does not turn upon theological reasoning alone. It is established by centuries of veneration, by generations of being "People of the Book." Its familiar Surahs are recited at birth and in bereavement, repeated in the crises between, and breathed in the long piety of all the generations. The superstitious and the ignorant have charmed away evil with portions of the Holy Book. Children of the mosque schools through the centuries have washed their slates and cherished the water so made sacred. The Qur'ān has been their grammar and their literature. Its chanting is the chief music of the worshipper. Its sentences are the chief adornment of the mosques. The centrality of the Qur'ān has made calligraphy the most characteristic form of Muslim art. Its memorizers have been those who alone were qualified to pass into further realms of legal study. Commentary on the Qur'ān has been since Al-Ash'arī the main activity of Muslim theology. The periods, the reiteration, the warnings, the refrains, of the Qur'ān have been the constant companions of the devout for almost fourteen Muslim centuries.

If some thinkers in Islam today have come to look upon the Qur'ān with some modifications of the older theology, and tend to think of it in less supernatural terms than their forebears, this has not altered its place in their affections. An Indian Muslim leader of the nineteen-twenties records how he rediscovered the power of the Qur'ān while a political prisoner. "Ever since," he writes, "this book has had the invariable effect of intoxicating me with its simple grandeur, its intense directness and its incessant flow of motive power for the manifold activities of life." [9] He holds that to soak oneself in its sentences is to find all the philosophy one needs for life and death.

An illustration from another witness may be cited from a narrative of Arab dhows and Arab sailors in the Red Sea and the Persian Gulf. The English author spent several months in one such craft between Aden and Zanzibar. He describes the daily prayers of the crewmen and the frequency and evident reverence with which they listened to a Qur'ān-reader in their midst.

> I found the timelessness of things and the utter dismissal of the modern world were easy to become accustomed to. The only book on board was a copy of the Quran, in which the passengers often read. When he came to a good part, Hamed would often call a small group together and read aloud, in a very pleasant and well modulated voice, and they would discuss whatever they read for hours. They seemed to find perfect content in this book and never tired of reading it. Sometimes one or another of them would chant chapters from the Quran from memory.[10]

It would not be difficult to multiply such examples of the place the Qur'ān occupies in the devotional and mental life of the Muslim. When every allowance has been made for secular pressures, the Holy Book of Islam remains among the most continuously formative volumes in human history. Those who would bring into the ken of its people the deep content and meaning of the Bible as the record of the mighty acts of God must surely aspire after a patient understanding of the Book which comes between.

VIII

In the inner life of the contemporary Muslim is a deep sense of the Islamic past, sometimes nostalgic, but always a factor in the current scene. "The past in the present" might well be the theme-title of an analysis of Islam today, and the issues it faces. The sense of history and what it involves constitutes yet another area where discernment and sympathy are imperative. The

Muslim is keenly conscious both of the glories and the twilights of that history, though he is not always of one mind in identifying them. Primitive Islam, the times of the Prophet and of Abū Bakr and 'Umar, the first two Caliphs, are the days of pristine purity. In that period may be sought the true patterns of Islamic rule, even the prototype of socialism and the welfare state. There is less assurance about later periods. But for those who are concerned with splendor rather than with entire fidelity to the primitive qualities, there are the golden glories of Umayyad Damascus, of Al-Mansūr and Hārūn al-Rashīd in Baghdad, of Fātimid Cairo, of Salāh-al-Dīn, of the Mughal Emperors and Sulaymān the Magnificent among the Ottoman Turks. Through political vicissitudes runs the stream of science, philosophy, medicine, and astronomy. There are great names like Al-Fārābī, Ibn Sīnā, Ibn Rushd, and Ibn Khaldūn, to whom Western thought is much indebted, Al-Tabarī, Al-Bīrūnī, and Al-Rāzī who have a secure place in the advancement of knowledge. Despite the restraints upon creative art in Islam, there has been a great tradition of builders, designers, and craftsmen. The Muslim world contains endless wealth of architectural beauty and "sermons in stones." How diverse, for example, are the minarets we have here particularly in mind: what riches of design and adornment, of proportion, color, line, and structure have been invested in their purpose! Imagination can give us ready entry into a Muslim sense of the past in so far as it may be mediated through its monuments.

The Muslim's awareness, however, of his faith's past greatness is not only a happy indulgence in the sense of time-transcending community. It is also, in some degree, a painful problem. For that sense of history includes the knowledge that somehow it has not always gone aright. The Muslim feels himself part of a chosen people, in that to him and his has come the supreme favor of God. He is not among the *mushrikūn* and the *kāfirūn*, the idolaters and the unbelievers. Being the ultimate community of God, the destiny of Islam is to lead the world and to manifest the success of the Divine election. In the greatest periods, Islam believed that so it has been. In its triumphant origins as an imperial religion Islam conquered large portions of the two existing Empires, the Byzantine and the Persian, within a single decade. Within a century of the Prophet's death, the faith had been carried victoriously across the Pyrenees in the West and the Oxus in the East. Then, indeed, God was with Islam. Things, then, were as they should be.

But in later times it seemed that God in general history had half forsaken Islam. The Caliphate fell on evil days. At times there were at least three competing Caliphs. It was true that conquerors of Muslim hearthlands coming out of Asia, Seljuk Turks, Mongols, Tartars, Ottoman Turks, sooner or later became Muslims. The Islamic heritage might change its political masters but it always emerged religiously and culturally dominant. In modern times even this comfort became dubious. In the eighteenth and nineteenth Christian centuries the historic lands of Islam came increasingly under the domination, if not political, certainly economic and cultural, of Western powers representing a non-Islamic faith. India fell from a position of hegemony in Islam to be the "vassal" of the East India Company and then of the British Crown. Victoria occupied the heritage of Akbar and Aurangzīb, while Ottoman rule, looked at from the West, was the sick man of Europe. It seemed as if the course of Islamic history had gone awry, as if the God of the Prophet had forsaken His people, as if the Divine election had miscalculated.

To make the plight of the Muslim even more painful, there came the Industrial Revolution and the steady growth of applied science giving immense advantages, in world relations, to those few European nations and later the United States. who by happy coincidences of history and geography, had enjoyed a long start in the race to technology, leaving the whole remaining world in relative backwardness and exploitability. This was the Europe which had barely preserved itself from Islam, on its western approaches in the eighth century and its eastern in the sixteenth; Europe which had languished in barbarism when Muhammad lived in Arabia; Europe which owed its Greek philosophical and scientific education to Arab, or rather Muslim, schoolmasters. For the Muslim of the nineteenth century it was not simply that the Muslim world was far behind Europe in scientific advance, but that it was an old tutor bettered, indeed humiliated, by an early pupil. Though the debt of Europe to Muslim science was perhaps idealized by these interpreters, there was enough truth in that reading of the situation to leave the average Muslim bewildered, resentful, and uncertain. This mood produced many understandable, if sometimes ill-conceived, reactions, from the Indian Mutiny to Wahhābism.

In this long perspective of Islamic history, it is wise to see in much of Muslim thought and action in our time the urge under God to rectify the past, to put history in harmony again with Islamic destiny, to recover the success and the leadership proper to the household of Islam. In so far as that urge prospers in its purpose, so much the more are assurance and confidence restored to Islam. Pakistan is perhaps the most conspicuous example of the attempt to recover the historic nature of Islam, to retrieve the un-Islamic in Muslim history. But what Pakistan means is reproduced elsewhere in Islam beyond its borders. No outsider can enter into the present-day mentality of Islam without appreciating the nature of its relationship with its past. There is the recovery of one past, the appropriate, and the retrieval of the other past, the inappropriate. Both emotions are powerful present factors.

IX

This distinction leads into a final aspect of interior Islam, suggested in Chapter I above. The Muslim mind is not able to find complete unanimity as to the identity of the appropriate and the inappropriate in its own past. There is general agreement that the one is loyalty and the other decadence. But what is the loyal and what the decadent? And why? And how did the latter come to be? These questions are differently diagnosed according to whether the observer is conservative or "modernist." There is a strong tendency to blame the decline upon *taqlīd*, the spirit of traditionalism and uncritical veneration. Iqbāl, in his diagnosis of Islamic weakness, identified this petrification as the true cause of failure and called for a new dynamism to replace it. In this he was supported by numbers of other critics in all parts of the Muslim community. There is nothing wrong with Islam, what is wrong is worthless Muslims, is the reiterated cry. The new dynamism, however, with its call for freedom from ancient exegesis, from conservative commentary and static interpretation, is not always recognizably Islamic, at least in the eyes of those who fear an avalanche of reinterpretation, sweeping away their old mental securities. It is one thing to reproach unworthy Muslims; another to decide in what precisely their reproach lies. Were they too literal or too lazy? Too hidebound or too venturous? Is the way back the way forward? Have Muslims been disloyal in departing too little from the letter or from appealing too much to the spirit? To correct what is wrong do we need to shake off authority or to reassert it?

Muslims are divided in their answers to these questions. Some are inclined to blame the shaikhs and 'ulamā', others to vindicate them. Some regard reformers as too drastic; others as too timid. A great debate is in progress about the Why's and the Whither's of Muslim diagnosis and destiny. Examples are on every hand. It is not simply the fact of the debate, but the larger question it raises as to recognizable organs of development, or valid reform, in religion. Who is ultimately to determine what is legitimately altered and what not? To this most important issue, *Ijtihād* is not a complete answer, hedged about as it is by many provisos and suspect in the eyes of many. Would it be unfair to say that the Muslim mind in general tends to be disparate in its attitude and can rest content with a number of different truths and attitudes, without bringing them into strict cohesion or inclusive rational order? Moreover, since Al-Ghazālī and the twelfth century, there has been a general tendency toward authoritarianism and away from intellectualism in Muslim theology. This has produced an attitude of caution and an abeyance of many urgent questions which come with accumulated pressure upon Muslims of today. It may be said that finally Islam is what Muslims believe. But this leaves one searching for a definition of the Muslim. One cannot say: "A Muslim is he who professes Islam" if one does not wish to be arguing in a circle.

Our desire for communication with Muslims, then, must reckon with the fact that Islam itself is undergoing a process of redefinition. There is bewilderment in some circles, assertiveness and extravagant claims in others. We must be ready sympathetically to hear Islam equated with true democracy, perfect socialism, innocuous capitalism, and abiding peace. We must be prepared to understand what a prominent leader had in mind when he wrote: "I do hope I am a Muslim." It is the view of one Muslim editor that there is more (true) Islam in the United States and Britain than in Pakistan! It would, of course, be entirely unjust to stand by Lord Cromer's famous (and foolish) dictum that: "Islam reformed is Islam no longer." [11] We have neither right nor desire to insist that Islam shall remain perpetually what we have at one time thought it was. Like all living things it changes, adapts, "decomposes to recompose." While never ceasing to be recognizably itself, it can often puzzle us with what that self is and is becoming. If it puzzles us, how much more may it puzzle, distress, or vex, and yet exhilarate, those who feel the burden of these changes because, unlike the outside spectator, they are inward adherents. This realization of Islam as on the move is no small element in our Christian duty of understanding and discernment, in our would-be relationship in Christ with the people of the minaret. The call of the muezzin to the Christian demands first an attentive ear. It also demands a willing hand, and to that we now turn.

NOTES *to Chapter VII*

1
The preacher was Joseph Hall. The passage is cited from Chew, Samuel C., *The Crescent and the Rose,* New York, 1937, p. 445. This work is a mine of information on Islam in the literature of Europe in the centuries before and after the Renaissance.

2·
Cf. 'Alī Khān, Liaquat, *Pakistan, the Heart of Asia,* op. cit. and Naguib, Muhammad, *Egypt's Destiny,* New York, 1954, *et al.*

3
Cf. Grunebaum, G. E. von, *Medieval Islam,* Chicago, 1946.

4
Husain, Taha, *Mustaqbal al-Thaqāfah fī-Misr (The Future of Culture in Egypt),* Cairo, 1938, translated by Sidney Glazer, Washington, 1954.

5
Trimingham, J. Spencer, *Islam in Ethiopia,* London, 1952, p. 273.

6

Gairdner, W. H. Temple, *The Phonetics of Arabic*, London, 1925.

7

Selection is perhaps a little invidious but mention may be made of Ziadeh, Farhat, and Winder, R. Bayly, *An Introduction to Modern Arabic*, Princeton, 1955; Young, Edward J., *Arabic for Beginners*, Grand Rapids, 2nd edition, 1953; Frayha, Anis, *Essentials of Arabic*, Beirut, 1953.

8

Nida, Eugene A., *God's Word in Man's Language*, New York, 1952, p. 45. The people concerned are the Zanaki on the shores of Lake Victoria.

9

'Alī, Muhammad, *My Life a Fragment*, Lahore, 1942, p. 124.

10

Villiers, Alan J., *Sons of Sinbad*, Charles Scribner's Sons, New York, 1940, p. 35.

11

The prominent leader was Muhammad 'Alī, the Khilafatist (see note 9); the editor is Mazharuddīn Siddīqī, editor in charge of *The Islamic Literature*, Lahore; Cromer's dictum is found in his *Modern Egypt*, 2 vols. New York, 1908, vol. 2, p. 229.

···
viii

THE CALL TO SERVICE

A RECENT French novel portrays a doctor and a priest ministering together in the midst of a raging plague. The doctor questions the meaning of the pestilence and finds it irreconcilable with a Divine goodness. "Perhaps," suggests the priest, "we have to love where we cannot understand." "I don't want to start a dispute with you," the medical man replies. "We are working together for something that unites us. That is all that matters." The priest was very moved. "Yes!" he said, "you also work for the salvation of man." With an effort to smile, the doctor observed: "The salvation of man—that's too big a word for me. It's his health I'm interested in; his health, first of all." [1]

There are no doubt many who, likewise, as a refuge from their own wistfulness, would limit themselves to the smaller purpose. Health alone seems a big enough objective: yet, as the Christian sees it, so big that it must take in salvation, too. For it is to this and no less that God in Christ has set His hand. Since God's enterprise is "salvation," ours must be also. The word must be understood in its full Biblical quality, so as to forbid an idea of welfare that takes no account of forgiveness or a concept of redemption that excludes the here and now. For the Christian mission is not organized philanthropy in dissociation from the love of God at work in Christ. Nor is it a rescue of the soul that is content to ignore society. If we may not say: "Their health is all," neither may we say "Their health is nothing." We must be dedicated to what the Psalmists called "God's saving health"— the fullness of personal life, of body, mind, and spirit, within the redeeming intention of God.

So the service of the physician, the nurse, the midwife, the agriculturalist takes its place within the Church's mission among men. The loving compassion, which Christ teaches, within their skills and knowledge embodies in part the meaning of the Kingdom of Heaven. It exemplifies the gift and character of Him Who said: "I am among you as he that serveth." In thus expressing the lessons of Christ's life, we make it possible to proclaim more fully the power of His death. The heavenly meaning of salvation is discovered in its earthly impacts. Our concern in this chapter is for some of the aspects of the abounding human need in the Muslim world of our time and their call for a manifold and imaginative compassion.

II

But this part of the Christian world-duty is beset more and more in these days by strong misunderstandings on the part of those for whom it is offered. The growing sense of state responsibility for medical and social needs, generated within the new nationalism, makes the Christian, and often alien, sources of ministry suspect. To the patriotic Egyptian, or Pakistanī, or Indonesian, it is an embarrassment to find medical and educational service to people in his villages or towns pursued by Christians and linked closely with what he sees as Christian "propaganda." These emotions readily develop into the charge that such ministries are only incidental to objectives like conversion. The critic may go further and find in them a calculated "exploitation" of the poor through their poverty, or the sick through their disease. He may see the evangelist as taking mean advantage of ignorant people at a most impressionable point in their lives. Evangelism may become for him the Gospel capitalizing on human wretchedness.

It is not enough simply to protest that this is a travesty of the fact and far from the intention or the nature of the Church. That is true. But the Muslim individual finds it harder to see than we. The Gospel, to be sure, never capitalizes, any more than holiness profanes, or honesty lies. But we must put ourselves where the Muslim is and hearken to the apostolic injunction: "Let not thy good be evil spoken of." How shall we greet the view that takes service ill?

Not only by affirming that large numbers of his fellow countrymen have seen the thing another way. Nor yet by dismissing the charge as malicious, since potentially sound thoughts may underlie it. Nor can we solve the problem by terminating the preaching. For then we betray our deepest trust. We also make the situation worse by failing men at a deeper point than their poverty or disease. We become liable to the accusation that we are mere busybodies, or searchers after merit; or we are indulging in the sense of superiority that some find in the presence of the visibly inferior, that is, the needy. Or we may be thought the advance guard, or the rear guard, of political imperialism. Only by a steady, careful, articulate relation of our offered "works of mercy" to the mercy of God implicit in the Gospel of Christ can we give the lie to every false interpretation.

We cannot, on the other hand, escape the original charge, by abandoning, not the preaching, but the serving. For then the preaching becomes an isolated Gospel, impoverished in its concept of love and salvation alike, and the evangelist becomes one, like the priest and Levite in the parable, "passing by on the other side." Jesus Himself taught as He healed, healed as He taught. Though He decisively refused the temptation to be only and perpetually bread-maker, He did not commit Himself to saying that man shall not live by bread at all.

The only satisfactory answer to potential misunderstandings of Christian ministry to human need is a sound theology of its place in the mission, a deeper apprehension of the meaning of Christ's salvation among men. The issue was well stated by M. A. C. Warren in an address to the Willingen Conference in 1952:

> Has the missionary movement really integrated its acts of mercy with the central message of the Gospel? By acts of mercy I have in mind its educational service, its ministry to the sick in body and mind, its attempt to

grapple with under-nourishment, by bringing a theology of the soil, in relation to its theology of the soul? There is . . . confusion about all this . . . due to an altogether inadequate appraisal of the nature of evil and its wide-ranging effects upon the corporate life of man—indeed its cosmic range. Our theology of missions has been much too much concerned with the rescue of souls and the floating of little arks of salvation, and all too little with the assertion of the Crown Rights of the Redeemer in all parts of His Dominion. We have taken too poor a view of grace and too limited a view of sin.[2]

The answer is a truer relation between what we strive to do and what we are commissioned to preach. We are to be militant in deed as well as word, against all that impedes the rule of God. We must do everything possible to dissociate works of service from the inward urge to baptism, remembering always Christ's rebuke to the multitudes He fed: "Ye seek Me because ye did eat of the loaves." Christ's own healing ministry must be our pattern. His miracles might represent what God's Kingdom meant and brought, but they were in no sense an inducement to discipleship. They might invite, but they did not of themselves induce, allegiance. They exemplified the fruits of faith; they did not displace them. Discipleship, even for recipients, remained a free, voluntary, rational submission. So it must be with those whom we would win. And as with Christ there was a careful priority of His redeeming purpose for all, above His particular healing for any, so it must be still. In these proportions our response to human need will demonstrate and commend the Divine Love, without intruding upon the soul's response to the Christ it bespeaks and from Whom it derives. Only so will a truly Christian balance be maintained between the missionary aspects of "faith and works"—the faith of the receiver, the works of the sent. Misconceptions may persist. But in proportion as we can conceive of school, hospital, or clinic in these terms, the force of these misconceptions will be broken. In service the Gospel is implicit; in preaching it is explicit. They are the illustrative and the interpretative in the labor of the missionary Church.

III

What, then, are the human needs in Islam in which, under such a concept of service, we must recognize a call? The minaret looks out in truth upon a needy world. The burdens of human existence in great cities and impoverished villages lie heavily upon multitudes of our fellowmen—despite a native capacity for living uncomplainedly under trials, and despite strong and growing efforts on the part of governments becoming alert to their social duties. There is no opportunity here for any adequate analysis of the underlying causes of social ills and economic distress in the Muslim world. Our concern must rather be with what those evils mean in the personal lives of men and women—with the struggles against poverty, disease, ignorance, inequality, and malnutrition. It was said of William Cobbett, author of *Rural Rides* and a courageous prophet of the dangers of the new industrialism in nineteenth-century England, that when he contemplated the Industrial Revolution he could not see the way out, but he could certainly see the way in. It was to discern, to criticize, and to expose the evils of the new day in the sufferings and privations of thousands of ordinary people. In our time we may be unable to see the way out of the human problems of the world. But the way in is clearly evident. It is to invest our lives in the service of those problems as they bear upon people. Indeed the meaning of Christian compassion is that problems become persons, and cases people.

The physical needs of the Arab world can perhaps most fittingly be presented in the pictures drawn by one of its justly celebrated writers, the blind litterateur, Dr. Taha Husain, of Cairo. In his *Al Mu'adhdhabūn fī-l-Ard* he draws moving portraits of earth's suffering folk as he has observed them.[3] The evil he sees in society he makes the reader see as a struggle in the soul that is caught in its toils. Each individual is representative. Each story tells the personal measure of the evil it mirrors; imaginative multiplication of the instances gives the total dimension. The stories charm, but also appall. There is the village girl who marries, at her father's will, into an unhappiness that ends in suicide. One day she goes with her waterpot to the river but does not return. All

214

the promise of her beauty has been blighted by a system of marriage which thwarted the course of natural love.

Another moving story likewise ends in a watery grave. Qāsim, the consumptive fisherman, begins another day of his long and weary struggle for existence, going out to the river to fish. On the way, in the darkness of the early dawn, he hears the muezzin calling that prayer is better than sleep. Through his mind there runs a verse his brother, a shaikh, had taught him about the remembrance of God. He performs the prayer in the mosque and that day the heavens smile. He takes a superb fish which a youth helps him to carry to the house of the *'Umdah*. Overjoyed with his success he goes to the market to buy food for his wife and daughter and anticipates their pleasure at his news. For "carrying his body more often than it carries him" and spending as he does many waking hours in listless, wordless despair, this is indeed a day of days. But the very night of his successful venture his seventeen-year-old daughter, Sakīnah, has allowed herself to be seduced by the husband of his sister, who, though a man of pious reputation and a pilgrim, is unhappily one of those who win or bribe the poor to shame. Qāsim finds his wife, Ammūnah, and their home shattered by this tragedy. In misery, he cries out that the poor should never beget daughters. The next night he again seeks the river never to return. The dawn muezzin greets the silence of the daybreak, but Qāsim is as one without ears, driven by a compulsion of wretchedness to final exit from a world that had no health or peace or rest to give him. It is a world that, as Taha Husain sees it, is full of Shakīnahs and Ammūnahs and Qāsims. But most of their human neighbors are too busy to sense or glimpse their tragedy.

There is the story of Sālih, a village lad, who is always punished at school, since being poor he has no sweets or melon seeds with which to bribe the helper of the blind schoolmaster. He has, however, a mentor from the same village, who may well represent the author himself. But the burdens of poverty never lift from Sālih's shoulders and at the close he meets death at a railway crossing. Again the author insists that there are a thousand Sālihs whom the wealthy blissfully ignore. The chapter on *Sakhā'*, Munificence, is a sardonic denunciation of the insensitivity of the well-to-do, their shameful preoccupation with their own luxury. For Egypt is sick. The writer has a mission to feel for its ills and to write for their retrieval. Thus he prefaces his collection of stories with these words:

> *To those who are consumed with the passion for justice,*
> *Whom fear of justice makes ever wakeful,*
> *I address this study.*
> *To those who come by what they do not need*
> *To those who do not come by what they need*
> *Is this narrative addressed.*

Taha Husain's portrayal of what it means to be poor and needy and sick in the areas of humanity with which we are concerned takes us to the heart of its meaning in the personal realm. Salient in any diagnosis of its external causes is the system of land tenure. The vast majority of the peasantry in the Middle East are simply share-croppers with a low level of subsistence. In Egypt, prior to the advent of the present regime, less than one-half of 1 per cent of the landowners owned over 36 per cent of the land, while 72 per cent of the owners, with less than one feddan each, owned less than 13 per cent of the land. Less than two hundred persons, including ex-King Fārūq, owned 12 per cent of the country. There were one and a half million entirely landless laborers. The standard of living is precarious in view of the acute pressure of population. In the opinion of some observers, failing any drastic new measures and pending schemes of Nile development which may take twenty years to achieve, the maximum possible increase in cultivable land will hardly do more than keep pace with the population increase.

Industrialization in Egypt might be a possible remedy, were it not impeded by a lack of capital, power resources, and skilled labor. The industry which might cure rural poverty is itself impeded by it. The vigorous and ardent reforms of the new regime in Egypt, with strict land limitation and redistribution, have made some impression on the problem but are not of themselves a complete solution, still less a full satisfaction of the land-hungry. Though the infant mortality rate in Egypt has been, tragically, one of the highest in the world, the growth of population continues apace from fourteen million in 1927, and sixteen million in 1937, to over twenty-one million in 1955. There has also been a significant movement of population into the cities. Only about 15 per cent of the population was urban in 1917: 23 per cent was the proportion in 1947. Cairo's population rose 60 per cent between 1927 and 1947. It is true that due to active measures of governmental social welfare and the establishment of village clinics, the first five of which date from 1941, much has been done to alleviate the lot of the fallāhīn. There is happily less truth now in Dr. Wendell Cleland's explanation in 1936 of the reason why the population problem was allowed to aggravate itself:

> It is in connection with the ill-health of millions of these peasants . . . the endemic diseases of bilharzia and ancylostoma . . . that one finds a clue to the tolerance of the extreme density and abject poverty, in that the anemia resulting from the widespread worm infections so depletes energy and lowers ambition, without at the same time causing early death, as to fill the land with half-living, listless people.[4]

Perhaps "tolerance" is hardly the word about what was then apparent inevitability. But at least it is true that attempts to grapple with these diseases indicate an increasing sense that a population's welfare is to be measured qualitatively, not jeopardized by quantity. These measures and remedies have still far to go. The ills and sorrows of human existence will for several generations weigh more heavily upon the Eastern world than upon the comfort-cushioned civilization of the West. And that for the Christian is call enough.

Father Henry Ayrout's: *The Fellahin*,[5] is a moving, factual description of the actual lot of the Egyptian peasant, his daily round, scant food and ancient poverty, his traditional faith, and the unchanging repetition of todays. For few fallāhīn have leisure to look far ahead into the future because of an exacting present. Any ministrant who penetrates their plight can find the most rewarding toil. He will discover villages with a tragically high incidence of blindness or eye afflictions, involving in some cases

217

more than half the local population. Amid such privations the active love of men for Christ's sake must pursue its vocation. The road to Jericho runs through many a village world. The thieves that prowl it are disease, poverty, and insecurity. These jeopardies, like robbers, are everywhere.

For those who have known it from within there is a fascination about the rural life of Egypt which can be sensed by any imaginative traveler by air. The Egyptian sky is indeed the surest place for an apprehension of the Egyptian scene. A precariously narrow belt of green stretches from south to north across the landscape that pales into the distances, west and east, into dull and largely lifeless miles of brown or gray. The precariousness is in one sense apparent only, for the mighty Nile is a guarantee of fidelity in the center of the strip of green. Its age-old resources are fed from distant hills. But in creating a nation from immemorial time the Nile has kept its people in perpetual proximity to its own banks. The Egyptian is thus by nature instinctively gregarious. Unlike his neighbors in Syria and Lebanon, he rarely emigrates happily. His river-shaped country makes a community in which there is little privacy, little opportunity to venture safely outside the range of human concentration. The present virility of the population, with the aid of new science, reducing mortality, makes the community steadily larger, steadily closer, steadily heavier in its pressure upon the available resources. Engineering and science will do well if they can develop these enough merely to keep pace with the incessant demands of multiplying humanity. Among the villagers and the poor of the capital is where the stress of this situation most sorely falls.

Pressure of population, however, is far from being the only factor tending to a hard struggle for a higher standard of living. There are wide areas of the Arab world where there is ample room for growth but physical and economic conditions are no less exacting. A young Turkish author, Mahmut Makal, has given recently eloquent expression to the harsh conditions in rural Turkey. His two works have occasioned sharp controversy in some circles but there is no doubt that he speaks with an authentic voice for the Anatolian peasantry from whom he comes. He mirrors in passionate prose the aspirations and frustrations of a scholar-teacher in an austere setting that had little patience with his hopes and remained bewildered by his intimations of a new world.

I write these notes as we dig in the vegetable field. The sun wearies me and makes me sweat. The crops are ripe now; my father is alone. It wouldn't do not to help him, but when I leave to go off to the fields I take with me books and paper. As I write these lines we are hoeing watermelons like everyone else—mother as well. The heat is overpowering; at last I can stand it no longer and look for a patch of shade. I stretch myself out in the shade of the maize, and, as I write, my mother's voice reaches me. She is singing:

"Were you cold in the snow that fell on the hills?
You couldn't guess then how the heat would scorch."

"Mother, when one comes to think of it, what good is it all?" "Well, what do you expect? You shouldn't have left the house." There's not a soul left in the village; everyone is occupied. And shall I be the only one to stay at home?

Away stretch the steppes, as bare as your hand. The flocks go off to the village to be milked, hungrily picking their way through the dry clods of earth—if, indeed, there can be anything worthy to be called milk in their udders. It is evening; we are back at home. Tomorrow we shall go and gather vetch. I shall have to spend a bit of time there too. So the wheel of fate grinds out our lives, turning and turning as it has done for the last thousand years. Ah, if only my pen had the power to tell these things as they should be told! Where are our artists? They should be witnesses of these scenes with their own eyes!

Turning from "The Struggle for Existence" to "Scenes from Village Life," Mahmut Makal continues:

Our large towns will remember the oil lamp, and think of it as an antiquated contrivance belonging to the past.

But the lamp as an instrument of civilisation has not penetrated to many of our villages. On the day that I first lit our own lamp and set it up in a place all distempered with soot from dung and resinous wood, with a wooden nail which stuck to my hands like pitch, I felt like some great military leader squaring his shoulders after a famous victory. The children were astounded.

"Look, mother! It's burning from *inside,* not like our bit of resin wood!"

However, when I go away, that is not the light they use. And should I ask my father and mother why they don't light it, they tell me: "In the summer, when you're home for the holidays, you can light it yourself: if we use it now, how long do you suppose our oil would last? What's more, if the thing falls, it may break into a thousand pieces." [6]

Describing the village from within, this Turkish author is a pioneer in whom vast numbers of peasantry begin to be articulate. Yet the physical alleviations of the severities of existence for which he pleads are not of themselves the whole answer. Indeed, they create, as he insists, new vacua in the souls of men, new dimensions of need, and new emotional insecurities.

IV

The changes of modern technology do not necessarily increase the sum of human happiness. They may simply alter the conditions under which the masses suffer. The steady diminution of nomadism, for example, a major element in contemporary change not least in Syria, does not inevitably mean betterment. Bedouin settlement has been proceeding often so imperceptibly that even those most affected have failed to realize its full extent and implications.

The conflict between the desert and the town has gone on from time immemorial, and not only in Syria. Life in the desert has always been hard but it has been free. No organised government from outside could ever penetrate to the heart of the desert, where the Bedouin lived their own lives in their own way. Their existence depended upon the camel and upon their isolation. They lived by the adaptability of the camel . . . their other source of income was raiding. . . . Now it is all different, in consequence of the invention of motor transport. Nobody buys camels any more; and the motor car is rapidly taking over transport in the desert itself. What is more significant, with the coming of the armoured car and the aeroplane the government can reach any point in the desert within a few hours. . . . The Bedouins are slowly but inevitably losing their financial as well as their political independence.[7]

Resettlement in villages, though it tends to overtax plans for rural improvement, must be regarded as a step in the right direction, since it enlarges the possibilities of human life that are always meager under nomadism. Nonetheless there remain—to continue the source just quoted—"problems of social tension quite out of proportion to the actual improvement in social welfare so far accomplished." For social distinctions become vastly more visible than they were. Formerly "when they journeyed, the rich man rode and the poor man walked, but the difference was only a few miles a day in journey done. [Now] the poor man still walks on a dusty road and a motor car throws dust in his face as the rich man rides by." All the parallels of Western history emphasize that industrial and technical changes are not of themselves panaceas. They may aggravate distresses even while they alter circumstances. While they inevitably transform they do not necessarily improve. Only by the active ministry of the social conscience and a passionate human concern can their potentialities for good be actualized and their evils mitigated. The call to such service is as wide and exacting as technical changes are manifold.

Nowhere is this truth more evident than in the great urban centers. Sprawling and multiplying city populations in Beirut, in Cairo, in Karachi, in Casablanca, in Teheran, present a picture of contrasted splendor and privation. Everywhere there are large palatial structures, buildings for government ministries, official residences, business houses, and the apartments of the prosperous. Architects and engineers have had innumerable opportunities in the last decade to reshape the urban skyline. The hearts of many capitals are being steadily transformed by new monuments of civic pride, new edifices proclaiming new times. But it takes longer to transform the dwellings of the masses and to correct and purge insanitary conditions made more painful in their survival by the contrasts that are close at hand. The East is not alone in its slums. But neither does it lack them. For cities tend to play a disproportionately dominant role in the economy of Asian countries. City merchants in many areas exercise undue power over rural productivity. In the general absence of direct taxation, the prosperity of mercantile elements does not contribute adequately to the total welfare. Most cities have communities of absentee landlords often negligent of human welfare on the estates they own. The urban conglomerations of population reflect the consequences of maldistribution of national wealth and also the discordant interests of country and city as the two are frequently related under existing conditions. The evil of the callous landlord—a bitter phenomenon in many national literatures —has been made the center of a powerful novel of Cairene life by an Egyptian writer, Albert Cosseri.

> Perched at the top of the Alley of the Seven Daughters the house owned by Si Khalil, the detested landlord, groaned in the blast and almost collapsed. The bitter truth must be told: it was simply a miracle that the house was still standing. Only poor wretched creatures blinded by their abject misery, could find shelter for their precarious existence inside those dilapidated walls. A mere vegetable pushcart, passing through the alley, would shake the house to its foundations like an earthquake. To forestall further damage, entrance to the alley had been forbidden to all types of vehicles and even to certain street vendors whose powerful cries might precipitate catastrophe. . . . As for its tenants, they were people hardened to everything, long accustomed to the terrors and delusions of the poor. Their miserable state did not allow them to protest. Besides, what was

the use of protesting? From where they lived no one could hear them.

Is there something Dickensian in the incredible portrait of the owner?

> Si Khalil was the worst kind of landlord. . . . Getting together a little capital, he set out to buy some tumbledown shacks, unspeakable ruins whose owners, only too glad to be rid of them before they collapsed completely, let him have them for a song. . . . His ability to reconnoitre and evaluate the future ruins of the city was almost legendary. At present he owned about ten of these suspended avalanches, scattered round in different alleys of the native quarter. However, Si Khalil did take some risks in the business, because these houses might well crash before they had brought in any income.[8]

A caricature surely, and yet, as with Dickens, a caricature with the passion of reform. *The House of Certain Death,* in its own way, is an attempt, no less than *Bleak House,* to bring the scorn of the novelist and the conscience of awakened readers into line against a social wrong. A contemporary crusade for social justice in popular writing is taking shape and aspires to do for its own context what Charles Kingsley and Harriet Beecher Stowe attempted last century in theirs.

Cosseri, admittedly, is not altogether an appropriate example since he resides in Paris and writes in French. A more sober and convincing witness was Ahmad Amīn, for whom Cairo was always home. His *Autobiography* makes no effort after histrionics but relies on a quiet, factual simplicity. Writing of his own childhood in a Cairo quarter in the last decade of last century, he remarks:

> The proportion of births in the quarter was in inverse relation to the classes. The poorest class was the largest in number. The wife gave birth to six, or eight or ten children, while the one rich house had no child. And just as the number of births was large, so was the number of deaths. The sanitary state of the quarter could

hardly have been worse. There was no attention paid to the purity of water supply or cleanliness of food. The people did not even know a doctor. Whenever a person became ill, every visitor, man or woman, treated him. Each prescribed some medicine from the druggist he had tried successfully, while the sick one was at the mercy of fate. . . . Contagion was very readily contracted. In this way death carried off my friends among the children around me.

> *"Do not marvel at the perishing—how he was taken. Marvel rather at the healthy—how he was saved."* [9]

Happily the half a century since the writer's childhood has seen remarkable developments. But, if European precedents are a sure guide, a half century is brief enough time to achieve the eradication of physical ills of such long standing.

Before we leave these cities to consider a few miscellaneous statistics, there is a further observation from the autobiography just quoted. It might seem unfair to quote a source relating to 1900, were it not for the truth already noticed which Ahmad Amīn incisively confirms elsewhere. An inner discontent is generated by the new contrasts of the technical age long before the physical opportunities to satisfy it are opened to all. For all its insanitary misery, the Cairo suburb described in *Hayātī* was uninvaded by the consciousness of difference, by the paraded contrast of Hollywood and the sorry disenchantments of the local cinema. The masons, bleachers, tailors, cooks, and street vendors and their ill-housed offspring "were wretched without feeling their wretchedness . . . Despite the class difference, we were all— we small children—democratic. We did not give much weight to wealth or poverty, to learning or ignorance. We played together and spoke one language in which there was neither arrogance, nor servility." [10]

The contemporary generation, however, is in a far more exacting world. Though the conditions of poverty have been partially improved, the consciousness of poverty is intensified. Pundits may debate the proportion here of loss or gain. He who sees in all things a sphere to serve Christ knows there is everywhere a loss to accelerate and a gain to enlarge. He ministers that men may lose both their fears and their evils, that they may gain both health and life. Both the loss and the gain he knows to be implicit in the meaning of salvation.

V

Let city and countryside be put together in a few basic statistics—always with the recollection that, because of the imperfect methods of recording and the difficulty of the terrain, statistics in Asia and Africa at least when they concern sickness and suffering, should be taken as not usually excessive. There is a familiar Iranian saying that in spring the peasant swears by the life of his child and in winter by its tomb. In 1950, a sample survey in 173 villages in districts near Teheran revealed an infant mortality rate of 217 per thousand live births and the neo-natal mortality at 87 per thousand live births. Diarrhea and enteritis are frequent causes of infant mortality, mainly because of the pollution of water supplies and the use of excrement as fertilizer.

There are no modern facilities for the disposal of sewage in Iran except in Abadan, and no treated municipal water supplies except in Abadan, Shiraz, and now in Teheran. Other intestinal diseases, as well as malaria, trachoma, tuberculosis, and typhoid fever are frequent in most of the countries. In 1950, at least 233 per thousand in Baghdad were affected by trachoma. Local Irāqī authorities in the vicinity of Kirkuk and Basrah put the incidence of tuberculosis in certain villages as high as 25 or 30 per cent, active or latent. In Afghanistan, where there are no available statistics, estimates indicate that between twenty and forty of each hundred infants born die before reaching maturity. There is an even higher figure in Saudī Arabia. Figures for Turkey are available only in the form of selected studies. In 1951, infant mortality per thousand live births was 138 in Istanbul, 196 in Ankara, 201 in Izmir, and 272 in Adana. The usual life-expectancy in Saudī Arabia is between thirty and forty years. Conditions of housing, both urban and rural, congestion, lack of food and sanitation, nutritional diseases, and tragically inadequate public health measures, all contribute to the total sum of human sorrow, sickness, and pain.

A bare and casual listing of random figures has to be repossessed by the imagination and transformed into flesh and blood, into haunting fear of death and wistful apprehension about life, into hearts beyond numbers, if we are to count them truly. The "other side" of the Eastern road is fatally easy to take, insulated as we may be by distance or inured by an unthinking familiarity with the misery of which we merely read. To be discipled to One Whose compassion was inclusive and Whose offer was to the weary and heavy-laden is to be under exacting obligation, wherever the minaret calls from out the dimensions of human travail. For does not its cry unto good involve its vicinities of pain or poverty? The political and the economic ordering of human society lies properly in the hands of those who comprise it. This is the principle of national sovereignty in self-responsibility. But the ministries that are personal and compassionate have a quality of response to human need that no organs of state welfare can of themselves replace. For beside these and beyond them must be the concern that has learned to penetrate all the corollaries of the ills it serves. For the Christian, it is Christ Who empowers such a compassion both as an obligation exemplified and a grace enabled. His tenderness is a living legacy. In skilled devotion it is still at work. In the Quetta Hospital on the North West Frontier, a single eye surgeon in nearly half a century of missionary surgery removed 60,000 cataracts from the sightless eyes of Pathan tribesmen. "Let there be light" is a Divine *fiat*. But sometimes it is allowed to men to say it, too.

It has been insisted throughout that Islam is not apathetic to its human problems and that our service must be alongside. The new nationalism is developing both the principle of state responsibility and its active fulfillment. Some of the achievements and the staggering tasks of this governmental response to social needs may be noted here.

In most of the countries with which we are concerned, from Turkey to Indonesia, Ministries of Health and of Works, or of Social Affairs, have become responsible for curative and preventive medicine, for hospitals, sanitation works, and nutritional problems. Some are of very recent creation, and the facilities through which they operate are only painfully being established.

Red-Crescent societies, anti-tuberculosis societies, ophthalmic institutes, and similar units on a voluntary basis support and amplify their efforts. In many capital cities and large centers, government hospitals are increasingly active. The rural problem, however, is very pressing. For example, the aggregate of hospital beds in 1951 in Iraq was 4,901 (population around five million) but 2,086 of the beds were in Baghdad and 534 in Basrah provinces alone. In Iran in 1947, there were 4,428 beds in hospitals operated by the Ministry of Health for a population of just under twenty million and over 40 per cent of the total in Teheran. Likewise in Syria in 1951, there were 0.7 beds per thousand of the population, in Indonesia 0.8. In Afghanistan the figure is some 1,250 beds among twelve million, or one bed per ten thousand. For Turkey it is a little over one bed per thousand. The Ministry of Health of Saudī Arabia, formed in 1951, operates nine hospitals, the largest being at Mecca, among a population of several millions.[11]

Great efforts have been made to take government health services into the villages, on the principle of helping the villages to help themselves. The Ministry of Social Affairs in Cairo, with vigorous leadership from Dr. Ahmad Husain, began in 1939 an ambitious program to establish rural clinics throughout the Egyptian countryside, each staffed with a resident doctor, nurse, and agricultural advisor. Likewise in Indonesia, the Constitution lays it down that the family is entitled to protection from the state and that the latter "shall provide for the needs of the poor and waifs." In its last decade the Dutch administration had initiated schemes of social welfare mainly in Java. The young Indonesian Republic has enlarged and extended these and aims at a hygiene office for every *desa,* or village. Ninety per cent of the population is rural. The Ministry of Health has taken up vigorous measures, notably for the control of framboesia, which has been a persistent scourge. Though these programs have done much to obtain their objectives, the deepest urgency here as elsewhere is personnel. Figures for doctors and nurses in all the countries show both inadequate numbers and uneven distribution. There are less than 200 qualified physicians and surgeons in hospitals in Saudī Arabia including some forty on the staff of the Arabian

American Oil Company. In Turkey there was a total of 7,699 registered physicians in 1951, but over 40 per cent of them were in the Istanbul area and the provinces of Istanbul, Ankara, and Izmir claimed almost 60 per cent. About three quarters of the private physicians of Iran are in Teheran alone. The same proportion of the dentists of Syria are to be found in Damascus. In 1951, around 700 physicians were practicing in Syria with about one half of that total located in the province of Damascus. Iraq had 811 registered physicians in 1950, 444 of whom practiced in the Baghdad area. One third of Indonesia's 1200 doctors among seventy-eight million people operate in Djakarta.

Selective as these figures are, they give the imaginative reader a significant clue to the situation. They might readily be paralleled throughout Asia. It must be remembered that state responsibility has massive internal obstacles to overcome—inertia, apathy, distance, space, custom, and habit. A recent issue of *Pakistan Today* features the new nurse in Pakistan and rejoices in the readiness of many girls to enter the nursing profession, whose mothers were raised in purdah. But the difficulties are still tremendous. The awakened Islamic consciousness of responsibility has great tasks before it. In proportion as the negative aims of nationalism are fulfilled these constructive and positive aspects call for a vigorous devotion.

The political concomitants of independence, however, do not always help. Until very recently in Egypt the agitation over Suez and the Sudan and British relationships preoccupied the public mind to a degree that permitted either the tolerance or the neglect of clamant social issues, which—politics apart—had an emphatically prior claim. Similarly in Pakistan, the urge to realize an Islamic separatism monopolized patriotic concern to the practical disregard of crying social distress. There were many bitter protests to this effect during the long debates through seven years of the first Constituent Assembly's existence in Pakistan. Thus Begum Suhrawardy Ikrāmullāh on the final day, in October 1953, on which the Report of the Basic Principles Committee was debated, urged that the Assembly call a halt to claims about Islamicity and the quotation of poets, and embody in deeds the meanings of Islam. She declared that the Government had failed to provide adequately for the social and educational needs of a nation in misery and decried the preoccupation with constitutional theorizing at the expense of genuine action. Other speakers, though not all from the Muslim side, made similar charges.

It may be argued that these political sources of delay or confusion on issues of social reform are a necessary price of what some would call the priority of politics. But to concede the priority of politics is to admit the relegation of social reform. Postponement of what is chronic rarely facilitates its correction. In Iran extreme political nationalism, overrunning the restraints of a reasoned patriotism, sacrificed the revenues of a constructive seven-year plan. The country thus victimized itself socially by preferring, in extreme form, the priority of the political. Egypt, Pakistan, and Iran are no more than examples in this respect. Everywhere, too, there is a sad diversion of national wealth from social reform to military defense in the unruly world where these nationalisms have come to maturity.

Nevertheless, despite every difficulty, external and internal, physical and moral, national schemes of state concern for health, food, housing, irrigation, sanitation, hygiene, medicine, and research are in being and will enlarge in scope, effectiveness, and resources. The government hospital steadily becomes a familiar item in the life of towns throughout the Muslim world. All too slowly no doubt, but steadily, it may be hoped, the government clinic or the itinerant state medical service will penetrate into remoter villages. These in turn will be more and more susceptible to the refinements of modern living. Electrification, for example, is a near-reality even in the remote regions that border Afghanistan and Pakistan. The potentialities of atomic energy for heating, transport, and industrialization are such that parts of the world, where conditions resemble the old American frontier, have before them a destiny like that which transformed and subdued the North American continent. Indeed, one way of summarizing the significance of our time is to say that many of the possibilities which made the American frontier, ideally understood, are everywhere present across Asia. It is not that there is everywhere the same relative emptiness or the same latent productivity. But technical man is everywhere on the march to possess nature. It may be assumed that the new Muslim nationalism, in varying degrees and with local diversities, will everywhere ally itself with these imponderable forces of change.

VI

It must be assumed also that the Christian mission in its call to compassion must likewise undergo many external changes. The old classic patterns of the mission hospital as the sole institution, ministering without rival in a world otherwise empty of healing has ended, is ending, or will ultimately end, all over the world. Of old, missionary doctors in Isfahan, in Quetta, in Aden, by the Persian Gulf, in Hebron, in Tiberias, in Damascus, in Tripoli, in Old Cairo, every one a center of amazing Christian medical ministry, took up their posts for a lonely warfare against disease and misery. What the pioneers did can still be paralleled and their legacy of good will endures to create many a present opportunity. But more and more the activities of government medicine or of quickened local initiative will properly come into their own. Their coming is to be heralded with grateful satisfaction, for the Christian seeks no monopoly rights over human healing, where no monopolies can ever be desired.

How is the continuing compassion of the Church to be fulfilled in this new day? Adaptability, resourcefulness, and love are the answers. Christian works of mercy can always find new areas in which to pioneer. Particular techniques or specialist service requiring peculiar skills can be developed. Imaginative insight will see the gaps and fill them in humility and discernment. Within the national medical enterprise there is the place and contribution of the local Church. The mission hospital, originally founded and sustained by private gifts from overseas, becomes a national hospital, governed and administered by local leaders in full responsibility. The Old Cairo Hospital, for example, after long years of service as an English institution is now wholly managed by a local board. This kind of change fits the pattern of the new day, while insuring the continuity of the old traditions and attitudes in healing and nursing.

It is precisely in these realms that the medicine within the constraint of Christ is most significant. Funds and buildings, even skills, are not all. The transforming concept of ministry is indispensable to a true house of healing. Governments, as such, East or West, cannot, with all the will in the world, create an ideal hospital. They may provide the resources and the machinery, as also may private foundations and assistance programs. But the personal devotion on which the hospital's activity as a community of love must turn can only be assured in that consecration to human need which is born of the Divine compassion.

Such good will is no easy growth, no chance product. It comes in contemplation of the Cross, in the imitation of Christ, in the power that springs from the Divine grace, in the hope that believes to see the repair of human nature. The task of the Christian Church in the medical realm will always be to demonstrate the meaning of health as wholeness and salvation and to live in the power of the love of Christ.

National welfare, medical service, and public programs have potential resources of men and means which Christian missionary enterprise could never match. The finest mission hospitals, considered from the point of view of the totality of need, were never more than a gallant gesture, oases in a vast desert, barren of medicine, serving a province, while being adequate hardly for a suburb. Governments are dealing increasingly with a problem which the missionary Church could never handle, in the full dimension of physical need. The old missionary medicine emphatically needed the newer state medicine; but in the dimension of the Spirit, the newer needs the old. "There is a blessing in your hands," whispers a suffering Muslim woman being tended in her pain. "Christianity taught us to care," says another as he explains his new understanding of the wistfulness of the sick. Will there ever be a lack of opportunity in this needy world for those who can thus bring even a faltering Christ-likeness into the midst of human sickness and poverty? Does any medical man with a Christian life-commitment seriously doubt that the Asian or African world will have no place for him? Rather the doctor, the agricultural expert, the social worker, dedicated to Christian discipleship, can invest himself a thousand times over in today's world.

When some forms of service cease to be available, others open. In 1948 the Hospital of our Saviour in Ado Ekiti in Western Nigeria was closed. In 1953 a new hospital for maternity and child welfare was opened in its place on a different site and with a new name. It was called Ile Abiye meaning "The House of Birth to Life"—life in its fullest sense. The African Christians themselves chose this name. For, to many Africans, disease is perpetual and a hospital resembles a shop where you pay your money and get temporary stay of illness through a bottle or injection, the most efficacious medicine going to the highest payer. The new name epitomizes a larger idea. Health is not a precarious interlude between periods of dysentery, worm disease, or malaria. It is the plan and gift of God to be nourished and sanctified by care and reverence. The sick are to be lifted back to health of soul and body. The Minister of Health for Western Nigeria himself opened the new hospital and the churches of the area contributed no less than five thousand dollars to its erection.

Such examples might be multiplied. There is a great, long, uphill battle to be waged against ignorance and neglect. It calls for consecrated people as well as multiplied government action. To provide such people is often one of the ways in which Christian enterprise can serve the new day. For many years now the Quetta Hospital has run a regular course of training for male nurses, its candidates being the first such to qualify in North West India. They are now working in all kinds of hospitals and sanatoria throughout the sub-continent. Spiritual training went side by side with professional study. It has borne fruit in devotion and capacity for leadership and sacrifice. One graduate wrote: "I shall never forget that you made a man of me when I was weak. You brought me to God the Father and Jesus Christ, and showed me the way to new life." A similar and much larger training ministry for Indian women is undertaken at Ludhiana and Vellore. Similar efforts are being made to foster the intelligent vocation to nursing in Eastern Arabia. This development of the human resources of potential compassion under Christ is a mighty task of our time. It is far more important than bringing the white man's impatience for organization that overlooks the need for the nurture of initiative by those for whom it is needed. Every community cries out for those of its own people who will say:

> *'Tis ours to give and spend ourselves*
> *Nor grudge the labour and the pain*
> *To sow the seeds of noble worth:*
> *Yet without Thee our toil is vain.*
> *Great Lord of life 'tis Thine to give*
> *The quickening breath by which they live.*

VII

There is one area of human need among Muslim peoples which requires special notice in any summary of the call of the minaret to Christian compassion. That area is refugeedom. When Pakistan was launched one person in every five was a refugee. Some twelve million people on both sides of the partition were caught in the pain and bitterness of migration, while some half million more forfeited life itself. The Pakistanī share in this colossal human tragedy was slowly faced. In the course of the seven years since partition the scars have begun to heal. One of the factors has been the bold planning in the development of greater Karachi. Crowds of refugees flocked there in 1947. The Central Government took over from the Municipal Corporation. Today there are one and a half million in an area covering nearly eighty square miles. Hundreds of new houses have been erected and many refugees have remained as permanent citizens. Ultimately a greater Karachi, covering almost as large an area as greater London, will become a fact, a vast witness to Pakistanī effort in emergency. It will take more than the present decade to settle the problems of homelessness and poverty in Pakistan, with an economy all too dependent on a few export commodities like jute and cotton, all too sensitive to world fluctuations, and an agriculture whose irrigation needs

233

still await sound political and technical solution. The enlightened Pakistanīs themselves are only too keenly aware that the genesis of their state has been accompanied by human travail which, unlike the births of nature, long outlasts its infancy.

But the plight of Pakistan, for all its costliness, has coincided with the exuberance of new beginnings and the incentives of hopeful reconstruction. The new nation has been master in its own house. The decisions which made the partition had been fully shared and willed. The sub-continent was partitioning itself and its pain was, therefore, its own. With the Arab refugees of the Near East the case is different. In numbers they may be fewer, but in bitterness and hopelessness they are unmatched.

In his *Rebirth and Destiny of Israel,* David Ben Gurion, Prime Minister of the State of Israel, through most of its existence, remarks of the Arab departure:

> This has changed the face of Israel utterly. In March 1947, the population of Palestine was 1,850,000—614,000, or 33% Jews, 1,200,000 or 64% Arabs and 36,000 Greeks, English and others. We took the first Israel census in November 1948, not reckoning all the Arabs, since Galilee was still embattled; the population then was 782,000 —713,000 or 90% Jews and the rest Arabs. At the end of 1948, hostilities over, it was estimated at 867,000— 760,000 or 87% Jews and 107,000 or 12% Arabs.[12]

905,986 is the latest official United Nations' figure for these Palestine refugees. Birth rates running high have increased the refugee population in the eight years of their ordeal, but there has been little appreciable diminution by resettlement.

Here is a moldering of humanity in tented concentrations of wretchedness: survival by international dole, with little prospect of the longer future. Its former lands and villages are occupied by a population which, whatever may be said about the circumstances of their occupancy, has possession and intends to remain. There is the haunting fear that the present truce may be consolidating the means—and the arguable necessity—for further *Lebensraum,* again at Arab expense. Much of the occupancy, too, is within sight of the erstwhile owners and tillers, who live in

villages, sundered in many places from their fields and vine-
yards. If desperation often leads to the stealthy crossing of that
frontier, it may be called provocative, but it can hardly be called
inexplicable.

The tragedy is not lightened by the realization that the refugees' plight is in part the fruit of earlier years of self-seeking
by money-loving Arab landlords, as well as of divided Arab
counsels and incompetent leadership. The sense of being the
focal point in suffering of a strange and bewildering conspiracy
of events in Jewry, in Germany, in Lake Success, in London, in
Tel Aviv, in Washington, bringing high finance, power politics,
selfishness, racial idealism, and honest bungling into one tragic
final act, kindles intense bitterness. The refugee is the victim
of a cruel past and a seemingly hopeless future. His leaders
believe they cannot abandon in his name the policy of repatriation, though no "patria" remains, or could feasibly be repossessed without catastrophe. Yet to forego repatriation, Arab
statesmanship affirms, is treason to the Arab cause. The refugee
has paid the price of the establishment of Israel. He must also
go on paying the price of its non-recognition. He is caught between the Israeli entrenchment on his land and the Arab entrenchment in the fact of his exile. He can repossess neither his
soil nor his soul. Few national tragedies in the modern world
are fraught with greater cynicism and despair.

If these are some of the tormenting features of the refugee
situation as it bears upon the minds of those who suffer, its
physical aspects are equally appalling. The United Nations' allowance of flour, sugar, dried vegetables, rice, and fats is a bare
minimum and provides a daily diet of only 1500 calories. It
permits survival and little more. If the politicians cannot soon
decide the question: survival for what? even this policy of barely
sustaining existence may collapse. Palliatives are never medi-
cines and no prolonging of their use can create a cure. What
is to be said of a policy which can neither cease nor succeed?
The tents of many of the refugees are not suited for continuous occupation. In summer in the Jordan valley, they are veritable ovens; in winter they are at the mercy of cold, wind, and
rain. In the Gaza strip, which contains some 200,000 refugees,

and to a lesser extent in Jordan, the influx of refugees has seriously overstrained the local economy, forcing into poverty many in the resident population, not strictly refugees, and therefore not recipients of the United Nations' rations. It is little wonder that accurate statistics of deaths are hard to come by. A death means the loss of a ration card—a calamity to be avoided by concealment.

Medical action, mercifully, has been successful, in the main, in checking serious epidemics, though they have been a constant threat. But there has been and remains a very wide incidence of eye-disease and dysentery. In 1951-2 there were over 280,000 cases of trachoma and it is reckoned that about half the total refugee population has some form or other of serious eye disease. Frustration, privation, and bitterness have led to a steady deterioration even in physical quality. This deterioration is accentuated by the fact that the more enterprising among the refugees have left where possible, to search for their own rehabilitation in the oil industry of the Persian Gulf area, in Libya, or elsewhere. Though few in numbers, the departure of these elements lowers the general level of initiative and self-help. These last are virtues hard to retain, harder still to practice, in the conditions to which events have condemned these thousands.

Nor should the Palestinian tragedy be measured only in terms of refugeedom as officially defined. The State of Jordan, now comprising territory west of the river, incorporated after the fighting of 1948, is burdened with a considerable new population still residing where it always did but reduced by the Palestine debacle to a position of joblessness. In the main a desert country, with only a tenth of its land potentially cultivable, it has some 120,000 inhabitants who no longer have access to their former lands; villagers, in addition to the half million refugees, whom the United Nations Relief and Works Agency is not authorized to help. Some rectification of the frontier would restore arable lands to villages bereft of them. But there are long-range problems of water development and irrigation which presuppose an agreement with Israel. Meanwhile a country, almost half of whose population is refugee or near-refugee, faces a perpetual problem of economic viability.

How does the minaret's cry sound in the camps? *Hayya 'alā-l-falāh*—"Come ye unto the good?" No circumstances would ever induce the muezzin to change the sacred words. But who will help the refugee to understand what the good is and where, from out a refugee camp, it can be found? The Christian answer is not wholly blankets and shoes, though Lutheran World Service alone has helped to clothe 200,000 refugees in a single year. Nor is it only education and the effort, against fearful odds, to renew faith in human dignity and to kindle hope in the hopeless. Yeoman service has been rendered in this sphere by specifically Christian activities under the aegis of the Refugee Committee of the Near East Christian Council. Nor yet is it only the duty to pray and work for the solution of the political issues, where deadlock means the perpetuation of misery. It is all these together and yet more. It is witness to the Biblical significance of an earlier Palestinian exile and the sharing and the illuminating of the mystery of suffering and redemption. It is the preaching of Jesus, crucified and risen, the Christ Who once loved the haunts of these displaced Palestinians and was moved with the compassion which, since His crucifixion, has become the Gospel.

Should we not expect that the contemplation of the Arab world today, with its refugee tragedy at the heart of its restlessness, will call out a deep response of Christian life-investment? The early Church rightly broke out beyond Palestine into the wider world. But what it set forth to be and do is nowhere more desperately needed now than in the area from which historically it came.

VIII

We are still far from a comprehensive survey of human need as it might have been seen from the minaret. Not all the call is for healing: not all the ministry is medicine. The wholeness of man is also to be sought and served by education. The school and the college have long been a familiar element in missionary enterprise. This is so, not because education in itself is salvation, but because the awakened mind, the power to read and think, emancipation from the fears of ignorance, are all part of the birthright of man as the loved of God. The Christian service to the minds of men, like that to their bodies, is a sacred trust. Both its content and its method should proclaim the nature of the Gospel of Christ. As it brings science and history, biology and biography, it mediates knowledge, liberates and enlarges the mind, and proclaims the wonder of truth. By the reverence of worship and the honesty of scholarship it exemplifies more truths than it may directly teach. Most of all it exists to transmit the sacred knowledge of the saving deeds of God.

Local conditions and regulations may seriously hamper the full scope of Christian education. There have been situations, in Turkey for example, where it had seriously to be debated whether educational projects were any longer a feasible Christian enterprise under the restrictions obtaining. Though there must always be difference of opinion on such points, it is clear that Christian meanings can be exemplified in education even where they cannot be doctrinally explained. Student-teacher relationships, attitudes of mind, treatment of themes, can all partake of Christ even when Muslim state policies disallow an articulate Christianity.

There remain wide open doors in many places for the contribution of the Christian educator who is willing for loyal and discerning partnership with national leaders in the service of the new generation. State education, it is true, is growing everywhere and there is increasing state supervision of all schools. If state action often supplants Muslim religious schools there is no cause for surprise if it also curtails and controls the work of the Christian schools. But as with hospitals, so with the schools. There is a vocation to face the difficulties patiently, and as far as opportunity offers to make the quantity of the work and of the product effectively plead their continuance. Some schools and colleges have been obliged to close down when laws made their Christian self-fulfillment impossible. Even that, however, is not necessarily the end of their influence, for the good school remains a factor through all the adult years of its members. The possibility, too, of Christians filling secular teaching posts for the sake of their scope in ministry should not be overlooked. There are also parallel activities such as hostels for university students, recreation centers, "Schools without walls," and social service projects, all of which can be pioneered to meet new needs and situations.

Dotted over the whole Muslim world in well-known cities are scores of Christian colleges. Some have passed into history: others have grown and blossomed into great universities. But all of them, with the lesser schools that have fed them, have left a permanent mark upon the youth, and so upon the nations, they have served. Their graduates are among the prominent citizens and leaders of their countries. The task in our generation is to find ways of maintaining that ministry through every change of circumstance and of developing a worthy educational service to the new age. The opportunities those institutions grasped do not everywhere persist. But to see the new ones and to be spent in redeeming them is to be worthy of the succession. When Samuel Martin Jordan went to Teheran in 1898 he was destined to become one of the most influential servants of Persian youth. With the help of able colleagues, he built a boys' school in the Persian capital into a great college. Every student he and his wife reckoned an adopted son. He stressed personal character, honesty, and discipline. Muslim fathers readily entrusted their sons to his care, knowing that the school was a place of Christian conviction and nurture. A Persian in the provinces once referred to it as "the factory in Teheran which makes men." Courses on the Gospels provided an impetus which has since been registered in the lives of Persian landowners who today practice among their tenant peasants what they discovered in the school. More Muslim students are said to have found faith in Christ in this Teheran school than in any other school in the world. When Samuel Jordan died in 1952 his long years of educational service in Iran were signally honored by the highest in the land.

This record provides one outstanding example of the meaning of educational ministry. Samuel Jordan's generation in Iran is not ours. But despite all the changes which today qualify the work that would emulate his, there remains a rich educational opportunity for those who know themselves called to a ministry serving the growing mind. The example of the Alborz College in Iran has been taken only because it measures the vocation and because there is no space here for a larger discussion of the theme. All such service must be in the spirit of another "Iranian" educator, Clifford Harris, who died in Isfahan when his work was scarcely begun. He is best remembered in the words he prayed.

> O Thou Who art heroic love keep alive in our hearts that adventurous spirit which makes men scorn the way of safety so that Thy will may be done. For only so O Lord shall we be worthy of those courageous souls, who, in every age, have ventured all in obedience to Thy call.

IX

There is one other area of education, at the opposite end from the college and whose "campus" is everywhere in Asia and Africa. Here there is endless room for adventure and a fully open door. It is the bringing to illiterate masses the will and skill to read. Such literacy ventures have come greatly to the fore since the nineteen-thirties in the Christian mission. The idea of opening new worlds of opportunity to the adult illiterate, whom education overlooked when he was a child, has a worthy Christian ring. The impulses which set Luther and Tyndale translating into "the vulgar tongue" inspires the desire to unlock the Scriptures through the key of reading. This liberation of the sacred text through literacy is also the liberation of the new reader from the shackles of ignorance. Lovers of the Scriptures become the pioneers for all books. This thought must give us pause, as well as gratitude, though what men may do with new skills is no reason for withholding them. Much of the first reading material of new literates under these auspices is the simple "Life of Jesus." There remains a crying need for literature to meet the more educated public. The relative ease with which "Each one can teach one" also provides a ready channel for the practice of neighborliness and mutual help. So the program has more lessons than the letters.

Again in this field, state action is taking up new duties. Government programs are going forward, sometimes in company with, sometimes parallel to, the Committee for World Literacy and Christian Literature. There remains very much land to be possessed. Literacy and the more exacting ministry in literature to the world's new readers can more than absorb the devotion of a generation. The desire to read and the magic quality of letters are strong among Muslims, if only for the fact of the written revelation. Literacy figures, especially among women, are low in many areas. In Turkey, where since 1928 there has been a modern script and great emphasis on education, the illiterate proportion of the population decreased from 90 per cent in 1923 to around 50 per cent in 1950. Iran has a population from 80 to 90 per cent illiterate, since compulsory elementary education only began in 1943. Outside of Damascus, literacy rates in Syria do not exceed 40 per cent among men and 10 to 20 per cent among women. Figures are better in the Lebanon, Beirut having a literate proportion equal to over three-quarters of the population. West Jordan authorities in 1951 calculated that about two-thirds in all age groups there were illiterate with higher proportions for East Jordan. The rate for Iraq as a whole is some 10 per cent literate with 40 per cent as the proportion in Baghdad. Ninety per cent is the estimated illiterate figure for Saudī Arabia. Assuredly these figures will steadily improve on every side. But to the imaginative they are an invitation to minister with humility and grace and thus to enlarge the dimensions of many an imprisoned mind and to open the gates of new life through the printed page and beyond to "the Word made flesh."

Here, then, are "situations vacant" throughout the Muslim world—posts to be manned within earshot of the minaret, by servants who have heard the mute summons from their fellow men for the things that they can do and be. It is sometimes said that the art of politics is to listen, not to those who talk, but to those who are silent. Be that as it may, the Christian in his realm of ministry learns to hearken to the silent eloquence of human need, to the low whisper of its wide appeal. Salvation is a big word with which to answer. But no smaller word will suffice. He aspires to be as one of whom John Buchan wrote: "He has the Greek quality of Sophrosyne, which means, literally, 'the possession of saving thoughts.'" And thoughts that intend salvation turn thereby into deeds.

NOTES *to Chapter VIII*

1

Quoted from MacKinnon, Donald M., *Christian Faith and Communist Faith,* London, 1953, pp. 149-50. The novel is *La Peste,* 1947, by Albert Camus.

2

Warren, Max A. C., "The Christian Mission and the Cross," in *Missions under the Cross,* edited by Norman Goodall, New York, 1953, pp. 35-6. Quoted by permission.

3

Husain, Taha, *Al Mu'adhdhabūn fī-l-Ard,* Beirut, 1951; On "Khadījah," pp. 44-55, on "Qāsim," pp. 26-43, on "Sālih," pp. 4-25, on Sakhā', pp. 129-36. See also Schoonover, Kermit, "Taha Husain," in *The Muslim World,* October 1955, Vol. 45, No. 4, pp. 366-7.

4

Cleland, Wendell W., *The Population Problem in Egypt,* Lancaster, Pennsylvania, 1936, p. 108.

5

Habīb-Ayrout, *The Fellahin,* translated from the French by Hilary Wayment, Cairo, n.d.

6

Makal, Mahmut, op. cit. pp. 36-7 and p. 57. Translated by Sir Wyndham Deedes, Vallentine, Mitchell & Co., Ltd., London.

7

Carleton, Alford, "Syria Today," in *International Affairs,* January 1954, Vol. 30, No. 1, pp. 29-30. Quoted by permission.

8

Cosseri, Albert, *The House of Certain Death,* translated from the French by Stuart B. Kaiser, Norfolk, Connecticut, 1949, p. 8 and p. 61. Copyright 1949 by New Directions.

9

Amīn, Ahmad, *Hayātī (My Life),* Cairo, 1950, pp. 32-3.

10

Ibid. p. 30.

11

Statistics in this section are taken, by permission, mainly from Stevens, J. S., Whayne, T. F., Anderson, G. W., and Norack, H. M., with collaborators, *Epidemiology, A Geography of Disease and Sanitation*, Vol. III, *The Near and Middle East*, J. B. Lippincott Co., Philadelphia, 1954.

12

Ben Gurion, David, *Rebirth and Destiny of Israel*, New York, 1954, p. 542. This work was edited and translated from the Hebrew under the supervision of Mordekhai Nurock. Quoted by permission of the publishers.

ix

THE CALL TO RETRIEVAL

A̶MONG the great faiths of the world Islam is unique in its relation to Christianity. Though indebted in part to Christian parallels, Islam has proved in history the supreme displacer of the faith of Christ. Displacement of an earlier by a later religion is no unusual phenomenon. The Church of the New Testament called itself "the new Israel" because it believed itself heir to the promises of the old, and found in its experience of Christ the grace and truth that abrogated by fulfillment the law which came by Moses. In the theological expression of this relationship to Israel, St. Paul dwells on the thought that the Jew in Christ has received the consummation of his inheritance by that in which his very Jewishness is superseded. This as the Christian sees it is displacement by fulfillment.

Islam holds a similar conception of its relation to the Christian faith—though with no sustained effort to show how Islam does better justice to the meaning of Christianity than Christianity does itself. The Qur'ān offers no theology of a Christianity made ultimate in Islam, as the New Testament does of a Judaism fulfilled in Christ and the Church. But the claim is made that Islam represents what Christianity should have been and failed to be. Islam is the correction of what is erroneous and the more perfect expression of what is legitimate in the religion of the followers of Jesus. There is a familiar Muslim parable of the three caravans that set out across the desert. The first halted and encamped while the other two went on. By and by the second halted and encamped, leaving the third to complete the journey alone. The caravans were, respectively, Judaism, Christianity, and Islam.

Islam, then, as Muslims see it, has arrived, whereas Christianity has fallen short. If, therefore, we wish to know what the religion of the Prophet Jesus was truly meant to be, we go, not to the existing Gospels which are themselves corrupted by the disloyalty of Christians and the deviations of their impure faith, but to the Qur'ān. While it is common in some circles to speak of Islam as "a Christian heresy," for Muslims the Christian "heresy" is Christianity itself. Islam claims that in its historic faith the Church has misconstrued the mission of Jesus. Since these "errors" involve the central points of the Christian's understanding of Jesus, His Incarnation, and His death upon the Cross, the issue admits of no reconciliation. The Muslim sees Islam correcting Christian "distortion" of Jesus and of God. The Christian sees it disqualifying the heart of his understanding of both.

Among the factors contributing to the rise of Islam was the Christian failure of the Church. It was a failure in love, in purity, and in fervor, a failure of the spirit. Truth, as often before and after, was involved to its hurt in the spiritual fault of its trustees. Islam developed in an environment of imperfect Christianity and later by its own inner force gathered such strength as to become, and remain, essentially at odds with the pure faith beyond the imperfection.

This is the inward tragedy, from the Christian angle, of the rise of Islam, the genesis and dissemination of a new belief which claimed to displace what it had never effectively known. The state of being a stranger to the Christian's Christ has been intensified by further failures of love and loyalty on the part of institutional Christianity in the long and often bitter external relations of the two faiths through the centuries.

It is for these reasons that the call of the minaret must always seem to the Christian a call to retrieval. He yearns to undo the alienation and to make amends for the past by as full a restitution as he can achieve of the Christ to Whom Islam is a stranger. The objective is not, as the Crusaders believed, the repossession of what Christendom has lost, but the restoration to Muslims of the Christ Whom they have missed. All that the minaret both says and fails to say is included in this call to retrieval as the listening Christian hears it.

This chapter concerns itself with Islam from this angle of its unawareness of Christ, and with the Christian responsibility for that unawareness. Its twin topics are: Muslims as Strangers to Christ and the Christian Sources of Muslim Estrangement. We take up, as it were, the study of a veil, of a process of obscuring by which the fullness of Christ has been lost. The two disciples on the road to Emmaus, in St. Luke's story, mistakenly took Jesus for "a stranger in Jerusalem." The Christian who seriously contemplates Islam is led sometimes to a similar, but sadly unmistaken, question: "Art Thou always a Stranger here?" The days before the advent of Muhammad are commonly called by Muslim historians *Ayyām al Jāhiliyyah*—"The Times of the Ignorance." They were dark and sad because of what was yet unknown. As the Christian sees it there is a *Jāhiliyyah* still within Islam—a *Jāhiliyyah* about Jesus.

II

Most Muslims would probably protest at once that they are very familiar with the name and the prophethood of Jesus Christ and that they are far from unaware even of the Christian account of Him, since it is the duty of their faith to repudiate a part of it. They know well the Jesus they acknowledge and enough about the Christian account of Him to refuse it. How then are they strangers? If we press the matter, we intend no reproach—except upon ourselves. We mean only that the question compels a deeper investigation. We begin with Jesus Christ and His Church in the present assessment of Muslims and move backward in history in order to come finally to the circumstances of Muslim "Christian" knowledge in Muhammad's day.

The study of Muslim society called *Al 'Adālat al-Ijtimā'iyyah fī-l-Islām* (Social Justice in Islam) by Sayyid Qutb, referred to in Chapter v, ends with a final assessment of Muslim duty in relation to communism and capitalism. In the course of this discussion the writer remarks that Christianity is opposed to materialism but adds:

> Christianity, as far as we can see, cannot be reckoned as a real force in opposition to the philosophies of the new materialism: it is an individualist, isolationist, negative faith. It has no power to make life grow under its influence in any permanent or positive way. Christianity has shot its bolt so far as human life is concerned: it has lost its power to keep pace with practical life in this and the succeeding generations, for it came into being only for the limited and temporary period between Judaism and Islam. When it was embraced by Europe owing to specific historical circumstances, and when it proved incompetent to keep pace with life as it developed then, Christianity confined itself to worship and to matters of the individual conscience, ceasing to have any control over the practical affairs of life; for it had not the power to persevere, to develop or to grow. Christianity is unable except by intrigue to compete with the social and economic systems which are ever developing, because it has no essential philosophy of actual, practical life.[1]

There is no need to suppose that the writer here is malicious, or willfully perverse, nor yet that he is preparing the ground by contrast for the perfect social system of Islam. The ignorance of Christian thought and history displayed in his dismissal of Christianity *is* ignorance, sharpened perhaps by instinctive animosity. The faith which believes God Incarnate is truly far from "isolationist," since it believes in a Divine involvement of love in all our human needs and hopes. Nor can it be rightly called "negative," since its positive ethical commands are love toward God and one's neighbor. Nor is its worship a private obsession. Worship in Christianity is that context of Godwardness in which alone both the person and society are fully and securely alive. How shall we describe as "individualist" that which lives in the fellowship of the Holy Spirit and which robbed even the most stubborn divisions of the ancient world of their finality? "In Christ there is neither Jew nor Greek." And not the ancient world only. Has the writer forgotten, ignored, or simply not heard of William Temple and F. D. Maurice, Wilberforce, Shaftesbury, and Livingstone, and other exponents of the social meaning of Christianity in both thought and action? And then the writer's sense of history. What are the "specific historical circumstances" by which Christianity came to Europe? Was St. Paul's response to the Macedonian call "isolationist" and St. Augustine's vision of the City of God "individualist"?

Here, however, we are not concerned with refutation; only with the measure of unawareness. We must avoid the easy temptation to vindication. For these misunderstandings will be set right, not so much by argument as by a constructive effort to discover and correct the sources from which they come. Assertiveness such as this is not overcome by its like, but rather by the patiently objective. Here are not simply arguments to be refuted: here is a tragedy to be redeemed. What matters is not that men have thought ill of Christianity but that they have forfeited the Christ.

Sayyid Qutb, sadly, is representative enough. A score of Muslim depreciations of contemporary and historical Christianity could easily be cited. The Christian Church is incurably compromised with hypocrisy and vested interest. The Christian ethic is vague, impracticable, other-worldly. It has set impossible standards of moral purity while every form of corruption, prostitution, and vice has flourished behind its idealist façade. Better the sound, moderate, feasible sanity of Islam, with its recognition of the weaknesses and limits of the natural man, than the futile idealism and real shame of Christian society. Christian history, likewise, is a sordid record of compromise and bigotry, broadening out into the proliferating sins and scandals of Western civilization. And now Christianity is jejune, effete, misguided, and discredited. Its origins are erroneous, its story tarnished, and its energies spent.

III

The disqualifications of Christianity are carried into theological realms and involve considerable discussion and devalidation of the New Testament. Prominent in this area of Muslim criticism of Christianity is the Ahmadiyyah Movement, or rather Movements, which developed in Indian Islam in the last quarter of the nineteenth century and were named after their common founder, Mirzā Ghulām Ahmad. In the present context, it may be appropriate to discuss his legacy briefly, though it would be misleading to see in him and his followers a representative expression of Muslim criticism of Christianity. The reason for citing the Ahmadiyyah attitudes is that, though they go further than orthodox Islam approves, they provide a measure we cannot ignore of the extent of Muslim unawareness of Christ.[2]

Mirzā Ghulām Ahmad claimed to be a renewer of Islam and in the opinion of many Muslims laid claim in some ambiguous sense to prophethood—an issue which contributed to the division of his followers, after 1915, into two sections known as the Lahore and the Qadiān (now Rabwah) Ahmadiyyah. The former, interpreting their founder's claims modestly, have tended to come steadily closer to orthodoxy. The latter have held to the idea that their founder was a "prophet" or at least a "renewer" capable of being succeeded by a Caliph. They are now governed by his second successor, and son, Bashīr al-Dīn Ahmad. Their community was obliged to move from Qadiān to Rabwah when the partition of the sub-continent left the former outside Pakistan. But they still look back with great reverence to their old local ties. Both groups have engaged in extensive Muslim missionary work and have mosques and representatives in many parts of the world.[2]

Among the factors generating Mirzā Ghulām Ahmad's activity was a sense of the need of Islam for revival and a belief that it suffered from a certain inferiority consciousness vis-à-vis Christianity. Islam needed to be more militant and assertive and to rid itself of a sense of positive relatedness to Christianity. To achieve this he was prepared to jettison certain Islamic beliefs which, in his view, compromised the standing of Islam in relation to Christianity, and thus to make some sacrifice of orthodoxy in the interests of a more vigorous anti-Christianity. He was stimulated in part by the presence of Christian missionaries in his locality and in part by the sense of Muslim subservience to British rule in the India of his time. In pursuit of his resolve that Islam must be cleansed of a lingering excess of respect for Jesus, he sought to eliminate those traditional beliefs, which had come into Islam after its expansion, relating to Christ as returning from Heaven to the world in order to subdue anti-Christ and bring in a Muslim millennial state of bliss and righteousness. Though embedded in orthodox faith, these beliefs regarding a future role for Christ were traditional and not Quranic. Mirzā Ghulām believed that Islam would be more robust without them.

As for the Qur'ān, what it actually said bearing on the point at issue could be reinterpreted. The Qur'ān quotes Christ (Surah xix. 33) as referring to "the day I die"—which Muslims have understood as applying to a post-millennial death, yet to occur, since Christ did not die on the Cross. In the famous passage (Surah iv. 157) the Qur'ān says of the Jews: "They did not kill him, they did not crucify him, he was resembled to them," meaning that someone else, made to look like Jesus (supposedly Judas), was crucified in His place, while Jesus ascended into Heaven. Instead of the orthodox belief that Jesus was never actually nailed to the Cross ("They did not crucify Him"), the Ahmadiyyah interpretation affirms that Jesus was so nailed and later taken down, still living, and laid in the cold tomb. Thus they did not succeed in killing Him by crucifixion. He revived in the tomb, escaped, and later journeyed east, to die at a great age in Kashmir, where, near Srinagar, his tomb may still be seen. This is what the Qur'ān means by the phrase: "the day I die."

By means of this interpretation it is possible to retain Quranic authority for a view of the Cross which rejects not only Christian history but also much Muslim tradition. Though the Lahore group has corrected its unorthodoxy on points relating to the status of the founder, it has sustained these interpretations of the role of Christ and shares them with the Qadiānī group. A recent publication *Jesus in Heaven on Earth* expounds and argues this view in considerable detail.[3] There can be no doubt that the attitude sharpens the gulf between Christians and Muslims to the degree that it displaces or modifies that veneration for Jesus in Islam which derives from traditional expectations centered in Him. Islam had retained a second-Advent Jesus though it lacked a crucified and risen Jesus. The effect of the Ahmadiyyah Movements, as far as they succeed—and they are very vocal—is to sunder even that tenuous link with a Christian view of Christ.

It should not be thought that this of itself makes all Ahmadiyyah writers derogatory of Christ as a leader. Some of them, it is true, have carried their anti-Christianity to a point of vilification far removed from characteristic Muslim attitudes, suggesting, for example, that there is something unsavory about the relation of Mary Magdalene to Jesus, that He was offensive to His mother in the wedding feast at Cana, and that the cry on the Cross: "Why hast thou forsaken me?" was cowardly and pathetic, even ignominious. This contemptuous attitude to Jesus is checked, and in many cases excluded, by the Muslim recognition of Him as "one of the prophets." Nonetheless, in so far as the Ahmadiyyah Movements have changed Muslim attitudes toward Christianity, they have done so in the direction of greater alienation and a more rigid Muslim self-sufficiency. It is one of our sorrows that here a serious compromise of Muslim orthodoxy has been made, not to facilitate Christian relationships but to aggravate them. This brief discussion of the Ahmadiyyah Movements is ample evidence of our immediate argument, that Islam is in a state of not-knowing in respect of Christ. "Behold I stand at the door and knock," He says. But Ahmadiyyah is putting more bars to the door, or withdrawing further into the shuttered house.

IV

To return from this digression. If the Ahmadiyyah Movements must be seen as arming a state of unawareness against what might dispel it, there are other forces, too. Disinclination to look beyond Islam, complacence and self-sufficiency, animosity politically engendered but religiously operative, misconceptions about the West, all help to complicate and perpetuate the state of strangeness to Christ these pages argue. A few examples should be cited.

One of the great leaders of Muslim India in the decade after the First World War, was Muhammad 'Alī, advocate of all-Indian unity and of Pan-Islam, a thinker to whom the idea of Pakistan, or any "Islamistan," would have been anathema. During his imprisonment under the British, he wrote a "fragment" he intended as a personal introduction to a much larger work on the Qur'ān and Islam which he was never able to complete after his eventual release and reabsorption in political activity. *My Life—A Fragment* is a moving piece of Muslim autobiography from which we have earlier quoted in discussing the place of the Qur'ān in Muslim life. When Muhammad 'Alī takes note in it of Christianity he is sharply, almost disdainfully, hostile. The classical expression of Christian faith in the decisions of the Council of Chalcedon, he argues, makes too great demands upon our credulity. At the same time the liberalism of modern Christianity has left that old faith almost unrecognizable. Islam is saved all this confusion by its simplicity. The Apostle Paul had no knowledge of, or care for, the teachings of Jesus and evolved of himself a doctrine of Christ which had no historical validity. "The only trace of the Christianity of the disciples of Jesus and the members of His family left after the fourth century was to be found in certain Jewish rites like circumcision practiced in Abyssinia." [4] The New Testament is a broken reed and the Christianity which runs through St. Paul, Athanasius, Aquinas, Luther, Wesley, and Kierkegaard is a pseudo thing.

The familiarity that is evident here with the historical discussion of Christian origins by scholars within the Christian tradition is not unique among Muslim authors. Their interest in the internal theological debate in Christianity is a natural consequence of the fact that the Muslim view of Christ is there involved. But unhappily few, if any, Muslim thinkers have penetrated into the Greek New Testament or opened themselves to the convictions that, arising from historical scholarship, point strongly to the authenticity of its general witness and the unity of its presentation. They have been too easily content with what has seemed to confirm their prejudgment. We are in great need of trying to stimulate a Muslim study of the New Testament which will face responsibly all it contains.

A recent Muslim study of Christ in the Gospels created some expectancy that the time might have arrived. 'Abbās Mahmūd al 'Aqqād in 1952 published his popular Arabic study under the title *The Genius of Christ*. It has had a wide circulation and shows deep reverence for its hero. Much space is given to the Messianic concept in history and to the birth and teaching of Christ. Muslim metaphors are used to illustrate the meaning of Christ's words and stress is laid on the importance of the disciples. But the author drew back from any commitment as to the Cross, ignoring the sense of final suffering running through so many parables and sayings of our Lord, and declaring that beyond the point of Christ's arrest in the garden nothing assuredly historical is known. Thus he bypasses the Cross and Resurrection and derives the spread of Christianity from the zeal of the disciples and the suitability of their message to the world of that time. Though the work is in popular format, it represents a sincere and reverent attempt to comprehend Christ within a Muslim scheme. It is an interpretation of the Gospels without the climax which brought the teaching to its consummation and generated the Gospel that made the Church. It is a tribute which nevertheless insists: "Come down from the Cross." It is, therefore, for all the welcome interest it shows, a measure of the distance many Muslims, even with good will, still are from the Christ of Christianity.[5]

Another noted Egyptian writer Muhammad Husain Haykal, one-time President of the Egyptian Senate, prefaces his long and painstaking *Life of Muhammad* (1935) with certain remarks on the Christian faith. Christianity he characterized as unfitted to be the religion of the West by virtue of its ascetic renunciation. Christian antipathy to Islam is entirely due to doctrinal errors; to the substitution of Trinity for Unity; to the idea of redemption, as incompatible (as it is thought to be) with belief in a Day of Judgment; and to the assertion of Christ's being Divine.

There is little point in multiplying witnesses if the fact is clear. A popular Indian Muslim's biography of Muhammad, K. L. Gauba's *Prophet of the Desert* must be the last. After remarking that Muhammad was practical and successful, the author observes:

> Poor Jesus Christ expressed the noblest sentiments on charity and forgiveness; thus upon the Cross, persecuted and crucified, he forgave his enemies—"They know not what they do"—But it was never in Christ's good fortune to have his enemies reduced to impotence before him.[6]

Reflection on this verdict will surely provide the measure of the extent to which Muslims are unaware of Christ. The writer here is clearly discounting Him on the wrong counts. The supreme glory of Christ has become in his view something that renders Him pathetic. It is not simply that Christ goes unrecognized in the hidden majesty of redemptive love, but that the criteria of majesty are devalued and "good fortune" given precedence over "great grace."

These are the attitudes which await the patient ministry of Christian interpretation. For all their incompleteness and their intermittent bitterness, they are evidence that Jesus is not unknown. Yet neither is He known, since the secret of His significance remains undiscovered. The part, in fact, obscures the whole; the partial truth, blind to the full truth, becomes at the same time untruth. For it withholds more than it gives and forestalls its own completion. This situation between Islam and the Christ of Christianity is what demands retrieval.

v

If we have tried to sense that situation by reference to a few recent writers who present the general mind, we can also let it kindle our imagination by historical reverie. A geographical journey can impress it on our minds as well as an excursus into books. So much of the area of Muslim predominance in the world was once Christian. The minaret stands often in the very precincts of a departed Christianity and in some cases the mosques are the transformed cathedrals. When Damascus capitulated to the forces of the second Caliph 'Umar in A.D. 635 the great Cathedral Church of St. John the Baptist was divided into two parts, while half the churches of the city were taken over for mosques. For some seventy years the Cathedral housed the two religions until Walīd I, in whose reign the Muslim armies crossed the Straits of Gibraltar, decreed its complete absorption into Muslim use. When the Christians appealed, his successor, 'Umar II, was advised by the lawyers of Islam that the former Christian half, taken into Muslim prayer, could not be alienated to Christian use again. There was a symbolic truth in that uneasy and impermanent partition as well as in the ultimate Muslim possession of the whole. For a partition there truly was —a barrier between the rite that read the Gospel, commemorated the Cross, and epitomized the fellowship of the risen Christ, and the rite which prayed toward Mecca and understood God according to its Prophet.

Ousted in two stages from the Cathedral in Damascus, Eastern Christianity everywhere gave ground to Islam—not territory alone, but numbers, vigor, vitality, and tradition. It persisted, isolated and introspective, in a constantly growing Islam that had all the prestige of success and victory. There is no space here to tell in detail the story of the submergence of the Christian Church in wide areas of Asia and Africa, including its own birth lands and the cities of its early splendid story, like Jerusalem, Antioch, Alexandria, and Carthage.[7] If the old and oversimple thesis that Islam was spread by the sword needs modification, so does the popular counter-story that the faith from Arabia was a tolerant option freely chosen. It is true that Islam was capable of considerable toleration and that it was prepared, on conditions, to allow Jews and Christians to remain what they were. It is also true that when active persecution did occur it was the work of particular Caliphs and of local fanatical officials, not representative of the best in Islam. The idea of a sword at the throat of every Christian, compelling him to Islamize, is a crude and overdrawn picture. There were martyrs and there were those dispossessed; fear and discrimination played on the motive of vulgar passions. But there was also the possibility to continue as a Christian if one was ready to shoulder fines; wear distinctive dress; surrender some of one's churches and never build new ones; and suffer indignities and curtailment of opportunity—unless one had a craft or a skill of which society or government had need. If Christianity did not persist in more robust quality the fault was not wholly with Islam.

At the same time it is important to keep clearly in mind the imperial form of Muslim expansion, and the essential contrast in the fashion of the world outreach of original Islam and original Christianity. The latter did not attain imperial status for three whole centuries, during which it was, in the main, a persecuted minority, recognizing and paying its civil duty to the Roman Empire and defying it only where it found that Empire incompatible with its first allegiance, as in Emperor-worship. Christianity was a faith to which, after three centuries of almost overwhelming odds, an Empire turned. The history of Islam, by contrast, contains no Constantine. Muhammad was from the outset its Constantine as well as its Prophet. From the time when Islam established itself as a city state in Medina, it was a form of rule as well as of worship. It came upon the Eastern world, not simply as a creed but as an allegiance, a state, and a sovereignty. Its tokens were not baptism and the bread and wine; its tokens were prayer and the Caliph. It would, therefore, be both unhistorical and un-Islamic to suppose that when multitudes of Christians, in ancient Christian bishoprics, turned to Islam, they did so merely out of intellectual persuasion and never out of prudential realism, or that what they accepted was a creed only and not also a conquest.

But our immediate concern is the nature of the retrieval which this story imposes on Christianity today. Let it be clear that the retrieval is not territorial. Christianity is not a territorial expression. The retrieval is spiritual. It aims not to have the map more Christian but Christ more widely known. We are not concerned with the comparative strength of Islam and "Christendom" but the absolute loss of Christ. The retrieval to which we are called does not mean taking back cathedrals from

mosques, but giving back the Christ. The external tokens of
His displacement are important only because of the displacement they symbolize. To restore Christ transcends all else.

If, then, we make a brief mental visit to the areas of such
displacement, it is to feel the force of this aspect of our duty
to Islam. Take the Sudan. How many Christians in America
or Britain would naturally think of it as a Christian country,
or of a Sudanese Christianity other than that planted by recent
missions in the pagan south? But Christianity had its first contacts with Negro races in the earliest days and there was a
Nubian Christianity with its capital at Maqurra from the sixth
to the fourteenth century. It may have been an isolated and
at times impure Christianity and the reasons for the Muslim
penetration and displacement, seven centuries after Muslim success in Egypt, may not have been entirely external. But, for all
its imperfection, that Sudanese Christianity had deeply affected
the life of a vast region of Africa. Its disappearance left Ethiopia the last remaining representative of a Christian Africa.
J. Spencer Trimingham, who surveys this story in his *Islam
in the Sudan* has this footnote to his narrative:

> Remains of red brick Churches of the Alwa [Christian]
> Kingdom exist at Soba, Rudis, Elti, Kutranj, Kasemba,
> Bronko, Hassa, Haisa, Kamlin, Arbaji, and Sennar, on
> the Blue Nile and at Qataina on the White Nile.[8]

Ezekiel might have added: "Can these bones live?"

Remains, no doubt more familiar and no less eloquent, lie
across North Africa. Tertullian, Cyprian, and Augustine made
North Africa a classic Christian world. One of the justly loved
writers on the Christian relation to Islam, Constance E. Padwick, reflected in a "North African Reverie," on the living appeal of its shattered past.

> Standing . . . amid the forest of broken pillars that
> represent the Christian basilicas of Roman Carthage,
> one tastes the victory of Islam as though it took place
> only yesterday . . . Those broken columns, all that is
> left on earth of a Church of many bishoprics, speak

to Christendom with a voice shattering to complacency.
. . . Here it was said to the Church as it was said to
the Virgin Mother of old: "Yea, a sword shall pierce
through thine own soul also that the thoughts of many
hearts may be revealed." [9]

Today the few and scattered representatives of the Christianity
that once found passionate expression on that southern Mediterranean shore are engaged in reparation. Their task is to utter
anew the faith and love which once lived within these ruins
and so to break the silence of the centuries. It is to wake the
echoes of a history long old and make them vocal in the ac-
cents of today, to build again the worshipping community beside the old basilicas. Here, exemplified in Barbary, is the call
to Christian retrieval which comes in the very silence of the
Christian past around the minaret.

Where the Christian past has unbroken continuity and the
faith lives side by side with Islam, as in most of the Arab world
(outside Arabia), in Ethiopia, and in Turkey, there is still a
partnership of Christian reparation with the ancient Churches.
For centuries of Muslim predominance have not left a continuing Christianity untouched. The price of continuity has been a
certain introspection and a habit of aloofness. The relation of
the Western Christian to Eastern Christianity will call for consideration below, and mention of the question here is made
only lest it be supposed that tasks of reparation are confined
to those areas where a former Christianity has altogether ceased
to be.

VI

But we merely *illustrate* what is meant by retrieval when we
take stock of Muslim writing about the Christian faith and
ponder its displacement in many historic territories. These are
only symptoms and parables of the Muslim unawareness of
Christ. To *know* it in itself we go to the Qur'ān and the place
of Jesus in Muslim revelation. Here is the longer of the two
largely parallel passages relating to Jesus' birth as found in
Surah xix. 16-34.

Remember Mary in the Book, how having withdrawn from her people to a place eastward and secluded herself from them, We sent unto her our Spirit and he appeared unto her as a perfect human being. And she said: "I seek refuge with the Merciful from thee. If thou art one who fears God [leave me.]" He said: "Indeed I am a messenger of your Lord unto thee to bestow upon thee a pure child." She said: "How shall I have a son when no man has touched me and I have not been a harlot?" And he said: "So has thy Lord said: 'It is an easy thing for Me and in order that We may make him a sign unto men, a mercy from Us.' It has been so determined."

Thus she conceived him and withdrew with him to a remote spot. And her travail-pains drove her to the foot of a palm-tree, crying: "Would that I had died 'ere now and become oblivious in oblivion." Then he (the child?) called to her from beneath her: "Do not grieve: thy Lord has provided beside thee a flowing stream. Shake the trunk of the palm-tree towards thee for the ripe fruit to fall. So eat and drink and be gladdened. If you see any human person tell him: 'I have vowed a fast unto the Merciful: I will speak to none this day.'"

And she brought him to her folk, carrying him [in her arms] and they said: "O Mary, this is a shocking thing you present us with! O sister of Aaron, thy father was not an evil-doer, nor was thy mother a harlot." She motioned towards him. But they said: "How can we address one who is a child in the cradle?" And he said: "I am the servant of God. He has brought me the Book and made me a prophet. He has blessed me wherever I be and has enjoined on me prayer and almsgiving as long as I live; and [made me] honourable towards her who bare me. He has not made me a miserable lordling. Peace be on me the day of my birth, the day of my death and the day of my resurrection alive."

> This was 'Īsā, son of Mary—the true saying concerning which they are dubious.

The passage goes on to deny that the one so born is in any sense the Son of God—a notion unfitting. The parallel passage in Surah iii. 35-60 gives further details about the birth of Mary herself and of John, son of Zachariah. Repeating that Jesus is, like Adam, only man, it puts into His mouth the words: "I have come unto you with a sign from your Lord. I create for you out of clay the likeness of a bird, I breathe into it and by God's permission it is a bird. I heal the blind and the leper and I raise the dead by God's permission and I proclaim unto you what you may eat and what you may store up in your houses."

This bare and somewhat enigmatic statement is almost all the Qur'ān knows of the ministry of Jesus in the Gospels and of His parables. Surah v. 112 refers interrogatively to Jesus and a table of food from heaven, perhaps dimly echoing the feeding of the five thousand or the Last Supper, or simply transposing the like question once addressed to Moses. It should be noted that the Qur'ān throughout refers to Jesus under the name 'Īsā, corresponding to the Esau of the Old Testament. Though there are many theories relating to this name, its use remains a mystery. Christ is then a prophet, a teacher, a healer of the sick, a spirit from or of God. To Him is given the Gospel—not the Good News about God in Christ, but a Book of words or preaching, which the Qur'ān does not anywhere reproduce, except in very occasional references, like those to the camel and the needle's eye and alms in secret. The only element out of the background of our Lord's ministry, apart from His healing, is the fact of opposition, in face of which Jesus relied upon His disciples, for whom the Qur'ān has a high regard. But it presents no picture of Jesus' deep education of those disciples, nor does it allow that the opposition to Jesus issued in His crucifixion. Indeed, this is specifically denied in vehement terms along with the whole idea of the Incarnation. Thus the ascension of Christ is an arbitrary kind of exit from the human scene.

There are certain passages in the Qur'ān which might be regarded as conciliatory towards Christians. Surah v. 82 says: "Thou wilt find the nearest [of mankind], in affection, to those who be-lieve, those who say: Lo! We are Christians. That is because there are among them priests and monks, and because they are not proud." But there are other verses bitterly denunciatory of Christians and of priests. Surah ix. 30-31 reads: "God Himself fighteth against them. How perverse they are! They have taken, as lords beside God, their rabbis and their monks and the Mes-siah, son of Mary, when they were bidden to worship only one God." It is hard to resist the impression that Muhammad's at-titude changed, when he discovered that his claims failed to receive the hospitable welcome he had first expected from the people of the earlier Book.

The foregoing is a summary of all that the Qur'ān contributes to a knowledge of Jesus Christ. Allowing for repetitions of warn-ings against His Divinity and the duplication of the Birth narra-tive, it could be written in three or four pages. Though there is much fuller material in the Muslim traditions—much of it de-rived from Christian sources during Islam's expansion—it is con-cerned mainly with eschatology and adds nothing which is ex-pressly excluded by the Qur'ān itself. The chief note in the tra-ditions about Christ is that he was a homeless wanderer, *Imām al-Sā'ihīn,* the preacher who had nowhere to lay His head, but the final nature and the ultimate quality of this homelessness are all unknown.

If one sought a single justification for the Christian mission to Islam one might well be content to find it in the Quranic pic-ture of Jesus of Nazareth. It is not simply what the picture fails to tell, vast as that is, but also what it disallows. Worse than the silences are the vetoes. A partial portrait can be filled out. But what if it has negated in advance its own completion? For love of Christ retrieval must be made.

Consider the Quranic Jesus alongside the New Testament. How sadly attenuated is this Christian prophet as Islam knows Him! Where are the stirring words, the deep insights, the gra-cious deeds, the compelling qualities of Him Who was called the Master? The mystery of His self-consciousness as the Messiah is unsuspected: the tender, searching intimacy of His relation to the disciples undiscovered. Where is "the Way, the Truth and the Life" in this abridgment? Where are the words from the Cross in a Jesus for whom Judas suffered? Where the triumph of the Resurrection from a grave which was not occupied? We have in the Qur'ān neither Galilee, nor Gethsemane; neither Nazareth nor Olivet. Even Bethlehem is unknown by name and the story of its greatest night is remote and strange. Is the Sermon on the Mount to be left to silence in the Muslim's world? Must the story of the Good Samaritan never be told there? the simple, human narrative of the prodigal son never mirror there the essence of waywardness and forgiveness? Is "Come unto Me all ye that are weary . . . and I will give you rest" an invitation that need not be heard, and is Jesus' taking bread and giving thanks a negligible tale? Should not all mankind be initiated into the meaning of the question: "Will ye also go away?"

In sum, must not the emasculated Jesus of the Qur'ān be rescued from misconception and disclosed in all His relevance, in words, deeds, and sorrows, to the whole plight and aspiration of men? To do this is what is meant here by retrieval. Our concern about assaying it will surely measure our own estimate of Who and what He is—the Christ Who questioned His disciples on one crucial occasion: "Whom do men say that I am?" The answer matters, to Christ and to all the world. We have no right either to suppress the question or to neglect the response. Rather, inseparable from our Christianity, is the duty so to bring men to Him Who asks that they may answer for themselves.

VII

Unhappily this state of not knowing Jesus in Islam, which has now been illustrated, goes back to Christian failure, so that retrieval is also restitution. Could Christ otherwise have been so obscured and lost to sight and knowledge? Does not the New Testament inseparably link the fullness of Christ with the Church which is His body, in the sense that the one instrumentally depends upon the other? "The light of the knowledge of the glory of God in the face of Jesus Christ . . . this treasure in earthen vessels." So run St. Paul's metaphors. The loss of Christ necessarily argues a delinquent Christianity. Arabian and Eastern history confirm the fact. In analysis of that tragedy we must begin with the Christianity in which Islam first developed, "the dimness," as C. E. Padwick has it, "from which Islam drew at its beginning so blurred, so veiled, an outline of the Son of Mary—mysteriously born and lord of many a miracle, but not of love's paramount miracles of the divine Incarnation, the Cross and the Resurrection." [10]

The Qur'ān took up and laid the sanction—and sanctity—of Divine revelation upon misunderstandings for which the Church must bear its measure of responsibility. Misconceptions as to the Trinity and Jesus make clear that Muhammad was never in a position to know at first hand the authentic Christianity of the New Testament. The Christians, with the Jews, as "People of the Book," may well have been, as we have seen, the historical source of the germinal idea that blossomed into the conception of "an Arabic Qur'ān." But the full witness of that Christian Book seems never to have been available to him. Certainly the Bible did not then exist in the Arabic language and the Greek, Syriac, and other versions could only have been open to him indirectly, through personal contacts.

However we may decide the question of Muhammad's illiteracy, noted in an earlier chapter, it seems clear from the contents of the Qur'ān that Muhammad's Christian knowledge was wholly oral in origin. It also appears that either the range or the quality of these contacts was insufficient to constitute an authentic encounter with Christ. It is true that we must also take account of the originality of Muhammad himself, the yearning for an Arabic answer from Heaven, for an "indigenous" revelation, for a direct, Divine message to the situation in Mecca. All these are factors which might have operated, even if Muhammad had enjoyed the fullest opportunity to know the purest Christianity. The facts, or at least some of them, seem patently to reproach Christianity itself for Muhammad's belief that God in the Qur'ān was superseding it. Could his antagonism have been wholly Arabian self-assertion? Could it have sprung only from Muhammad's will to be a prophet? For at the outset that will was not consciously formed. Could it have been only the Prophet's growing communal confidence making him independent of all parallel sources of ideas such as Jews and Christians? For he had at least begun, or so it seemed, by being in debt to them. If the displacement of Christianity was not due only to these motives, must there not have been other factors for which Arabian Christianity was directly to blame? Islam was generated as a new faith because of the conviction that a new one there must be. But why?

Christianity on the borders of Arabia was torn by ecclesiastical disputes which poisoned theological controversies. It was embittered by partisanship and compromise. The Ghassānids and the Hīrā Christians on the Syrian and Irāqī frontiers of Arabia were responsible for some Christian penetration but they occupied buffer areas in uncertain relation with Byzantium and Persia. The southern Arabian Christianity of Najrān and the Yaman is known to have suffered much persecution and did not succeed in making any lasting foothold in the Hijāz itself.[11] The pre-Islamic Arab poets refer to Christian hermits, Christian wine, and Christian bells. Does the conventional paganism of poetry alone explain why Arab Christianity produced no religious literature of its own? The ancient poetry of Arabia offers no conclusive evidence that Christian ideas had made any abiding impression upon the Arab mind and heart.

Ideas of a Divine judgment, of a revealed Book, of resurrection and the Divine will were present in the Jewish-Christian background, but they only came to fervency in the intense conviction of the new Muhammad, conviction so intense that it received them as in a new Divine action of inspiration, displacing their old guardians and diverging widely into a new entity. Perhaps in the formative years of Muhammad's quest a more virile, a less dubious, Christianity could have satisfied his sense of need and obviated the great "other" that Islam became. We cannot tell. We should beware of reproaching Arabian Christianity in a situation in which so much is obscure. But the new religion did emerge and as it hardened into self-sufficiency Christians had no longer any means of demonstrating that Muhammad had misunderstood their teachings. It became part of the very dogma, not to say the vested interest, of Islam that Christianity was now replaced.

The rise of Islam will always remain a painful puzzle for the Christian mind. Mystery must always surround the genesis of so great a phenomenon. But Islam is the only great post-Christian religion and as such was not generated in isolation, either geographical or mental, from the Christian world. The latter, therefore, can never exonerate itself from responsibility. To define that responsibility in detail is impossible. How to face the fact of it is now the question. For whatever we may learn from the failures of other generations to be the Church, we have to strive to be it worthily in our own. We have also to recognize that more Christians than those contemporary with Muhammad have compromised their Christianity and perpetuated Muslim antipathy. There is space to consider only a few examples.

The first belongs to the twelfth and thirteenth Christian centuries, the era of the Crusades. Though it is almost seven and three-quarter centuries since the Latin Kingdom of Jerusalem collapsed, Islam is still conscious of the crusading temper of that Latin Christianity as a bitter tradition. This lingering sense of crusading wrongdoing in the Arab East is a reproach for which in the Christian Church we should be thankful, since it is a recognition that the Crusades were a piece of Christian history unworthy of the name and treasonable to the nature of Christ. It is no doubt easy to adopt an attitude of superior criticism of the Crusaders, who from 1096 to 1291 strove to recover and retain the fields of Palestine for "Christian" powers. A complacent and comfortable critic may well forget the sacrifice, endurance, and valor of numberless volunteers, whose bones were left to rot on Anatolian roadways and whose spirits languished in frustrated sieges. The Crusades were served with a devotion that, had it been as wise and true as it was fervent and undaunted, would have blessed the Eastern world.

But devotion was ill-served, misused, misguided, and betrayed. The Crusades were generated in contradiction and pursued in ambition. The relations between Western and Eastern Christendom and between individual leaders within the Latin forces were, for the most part, lamentable. Sacrifice was demanded and sacrifice was squandered. Duplicity, self-seeking, stupidity, and plain human frailty besmirched the name of the Church. In man power the Crusaders were at a disadvantage; their main military asset was the dividedness of their enemy. Once the great Salāh al-Dīn (Saladin) had consolidated an energetic and resourceful resistance the Latin Kingdom was doomed, and its fall proved in the end an irretrievable disaster.

That final frustration of futility, however, only confirmed the Christian confusion of mind in which the Crusades were conceived and pursued. The important matter was not the possibility of pilgrimage but the obligation of witness. Christ's concern was, and is, for men not monuments, for souls not sanctuaries. What had been lost, and remained lost, to Christendom, was nothing to what had been lost, and remained lost, to Muslims. The gain of Jerusalem had no merit to supplant the giving of Christ. But these insights few saw. The Crusades were a mistaken gesture of a disloyal Christendom.

> Deus le vult—of that they were sure. What then does He will? The deliverance of "those holy fields"—yes, and hence enmity to "the Paynims." The literature of the period gives us glimpses of what were the jokes of a crusading army in a camp where a Baldwin or a St. Louis prayed—tasty tales about serving Paynims with pork or even with bits of roasted Paynim—probably no better and no worse than the talk of other armies, but far from any saving thought on behalf of Muslim souls.[12]

There were contemporaries with great saving thoughts, notably Raymond Lull, who, in his oft-quoted words, saw ". . . many knights going to the Holy Land, thinking they can acquire it by force of arms." But they were rare. The multitudes failed to recognize that "He who loves not, lives not" and that the only way to serve Christ and the world is by "the pouring out of tears and blood." If Lull's vision measures by contrast the tragic misguidedness of the Crusades, then these in turn measure the dimensions of Christian reparation. The Crusades did not merely postpone an authentically Christian answer to Islam. They intensified both its urgency and its difficulty. History has not yet outlived the legacy of their reproach.

IX

Indeed, history has in part repeated it. The Crusades may seem very far away. Much nearer our own time there have been other forms of "Christian" disservice to the faith. The Western world no longer advances on the Eastern in the name of religious repossession of forfeited sanctuaries. But for almost two centuries the science, industry, and commerce of the West have steadily permeated the world of Asia. Nations belonging to the continent of Europe—Britain, France, Belgium, Holland, Portugal—established themselves as the governing powers over wide areas of Asia and Africa, taking advantage of the long start which circumstance and ambition had given them in the pursuit of empire and trade. What matters here is not the details of that story but how it seems in retrospect to numerous Muslim peoples who have only lately broken free into their own nationalism. The retrospect is naturally conditioned by their struggle and their aspiration. They tend inevitably to identify Christianity with the lands where it was traditional and whence the material and political domination came. That identification in the absolute sense is, of course, false. Its falsity, as we shall note elsewhere, is one of our large tasks of interpretation. But the responsibility of Christianity in "Christendom" we cannot seek to escape. The faith of the Christian Church, as Muslims have read it in the behavior and the attitudes of Western powers, Western commerce, and Western culture has been deeply and sadly obscured, sometimes entirely dimmed. In so far as the faith acting—as it only can—through Christians failed either to correct these relationships, where it could, or repudiate them where it could not, it is involved in a compromise that demands retrieval. It may be argued that no generation of the Church can bear more than its own immediate burdens. But this does not release us here and now, since, in the solidarity of the Christian fellowship, these past delinquencies have entered, and do enter, into our own burdens.

The past as the past cannot be undone in the present. But part of the present duty is the correction of the past. We have to carry the burden of what the Church has been, of what it has failed to be, and the burden of what the Muslim supposes Christianity to represent. Examples of the need of reparation in detail would mean writing again the history of East-West relationships, as well as trying to disentangle what resulted from actual Christian disloyalty and what from Western rejection of Christianity. That would be impossible. The Muslim, anyhow, is not likely to make the distinction. He knows, perhaps, that government inquiries into vice in Teheran have traced it in part to the influence of American films; that low Western journalism has inspired a flood of similar publications in Cairo and Beirut; that flaunted Western wealth has broken down many old conceptions of commercial integrity among Muslim merchants; that the "invisible exports" of the Western world—secularity, indulgence, cheap love, commercialized sex—are all too visible in their impact upon the Eastern mind.

Trade relationships on the part of the West have been too often conceived in terms of markets, not of people; of sales, not of society. Diplomatic relationships are liable to be preoccupied with bases for our defense or the global contributions of others to our security. In too many ways the Westerner tends to be condescending or patronizing, so that even his good will is suspected and his genuine sympathies misunderstood. Emotional susceptibilities on the other side have no doubt some responsibility. But no Christian, who considers seriously the combination of contempt and fascination with which the Muslim East regards the West, can doubt that if Christ remains in so urgent and so deep a sense a stranger, the fault is plainly ours.

We may perhaps adapt the words of His own question to Philip the disciple: "Have I been so long time with you and yet have *they* not known Me?" In the New Testament understanding of the Church, the Christ of all the world comes to belong to humanity through witness only in proportion as His Church belongs to Him in loyalty. "Let not those who seek Thee be confounded through me" cried the Psalmist. The fear that they may be—the fact that they are—these must be ever with us. Perhaps another question may be borrowed. "Understandest thou?" Philip the deacon asked the man of Ethiopia. Today he might have answered: "How can I, if some man misguide me."

All that should be said about retrieval as an aspect of the Christian duty to the people of the minaret leads directly into the very heart of the matter. The surest way to repair what we have been is to tell what Christ is. Estrangement will best pass in the presence of the Stranger. Retrieval leads into Interpretation.

NOTES *to Chapter IX*

1

Qutb, Sayyid, op. cit. p. 278-9. Quoted by permission of the American Council of Learned Societies.

2

The literature of the Ahmadiyyah Movements is large. Among the important publications of the Qadiānī Ahmadiyyah are: Ahmad, Mirzā Ghulām, *The Philosophy of the Teachings of Islam*, London, 1910, Washington, 1953; Ahmad, Mirzā Bashīr al-Dīn, *Ahmadiyyat or the True Islam*, 1st edition, Qadiān, 1924, 3rd edition, Washington, 1951; *The Holy Quran: English Translation and Commentary*, Vol. 1, Qadiān, 1947.* The Lahore Ahmadiyyah has published, *inter alia*, 'Alī, Muhammad, *The Religion of Islam*, Lahore, 1936; 'Alī, Muhammad, *The Holy Quran, Translation and Commentary*, Lahore, 1920. For the history prior to the schism, the reader may consult Walter, Howard A., *The Ahmadiyyat Movement*, London, 1918.

3

Ahmad, Al Hājj Khwāja Nazīr, *Jesus in Heaven on Earth*, Lahore, 1952.

4

'Alī, Muhammad, *My Life—A Fragment*, op. cit. p. 160.

5

Al-'Aqqād, 'Abbās Mahmūd, *'Abqariyyat al-Masīh*, Cairo, 1952. See "The Genius of Christ" in *The East and West Review*, London, July 1954, Vol. 20, No. 3, pp. 88-96, for a résumé of the contents of this work and a discussion of its Christian bearings. A still more noteworthy Muslim treatment of Christ is that by Husain, Muhammad Kāmil, *Qaryah Zālimah* (City of Oppression), Cairo, 1954, where the author reconstructs imaginatively the tensions, fears, and bigotries involved in the desire to crucify Christ—a deed which he describes as humanity's crucifixion of its own conscience.†

---

* *The Holy Qur'an, Arabic Text and English Translation*, Rabwah, 1955.
† See "City of Wrong," *The Muslim World*, April and July, 1956, Vol. 46, Nos. 2 and 3, pp. 132-43 and 225-36.

6

Gauba, Khālid L., *Prophet of the Desert*, Lahore, 1934, pp. 293-4.

7

The story has been admirably recounted in Browne, Laurence E., *The Eclipse of Christianity in Asia*, Cambridge, England, 1933. Arnold, Thomas, *The Preaching of Islam*, London, 1913, was a notable contribution to the investigation of Muslim expansion and sought, as its title implies, to emphasize and document the "religious" presentation of Islam in the conquered territories. While Arnold did much to qualify earlier extreme views, his examples were in part ill balanced and his thesis nowhere took adequate account of the Islamic law of war and peace and of the fundamental fact that preaching was inseparable from conquest. It should also be remembered that while "readers" might explain Islam, the Qur'ān as such was not translated or given into the hands of unbelievers. One only had access to the supreme source-book of Islam after one had become a Muslim.

8

Trimingham, J. Spencer, *Islam in the Sudan*, London, 1949, p. 79, fn. 1.

9

International Review of Missions, July 1938, Vol. 27, No. 3, p. 341.

10

Ibid. p. 341, fn.

11

Its semi-pagan quality can be gauged from an examination of the archaeological remains. See Winnett, F. V., in *The Muslim World*, Oct. 1941, Vol. 31, No. 4, pp. 350-52. The evidence indicates that Jesus had been incorporated into polytheism and that animal sacrifices were offered in His Name.

12

International Review of Missions, op. cit. p. 343.

X

THE CALL TO INTERPRETATION

ESCUE a word . . . discover a universe" suggested an eminent Cambridge New Testament scholar to his hearers, in preaching before the University. "Can we bury ourselves in a lexicon," he continued, "and arise in the presence of God?" [1] Dictionaries are, indeed, places of unexpected wonder for all who have felt the fascination of words, not least the Greek lexicon which serves New Testament study. All words, in fact, have histories, and some of them extraordinary adventures. Who would normally connect the attic of his house, a place of discarded things, with the Attic architectural glory of ancient Greece, or "bunk" with a constituency in North Carolina, whose Representative felt he had to speak for it even if what he said was nonsense? How many remember that "oxen" and "beef," "pigs" and "pork," are a usage which goes back to the Norman Conquest of England, when the Saxons became the herdsmen and swineherds who kept the beasts, and the French Normans ate the meat? So the animals have Anglo-Saxon names and their meat French ones.

History is hidden in language. Meanings may subtly change until they almost reverse their originals—like "comfort" and "security" and "simpleton." For words are meaning being exchanged. They are the counters of intellectual intercourse. A single language agrees upon a particular sequence of letters written or sounds uttered, to convey a certain sense. When the print says "Man" or the speaker cries "Fire!" a particular impression is conjured up in the mind of the reader, or the listener. He has at once a mental image that the word has inspired within him at the behest of the mind intending that result. Words are the highways of the traffic of ideas, sentiments, emotions, and relationships, and the work of the world is done by them.

The trouble with a foreign language is that the symbols are not part of a familiar system. They are to the listener a sequence of meaningless sounds, to the reader a jumble of indeterminate shapes. The art of translation is to take over what was carried in one agreed frame and to convey it in another. No meaning is received save in terms of what is already known. The word is the point of exchange.

These considerations, obvious enough in themselves, illuminate that most comprehensive of New Testament descriptions of Christ as "the Word." The English Bible has wisely used the capital letter. As the Christian faith understands and receives Him, Christ is "the Word of God." He in Himself constitutes what God wants to say. God, that is, engages in speech. He is not content that there should be a barrier of silence and, therefore, of unknowing between Himself and man. Whereas the ultimate speech of God for Islam is prophecy, "sealed," as the phrase goes, or accomplished, in Muhammad, the speech of God for the Christian is personality—a human life in all the revealing human situations, the Person of Jesus Christ in the flesh, Whose antecedents, character, history, and meaning for men are sufficiently recorded in the Bible. The Bible thus becomes a secondary "word" —the written word preserving and expressing the incarnate. There is the Life that reveals; there is the history that describes. The latter is the means to the continuing accessibility of the former.

Thus the Bible is very differently conceived from the Qur'ān, where the revelation is essentially the "scripture" written. But the immediate point is that God is understood to have spoken. As both Muslim and Christian agree, it takes God to reveal God. God Himself must say what He has to say, though He may depute the task to servants, to prophets, to seers. But what they say must be intelligible to man otherwise no meaning is conveyed and the speech, if it is spoken, is nevertheless not heard.

Christianity rests on the conviction that the surest method of revelation is personal; that the unmistakable terms of Divine disclosure for us are human life. So in the mercy of God the Life was lived, the deeds were done. We need make no mistake about God after we have known Christ. "He that hath seen Me hath seen the Father" was His claim.

Using, then, the image of human life, God uttered Himself in terms already within our ken, in a manger and village carpentry, in synagogue and field, in Gethsemane and Emmaus: God Himself the Interpreter and the Interpreted. The very substance of human life has become the vehicle of the Divine. Listening to this language we discover God. We learn what God intended for humanity. "The Word was made flesh" (John i. 14).

But like all other speech this Divine Word can be silenced by inattention, by indifference, by being out of range or mind. So it is that what God says may go unheard and unknown. This is variously true of all men. We have seen in the previous chapters something of the particular form of Muslim "unawareness." The Word divinely spoken stands in need of witnessing expression. We have to "rescue the word and discover the universe" of God's revealing love, in Christ. We are called to be interpreters of God's interpretation of Himself. A frequent phrase in St. Matthew's Gospel may serve us here: "Thou shalt call His name Emmanuel which, being interpreted, is God with us" (Matt. i. 23). "Being interpreted" is a mighty condition. It stands between everything and nothing. It is the hinge upon which "Emmanuel" turns. For "God with us" is not simply a statement. It is a conviction. More than an announcement, it is an experience. Unless it is heeded, pondered, and believed, it might as well have never been. Meanings not conveyed are meanings frustrated.

The amazing reality behind and within the Christian mission in the world is this task of interpretation. Our duty is to carry over the Word which God has uttered, to be the translators of His speech into the language, the idiom, and the minds of ordinary men. Our words are to be the servants of the Word, our lives of His Life, our persons of His Person. Men are to take from us their knowledge of Him, from Whom God would have them take their knowledge of Himself. There is the sequence: "Thou in Me and I in them" with the purpose "that the world may know that Thou hast sent Me" (John xvii. 23).

The interpretation by the Christian of the Word which is Christ must learn to face all obstacles and subdue them to the master-purpose. What is worthy of all acceptance must be capable of all acceptance. The interpreter refuses to believe that the language of God in Christ is beyond anyone's understanding given patience, lowliness, resourcefulness—and the Holy Spirit. Like every wise translator, he will be indefatigable in seeking his clues in all areas of life. He will be patient with all contrariety, knowing that wherever there is opposition there is also relevance. Indifference, on the one hand, or conscious "difference" on the other, oblige him to find the way in. Islam is particularly calculated to put the Christian interpreter on his mettle since it forces him to a radical and patient expression of his faith. By the very vigor and cruciality of its objections, Islam compels the Christian to delineate Christ more deeply. The grounds of misunderstanding must be made the theme of more patient exposition. Every difficulty must be made an opportunity.

This interpretation involves a person-to-person relationship. The institutions in mind in "The Call to Service" may provide the framework and the occasion. But the progress or the contagion of the Kingdom of Heaven is "soul by soul." We cannot institutionalize the world into God's Kingdom. Nor can we fulfill our ministry except by an intimate relationship with ordinary people. For they are the crux of the Gospel. As Christians we are committed to the infinite significance of the person. The metaphors which describe our task are those of shepherds and sheep, pastors and people. We are called to a tender solicitude for the minds and wills of men. The Word which is Christ has to come into their vocabulary. So we must study what they mean in all the moods, the overtones and undertones, of their existence. It is our life-task to make bridges into their minds. This means being near enough to be heard; getting near is a large part of our problem. But our first confidence must lie in the worth of the story, if only we serve it as it deserves. "Hearing comes," said the Apostle, "by the word of God" (Romans x. 17). Only when something is apprehended is it being communicated.

What, so understood, are the main contents of Christian interpretation to the people of Islam? Five important areas at once suggest themselves, in a sequence which almost decides itself. These are the Christian Scriptures, the Person of Jesus, the Cross, the Christian Doctrine of God, and the Christian Church and a Christian society.

A. INTERPRETING THE CHRISTIAN SCRIPTURES

II

There are two excellent reasons why interpretation should begin here. The first is that the Muslim has an instinctive sense of "Holy Books"—the highest and greatest of which is the Qur'ān. He expects religion to have this "scriptural" quality. The second is that ultimately all presentation of Christ and of God must hinge upon the Biblical and, particularly, the New Testament expression. A large part of our task is to bring the Muslim to a patient and hospitable perusal of the Gospels and the Epistles.

But these two sound reasons also locate for us the supreme difficulties. The nature and role of the Christian Scriptures in Christianity are so strangely contrasted with the Islamic role of the Qur'ān. The strangeness is not merely that of vocabulary, important as the distinctions are between Christian and Islamic religious Arabic. There is a much more inclusive unfamiliarity persisting beyond all problems of language and textual translation.

The Muslim who addresses himself to the Bible finds a variety of books of independent authorship, stretching over more than a millennium. Within the New Testament he finds four different Gospels, and a sequence of various Epistles. All are in evident contrast with the Holy Book of Islam, which came via one human instrument, through some twenty-three years of Meccan and Medinan history. It is difficult to comprehend why there should be four Gospels, when the Gospel, or *Injīl,* entrusted by God to Jesus the Prophet was reputedly a single book. The assumption is immediate that because there are four, none of them is valid. Indeed there is a widely current Muslim explanation. The early Church lost the original "Gospel" *from* Jesus and several leaders set themselves to making good the deficiency, with the result that they all differed and they were all wrong.

Involved in the question is the larger one about what the Gospel in truth is. On the Muslim view of revelation all prophets are bearers of words from God, understood to be entrusted to them in complete form, not as a result of a Divine enabling of their mental and spiritual powers, but as a verbal transmission from heaven. Thus the teaching of Jesus, properly understood, is a body of words, now lost, but happily safeguarded in the culminating revelation of the Qur'ān. This view does not envisage a Gospel in, as well as through, Jesus—good news of a Divine initiative for man's salvation in His Presence among men and His history there. It is, of course, upon this latter concept of the Gospel, the Gospel of God in Christ, that the character and the very possibility of "the Gospels" according to the four Evangelists rests. On the Christian view, it is not only comprehensible, it is desirable, that the significance of that Life and Death should be recorded as it impressed itself upon minds within the Church. The Gospels bring a cumulative witness to a central Figure without conspiring to eliminate secondary divergencies. They arose in the heart of the Church to perpetuate its saving memory of Christ, when time was thinning the contemporary generation and the wider world beyond the Palestinian was entering the fellowship. Thus their existence is in no sense a gesture of recovery that failed, but an act of affirmation that was achieving its universal purpose. They exist not to replace the irretrievably lost words of Jesus, but to report His significance—words and deeds—as a glorious possession.

To take across into the Muslim mind this truth about the Gospels is a primary duty. It has another aspect. The Qur'ān for Muslims is the Word of God to Muhammad immediately reproduced for men to hear. It is not what men reported Muhammad to have said as Prophet. Such reports constitute Tradition and are, as we have seen, of lesser status, though indicative of the Divine will. But the Qur'ān does not go through the mental understanding of reporters, any more than—as understood by orthodox Islam—it goes through the conscious processes of the Prophet's mind. It is more assuredly God's if man is in entire abeyance.

Not so the New Testament. Though the Gospels undoubtedly contain verbatim accounts of what Jesus said, there are many places, not least in St. John, where the evangelist merges imperceptibly into his material. There is condensation and editing; there is choice, reproduction, and witness. The Gospels have come through the minds of their authors and, in deep measure, through the mind of the Church behind the authors. They represent experience and history. They are history told out of the experience to which it gave rise. This may be seen as eminently suitable, distinctly appropriate. For "the Word" is a captured significance, a realized meaning. To have Christ as the Church found Him is to have Christ more validly than He could be had in some hypothetical but unattainable abstraction. For all history is experienced fact and cannot escape the interpretative element. Such interpretation might be suspect if it were uncongenial, unsympathetic, as an abstract record that had not participated. But the New Testament has escaped this danger and enjoyed its contrary by the very involvement of the writers in the impact and meaning of what they report. We have, then, to help the Muslim conceive of a Divine revelation that is primarily personal, not oracular; that proceeds by enabling not overriding the minds of its writers; and that gathers into its written "word" the comprehension of the hearing of the Word Incarnate.

III

In this context, also, we must present the Epistles. On the Qur'ān's hypothesis they must be deeply mystifying, even inexplicable. How can personal correspondence be Divine revelation? If St. Paul chooses to address himself to Galatia, how can that constitute a piece of a preserved volume in heaven? The objection is worth facing because the content of the answer is so rich.

The Epistles in the New Testament are the clearest evidence that Biblical revelation co-operates with human experience in order to complete and fulfill itself. For the revelation is not simply of a law to be followed, or a set of facts to be believed, or even a history to be accepted. It is the offer of a relationship. It *brings,* it is true, a law to obey and involves facts and history, but it *is* essentially a relationship to be received and experienced. Its doctrine of God means fellowship with God: its doctrine of man means repentance, forgiveness, and regeneration. All that it proclaims and asserts, it offers and imparts. It is proclamation unto experience. Thus what it means cannot be expressed out of connection with its reception. In the Epistles, therefore, we find St. Paul and others explaining the converts to themselves, showing them in detail the nature of their faith, its impact upon their character and their behavior, its meaning as a break with the past and as a promise of the future.

The evangel recorded in the Gospels is experienced in the Epistles. It is out of that experience, analyzed and elucidated in the Epistles, that the Gospel records were written. Herein is the essential unity of the New Testament. The Christian, as the earthly product of the faith, the human consequence of the Divine grace, is in this sense part of the revelation. To explain him, to discipline him, to describe his making and his behaving, is the work of the Epistles. In them the nature of what God says is being apprehended, not by Divine dictation to a scribe, but by apostolic education of the early Church, under the Holy Spirit, into the meaning of its own life and the shape of its proper fellowship. The Divine communication is completed in the representative description of its actual consequences in human destiny, both personal and social, as those consequences were to be seen in Corinth, Rome, Ephesus, or Philippi.

Another reason why an apostle's correspondence can take its appropriate place in the volume of revelation involves a further point, applicable to the Bible as a whole and not least to the Old Testament. This is the "occasional" nature of Biblical revelation. It is rooted in history and in particular events. It arises out of representative situations. St. Paul may be dealing with questions peculiar to Corinth (idolatrous meats in the market place), or to Galatia (the temptations from the Judaizers). But the principles on which he bases his discussion are abiding. The instance illustrates their application, and may well recur, in recognizable, if not identical, form elsewhere. If not, the principle remains. Those churches of the Epistles with their problems and vagaries are to be regarded as symbolic. The apostolic attitude to the "occasion" has a relevance beyond it. For the occasion is inclusive of much more than itself. The Epistle to the Romans belongs to more than Romans. Even the letter to Philemon, so intimately personal, has an ageless relevance beyond the issue of Onesimus, the slave who ran away.

Here is the pattern. Without the instance, the universal might be mere abstraction. Apart from the abiding truth involved, the instance would be ephemeral and negligible. In the concrete universal, in the significant particular, comes the down-to-earth revelation. It is not only precept but demonstration. It not only enjoins but saves. The Biblical revelation borrows endless "occasions" of human existence that in them it may representatively reveal the pattern of the Kingdom of Heaven. How appropriate this is to the faith which believes the Word to be made flesh, how remote and mystifying to the Muslim until interpretation facilitates his understanding.

"Occasions," too, explain much of the Old Testament. H. G. Wells in his *Short History of the World* impatiently complained that the Bible spent too long rehearsing the story of a very insignificant people with a very undistinguished succession of kings. What he failed to see was that the Biblical interest in Israel was, among other things, illustrative of the doctrine of man. Events are recorded from Abraham, through the Exodus, in the exile and beyond, not because they exhaust what is significant in the human story, but because they are representative of human waywardness and because their particular sequence has its place in the preparation for redemption in Christ. Since Biblical revelation turns on events, and since events in history are potentially innumerable, it proceeds by inclusive selection. The relation of God to all history is made clear in a particular history. A special history prepares and introduces that which illuminates and redeems all history. So the Bible covers not the two decades of a single prophet's ministry, but the eighteen or so centuries between Abraham and St. John, between Ur of the Chaldees and the Isle of Patmos. Its revelation lies in the varied, always selective, always representative, reaction of men in rebellion and in obedience, to the Divine will and word.

Thus the greatest prophecies are incomprehensible apart from historical occasions. Amos is not to be understood apart from the iniquities of Omri and the rise of Assyria. "Can two walk together unless they be agreed?" (Amos iii. 3). It was events that made clear to Amos in Tekoa how the historical causes producing a punitive Assyria were controlled by the righteousness which required the retribution of Samaria. The domestic tragedy of Hosea is found illuminating the Divine relationship with a harlot nation. Jeremiah, Isaiah, Ezekiel, are all prophets who must be measured and understood against the background of history. They are the interpreters of particular events that all history may be understood.

Likewise the Psalms, as poems of lament, complaint, fear, or dismay, will hardly seem to a Muslim what God could have supposedly revealed. But in their accumulative witness to the meaning of God in human life they communicate the "felt" significance of the truth God willed men to understand. As men wrestle with their situation in the context of what they know of God He enlarges and deepens that knowledge and brings it to light and life for all who read. The revealing process, so to speak, enlists and allows the mental and spiritual capacities of particular men, through whom it addresses the minds and spirits of all men. And when the Psalmists are lifted into exaltation and doxology their witness is to the apprehended meaning of the truth made known. Theology passes into doxology, which is its most communicable form. If the Qur'ān contains no Psalms and little history and is the fruit of only one prophetic experience that fact is the measure of the difference in the Biblical and Quranic concepts of revelation and so in turn of the extent of our interpretative task.

Much more might be said in this context. It must suffice to add one further point about the nature of Biblical revelation —its honest realism in describing man. Whether it be the story of Abraham or David or the portrait of the disciples, they are there, as Cromwell might have said, "warts and all." No attempt is made to hide their shortcomings or minimize their frailty. In this they are a measure of the humanity that God would redeem. Since we perceive them to have been "men of like passions" with ourselves, we may have hope and faith for ourselves. Though the average Muslim is well aware of the frailty of man because of the doctrine of the compassionateness of God and so is prepared for human weaknesses, he does not readily associate these with patriarchs and prophets. Moreover, the Qur'ān emphasizes very strongly the difference between Islam and non-Islam in terms of belief. The *Muslimūn* or believers are "the gainers," the *Kā-firūn* or disbelievers are "the losers." Though there are strong moral distinctions in the Qur'ān, they normally follow distinctions of creed. Thus there is less tendency to recognize any inward wrongness within the community of the faith. This is natural in a revelation concentrating on law. Whereas law condemns all that is outside it and approves what is within it, redemption proceeds upon a sinfulness from which all suffer and from which all may be redeemed. This aspect of the Biblical idea of man under God may be one of the most important and difficult notes in a Biblical ministry to Muslims.

IV

It will be seen that all these are points arising from the contrasted concepts of revelation upon which the Qur'ān and the Bible proceed. The interpreter of the one to the readers of the other must, however, take note of certain duties, resulting from the Muslim attitude to the Bible. The Qur'ān contains material belonging to the same history as the Old Testament. It speaks of the creation and the fall, of the patriarchs and the law. It includes the two lengthy descriptions of Christ's nativity already noted. This fact of Quranic involvement in Biblical history and the claim of Islam to be the culminating revelation, gathering into itself all the pre-Islamic prophets from Adam to Jesus, have naturally given rise to a state of acute tension between the heirs of the two Scriptures through the centuries. The main and positive Christian task just described is complicated by much inter-Scriptural controversy. Though this must be kept in due perspective and never allowed to monopolize the business of interpretation in this field, the points at issue cannot be ignored.

Where there is variety or discrepancy in either Old or New Testament history between the Bible and the Qur'ān, the Muslim explains it under some form or other of the doctrine of corruption. The differences in patriarchal story, for example, are not to be examined in terms of Muhammad's sources of knowledge or his didactic purposes. They are explained in terms of a distortion in the present (i.e. the Canonical) versions of the original. This is emphasized, according to orthodox Islam, by the disparity between the Quranic picture of Jesus and that in the New Testament. Muslims reason that Jews and Christians, who in Arabia so manifestly failed to recognize and accept the mission of Muhammad, were not fit custodians of their own Scriptures. Quite evidently they tampered with them in various directions, suppressing what would have made them confirmatory of Islam and obscuring the true nature of their identity with the Qur'ān. The Muslim does not pause to consider that no *consciously* anti-Islamic corruption in fact occurred, since the Canon was made final three centuries or more before Muhammad's mission. Unconsciously anti-Islamic perversion is hardly an intelligent hypothesis.

But on the Muslim view, the point is that the Biblical Scriptures do not square with the Qur'ān; that their true original form did so square; and that, therefore, corruption has occurred. It does not matter that the alleged original form is irrecoverable. The Qur'ān embodies it sufficiently. The Muslim position thus begins with a hypothesis which is beyond proof or disproof, a hypothesis which ends where it begins. The Qur'ān is the infallible Book. All other true Scriptures agree with it. The Biblical Scriptures, as they are, do not agree. Therefore these are corrupted. But their corruption is offset by the Quranic embodiment of what they ought to contain.

Only a little imagination is necessary to appreciate how difficult it is to penetrate this closed circle of thought. To insist as we must that the Canon of Scriptures has not undergone any change since the fourth century and that it then recognized documents long established is sound history. But it makes little impression on dogmatic prejudice. If the two Holy Books are not the same, so much the worse for the Biblical. As scholars and historians, our task is to draw at least some in Islam into more objective and scientific attitudes toward the problem of inter-Scriptural relations. There are signs of some hope in this direction, but the path is not easy since the whole issue of what Quranic revelation is, and is not, will be found to be involved.

v

Imagination only need go a little further to realize the bearing of Christian textual and other criticism upon this situation. Educated Muslims are not unaware of the prolonged discussion in Christianity about the Bible. If very few have ever penetrated first-hand into that discussion or taken pains to acquire the necessary Hebrew and Greek disciplines which it requires, many have heard of Renan, Strauss, Bauer, and Kirsopp Lake. Not a few Muslim apologists welcome the suggestion that perhaps historical Christianity ought rather to be called "Paulinism." They are familiar with the hypothesis that a simple Galilean teacher was unwarrantably transformed into the Christ of the Creed—a hypothesis which, if established, would coincide in large measure with the Muslim picture of Jesus. This involvement of the Quranic Jesus in the discussions that have so long occupied Christian and secular scholars in the New Testament field have naturally sharpened Muslim interest in their studies. But unfortunately it cannot be said that the interest has yet produced a full or sustained study of Christ in which all the accumulated evidence on the subject is sifted and assessed. Rather the Muslim attitude in general has been to take the mere fact of this New Testament criticism as demonstrative proof that the Christian Scriptures are unreliable. Not understanding the demand for utter scientific liberty behind such studies, the average Muslim conversant with them assumes that quite evidently even Christians are all at sea about their Scriptures. He accepts without more ado the indication that the New Testament lacks the undisputed validity of the Qur'ān.

Furthermore, he finds the numerous versions of the Christian Scriptures bewildering and suspects in their multiplicity a confirmation of his doubts. It must be remembered that Muslims have only begun in the second quarter of this twentieth century to take kindly to Quranic translation in non-Islamic languages because numbers of non-Muslim translators had been at work. Consequently the Muslim mind does not readily appreciate variant renderings of Scripture, nor the idea that the essential revelation might require the suggestiveness of different versions before it is fully understood. We hope that with growing realization of how language is related to thought, these grounds of suspicion about the Bible will diminish and disappear. But meanwhile they persist as a source of unthinking surmise that the Christian Scriptures are somehow not what they claim to be.

There are certain other sources of misunderstanding when we try to express the Christian possession of the Scriptures to Muslims. One has arisen in the course of Christian missionary insistence on the Bible in the past. It concerns the fulfillment of prophecy. Early Christian apologists from Al-Kindi and John of Damascus used the argument that whereas Christ was prophetically foretold, Muhammad was not. The argument was popular down to the nineteenth century and, to Christians using it, it seemed valid and undeniable. But the Muslim counter-argument was not far to seek. It relied in part upon corruption and affirmed that prophecies about Muhammad were lacking only because they were suppressed. But they were not all suppressed. The Old and New Testaments do contain foretellings of Muhammad. The corruption of these Scriptures is not total. They have their valid parts and the Muslim is ready to adduce these on the basis of the essential oneness of all Scriptures. The Qur'ān itself exhorts him to consult those volumes antecedent to the Qur'ān. In doing so, he believes himself able, and also commanded, to identify those passages in the existing Bible which can bear positive Muslim exegesis. He will gladly demonstrate to the Christian where his own Bible foretells, describes, and commends Muhammad.

So it comes about that there is considerable Muslim exegesis of the Old and New Testament in a Muslim sense. It is as if the writers say: "Far from being unprophesied, Muhammad is amply foretold in your own Scriptures." The exegesis involved may often seem dubious and remote, but given the Muslim presuppositions and a certain inventiveness it can be given some semblance of plausibility. These Muslim interpretations of the Bible make a further demand upon Christian patience and ministry. Hindi and Parsee Scriptures have also been used in the same sense.[2]

The most painful and inclusive example of the problem is the familiar word translated "the Comforter" in St. John's Gospel: παρακλητος. It has the same consonantal sequence as the Greek word περικλυτος meaning "one worthy of praise." There is not the slightest textual reason for reading περικλυτος instead of παρακλητος in the New Testament. But the root from which the name "Muhammad" is derived in Arabic with its other forms —"Ahmad" and "Mahmūd"—means "a praised one" and corresponds roughly with περικλυτος. It has, therefore, been suggested, and it is widely held in Muslim circles, that the promise of the Paraclete means Muhammad, the subsequent Prophet. The change of the vowels by which "Paraclete" came to be read is then an example of Christian perversion. This charge and the Muslim alteration have no basis exegetically. Nor does the sense of the passage bear the Muslim rendering. But it is well to remember that the interpretation arises, in the end, not from exegesis but from presupposition. However painful the necessity, the Christian must cheerfully shoulder the task of distinguishing clearly between Muhammad and the Holy Spirit, and of appreciating how it comes about that the Muslim can be so confidently confused at this point.

There remains one further point to be kept in view when trying to relate the Christian Scriptures to the Muslim mind. Some differences between Islam and the Biblical faith may be explained by the former as due to abrogation. This is the doctrine that later revelation supersedes earlier revelation—a view held to obtain even within the Qur'ān itself.[3] Some Biblical statement may be entirely free of corruption, and yet be no longer valid. The full implications of this doctrine are too wide to discuss here. It explains the Muslim confidence that the Bible has nothing to add to the Qur'ān and that the latter is sufficient without the former. One need not defer too seriously to a faith which one's own has surpassed.

The Bible is from this point of view a treasure unexplored because it is thought of as possessed. It is a prisoner who cannot state his case because it is thought to have been already decided. In this situation, the Christian must rely on the inherent worth of the Scriptures, and press for a new attention to their contents. It may be that even faith in abrogation can be persuaded to show critically the sense in which the abrogated is perfected in the abrogator, and to study the former if only for this purpose. In any event, the Scriptures are capable of proving themselves an unpredictable treasure—a prisoner who, like Paul, can make a hearing even in his bonds. But in this case it can hardly be, without the intelligent and discerning service of those who appreciate how great "a prince imprisoned lies."

B. INTERPRETING THE PERSON OF JESUS

VI

"He does not beget and is not begotten," says the Qur'ān (Surah cxii. 3) in formal rejection of the doctrine of Christ as the Son of God. To allow such a doctrine is to "associate" a man with God, to deify the human and so lift it to the status of the worshipful which belongs only to God. It is to commit the supreme sin against the basic assertion of the Muslim *Shahādah* or Creed, that there is no god except God. Though the Qur'ān allows the Virgin Birth of Jesus, it is implacable in its opposition to the belief that the One so born is Divine.

Here, then, is another area of Christian interpretation with no escape from its demands. A simple reassertion of the Christian doctrine of Christ will not suffice. Nor do we circumvent the difficulty by transferring the emphasis to doctrines of God. For these, as we shall see, are inevitably involved already. Indeed the doctrine of the Incarnation is already a doctrine of God and is rejected by the Muslim on that ground. Islam does not so much resist the faith of Christ as "God manifest in the flesh," because it is unsuited to Christ, but rather because it is unworthy of God. Hence we do not dispense with the problem of explaining Christ to Muslims by taking what some might call a "theocentric" approach. Rather the more effectively we are

286

"theocentric" the more we find the problem with us. It was not for nought that Jesus said: "Ye believe in God, believe also in Me" (John xiv. 1).

Nor again can we escape the problem by shifting our emphasis to the human Jesus. To concentrate only on elements in Jesus that Muslims can at once accept is to fail Jesus Himself. We cannot leave Him in Galilee as if He were no more than a Prophet, when He Himself refused to stay there, but went on to Jerusalem to be crucified by men who would not have molested a mere prophet. We cannot interpret Him apart from the terms of His own understanding of Himself. These include those claims which gave rise to the Church's faith in His Divinity. Moreover, to be content only with the Prophet-Teacher would not be to do justice to the Muslim's need. The Christ Jesus of the historic faith is an inescapable Figure. It is He we must present to the world of Islam, in the fullness of His relation to the sins and bewilderments of men and in the fullness of His relevance for our understanding of God. Yet how we are to do this remains a problem and a burden. We must learn to communicate at all costs what it is to us to recognize in Christ the Incarnate Saviour, and we must do so in terms that Muslims can understand.

Our first step, no doubt, will be to convey to them the character and personality of Jesus as seen in the Gospels. Our surest way, supposing we have overcome the Scriptural difficulties just outlined, will be to acquaint Muslims with the New Testament narrative. Difficulties of expression await us in them all. St. Mark, for example, begins with the phrase "Jesus, the Son of God." The Muslim anathema is waiting at the first verse. This is unavoidable since the evangelists wrote from the standpoint of the matured faith. It is possible, and in some contexts wise, to use selected passages which allow the Muslim to make contact with the actual Jesus, without immediately provoking his resistance. But we do well to indicate that such passages are selective and introductory. They may well defer, they can never supplant, our fuller task.

Our final confidence must lie in the fact that the disciples and evangelists themselves came to their full faith as to the identity of Jesus from their experience of Him apart from those convictions. Our aim will be to lead Muslims by the same path: to let them begin where the disciples began. The final explanation of the Personality can hardly antedate its discovery. No Muslim is more a monotheist than were Peter, James, and John in Nazareth. We shall not err if we suppose that the order of Muslim experience will be the same as theirs. "What manner of man is this?" is a question Jesus is capable of compelling upon every generation, however predisposed they may be against the ultimate answer. Let us wait patiently. The confession: "Thou art the Christ, Son of the Living God" is not the outset of faith. We have no New Testament right to require orthodoxy, before we have presented Jesus.

The measure of what the presentation involves has already been indicated in the discussion of the Quranic Christ. Enlarging greatly that account by all those aspects of Jesus which remain unknown to Islam, we may lead into the Christian faith as to Who He is. We must remember that the revelation of Divinity is also the revelation of humanity. Christ is, to us, the measure of that fullness of human life which is the Divine intention and which is actualized when the human is perfectly related to the Divine. It must be made clear that the Christian doctrine about Jesus is not an imposition upon the facts but rather a conclusion from the facts. It must be our desire and prayer that Muslims so become acquainted with the real Christ that they come to understand why Christianity has explained Him in terms of the historic creeds. The whole faith as to Christ must not be left to seem a mere dogmatism or a piece of doctrinal subtlety, but rather a reasonable and legitimate ground of explanation. It is the Holy Spirit, through the Scriptures and the Christian commendation of Christ, Who leads the mind into that conviction about Jesus which compelled itself upon His first disciples. Our purpose is to put all men in the way of those facts and on the path of that experience, by which men first learned to speak in awed tones of the Son of God. The faith about Christ must never be dissociated from Him Whom it explains and from Whom it derives. What we are concerned first to communicate is not a doctrine but the experience which made it.

But when we have done all in our power to acquaint men with the real Jesus and His words and works, His meaning and ministry, we still have to explain the faith about him from the Godward side. If we are compelled in the earthly presence of Jesus to acknowledge a Divine quality, the meaning of this human manifestation of God still has to be related to what we believe about God. Or in New Testament language, what is meant by referring to God as "the Father of our Lord Jesus Christ"? (Ephesians 1.3.)

The answer must be stated as far as possible in terms which the Muslim already understands: the double belief about God—that He reveals and that He is Sovereign. We do not, at the outset, introduce the concept of Divine Love or the attendant mysteries of the Divine will. We can be well content with the two basic Muslim affirmations about God—that He reveals and that He is Sovereign.

It cannot be overemphasized that the Christian understanding of Christ is the Christian understanding of revelation: "God who at sundry times and in divers manners spake in time past unto the fathers by the prophets hath in these last days spoken unto us in His Son" (Hebrews i. 1). "By the prophets," "in the Son"; these are the preparatory and the culminating phases of the same enterprise of revelation. Against a background of interpreted history and into a concrete situation came a human life, a Personality, bringing into final focus and into unmistakable form the revelation of God. It was a revelation that was verbal in that He taught and preached, actual in that He lived and suffered, personal in that *He* was involved, and not only what He said. This aspect we can perhaps describe as "situational." Bethlehem, Galilee, the Well of Sychar, the Temple at Jerusalem, Bethany, and Golgotha brought into demonstration the character of the Person.

This, according to Jesus Himself and the faith He generated, was the Divine strategy. It may well be that the Muslim will not accept this account of the matter. But it is our first duty that he should know what it is he rejects. He looks upon our faith about Christ as an imposition upon the human teacher that offends against his place in the economy of revelation. But in fact it *is* His place in the economy of revelation. It would be blasphemy to turn a teacher into God; but to recognize that is not to deny that God Himself might come to teach. The sad fact about Islam is that it has refused the Christian faith about Christ on the wrong premise, on the basis, that is, of something which that faith does not say. We have not made a teacher into God, we have believed that God Himself undertook in Christ the education of mankind unto Himself.

It must be made plain that the faith about Christ is set in that confidence in Divine revelation which Islam holds, but represents a different concept of how revelation is achieved. Here, perhaps, it may be added that it takes God to reveal God. This profound truth finds some echo in Muslim thought itself in the saying that "God reveals Himself by, or in, Himself." If God is personal, knowledge of Him must be a personal revelation. He can never be only propositional. One does not know a friend as one knows Euclid's 40th Proposition. For a friend is more than a fact. "Who God is" lies deeper than the fact "that He is." And the "Who" cannot be fully known except in Self-communication. Words, teaching, ideas, propositions, must become "the Word"—experience, fellowship—before revelation is complete. It is this ultimate of revelation which Christianity finds in Jesus. God in revelation is God in Christ. Revelation is not simply recorded in a book; it is embodied in a Person. Is it not more fully, more appropriately, more effectively, revelation for that reason? The question may not be readily appreciated by the Muslim accustomed to the idea of a Book as the point of revelatory impact. But it must be made clear that what Christians believe about Christ belongs to the same realm of belief in a God Who does not leave humanity in darkness. The difference lies in a contrast in belief as to how God most fittingly dispels it.

When we speak of "God the Son" we mean God in the act of revelation. When we speak of Beethoven the musician, or Leonardo da Vinci the artist, we mean these men in their full personality in particular capacity, capacities which do not pre-

clude their having others, but yet involving them wholly. It is
necessary in the Muslim context, though not in the Christian,
to insist that the expression "Son of God" excludes all paternity
in the physical sense. On Christian premises the latter is unthinkable. The phrase means that Christ is God in Self-revelation, an activity which begets or generates an historical personality, wherein what God is in revelatory love, He is also known
to be in revelatory action. The Father begets the Son in the
sense that His "will" to reveal is translated into act. But all is
of Him and from Him and by Him. God is at once revealer
and revealed—the Father and the Son. By this faith in Christ
we recognize simply that when God reveals God what He gives
us is Himself. Our faith in the Divinity of Christ is not, as the
Muslim has believed, an affront to God, an offense against His
Unity, a supreme sin in doctrinal form. On the contrary it is
the genesis and the ground of our faith that the One Living
and Eternal God has Himself undertaken to tell men of Himself.

VII

We turn to the second fundamental conviction of Muslim theology, namely that God is Sovereign. For this too constitutes an
objection to the Muslim mind which can and must be turned
into an explanation of the Christian doctrine. Suppose, as we
have argued, that God reveals Himself. Is He likely to do so
in human life? Would not this be unworthy of His glory? So
runs the opposition in Muslim thought, with its constant sense
of a great gulf between the Divine and the human. It is true
that the gulf is bridged, since otherwise neither revelation nor
religion would be feasible. But God bridges it by intermediaries—by archangels and angels, by prophets and teachers who are
the means of His sending down of law and guidance for mankind. He does not bridge it of Himself. He sends rather than
comes. He gives rather than brings. To conceive of God in
Christ is for the Muslim mind an unworthy thing. God does
not become man. If He did, something unthinkable would have
happened to His Divinity. Muslims have resisted the Christian

interpretation of Christ on these grounds in the belief that they are safeguarding the Divine majesty.

Faced with this contradiction the Christian is compelled to look more closely at the sovereignty that is protected in this way. Are we right in forbidding anything to God which He does not forbid Himself? If God is truly greater than all, will there be things He will not do which we can identify and against which we can insist? May we perhaps be in the position of prescribing limitations to God, or of defending His sovereignty in ways He does not approve? May we be limiting God's sovereignty in the very act of, supposedly, defending it? These are the questions that arise. Is an enterprise of revelation, in its most appropriate form for mankind, an act unworthy of God? Must He not be left to determine the steps of His own purpose and shall we say to Him "Nay"? And if so, then we can never say that the Incarnation could not be. If it cannot be denied as a possibility, then any claims to occurrence cannot be ruled out in advance. They must be investigated as a matter of historical evidence. Such investigation brings us back to Christ in human history.

The burden of all these questions, put into the affirmative, is that what the Muslim desires to assert, namely Divine sovereignty, is in fact most gloriously in operation in Jesus Christ, "the Word made flesh." For is that sovereignty truly sovereign which fails to take action against the empire of ignorance and evil in mankind? Thought on the Incarnation here merges imperceptibly as it must into the Cross, since it was for redemption that God visited mankind. When we present Christ we ask Muslims to believe, not less but more, in the undefeated sovereignty of God. To believe that He stooped to our need and weakness is not to make Him less, but more, the God of all power and glory. With all patience, born of faith in this very sovereignty, we must invite men to seek and find in Christ the demonstration that God is God alone, and that all contrary powers are gloriously vanquished and subdued. For *Islām*, as a term, means the submission of the believer to the law and will of God. It is a relationship in which He must be all in all. God being "all in all" is the New Testament summary of the whole meaning of Christ. In either case the sovereignty and the submission belong together. Recognizing in Christ the Divine initiative of love manifesting its supremacy over all that otherwise would enslave men, the Christian makes his submission. It is a submission of worship and of confession. It is his *Islām* and Bethlehem is where it begins.

Our concentration here on the two Muslim themes of God as revealing and ruling does not mean that there are not other clues in Islam to the interpretation of God in Christ. These two are central and must be related to what we have in trust. Though God's relationship to man in Islam is basically that of law, a deep sense of the Divine mercy and favor is there. It has been intensely developed in Sufism. The Qur'ān itself speaks of the Muslims as being those upon whom God has been gracious, "not those with whom Thou art angry" (Surah i. 7). God is the merciful, who both cherishes and bestows mercy—a mercy which many Muslims down the ages have sought with strong entreaty and penitent petition. We must learn to relate what we find in Christ to all those aspirations, to the Muslim yearning for what lies beyond law, to forgiveness, renewal, and true piety. It may be said, in general, about the Divine mercy, as Islam conceives it, that it remains unpredictable. It is bestowed freely and in relation to the practices of Muslim religion. But it does not come forth to embody itself in a redemptive enterprise, or to articulate itself in inclusive events where men may know it indubitably. The belief that God is merciful in Islam admits of no doctrine of assurance, nor of sonship, so that men may say: "We know that we have passed from death unto life" (1 John iii. 14). "It may be"—"it may well be"—is the language we must use rather than "It is." We have, therefore, to present Christ as the focal point of the Divine compassion, the place where the Divine mercy fulfills itself in history, through One Who is both its pledge and its means, One in Whom we know God as forgiving and ourselves as forgiven. The assurance this active mercy allows us is not presumption. For it is God Himself Who, in Christ, leaves us no room for doubt. But, considered as the token of an ever-dependable mercy, the Incarnation is inseparable from the Cross, whither we must now turn.

C. INTERPRETING THE CROSS

VIII

"They did not kill him, they did not crucify him, it was made to appear so to them" (Surah iv. 157). So runs the Qur'ān in its familiar disavowal of the crucifixion. Once again the Christian interpreter has to begin from an explicit rebuttal of what he has to proclaim, and once again he must somehow turn resistance into understanding. But how?

In what follows it must be insisted that we have neither space nor intention for any comprehensive exposition of the Christian faith regarding Christ crucified—"the power of God unto salvation." Rather the aim is to investigate how best to bear witness to it in face of the Muslim rejection. It is implicit throughout that we must affirm the fact of the Cross always in the same spirit in which Jesus Himself suffered it. We cannot champion the Cross by attitudes which, had Christ taken them, there would be no Cross to proclaim. If we say, "In this sign conquer," it must be only the victory of meekness.

It is well to begin with the actual circumstances in the life and ministry of Jesus from which the crucifixion developed. The Qur'ān does not dispute that the Jews desired to crucify Jesus. The fact that they resisted Him strongly and resented His words is another instance in the Muslim mind of that hostility on the part of gainsayers to which all the prophets from Noah to Muhammad were exposed. The Qur'ān stresses that the messengers of God are always rebutted by the unbelievers, whom God in the end outwits and defeats. It is important to keep in view this fact of opposition to Jesus on the part of His contemporaries, even though the Qur'ān does not explain the underlying sources of it, in its profound silence about the content of our Lord's teaching. For this hostility shaped the situation from which Jesus was rescued, it is said, at the last from would-be murderers who crucified one—possibly Judas Iscariot—whom they were made to mistake for Him. Another suffered the full brunt of a hostility that was intended for Christ.

But why this belief in a Divinely arranged escape? Why this

strange rescue of the Christ? Here, it must be said, the motives are not historical but dogmatic. It is not that the Muslim is confronted with strong evidence that Jesus in fact circumvented death in this way and that another than He was substituted at the arrest and beyond. On the contrary, there is no such evidence —despite the efforts of several in the Ahmadiyyah Movement to find it in Kashmir. Rather the origin of the assertion about the history lies in the presupposition that hostility to the prophets should not succeed in slaying them. Such a climax would be a Divine failure to sustain them and corroborate their message. Such a failure would be unthinkable. Noah, Abraham, Moses, David, all saw the confusion of their opponents, and the vindication of themselves. Muhammad, though rejected by the idolatrous Meccans, lived to capture Mecca and destroy the idols. So also Jesus. God will not, cannot, leave His servants to suffer ignominy, nor allow their detractors a final triumph. So Jesus did not suffer. It was more appropriate to the nature of things, Divine and prophetic, that Judas should have taken His place—a proper end for him, a manifest outwitting of the Jews and a fitting climax for Jesus. How far indeed from the sense of the Gospels and "the cup which my Father hath given Me."

Truly, here is a gulf to be bridged by the interpreter—but one whose sources are in prejudgment not in history. A recent Muslim writer on Jesus in the Gospels remarks when he comes to the Garden of Gethsemane "Here the role of history ends and the role of credal faith begins." [4] He means that what happens after the arrest, history does not tell; faith, perhaps credulity, take over the story. But history is plain enough. If the Muslim does not follow it, it is because his prejudgment has intervened arbitrarily to break its course and to disallow there what it wills to reject.

There was the opposition, as we have seen. If its culmination in Christ's being crucified is a subsequent invention (as it can only be if it is not fact), did the Church then invent the faith which made it, creating the history which in fact created it? Was the historic Church, of which Islam must and does take account, constituted only in the teaching of Christ? Were the disciples only preachers of an ethic and not also bearers of a life out of death? Why then the Holy Communion commemorating, from the beginning, sufferings which never happened? And why the new Sunday, for "the third day" of the Resurrection became the first day of the week? Is historic Christianity, in short, explicable on the hypothesis of a substitute crucifixion?

But the whole matter goes deeper still. Apart from accounting for the Church and its genesis in faith in the Resurrection after the Cross, there is the deeper question which takes us beyond history into the thought of God, from which the Muslim rewriting of the Cross derives. What are we to say of the nature of a God Who behaves in this way or of the character of a Christ Who permits another—even if a Judas—to suffer the consequences of an antagonism His own teaching has aroused against Himself? Is this kind of victory the worthiest in prophets of God? The antagonism is there, on the Muslim hypothesis. The question is: What does God do, what does Jesus do, with it?

The answer unmistakably is that He suffers it. The Muslim reinterpretation offends deeply against all that the Gospels disclose about the self-giving of Jesus, His awareness of the inevitability of suffering and His surrender to the necessity. "The Son of Man" He said "must suffer." From beginning to end, He resisted the temptation—in the wilderness, on the road, in the garden, even on the Cross itself—the temptation to avoid the climax, to abandon Jerusalem, "to come down from the Cross." The Quranic account has turned those temptations into history, has rather abolished them, in a surrender to the easy way, with the added injustice of a substitute of a Judas. It has thus made havoc of the manifest continuity between what Jesus taught and what Jesus suffered. Though far from its intention, it has discredited the message in thus discrediting the Messenger. In conforming Christ to its own conception of the successful Prophet, Islam has robbed Him of Himself, transformed Him into an unrecognizable Jesus. It affirms that one was made to resemble Him. Rather—more tragically—He no longer resembles Himself. The Jesus of the Gospels is undiscernible in the shadowy figure who is made to quit the path of His own teaching and His own *islām,* or surrender, to the redeeming purpose of God. Truly here at the Muslim Cross we must say, as was said of old: "They know not what they do"—as true of philosophical rescuers as of Roman soldiers.

But what also of the character of God? The God of the Muslim Cross—of a substituted sufferer and an abstracted Prophet—is the *deus-ex-machina* God of the old Latin phrase; a God who turns the tables, opens the trapdoor, and confounds His foes; a God who deals not in the sure, if slow, processes of a moral order where love wins by suffering, but in the arbitrary assertion of the inscrutable. Yet it must be remembered that the Muslim rewriting of the crucifixion story is in the interests of God's glory. God, it is held, cannot be honored in the victory of a prophet's foes. He cannot be thought not to rescue His servant from such a people as the Jews. So the question moves into the realm of what is most appropriately Divine, what is most truly consonant with the Divine glory. Indeed, we may say, what makes God God and glory glory? How is God characterized as God? So deep do the issues go which are raised by the Muslim attitude to the Cross. It may be that the most we can do at the outset is to clarify what is here involved and simply let the issues stand. For beyond this point, argument is inappropriate. We are left with simple witness and the conviction we cannot enforce but only explain that "God was in Christ reconciling the world unto Himself."

IX

Beyond controversy, then, what does explaining involve? How does the Cross save? What is the meaning of the Resurrection? How was "God in Christ"? All witness to the faith of Christ crucified must surely speak out of the experience of salvation. We must show what the preaching of the Cross has meant in our own lives and proclaim the discovery of power and peace which has been made by multitudes through the faith that Christ died for them. Here Bunyan's pilgrim, with his burden unloosed at the Cross, becomes the parable of its significance in all the centuries. The terms in which this truth is expressed may differ, as do the New Testament metaphors themselves—liberation from bondage, ransom from sin, illumination of darkness, deliverance from evil, translation from enmity, and the rest. But whatever the language, the unanimity of confession leads to the Cross as the place of the transaction. Our task is to bear witness among all men to the fact of the power of Christ crucified in transforming human souls, breaking the entail of wrong and emancipating formerly selfish lives into the service of God and men. Behind every enterprise of Christian *caritas,* behind innumerable lives of sacrificial ministry, obscure or famed, lies the attractive and compulsive power of the Cross of Christ. Islam must share with all men in this witness. The question: "How does Christ save?" must be answered out of the experience that He does.

Yet the Muslim has a right to an honest explanation of what Christianity believes about the relation of the Cross to its consequences in human life and character. For this we must invite him to return to where we began—to the opposition of ungodliness, which as we have seen, Islam admits but deprives of its climax. Christian history believes that Jesus suffered the full length of that hostility, and that He did so willingly, as the price of loyalty to His own message. Jerusalem was the stronghold of those bigotries and evils against which in His teaching Christ had set His face. How, then, could His teaching remain out of relation to its most marked antithesis? Christ refused to stay in the safety of Galilee and went up to Jerusalem. But His going there—He being what He was and Jerusalem what Jerusalem was —could not but be costly. "Behold," He said, "we are going up to Jerusalem and all things that are written concerning the Son of Man shall be accomplished" (Luke xviii. 31).

This final and inclusive encounter Jesus faced, in full loyalty to His own doctrines, not rendering evil for evil, nor countering hatred with guile. Out of it only the Cross could emerge, if Jesus was not to unleash violence, appeal to force, or make Himself a King. Either He would withhold His witness or incur its consequences. Either He would resist those consequences by the only kind of action open to the resister, or He would suffer. These alternatives are plain and clear in the consciousness of Jesus in the Gospels. He chose to suffer. The Cross, as an event, is no artificial scheme. It is what happens when a love like Christ's encounters a world like Jerusalem.

Herein Jerusalem is the prototype of all. The Cross bore its superscription in Hebrew, Greek, and Latin. The human forces which made it what it was, as an act of men, are common to all humanity. A coalition of dark but representative human sins accomplished the death of Christ. There were political and personal sins of convenience and security in Pilate; ecclesiastical sins of prestige and pride in the chief Priests; social sins of compromise and brutality in the mob—all necessary to each other as allies in an evil deed. It is this representative character of the Cross as something that men did which is so clearly stamped upon the story. We recognize Pilate, Judas, and Caiaphas in our own hearts and in the soul of all peoples. It happened in Palestine, but it was what the whole world did. The Governor and the soldiers may have been Roman, the accusers Jews, but it was humanity in its waywardness to which they belonged. All understanding of the Cross must begin with the actual history and must recognize in the event, as a human deed, the representative expression of what men do in their wrongness. Before we can really participate in the Cross as redeeming, we must see ourselves involved in its revelation of humanity. It is the place where we discover what manner of men we are—we and our fellows.

But if the Cross was in these ways the act of men, it was also the act of Christ. How did He behave confronted with the worst that men could do? In fidelity to the course He had freely chosen, He endured the Cross and suffered the contradiction of sinners against Himself with forgivingness on His lips and in His heart. And from that forgivingness forgiveness flows. Had Jesus died in resentment or in blasphemy, in imprecation or sullen silence, there would have been no redemption. Only by bearing, does the Redeemer bear away the sin of the world. The words from the Cross—words which would never have been uttered had Jesus allowed Himself to be mercifully stupefied by the gall and the reed—illuminate the inner nature of His passion and proclaim the Cross as a supreme deed of redemptive sacrifice. Truly "with His stripes we are healed." Here we find a quality of love which makes an end of evil because it freely takes all its consequences upon itself. In revenge and hatred evil is perpetuated. In pardon and long-suffering it finds its term. For those who will acknowledge their inclusion here such redemption means a new beginning, where "the old things are passed away."

The meaning of the Cross as the redeeming deed of Christ will always defy a complete expression in theology. We can only put men in the way of its fullness. The majesty of Christ's suffering must be somehow communicated: His self-giving; His insistence on going to Jerusalem; His refusal to take ample opportunities to escape; His preoccupation with prayer, not flight, when Judas was already concerting His arrest; His silence before Pilate when a few words could have set the mob about his ears; His patient acceptance of the necessity of the passion as the price of love. All these take their place in the story. The Cross was no afterthought, no sudden tragedy. It was the conscious choice of Christ. It was what Christ did with His mission in the world, and with the accumulated evil of mankind. As the perfect fulfillment of the one it became the effective redemption of the other. If the Cross shows us what men are, it shows us unmistakably what Christ is. To disallow this climax, to preserve Christ from the Cross and forbid the Cross to Christ, is to separate what Christ, in being Himself, has for ever joined together.

Christian faith about the Cross goes on to believe that they were joined together in Christ's obedience because they were also joined together in the eternal purpose. If the Cross is to be seen as the act of men and the act of Christ, it is also understood in Christianity as, in a tremendous sense, the act of God. "God was in Christ reconciling the world unto Himself" (II Corinthians v. 19). Christ's obedience in the Cross is the fulfillment of the Father's will. All lies within the love of God. To see this is to be preserved from all mistaken theories that conceive of Christ as somehow placating a propitiating God from without, as if God needed some persuasion to the forgiveness of men. No! Rather the suffering of Christ expresses the Divine Love already active towards sinful man. For in every evil situation love must suffer. The great prophets saw this truth clearly. Jeremiah in some measure experienced it in his own person. The great sufferer for his people, described so graphically in Isaiah liii, was said there to have been "wounded for our transgressions." He was a vicarious sufferer because He took upon Himself, in all their pain and sorrow, the sins of His generation. The love and sacrifice wherein He suffered accorded with the very nature of God, so that it could be said: "The Lord hath laid on Him the iniquity of us all" (Isaiah liii. 6). Evil matters to God. It matters beyond our imagining, to His holiness and His compassion. Wherever by love an evil situation is redeemed, God is there. In Christ at the Cross that whole Divine concern for human waywardness, bearing its consequences in a great single deed, is seen in cosmic fullness. "Behold the Lamb of God which beareth away the sin of the world" (John i. 29). Here, the mercy of God accomplishes the forgiveness of the world within the pattern of suffering which is the necessity of the Divine nature.

All who have sought to express this truth have come to a sense of the poverty of all words and find themselves cast back upon the inclusive saying: "God was in Christ reconciling. . . ." The Cross is finally what God does, answering what men did there, and accomplishing His purpose in what Christ did. All preaching of the Cross is thus the proclamation of the inward meaning of man's act, Christ's act, God's act, meeting in a single event, where for all time the nature of sin and the victory of grace are disclosed.

x

What else may help us, under the Holy Spirit, to convey this "word of the Cross" to the Muslim? The power of the story itself: the illumination of the great Old Testament Prophets of redemptive suffering whom Islam neglects; the recognition in Islam that forgiveness is at once better and harder than revenge.[5] We must insist that there is nothing of truth in the thought that it is immoral for one to suffer for another. It happens. And when we are ready to submit to its power and live in its terms, it redeems. We must also banish all idle thoughts about the interplay of wills. Would there have been no Cross if Judas had not been a traitor and Pilate a coward? If not, are their treachery and cowardice responsible for the redemption of the world? These thoughts arise from misunderstanding of the inter-will character of this event and indeed of all events. The Cross has to do with sin. Sin sets the situation, but what love does in that situation is love's alone. One cannot rightly attribute the genesis of Islam to the idolaters in Mecca.

In segments of Islam there are far-reaching ideas of sacrifice, notably among Shī'ahs, and the sense that suffering innocently borne marks a place of Divine favor and power. Thus the remembrance of 'Alī, Hasan, and Husain may help to illuminate in some measure the Christian awareness of the Cross. The tragedy of Karbala when Husain and his retinue were massacred is interpreted in Shī'ah Passion Plays as a voluntary and redemptive sacrifice for the sins of Muslims. Husain is pictured as having acquired intercessory powers on behalf of his people by the effusion of his blood, and the thought of his resignation unto death stirs deep devotion.

But to mention these aids to interpretation is to realize that in truth the Cross has no parallel. It may be best to wait for men to see it by its own light. In other senses perhaps the very contrast is the clue. In the main body of Islam, outside the Shī'ahs and Sufism, the assumption has generally been that God's cause triumphs manifestly. The battles in early Islam are almost uniformly explained by Muslim writers as necessary to the survival of Islam. Had they not been undertaken the infant faith would have been destroyed. The hypothesis clearly is that force is valid in the Prophet's hands and name. So ultimately Muhammad rode into a prostrate Mecca and by that victory clinched the submission of the tribes. Jesus in Jerusalem chose to refuse external patterns of success. They were within His reach and to His hand. He rejected them for the way of the Cross. This contrast must be understood by all who would enter into the meaning of the Cross. It is all the more marked because the situations of Jesus in Jerusalem and Muhammad in Mecca are in some measure analogous. Both faced an opposition to religious truth based on prestige and pride. Both were rejected as upstarts, disruptive of the *status quo*. The Pharisees and the Quraish—though otherwise highly contrasted—are thus far alike. But there the similarity ends. Jesus did not conquer Jerusalem. He suffered outside its walls. The Cross became His throne.

It is necessary to present this contrast tenderly and without reproach. Until it is understood, the Cross as the key to the

Kingdom of Heaven can never be seen in its fullness. There are some Muslims who think Jesus pitiable in His very choice. But such voices are rare and might well be rarer had not historic Christendom so often taken the oppressive way and forsaken the pattern of the Cross. Freed to draw by its own force, the Cross remains the magnet of the souls of men. When the contrasted patterns of Christendom are cited let it be remembered that, though these reproaches must have their reckoning, it is the Christ of the Cross Whom we are calling men to seek and find. Faiths must surely first be understood in their architects, before they are assessed in their followers.

This then is the word of the Cross by which the Church lives. There always remains about it that which to some is an offense and foolishness. The recognition of the Cross as the place of pardon and peace, of Divine mercy in action for man's remaking, comes only in the Holy Spirit. Our task is to be wise and patient instruments of that Illuminator of the hearts, in Whose light men see light and through Whom they recognize as the Lover of their souls the One Who suffered and rose again.

> *Hath He diadem as monarch*
> *That His brow adorns?*
> *Yea, a crown—in very surety*
> *But of thorns.*

XI

What of the Resurrection, inseparable from the Cross, both in our Lord's anticipation and in the faith of His Church? Islam believes in a resurrection yet to be. When the Qur'ān reports Jesus speaking while an infant of the day of His death it refers to the future. Jesus did not die and without the Cross there is no victory. Ours it is to explain the Resurrection as the issue of the nature and quality of Christ's death. An event of unmistakable significance, it corroborates, vindicates, demonstrates, the ultimacy of the love in which Christ died, the inclusiveness and finality of His victory, and the identity of the Sufferer Himself. Because *He* died *as* He did, He rose again. The Resurrection is not an arbitrary finale to a situation which otherwise would have

303

been different. It is the intrinsic victory of Christ as crucified and of the Cross as Christ bore it, a victory which seals man's redemption and opens the doors of eternal life. It is the coming of the King of glory into His own, having proved Himself the King of love. Jesus and the Resurrection thus became the apostolic Gospel.

No doubt there are matters of historical evidence which need to enter into the presentation. For it was certainly not on the hypothesis of a resurrection yet to be that the Church was generated.[6] But important as these are, the crux of the interpreter's duty lies in the Cross where we have concentrated our thought. Was not Jesus recognized as risen because the disciples saw "the print of the nails"? To have by-passed the Cross is to remain unaware of Easter. The garden where there was an empty tomb is not reached save by way of the garden of the agony. We must strive to lead Muslims back to that interrupted pathway if we would bring them to the opening of the everlasting doors.

D. INTERPRETING THE CHRISTIAN DOCTRINE OF GOD

XII

There is a prayer in Surah xx. 27-28 which might well find an echo in the heart of a Christian who strives after an interpretation to Muslims of the Christian understanding of God. "Loose the knot from my tongue that they may understand what I say." For here Muslim susceptibilities are so many and Christian expression so difficult.

In one sense the interpretation in this exposition has already been made. For it is impossible to discuss the Christian Scriptures, the Person of Jesus, and the Cross without involving and being involved in doctrines of God and making these explicit. True as this is, there is need to gather together the full theological implications of these themes and present them concisely and in line with Muslim attitudes. In so doing certain other important points may be clarified.

It is, indeed, only this truth of the implicit theology which has allowed us to defer specific discussion of the doctrine of God until now. Whereas in his call to the Muslim we followed the muezzin in beginning with the affirmation of the Divine Unity whence all else derives, we are here content to take up the same theme as a sequel to other topics. This is not to suggest that God is not prior and supreme, the Eternal source of all things. It is simply that Christianity believes the Divine fullness to be known in context, in action, and in history, and that, therefore, thought on these may be the nearest and surest way to thought on God. Our exposition does not make God an afterthought. It follows the order of all personal knowledge, moving inward through experience to fellowship and through grace to faith. In the order of being, God is before all things. In the order of knowledge, there is much which properly precedes a full awareness of Him. He is the origin of our knowledge of Him. But within that knowledge He is Himself a culmination. We come to know Him Who always was and eternally is. In any discussion of our coming to know Him, we begin with what He has done in order to move towards what He is. Even the Muslim *Shahādah* itself expresses its great dogma in the form of a disavowal of an earlier and erroneous idea. It is impossible for any doctrine to begin *in vacuo*. The New Testament presupposes the Hebrew background and the creeds presume the New Testament valid.

In turning, then, to study the Christian doctrine of God we are exploring our own presuppositions when we discussed the Scriptures and Christ. There are at the outset two serious sources of misconception. The one is a misapplication of the criterion of simplicity, the other a misconception about terms.

XIII

It is widely thought, and often said, that the Christian doctrine of God is unnecessarily complicated, abstruse, and subtle. "The Father incomprehensible, the Son incomprehensible, the Holy Ghost incomprehensible—the whole idea incomprehensible"—as one wit had it, making crude havoc of the Latin meaning. The Christian faith about God, it is argued, is finally unintelligible: it collapses under its own intricacy. This view can be found expressed in numerous places in contemporary Muslim literature. Not a few Westerners, who have embraced Islam, whether travelers, like H. St. John Philby in Arabia, or disciples of Ahmadiyyah missions and mosques in the West, explain their decision in such terms. Christianity they did not understand because its central doctrines were confusing and elaborate. Islam is readily intelligible and entirely simple. Muhammad 'Alī, in *My Life—A Fragment,* earlier quoted, declares that for Islam a postage stamp would suffice, as far as theology is concerned. "There is no god but God and Muhammad is His Apostle" is all the Muslim's dogma and it makes no great call on his powers of thinking or his credulity.[7]

In view of these attitudes, it is important to make clear that the Christian doctrine of God is not intricate for intricacy's sake or that the issues implicit in its formulation were artificial and unnecessary. It is also important to consider the criterion of simplicity here assumed. "Simple solutions," A. N. Whitehead once declared, "are bogus solutions." Be that as it may, the higher the theme the less likelihood there is that it can be adequately formulated in simple terms. This is not to deny the simple and the unintellectual their awareness of God, or to overlook that such awareness may often come nearer to God than philosophic disquisition. Nor is it to deny that Fathers and theologians, like all experts, have not sometimes fallen into excessive love of their own pursuit of theological learning. This is not the place to attempt a definition of the necessity of formal theology to religion—though it may be observed that it would hardly be Islamic to deny it. But we are concerned to insist that doctrines of God are not properly to be evaluated by the criterion of simplicity. The latter is a mischievous notion as long as it remains itself undefined.

The simplest statement such as "God is One" or "God is Love" is only simple in the sense that subject and predicate are simple words and there are no complicating clauses. These simple statements, however, have a profundity no sincerity can evade or conceal. What the demand for simplicity in these realms is in danger of becoming, perhaps, unwittingly, is a demand for abeyance or, worse, disavowal, of thought. This should be resisted at all costs. Even a little reflection surely makes it clear that doctrines of God are not commendable merely by their ability to go on a postage stamp. Definitions are not quantitatively evaluated.

It seems necessary to make this point plain. The definition of a brick could conceivably be simple and being simple would supposedly be also brief. But the definition of God, though it might conceivably be brief, could hardly be always simple or necessarily be valid because it was either. Simplicity is too nebulous and undefined a quality to be, in this bare sense, a sufficient criterion of a sound theology. To insist on this fact is not to imply that theologians have never been tedious, or that Christian doctrine has never been clumsily expounded. It is to argue that properly understood the Christian doctrine of the Trinity is the formulation of revealed knowledge and personal experience, the continuity of which as a spiritual reality could only be safeguarded in this way. It is easy to join with Carlyle in ridiculing Christendom divided over a diphthong in its definition of Christ. It is profounder to enter with patience into the issue involved and to appreciate that no Church can live in or by a truth it is unable or unwilling to express.

Part, then, of our Christian task in this realm is patiently to dissipate the erroneous notion that Christian theology is a piece of dispensable subtlety encumbering the simplicity of true theism. The Muslim needs to be awakened to the profundity of his own simplicities and the relevance of what he considers the Christian extravagancies. Differences of view about God cannot properly be compared on the ground of comparative simplicity—not if He is truly their subject. The question must always be resolved into: How articulate is the simplicity? That question is only another way of asking: How adequately profound is the doctrine?

XIV

This leads to the second point—the misconception about terms. The Christian faith in God as Father, Son, and Holy Spirit is not a violation of faith in God's Unity. It is a way of understanding that Unity—a way, the Christian would go on to say, of safeguarding that unity. Perhaps our largest duty with the Muslim mind lies just here. For the Muslim, faith in God as Father, Son, and Holy Spirit does violence to the Divine Unity. For the Christian, it expresses and illuminates the Unity. The Muslim sees the doctrine of the Trinity as incompatible with belief in the Unity of God. The Christian finds these not merely compatible but interdependent. The issue, Christianly understood, is not Trinity and Unity, but Trinity and atheism. The Church's faith in God is defined in this way as the form in which such a faith is finally possible in this world of mystery and evil.

This claim will be the burden of the exposition that follows, when it is hoped it will be sufficiently sustained—though, clearly, no full presentation of the Christian doctrine about God, either philosophically or historically, is possible in this context. If our aim is to help interpret that faith to Muslims we must begin with this plea that the Muslim estimate and ponder the Christian Trinity, not as a violation of Unity, but as a form of its expression. We cannot proceed except on the understanding that we are both firmly and equally believers that God is One. We both stand squarely in the Hebrew tradition: "The Lord our Lord is ONE Lord." We are not discussing theism and tritheism. Christianity is concerned only with the first. Muslims who debate tritheism are not discussing Christianity. Where we differ is over how to define and understand the Divine Unity. What lies outside that issue is irrelevant to Christianity.

Here, before we go further, let it be said that "debate" about God is unseemly. It is un-Islamic and un-Christian as long as it is querulous, assertive, or doctrinaire. We are not concerned to bring cases to victory but minds to meeting. Though, where reason is involved, we have a right to be discursive and a duty to be positive, it is clear that thoughts of God can never be competitive thoughts. Over all theological partisanships must be heard the rebuking cry: "Who is this that darkeneth counsel by words without knowledge?" (Job xxxviii. 2) Our aim must be to mediate in intellectual converse and strong charity the fullness of the faith by which we live. Our plea must be to be understood for what we believe and not for some travesty of it. Our patience must undertake to differentiate the faith and the travesty. And let none suppose that the issues are unreal or that they can be avoided. If we shirk or silence them in the realm of God they will meet us elsewhere wherever we turn. We must banish the suspicion that a conspiracy of silence would better serve to peace.

But when we venture into word and colloquy we must remember that the theme is God.

Why then do Christians believe in Father, Son, and Holy Spirit—One God? What do they mean? Answer is only possible here in the barest terms. Two themes of thought about the Christian doctrine of God are suggested: its experimental origin and its propositional form.

XV

God, as we suggested above, came to be known for what He is from experience of what He does. Action and relationship become the clue to personality. We do not say only that the doctrine of the Trinity is a summary of the activities of God, for undoubtedly it is much more. What we do say is that those active relationships are indicative of God's being and nature. The first fact about this developing sense of God in active relationship with man is that it was experienced by men who were as adamant about the Divine Unity as the best of Muslims. Indeed the fundamental protest made by Muhammad against Meccan idolatry was implicit in the whole ethos of the Hebrew and Christian tradition. Muhammad's iconoclasm was desperately valid and necessary in the Arabian context. It had no validity, however, as a disallowance of Christian dogma, since that dogma could in no valid way be identified with paganism. The fact was that the Christian entity had made the same revolt as Muhammad in its own ancestry and context centuries before Muhammad made it in Arabia.

The Apostles, then, and the Fathers, were not thirsting to multiply deities when in the historic faith they interpreted their Christian experience. They began, as Muhammad began, with God, with *Allāh*, One Sovereign, Creator, Sustainer, Provider, and Lord, ruling and revealing. They knew that the universe derived from God's creative fiat. They understood creation as meaning that God's responsible will underlay all existence, not merely originally but momentarily. They recognized that God sought man's sole worship and obedience and that in His will was the secret of man's good and man's happiness. They knew that human life stood under the law of God and they believed that this law had been revealed and entrusted to a community or people—which people they were—who were to practice and commend this law as a truth for all mankind. In all these points they were akin to the Islam which Muhammad's mission constituted in the fresh enunciation of many of these truths. It is true they did not yet speak of God, except occasionally, and tentatively, as Father. But they knew Him as sovereign Lawgiver and merciful God. Their worship and doctrine recognized His Lordship and they entertained wistful hopes of His historic intervention in pursuance alike of righteousness and mercy.

In this context Christian faith was nurtured. These were the suppositions of Christ's own teaching. They were axiomatic to Christian theologians in and beyond the New Testament. From this point we move into that profoundest of all sayings: "Ye believe in God, believe also in Me" (John xiv. 1). The Greek original allows either verb to be indicative and either imperative. What matters is the intimate connection between faith in God and faith in Christ, between believing in Jesus and believing in God. Whence does this connection derive? Why is the nature of God such as to issue in something like the Person and mission of Christ? Why is the fact of Christ inseparable from a final understanding of God?

We can discern a double answer. God is by nature revealing. His will to reveal, being at once righteous and merciful, means also—in this world—a will to redeem. In our treatment of the Christian Scriptures we have seen this Muslim-Christian conviction that God makes Himself known in revelation, because He is related to His creatures in law and in love. He does not leave them in ignorance, or fail to bring to their reason the light of His will and purpose and nature. For the Christian understanding this revelation is finally personal and consummates all its words into a Word that lives and moves and has its being in our human ken. But further, this revelation—if it is of a living God—intends fellowship. God will not simply tell us what, but show us Who, He is. Revelation bringing God to us and us to God in knowledge means communion. The end of law is obedience; the end of education, understanding; the end of revelation, knowledge. God is not an idea; nor can He be obeyed, understood, or known merely as an idea. God, as Muslims and Christians suppose Him, in their common if contrasted traditions, is a God Who seeks worship and intends fellowship. Revelation overcomes not merely darkness, but distance.

At this point the Christian understanding of God encounters the fact of evil. The revealed law is manifestly flouted and the revelatory purpose frustrated by man's recalcitrance. The world in its history is defiant of God and goodness. This theme is interwoven in the Biblical revelation of God as also a revelation of man in his waywardness. The possibility of such a tragic reality is implicit in the possibility of fellowship. For man would not be a creature capable of responding to the Divine goodness, coming to him in revelation, unless he were also a creature capable of becoming a rebel against that goodness. Love and obedience cannot be compelled and remain truly themselves. Christianity, therefore, sees the possibility of sin as involved in the human-Divine situation as we know it, both in the idea of revelation and in the reality of human conduct. It proceeds from this possibility in thought to the reality in fact. It seeks to learn what God, the sovereign Good, does in response to this astrayness and disobedience of man. It finds the answer in Christ. It believes that all faiths, not least Islam, should be alive to this reality of insubordination, of disobedience, of *un-islām*, in the life of men in history.

It needs, perhaps, to be added for the Muslim's thought that the Christian belief in a real freedom in man to be and remain a rebel is not inconsistent with a faith in the ultimate sovereignty of God in His goodness. We have seen elsewhere something of the concern of Muslim theology on this point of the interrelation of the Divine and human wills. Suffice it to say here that a genuine, though limited, freedom in man even to defy God, while it helps to explain historical realities, is no compromise on God's reign or Unity, inasmuch as He in His permissive will allows and controls the situation in which man's defiance can occur, and inasmuch as the very possibility of the latter is implicit in the greater purposes of revelation and grace.

But the remedy of evil is more important than its genesis. If man is a creature, potentially defiant and actually rebellious, what of the law that revelation sends down, as the token and

311

measure of the Divine will? Shall it remain permanently flouted? Must not the revelatory purpose take cognizance of man's legal and moral non-submission? Can God remain sovereign apart from redemption? Must not recalcitrant man be brought somehow through his disobedience into that fellowship and love of the law's good which is the purpose of his being and the crux of his predicament? This is the final meaning of the whole idea of Messiahship, of God intervening in history to put man right and to renew the thwarted purposes of His righteous law. The ideal of that correction varied widely as long as it was in prospect. When Christ came, fulfilling and transforming it, it was seen to mean suffering and the crown of thorns. The significance of Christ as the anointed Redeemer, born, teaching, suffering, dying, is the most formative element in the Christian doctrine of God.

The contemporary generation after the Resurrection understood the Godward significance of their experience of Christ. They discovered the truth of His claim: "He that hath seen Me, hath seen the Father" (John xiv. 9). That God was in Christ was the only adequate hypothesis on which they could express and transmit what their experience of Christ had meant to them. So they spoke of Him as "the Word made flesh," "Son of Man" and "Son of God," "the Captain of their salvation," "the Author and Finisher of their Faith." Theirs was not the language of polytheists. These men were not idolaters. They were responding to a profound experience of God. They could find, as monotheists, no other ground on which to explain what Christ had been to them and had done for all mankind. God was not less God, nor less One, by this belief; He was more so. For the sin and disobedience, which formerly frustrated His purpose and defied His law, and which, uncorrected and permanent, would have constituted a contrary force unsubdued to good, had been triumphantly overcome, in a way which no punitive judgment could do. It is out of this realm of deed that Jesus had said to Jewish monotheists: "Ye believe in God, believe also in Me." Can we in our turn finally believe in God sovereign and supreme without believing in some enterprise like that of "God in Christ reconciling the world unto Himself"?

This is the truth we have in mind when we speak of the experimental origin of the Christian faith in the Holy Trinity. But the experience went further. It generated another fact. For this faith brought a new unity among men. It also entrusted new tasks of witness and proclamation. It was the occasion of a new joy and a new release of power and peace. The redeeming work of Christ on the Cross had its counterpart in redemptive transactions in the souls of men. The goodness the law intended now became a personal delight. Men found themselves transformed into a new likeness. Forgiveness brought a sense of joy and obligation. Moral power was released in men's hearts and a great new phenomenon appeared in the world, described as fellowship in the Holy Spirit. This was so manifestly continuous with the earthly life of Christ that man attributed it to the same source. It was so evidently of God that it was recognized to be God's. This new accession of understanding and joy was no less a Divine activity than the suffering and teaching of Christ Himself. God was evidently not only over men in creative sovereignty and for them in redeeming love. He was also in them and with them as an abiding Presence. "The Holy Spirit proceeding from the Father and the Son."

This Divine activity was not, of course, discontinuous with the Divine guidance and inspiration of the prophets and patriarchs. But now in the wake of Christ there seemed to have come an age of the Spirit which, though anticipated in its nature, was new in its fullness. For this reason Christians came to recognize that they must make room in their thought of God for His ever-present activity in their minds, their affairs and their hearts. They had a vitality not their own, inexplicable by circumstances and not deriving from genius of theirs. For ordinariness was their hallmark.

It may be worth observing that the Qur'ān recognizes in measure the sort of Divine relationship to man which underlies the Christian doctrine of the Holy Spirit. The Book itself is God's speech. He sends messengers and spirits, to whom He whispers His counsel. There are intermediaries between Himself and the world of time and sense. Clearly these communicative activities of God are differentiated from His creative activities. We have at least to think of God in different capacities. The basic contrast here is that Christianity takes these activities and gathers them into its understanding of God Himself. When we speak of God the Spirit we refer to God in this activity. Though He may use agents and instruments, it is finally God Himself Who is using them. In this sense the doctrine of the Holy Trinity is no more and no less than the idea of God as being in relationship with man, God Whose will sustains, Whose love redeems, and Whose Spirit orders and indwells the world of human life. A God out of relationship with man is certainly not theism, nor monotheism. Still less is He a God with Whom religion, as Islam and Christianity know it, can have to do. But God in relationship is precisely what we mean by the Christian Trinity—God so truly and unmistakably in relationship with us that we take the pattern of His relationship to us as the clue to His nature. What else, what better, should we take?

This then is the experimental origin of the Christian faith as to God. The genesis in experience cannot be too strongly emphasized. The Christian Fathers were not armchair philosophers, sitting down to evolve nice metaphysical theories. Their faith, when formulated, solves many outstanding philosophical problems but does not exist for that reason. It is profoundly significant that the sweetest and perhaps the earliest statement of this Christian faith places it in the context of experience where theology ends as it should in doxology: "The grace of our Lord Jesus Christ and the love of God and the fellowship of the Holy Spirit be with us all evermore" (II Corinthians xiii. 14). "For through Christ we all have access by One Spirit unto the Father" (Ephesians ii. 18). "Glory be to God most high."

XVI

Few would deny that belief needs to be formally defined. Only so can it be safeguarded from misunderstanding. Only so is it secure for the generations. The basic assumption that what God is can be formulated from what God does, made by the Christian theologians, would seem to have been a sound one. Dogma serves the needs of more than will admit it. The Church was profoundly right in requiring that its understanding of God in the experimental realm should be taken also into the definitive realm. The Christian community sought to embody in credal shape the nature of its experience, that all generations might enter into the same communion of saints—and of mind.

We have no time to do justice to the whole story. We must be content with one fundamental principle and some simple observations. The principle is that we must strive to introduce the Muslim heart to the faith within the Christian doctrine by the same path that the Church itself followed. We are to bring men to God in Christ, before we can justify to them what credally we believe about Him. Our duty is to demonstrate and communicate an awareness of the grace, love, fellowship which are the manward consequence of what God is. But we will not evade the intellectual tasks implicit in the credal forms. A few observations may be apposite.

The Christian Trinity is God the Father, God the Son, and God the Holy Spirit. It does not consist, as there has been a tendency among Muslims to suppose, of God, Jesus, and the Virgin Mary.

The terms "Father" and "Son" have no physical significance and are used analogically. The Divine solicitude for man in ignorance and sin "begets" or generates the activity of redeeming love which is evident in the historic Christ. That "God was in Christ" rather than that "Jesus was God" is the classic expression of this truth. James Denney set out the distinction clearly when he wrote:

> The word "God" as a proper noun identifies the Being
> to Whom it is applied so that it can be used as the sub-
> ject of a sentence: but it does not unfold the nature of
> that Being, so that it could be used as the predicate of a
> sentence. In the formula "Jesus is God the Son" . . .
> "the Son" introduces the very qualification of God which
> makes it possible to apply it to Jesus. In the same way
> . . . in saying that Jesus was "God manifest in the
> flesh," "manifest in the flesh" serves the same purpose.

The writer adds that the Fathers of Nicaea and Chalcedon "would have pronounced the bare statement that Jesus was God to have been as far from adequate to the whole truth they were desirous of expressing as the bare statement that He was man." [8] The phrase "God the Son" means God in self-revelation in the Person of Jesus, "God with us" taking perfect humanity into His revealing purpose and giving men that of which they may say: "This is the Lord: we have waited for Him, we will be glad and rejoice in His salvation."

There is absolutely no reason to insist, as some Muslims do, that the term "Father" necessarily implies paternity in the physical sense. No one using the phrase "Alma Mater" wishes it to be understood that the college or university has a womb. Terms are used for their rich significance in those senses in which they can appropriately be predicated. It goes without saying that God does not have children as His creatures do. This, however, does not invalidate the use of the deepest analogy known to human life—the more so since all fatherhood and family is the idea of God and takes its name, according to St. Paul, from Him.

Is the doctrine of the Trinity against reason? It may transcend our complete rational comprehension and also elude philosophical discovery. But being given it is certainly open to the fullest explory the mind can attain. If mystery remains, beyond the thinker's reach, this is not to say that his ambitions have no place. The theist has no need to be ashamed of the intellectual bearings of his faith. It illuminates many of the otherwise unanswered questions of philosophy. Moreover, it is well to remember that rejection of this doctrine on the grounds of mystery does not rid the unbeliever of the mysterious. The Christian doctrine lies precisely at the point where the supreme mysteries belong. If we reject that doctrine's account of them we still have the mysteries on hand. It is sometimes forgotten that while the onus is always on belief to make good its claim, there is a similar obligation for the skeptic to validate his unbelief. It is a false assumption to suppose that he has any easier task, and blindness to suppose he has no task at all. No doctrine can be justified on the ground that it is mysterious. But if the mystery is taken hold of and becomes luminous, then such doctrine where this happens may well be standing with the truth.

Reflection makes it clear that the idea of the Divine Unity can-

THE CALL TO INTERPRETATION

not be enforced in a mathematical sense, and that enforcement in such sense is the ground of most Muslim antipathy to the Christian Trinity. The higher we proceed in the scale of being the more rich and varied are the unities we encounter. Mathematical units are low in the scale of values, such as stones or a unicellular organism. The bricklayer on a straight wall may lay any brick that comes to hand because they are all alike and interchangeable. They are mere units. Not so the parts of a human body or the components of a flower. Here we have larger unities with differentiated parts. Human personalities are the richest and most diversified unities within our experience. William Shakespeare or Abraham Lincoln were single persons but what wealth of diversity lay within them. If the order of ascending unity reveals increasing fullness, who shall say that the Unity of God is not the richest and the greatest of all? Certainly we cannot disallow the doctrine of the Father, Son, and Holy Spirit on the ground that these add up to three. Was not Muhammad, Prophet, husband, leader, and example? He was no less one Muhammad. On whatever other grounds Muslims feel disposed to disagree with the Christian understanding of God, it cannot validly be on the ground that it is not a doctrine of Unity. For the only sense in which it can be thought not to be so is the one completely inappropriate, namely the mathematical.

A bare unity, philosophically understood, is a barren one. We have seen something of this problem in discussing the Qur'ān's relation to God, created or uncreated. For creation, to be meaningful as a loving transaction, must originate in a purpose that is already love within itself. We cannot say that "God is Love" and also say that "God is solitary" or, in this solitary sense, that "God is One." Entire transcendence is in the end a blank agnosticism. The Christian faith in the Holy Trinity only carries further the truth implicit in the Muslim faith in revelation and judgment. It is the Christian form of belief in a God Who has real and meaningful relation with men and the temporal world.

The formulation of the Christian doctrine of God was not a formulation of men in philosophic or scientific capacity, but in their capacity as the redeemed. As the credal side of the saving enterprise of God it should be set always in the center of its origin and of its abiding meaning. "God is most great" says the Christian *takbīr,* "because He has made Himself the Redeemer." His Lordship is both an experience and a hope. "Blessing and glory and wisdom and thanksgiving and honour and power and might be unto our God for ever and ever" (Revelation vii. 12).

XVII

There is perhaps one final question. Our attempt to interpret so far fails its glorious theme, is compassed about by so much weakness and beset with so many pitfalls and discouragements, that the temptation to desist is ever-present. Can we seek to build our Muslim relationships on less exacting grounds? There are many areas of non-theological intercourse and mutual enterprise that may be more fruitfully developed. Let us leave the irreconcilable.

But no! Though we may begin and build confidence and expression in less pressing realms, there is no properly Christian interpretation that is not concerned to give to all men the knowledge of God in Christ. The most tenacious and most widespread worship of the One God in human history and today's world, outside the Christian communion, has surely the most eloquent claim to the knowledge of "the God and Father of our Lord Jesus Christ."

For idolatry is far from being, as Islam supposed, the sole or even the most serious disparagement of the Divine Unity. Pagan idolaters multiply gods in ignorant ideas of celestial co-existence. But sinful men who deify themselves or their ambitions dethrone the One God. Their challenge to the Divine sovereignty is more heinous and more defiant. To refute the idolaters is one thing. But it should argue a passion that God should be all-in-all over every other challenge of evil and hate. The Christian tradition believes itself in trust with the knowledge of such a Divine sovereignty, reigning and to reign, in the majesty of redeeming love. The tragic irony is that Islam has mistaken the historic expression of that faith for a refined piece of the polytheism it was created to denounce. To find such a faith in such a situation is surely to make the fullest interpretation imperative.

XVIII

From the contemplation of our duty toward Muslims in the realm of Christian faith in regard to God and Christ, the Scriptures, and the Cross we pass to the realm of the Christian society and the Christian Church. Here also massive misunderstandings confront us. Some derive from the implications of misconceptions already studied, and others from the ambiguities of Christian history. As before, so now, our conviction is that occasions of misapprehension must be made themes of expression. All that can be attempted is a brief discussion of aspects of the Christian Church that are central to Christian definition and Muslim interpretation.

The nature of the Church is to be understood in the light of the nature of the Gospel. It is what results from the Divine initiative of grace in Jesus Christ. He had gathered around Him a nucleus of disciples who were both learners in His teachings and servants in His compassion. He bound them closely to His Person and taught them to center their faith and devotion upon His identity as the Messiah. This recognition had first to undergo the supreme test of the crucifixion, an event which seemed to give the lie to all their hopes but which in its issue both transformed and fulfilled them. The concept of the Christ, first tentatively, then triumphantly, confessed by the disciples bound them in spirit and heart to the long expectations of the people Israel. They saw in its fulfillment their own "social" continuity with their fathers in a community of hope and yearning.

It also bound them and their long antecedents in Israel to the whole community of faith resulting from the recognition in Christ of God's enterprise of human redemption. The initial group of disciples became the apostolic circle, born into a new solidarity of conviction and fellowship by the Resurrection. Jesus the Master was still the personal center and focus of their devotion. Yet now it was Jesus the Lord, so named and understood, not in the partial knowledge and therefore incomplete discipleship of the months between their enlistment and His death, but in the total assurance and commitment generated by His Passion.

It was in this sense that the Resurrection brought the historic Church into being. Legatee of the hopes and many of the patterns of the old Israel, and heir also to Christ's law and example, it was the new community of redemption resulting from the acknowledgment of Christ as Lord. Energized and guided by the Holy Spirit, it became the instrument in the world for the diffusion and demonstration of the good news of God. Almost three centuries elapsed before empire or government capitulated to it. Its essential nature as a community in, and yet not of, this world, a society within society, a fellowship deriving from Divine grace and human response, was by that time fully apparent.

This community of belief and fellowship was in a state of perpetual wonder at itself, exploring in its Epistles the meaning of its own genesis and the secret of its true being. Entrusted with the ancient Scriptures, it became the matrix within which the Gospel tradition was set down for the guidance of all the generations and for the lands which had not known a contemporary Christ. It described to itself through its Apostles' correspondence the meaning of its new life, the secret of its calling and its destiny. It knew itself heir to the promises. It was the body of Christ and a covenant society founded on the Divine mercy and pledged to show forth the praises of its Lord. It was at once a building for the habitation of God through the Spirit and an organism in which Christ, His truth and compassion, would still be active in the teaching and service of the world. It was an earnest of the meaning of the Kingdom of Heaven, the token in community of the power and the wisdom of God in Christ. It united the past of preparation with the present of realization. It lived to bear both into the future of man.

Embodying the meaning of the ages, it was also set for the healing of the nations. Its fellowship transcended the most obstinate divisions of the ancient world. In great historic decisions the Church broke away from the limitations of the Hebrew synagogue without sacrificing its debt to the Hebrew nurture. It welcomed Greek and barbarian into its life and came to use many of the concepts of the Greek mind to describe and define its credal faith. In pursuit of this openness of hand and mind it spread in widening evangelism across the Near East and into adjacent Europe, Africa, and Asia. In responding to the dimensions of the love of God in Christ, it learned more of its own nature.

Those Epistles and the subsequent Gospel histories of the Christ, Who had made their writers and readers what they were, came to establish themselves as authoritative Scriptures in the mind of the Church. This process of recognizing authoritative status, which was later finalized in canonization, did not endow those writings with authority or establish the Church as somehow superior to them. Rather it was a recognition, communitywise, of their inherent authority. Both Church and Scriptures together stood under the fact of Christ, Master, Saviour, Lord, from Whom both derived their being, the one as the written, the other as the institutional, consequence of all that He had been and was. But just as the writings argued readers and so a possessing community, the possessing community likewise argued a history and originating facts, and so in turn a Scripture and a record. The Scriptures were in the custody of the Church only because the Church was itself in the custody of the facts of the Scriptures. It gave the writings circulation: what they described gave it existence.

The understanding of revelation upon which this relation of Scripture and community rests has already been discussed. To the question: Did Jesus intend a Church? by which some Muslims have been attracted, the answer must now be clear. If His purpose was to teach and redeem, a continuing institution of hearers and redeemed seems inescapable. This is not to say that Christ intended all that historic Churches have become. But it does mean that the relation of disciples and believers to Himself involved their relation with each other, not simply as an agreement to associate, but as a corporate communal reality inseparable from a common allegiance. Faith is necessarily fellowship. To be in Christ is not to be solitary. Jesus as Teacher had taught His hearers to say: "Our Father . . ." When they entered the meaning of His Passion they found a new fullness to that implicit sense of community.

Muslim tendencies to disallow the Church belong to the partial

Muslim awareness of Jesus and would find their answer in the enlargement of the latter. But such tendencies are not universal. Many Muslim writers, in line with certain Quranic passages, lay great stress on the disciples and picture them as the devoted disseminators of His words after His removal from the earthly scene. This view picks up the Church after the hiatus of silence (where the Cross stands) and sees a continuity between a Galilean Prophet and the Apostles. But it must be asked whether the shattered disciples after Good Friday recovered their nerve and became evangelists only in terms of a Jesus Who had eluded death and was no more with them. The incredibility of such a hypothesis has been suggested already in the discussion of the Cross.

XIX

Apart from these Muslim attitudes to the historic origin of the Church, there are recurrent questions about its relation to human society at large. In this realm, there are issues at stake that are deep and urgent. The interpreter has to renounce contrasted distortions. The Muslim, as is well known, rejoices in his conviction that Islam knows no separation, ideally, between faith and society, between believer and citizen, between doctrine and culture. Islam is a practicable and feasible religion, relating to the whole of life. Several aspects of this quality we have studied in the chapter on "The Islamic Order." We have seen the general Muslim repudiation of "religion" as something distinguished from "the secular," from government and from the everyday, as if it were a private affair concerning only the soul and God.

There are aspects of this Muslim understanding of Islam which belong also, properly understood, to Christianity. There are other aspects which, unexamined, betray serious naïveté in the analysis of human nature and society. The patient examination of these can be greatly served by a simple exposition of the Christian case. Here perhaps more than anywhere we can most profitably dispel misunderstandings and at the same time deepen the level of realism in the discussion.

Many Muslim writers, past and present, upbraid Christianity for its failure to discipline and control Western civilization. It has not checked imperialism or corrected exploitation. It is, on the contrary, implicated in aiding and abetting Western dominance in the world. Even its missions are seen as a form of religious imperialism.[9] Other critics proceed upon a somewhat different hypothesis. Christianity, for them, is not so much reproached for involvement in Western mischief and selfishness, as for non-involvement. Christianity is absolved from positive implication by the contrasted charge of abstraction and withdrawal. It is a religion of high ideals and absolutist ethics, impossible of attainment in this human world. Society then goes on in partial lip-service to its ideals, but with little or no actual obedience. The faith itself, meanwhile, nourishes its ethics in individual seclusion or "monastic" isolation. Christianity, therefore, has not so much failed civilization as proved itself incompetent to try. In either case the faith of the Christian Church is wanting because it does not put the world to rights.

Any Christian attempt to face patiently the issues here involved might begin with a historical investigation of the debt of humanity, East and West, to Christian ethics, Christian love, and Christian sacrifice. But this of itself would not be a complete answer. Nor would an explanation of the failures of institutional Christianity in the world as due to inferior Christians, or disloyalty and non-practice within the Church, suffice to meet what is here at issue. We must be both radical and realist. We cannot claim all that is worthy, compassionate, and true in Western civilization for the credit of Christianity and explain the contrary as arising from neglect of Christianity. It is a Christian principle to be radical with ourselves and to take the diagnosis of sin into religion itself with no areas of spirit or mind immunized from the reproach that calls to repentance. We must recognize what failure implies for the religion so failing and not seek evasive exoneration in reprobating its confessors. For what the confessors are, or are not, is part of the record of the religion and some clue to its nature.

Beneath these considerations lies the heart of the matter. The Church is conceived in the New Testament as a society within a society. It is never properly thought of as coterminous, within history, with the whole of human society. "Christendom," though the term has validity, is not finally a Christian concept. The

Church is an *Ecclesia*—a called-out community. It is built upon the idea and the fact of redemption. It, therefore, involves an analysis of human nature as wayward and sinful. This astrayness is redeemed and corrected in Christ into newness of life, on the condition of faith and commitment. "To as many as received Him, to them gave He the power to become the sons of God, even to them that believe on His Name" (John i. 12). There is the "natural" man in his recalcitrance and the "spiritual" man in regeneration and pardon. The former no doubt penetrates into existing Churches. But the Christian understanding of how man is put to rights is that it happens personally and through faith.

Goodness and truth and love, then, are not actualized in terms of "natural" man, but of new-made man. The transaction is conditional upon repentance and faith, and is perpetuated in discipleship. These conditions of the transaction, being personal, are not social. Christianity belongs to and inheres in people who believe. It is never coterminous as such with any given society. Many social institutions, laws, customs, practices, habits, concepts, ideals, norms, may become "Christian." Christian truth relates to them imperatively. But they only become so derivatively from the Christian conviction and Christian regeneration of the people who shape or inhabit them. Thus the unit of Christianity, that in which it inheres, as fire in coals, is not society, but persons in society. Things are not the final locus of Christianity: people are.

Thus the Christian fellowship of people discipled to Christ as Master and Saviour is within, not identical with, a total population. It is always in nature, if not in fact, militant, antiseptic, regenerating its fellows as far as it can and resisting the un-Christian in the context as far as it may. It does not expect to identify itself with the whole. Not that it does not so desire: but because parts of that total aggregate withhold the vital allegiance which alone constitutes a Christian person. The Christian distinction between the regenerate and the unregenerate derives from a sense of the radical nature of human wrongness and the conviction that the true faith cannot be compelled. Man's response is his to bring or to withhold. In the degree to which men withhold it they count themselves out of the Kingdom it offers. The Kingdom in love will never let them go but it will never compel allegiance. For allegiance to this Kingdom can only be given.

This distinction between the natural man and the spiritual is basic to a proper understanding of the Church. The Gospel of grace does not suppose that men are perfectible by law. It cannot assume that because a revelation of law is given the heirs of that revelation are by that fact a perfect society. A community which confronts men with decision cannot at the same time be a community that recruits them all. Christianity, then, is not a political expression. Realist Muslims have recognized that the Islamic law has not at any prolonged time in history evoked a true society.[10] There has always been disparity between what was and what might have been. But Islam in general insists that the disparity is incidental. The people who have the Divine guidance as the clue to their life under law ought to be organized as a political expression and should be able as such to constitute the perfect human society.

The Christian mind, by contrast, believes that the society of the redeemed will always stand within the community, militantly, not identical with the whole. That whole, the secular world, must be free to organize itself. If we try to assume its conversion, it will belie our facile complacence. We cannot by legislation or assertion identify it with Christ. Its recalcitrance has to be recognized as part of its freedom and confronted patiently with the conditions of its retrieval. We only deceive it and ourselves if we suppose that no conditions exist.

This fundamentally is the reason why the Christian faith recognizes an ultimate distinction (and in that sense a separation) between the Church and the state. The distinction is the counterpart of its understanding of man in his need and God in His grace. The "separation" does not mean the non-relevance of Christ to life; it does not mean abdication of responsibility; it does not indicate indifference; it is not a withdrawal into a private and self-regarding piety; it is not dereliction of social duty. It is a refusal to regard man as being in no need of redemption, or the Kingdom of Heaven as unconditioned by repentance and a new heart. How patiently the meaning of this relation of the

Christian community to human society as a whole and to the criteria of goodness must be unveiled.

XX

Such a patient interpretation may serve to illuminate the fact that a totalitarian religious identification of faith and the state is not so realist as is sometimes supposed. Whenever religion is equated with the powers of this world the quality and worth of religion are inevitably reduced. It is by calling man out of his ordinary levels rather than by hallowing them as adequate that he, and indirectly his society, can be worthily transformed. This is part of our witness to Islam. The New Testament conceives of Christian life as more than we can manage—of ourselves. It is the gift of grace and the fruit of salvation.

It is imperative, however, at the same time to make entirely clear that the Christian Church is not indifferent about society and that the doctrine of redemption does not write off the "secular" world as hopeless and forsworn. On the contrary, its confidence in a redemptive purpose that has entered and is ever entering into history has the great "future tense" of hope. The redeeming Christ here and now brings the pledge of a sovereignty that will subdue all things unto Himself. The Church is not pessimistic when it is radical; nor piously preoccupied when it proclaims conversion. Christianity is not concerned merely with the eternal destiny of the individual. Nor is faith a private affair between the soul and God. To belong to Christ is to take up the Cross, to undertake costly responsibility for the world, to bear witness against social evil and strive for economic justice on all sides. To recognize that changing social conditions does not of itself change man is not to be indifferent about changing them. To appreciate that "things" as such can never be all that they should be, apart from the men who shape them, is not to be careless about how "things" are. Christianity is not to be written off as pious irresponsibility. On the contrary, the disciple who acknowledges his own redemption by the Cross is summoned to assert the rights of his Redeemer over the whole of life. The righteousness which saves him is an active righteousness. In Christ we learn to live responsibly for our neighbor and all that shapes his life—social, political, economic, and international.

For the Christian's faith in the Incarnation means that humanity is called to be expressive of the Divine nature. There could be no greater travesty than to suppose the Christian faith is either aloof from, or unfit for, a deep social conscience, fulfilled in action. We seek no exoneration from responsibility for Western wrongs and evils on the ground that they are no concern of the Christian faith. Rather we recognize failure in our moral duty. The truth just outlined that the Church does not look for a full redemption of man apart from faith does not mean we establish a universal alibi to excuse disloyalties in all our great, if subordinate, tasks of social militancy. We do not the less seek to humanize and hallow laws and institutions, because we seek finally to save men. He who writes Christianity off in this respect has not begun to understand it.

The clarification of the Christian's role in society should help to illuminate some interior problems in Muslim thought at the present time when a great debate is in progress. Does the "totalitarian" religion aim to dominate society and insure obedience by state authority and enforcement or does it seek to permeate opinion and rely solely on persuasion? Is there any sense, not harmful to religion, in which the political order should be free of religious dominance? If religion sets the desiderata of the state and of society, what is its true function in relation to these being actualized? Some Muslims today are by no means as confident as their forebears that the right way to serve the unlimited demands of the religious law is by the unlimited enforcement of religious sanctions. Christianity agrees that the claims of God are total and that nothing is exempt from their relevance. It does not agree that they can be met in a religio-political order externally established. At this point of difference there is a wide field for Christian interpretation with the nature of the Church as a clue.

XXI

Another area of possible Muslim misconception concerns the Christian ministry and sacraments. Islam prides itself on its freedom from "priesthood." Admittedly it has experts. No faith or law so intricate and meticulous could lack them and survive. The equality of all Muslim believers does not mean that any Sālih, Hasan, or Mustafā can claim to interpret the law. Sometimes "Shaikh-hood" has established a stranglehold over intellectual and religious life, resembling the worst features of priestcraft though from contrasted origins. But every believer in Islam has equal access to God and needs no human mediator. When Muslims, however, declaim against Christianity and deplore its priest-ridden-ness, they often overlook that they are proceeding upon assumptions which large segments of Christianity itself has repudiated and cast out. The New Testament knows of no such spiritual slavery to lords of God's flock. The Apostles themselves had most sober and humble estimates of their authority. There has also been a Reformation. We can only plead for that concept of ministry upon which our own understanding of the mind of Christ proceeds. It is, so seen, an instrument to God's truth, not a stranglehold on the believer. The role of the Christian minister in prayer and sacrament does not make the lay-believer his dependent. On the contrary, the minister officiates for, and by sanction of, the whole. Prayer does not cease to be personal and spontaneous for being sometimes liturgical. Just as the law of Islam is considered as necessarily in the custody of those who have consecrated their lives and studies to understand it, so the good news of God, and the ministry of Word and sacraments which serves it, are entrusted to men who have devoted themselves to this holy service and have been recognized by the whole body and equipped so to do.

As for the sacraments themselves, how little they have been interpreted to Muslims! Islam, in its own way, is sacramental. Washing before prayer, posture in prayer, the *qiblah* towards Mecca, pilgrimage and *Ramadān*—all these and much more are examples of material expression and spiritual meaning. There are clues in them all for an understanding of the baptismal water and the communion of the body and the blood. Concede the contrasted origins in law and in grace, the sacramental principle is the same. Indeed the Muslim might agree from the Qur'ān that the whole universe is sacramental, that it symbolizes and expresses the Divine majesty. So in our faith in the Incarnation we have the utmost focus of the truth that this physical realm of our world can become expressive of the living God. The Christian meanings in the bread and wine, emblems of the suffering of the Word made flesh, are almost unknown to the Muslim, fortified as he is by the prior disallowing of the Cross. But he has already in his own form that which may serve to illumine something of the principle, if not the heart, in the Christian usage. It might be well for us to remember that in the breaking of the bread Jesus was known to men whose eyes until then had been "holden" that they did not know Him. Perhaps we have not been careful enough to let the Muslim see the Church in its sacramental communion with the living Christ. Though reverent words can explain the objective meaning of the service only the reality of communion can show its fullness. Somehow the clues must be got through to "the strangers."

XXII

This reflection leads into two final points. The Holy Communion is the sacrament of one bread and one cup and, therefore, the sacrament of unity. The Christian explanation of the Church, in word and in life, must not evade the tragedy of division. Sectarianism and divisiveness afflict all great religions in varying form and measure. That the honest Muslim knows the problem in his own culture does not absolve the honest Christian from facing it in his. There are some sources of separated Christian loyalties that are not serious. Differences of language, heritage, and environment readily explain divergencies in expression and justify separate organization for worship. There are other differences in order and pattern that are softened, if not entirely obviated, by genuine co-operativeness and mutual fellowship. We must interpret to the non-Christian world the increasing significance of the Ecumenical Movement and the growing practical interdependence of many Churches. It is also true that deep and undeniable urgings underlie many historic divisions, urgings to freedom and conscience, to obedience in faith, to independence of usurping control, whose denial would be worse than schism, since they enshrine values that no mere conformity or external unity could outweigh. The lessons of those rebellions and their benediction even for the Churches they challenged are part of our heritage. Christian division is, in some senses, the high cost of a priceless thing.

Yet, when all these considerations are remembered, Christian disunity remains a perpetual embarrassment to Christian interpretation. Impressive as is ecumenical progress, there is a rapid increase in missionary sects dedicated to non-co-operation. Even more serious is the unjustified will to be different within the common heritage. Christians are still too much divided over too many issues for too little reasons. Some practical consequences will be considered in the next chapter. The interpreter's duty is a frank honesty with what we have failed to be and a frank sincerity about our vocation among Muslims. "We have this treasure in earthen vessels" (ii Corinthians iv. 7). But we have it. The Christ, even though we disserve while we serve Him, is the lover of all souls. It is Him we commend.

The other consideration is the obvious necessity of seeking wisdom and grace to be genuinely hospitable. The meaning of the Church is more often "caught" than taught. Too many theologians and ecclesiastics have gone astray in the past by seeking to locate the true Church when they should have sought simply to be it. In the end the Church will not so much identify itself by description, as be identified by others in recognition. We have the duty to explain what Christians are: we have at least as great a duty to be them. How better shall fellowship be understood than in a hospitable Christian community? Not a few Muslims have more readily discovered Christ in the home and family, even on the tennis court and wayside, than beside the pulpit or the platform. How important it is to invite the Muslim as such with no reservations into some active piece of Christian enterprise, some co-operative scheme of rural welfare or human service in which he may discover the impulse of the love of Christ. Here, perhaps, best of all he may face the meaning of life and discover what challenge and what mission Christ may bring. Like the first disciples some come to Christ because He leads them out to others: from the service of others they move onwards into the secret of His Cross. Service truly follows faith: but the faith that saves the soul may well be generated in the will to save others.

Active interpretation is, then, the final benediction. Let us strive so to conform our homes, our loves, our professions, our offices, our leisure and our affairs, to the allegiance of Christ that men may take knowledge of Him in what we have allowed His grace to make of us. Though the Church must surely explain its concepts, the bearings of its life, its origins, and its nature, it will most surely communicate itself in the men and women in whose hearts its doctrines of grace have become a personal hospitality to the needs and fears and hopes of their fellows. So men take knowledge of them that they have been with Jesus and that they are still in His company. So the Church is discovered: and in the Church all the rich meanings of God, the Scriptures, the Cross, and the Christ, which constitute its life in history and compel it still into mission to the world.

NOTES *to Chapter X*

1

Hoskyns, Edwin, *Cambridge Sermons,* quoted in Ramsey, A. M. *The Glory of God and the Transfiguration of Christ,* London, 1949, p. 6.

2

As examples of this Muslim interpretation one may cite: Dāwūd, 'Abdu Abū-l-Ahad, *Muhammad in the Bible,* Islamic Series, No. 2, Allahabad, 1952; Ahmad, Khwāja Nazīr, *Jesus in Heaven on Earth,* op. cit.; and Vidyarathi, A. H., and 'Alī, U., *Muhammad in Parsi, Hindoo and Buddhist Scriptures,* Islamic Series, No. 3, Allahabad, 1953.

3

The Quranic passages dealing with this theme of *Naskh,* or Abrogation, are Surah ii. 106, xiii. 39, xvi. 98 and 101. See Bell, Richard, *Introduction to the Quran,* Edinburgh, 1953, pp. 98-9. See also Chapter III, note 6, above.

4

Al-'Aqqād, 'Abbās Mahmūd, *'Abqariyyat al-Masīh,* op. cit. pp. 215-19.

5

Thus Surah xlii. 37 commends those who, when angered, forgive. The provisions of Surah lxv. 1, concerning the statutory delay before intending divorcées either separate in kindness or achieve reconciliation, may be taken to suggest the creative possibilities of forgiveness in which God may bring some new thing to pass. It is true that the Qur'ān uses the imperative *ighfir,* forgive, only in a petitionary sense, of God, and not in a hortatory sense, as to man. But it is clear that the Divine clemency is meant to be exemplary. Surah iii, in three verses, 16, 147, 193, echoes the petition of the Lord's Prayer: "Forgive us our trespasses," but does not add: "as we forgive those who trespass against us." Surah v. 45, after setting out the *lex talionis,* adds that to remit the vengeance is an expiation for the remitter.

6

Muslim writers who discuss the spread of Christianity confront a deep, historical problem, since they are obliged to explain the impact of Jesus upon the world, through the disciples, in terms of His words and teaching only. The place where the Resurrection stands in the Christian understanding of Christ is, for Islam, a blank. Yet its sequel cannot be ignored, even if, on the Muslim view, it has to be a sequel without a properly total source. Nevertheless, there is this measure of consistency in the Muslim account, in that, having disallowed the Cross, it rightly excludes the Resurrection. For they belong together. The Resurrection is the triumphant consequent of the quality of Christ's dying. Having forbidden actuality to the latter, Islam clearly can leave no place for the former.

7

'Alī, Muhammad, *My Life—A Fragment,* op. cit. p. 59.

8

In a letter, quoted by Baillie, John, *The Place of Jesus Christ in Modern Christianity,* New York, 1929, pp. 145-6, and drawn from *Letters of Principal James Denney to W. Robertson Nicoll, 1893-1917,* pp. 120-26.

9

As for example in Khālidī, Mustafā and Farrūkh, 'Umar, *Al-Tabshīr wa-l-Istiʿmār fī-l-Bilādi-l-ʿArabiyyah (Missions and Imperialism in the Arab World),* Beirut, 1953.

10

Cf. Qutb, Sayyid, *Social Justice in Islam,* op. cit. p. 228 seq., where the Umayyads are made responsible for a breakdown of valid Islamicity in matters political and economic, from which subsequent history has hardly, if ever, recovered. Also Al-Ghazālī, Muhammad, *Min Hunā Naʿlam,* Cairo, 1950, translated by Al-Fārūqī, Ismāʿil, under the title *Our Beginning in Wisdom,* Washington, 1953. On p. 141, he writes: "The reader may possibly ask whether Islamic socialism has been applied anywhere, and whether there is at present any living example of it . . . The answer unfortunately is, 'There is none.' The principles of Islam have been crippled in Islamic countries for a long time."

xi

THE CALL TO PATIENCE

I<small>N ONE</small> of Archbishop Temple's prayers occurs the petition: "Grant us to know when by patience and when by impatience we can serve Thee best." There are, it is true, situations which call for the impatience that rejects the plea of caution and refuses to evade imperative things by calling them precipitate. But in face of an obligation such as Islam presents there can be little question that patience is the evident need. Yet how difficult of achievement is the true patience that never lapses into apathy and indifference, that always keeps the clear vision of its purpose. Such patience is not the recumbent sort which Wordsworth once remarked in an old man of his acquaintance:

> *He is invariably subdued*
> *To settled quiet: he is one by whom*
> *All effort seems forgotten: one to whom*
> *Long patience hath such mild composure given*
> *That patience now doth seem a thing*
> *Of which he hath no need.*

The Church, on the contrary, has great need, in being summoned to restless effort in a field when visible external success is little found.

Under this theme of patience it is proposed to gather, in conclusion, certain aspects of the Christian mission to Islam with

333

which there has been no opportunity hitherto to deal but which are inseparable from what we have discovered of the call of the minaret to the Christian.

The question of converts, their number and their trials, is often raised in the home Church whenever the missionary effort among Muslims is discussed. People who know little else about Islam know that it has a tremendous resistant quality and that the way of Christian baptism is slow and hard. There are some who, in days of urgency everywhere and limitations of resources and man power, tend to approve the diversion of personnel and funds away from Muslim areas to more receptive territories. Or, sensing the dubious validity of such an outlook, they remain perplexed and dismayed about Islam, even when they continue dogged. The working missionary, who bears the problem in his own person, is similarly bewildered and burdened by the apparent fruitlessness of his devotion.

The first point to be made is that no Christian mission is constituted in its success, and none, therefore, is invalidated by numerical failure. The whole point of the argument has been missed if it is not clear that there is a Christian obligation to Islam which neither begins nor ends in how Muslims respond. It is rooted in the nature of Christ and of His Gospel. It derives from the nature of Islam in its unawareness. It springs from the situation we have tried to convey:

> *Over all things brooding*
> *The quiet sense of something lost.*

If Christ is what Christ is, He must be uttered. If Islam is what Islam is, that "must" is irresistible. Wherever there is misconception, witness must penetrate: wherever there is the obscuring of the beauty of the Cross it must be unveiled: wherever men have missed God in Christ He must be brought to them again. This book has failed in its purpose if it is not indubitably clear that in such a situation as Islam presents the Church has no option but to present Christ.

This is a categorical imperative. It should be plain to Mission Boards and subscribing Churches that the mission is not a calculus of success, but an obligation in love. Statistics do not make it, nor can they unmake it. Nor is it always a Christian thing to ask to know where we are going. It is not ours to see the full consequences or conditions of our duty. We may only have one clear light to guide us. But it suffices that it should be clear. All the corollaries of our obedience we may not be able to explain, or even understand. It suffices that we obey. As long as Christ is Christ, and the Church knows both itself and Him, there will be a mission to Islam.

When this is indubitably plain then it may be added that, precisely for the same reasons, response in faith and baptism is of vital concern and importance. We present Christ for the sole, sufficient reason that He deserves to be presented. But we cannot neglect that Christ claims discipleship and that His Gospel is something expecting a verdict. Part of our trouble, however, lies in our presuppositions about how the verdict shall be given and assessed. We are tempted to demand that it conform to familiar Western patterns and do not sufficiently allow for the unpredictability of the Gospel. Since all the nations, including the Muslim, are to bring their glory and honor into the Kingdom, we must be ready for the unexpected when Christ comes into His own in men's hearts and cultures. All that Christ will be to Muslims, only Muslims can declare.

At the same time it is true that there are historic patterns of discipleship, recognizably Christian, and that there is a traditional framework of response, even though "the wind bloweth where it listeth." We must, therefore, face the whole question of baptism in the Muslim context. A book such as this would have betrayed its readers if it failed to take up this issue.

II

It should be insisted first that baptism belongs to the personal realm. (It will be argued below that it is not necessarily an *individual* matter and attention is, therefore, called to the choice of the word "personal.") Baptism marks, confirms, and seals a personal response. The purpose of the Christian mission is not cultural displacement. It is the presentation of Christ as Saviour within every culture. The Christian Church, as we have seen in the last section of the preceding chapter, always supposes and concedes the co-existence of the external world. That world may be characterized by many varying patterns of life. The objective of the mission is not to make a nominal "Christendom" universal. The world which is the context of the Church, of whatever cultural character, is not, of course, exempt from its concern, its compassion, and its duty. The Church will be obligated in love towards all of it all the time. But baptism, bringing persons within the Church, means their incorporation by faith into the supranational fellowship of Christ. It does not, properly understood, de-culturalize the new believer; it enchurches him. That "enchurchment," as its impact widens, bears creatively upon all areas of its context. The new Christian becomes responsible to Christ for his old setting and to his old setting in the new truth. But he is not thereby "going foreign." All that is not incompatible with Christ goes with him into baptism. Conversion is not "migration": it is the personal discovery of the meaning of the universal Christ within the old framework of race, language, and tradition. But implicit in this view of personal faith is a concept of religion and society which Islam has not hitherto recognized. Here lies one of our deepest problems and our need for large patience.

The Muslim concept of toleration has been, from the beginning, that of freedom to remain what you were born or freedom to become a Muslim. It has never yet meant freedom of movement of conscience, or freedom to become. It was Muslims, rather than non-Muslims, who had the lesser range of intellectual and spiritual possibility. Islam has been traditionally proud of its toleration based on the famous Quranic saying: "There is no compulsion in religion." Modern Muslim commentators fully share that pride. Expositions of Muslim toleration can readily be found in a score of publications and journals. But the fundamental question as to whether there is personal freedom of the Muslim vis-à-vis Islam is not faced and is often not even suspected as present. It is assumed that Islam is a faith which no Muslim would ever conceivably wish to forsake. Consequently the option to do so does not validly or feasibly exist. Looked at from this side Islam is a faith which no adherent is free to leave.

And that which one is not free to leave has become a prison, if one wishes to do so.

On this point it does not matter whether the option is ever taken. A true understanding of freedom, as freedom of movement of mind, demands that the option should exist. Nor does it matter for what alternative the option is required. Islam ought to concede such freedom irrespective of any possible consequences as to its members. If it is to be a self-respecting faith it must possess its adherents in the sole strength of their freely willed conviction. Doubtless it does so hold multitudes of its people. But the test comes when the negative corollary is asserted that freedom of belief must include freedom of disbelief and freedom of adherence, freedom of non-adherence. The plain fact is that, hitherto, such freedom has not existed among Muslims.

When Islam was generated and expanded into the world, Arabia was required to be solidly and exclusively Muslim. But elsewhere, Scriptural minorities, Jews and Christians, and some others not implicated in idolatry, were permitted, as we have seen, to remain as tolerated and tributary minorities. Their physical and spiritual disabilities varied from age to age and from place to place. Their members might rise to positions of dignity and wealth or they might lead a harassed and precarious existence. But always Islam was the dominant religion, identified with the imperial power and enjoying its prestige. Minorities tended to become introspective, furtive, and depressed. Those born within them were not normally compelled to Islamize. The Armenian, Coptic, Syrian, or other Christian was not required to forsake the faith of his fathers. But there was often the expectation that he would. Circumstances were such that it took considerable tenacity, often a kind of hopeless doggedness, to remain Christian. Certainly there was no expectation of Christian revival and growth. There were prohibitions, for example, on the building of new churches which were symptomatic of the outlook. The freedom was a freedom to remain. The only direction in which one could become anything was the Muslim one. Movement of allegiance was all in one direction. The born-Jew, the born-Christian, had, paradoxically, an option which the Muslim

337

lacked. He could at least move into Islam. The Muslim could not move out.[1]

Some elements in Islam today understand and interpret Islamic nationalism and the Islamic state in the same sense. They wish to insure that Islamic society shall be self-preserving in the old authoritarian way. For when, in the modern period, Muslims came under non-Muslim rule in a complete reversal of the proper status of the Muslim the protection of Islam became a duty of some imperial or mandatory government. Now that Islam has in so many areas come back into self-responsibility, the conservative elements wish to insure that the traditional pattern will be resumed. Others, however, for practical or patriotic reasons, wish to interpret nationalism more liberally and to find some religious *modus vivendi*, with the concept of equal citizenship for all minorities. But not many are willing, or perhaps we should say able, to contemplate all the religious corollaries of equal citizenship. They are searching for some form of religious freedom short of the secular state.

Thus the present time sees a crucial debate on a very wide issue and great changes may be waiting in the whole concept of freedom in Islam in the next decades. The problem is now squarely on the shoulders of Muslims themselves. The foreign governments have almost everywhere withdrawn. The protection, sometimes the encouragement, of minorities is no longer a foreign duty or temptation. Here it may be noted in passing that much nonsense has been talked about the so-called partnership between missions and empire. It may be that imperial expansion facilitated missionary expression, but there are as many evidences of imperial policy curbing and frustrating missionary effort, as there are of its fostering and aiding it. But the point here is that a Muslim solution regarding what is to be done about the Islamic state, about religious freedom, and about the non-Muslim citizen has now to be evolved. Our duty is to strive to bear witness to the obligation of any self-respecting religion, however it be related to the political expression, to encourage and allow a veritable freedom of movement of worship and belief. For only so can it be in the truest sense a genuine religious faith.

The legal forms of such an ideal are hard to shape and actualize in a society so inured to one religious form. But the genuine test of any democracy is the freedom of the minority to become the majority if it can. Or stated conversely it is where the majority stands only in conviction. Several Muslim states in the United Nations have withheld their signature from the Declaration of Human Rights because of its insistence that freedom of religion means freedom to become as well as to remain. On the other hand, Sir Zafrullāh Khān, when Foreign Minister of Pakistan, made his now celebrated recognition of the right of all religions to peaceful self-propagation within a Muslim state, on the ground that Islam itself was a missionary religion. The right of propagation presumably includes the right to receive adherents and the right of all citizens to become adherents. But there are long legal and constitutional battles ahead on the question of such freedom.

The problem, moreover, is not only one of law. Law, in such a realm, must finally reflect and enforce opinion. If it is to be successful it must be believed to be right. Though the harsh penalties of the old Muslim law of apostasy—disinheritance and death—have been legally suspended or nullified in most areas, public attitudes, economic or commercial sanctions, and social ostracism continue to be potent adversaries of actual freedom. What is needed is a profound revolution in the public attitude in which religion will come to be recognized as not finally a fit realm for any kind of compulsion. This in turn needs powerful intellectual enterprise, *ijtihād* Islam might call it, to shape popular conceptions and insure their effectiveness. The issue is an internal one for Islam.

III

Our Christian duty is to serve this situation as patiently and sympathetically as we can, trying to uphold the ideal of a religious allegiance which is not even indirectly compelled, and endeavoring to communicate the gathered significance of Western trial and error on this very same point. There are many pitfalls. One is to base the plea for real toleration on the ground that religion is an entirely private affair, relating to the individual and God alone. That view is mischievously incomplete and ill-balanced. Neither Christianity, nor Islam, properly considered,

339

can tolerate it. Both in their different ways bear witness to the fact that the truths of revelation relate to the life of society and to the responsibilities of government. We cannot properly immunize the whole realm of the state from the significance of religion. Nor is any intelligent Muslim who understands his own heritage likely to accept such a position, unless it be in desperation. The purely secular state, like mere positivism in education, runs into too many weaknesses and errors, in the lack of a religious frame of reference. It has been part of the historic genius of Islam to insist on the close interrelation of faith and society, of religion and state.

But another pitfall is to express the necessary interconnection between the religious and the political in such a way as to jeopardize religious freedom. Something of the Christian concept of the two communities has been suggested in the previous chapter. A way has to be found to symbolize and make operative the truth that human life in all its aspects stands under the law of God, without so identifying that law with any religious authority or hierarchy as to limit the freedom of mind and conscience which is the prerequisite of valid religious conviction and allegiance. The Christian Church has much experience to share with Muslims at this point, if it can achieve the right relationship to transmit it.

One of the realms where religious forms in law and society are liable to become indirectly coercive is the law of personal status. As long as religious communities have an exclusive prerogative over matters of marriage, divorce, and inheritance, relating to their members, there will remain a serious infraction of genuine religious liberty. Change of status will not be freely possible if marriage rights, inheritance, and the rest are not brought into line. Only the existence of alternative procedures in matters of personal status can insure that communities do not exercise a stranglehold upon their members. The millet system, of which communal personal status law is a part, dies hard and has been provocative of much tribulation and backwardness. It is not Islam alone which clings to it. A recent attempt in Lebanon by a group of lawyers to secure a bill establishing secular marriage and divorce evoked successful opposition from the Christian hierarchy no less than from the Muslim. But such secular marriage would be a real symbol and means to the individual's being free from a community to which he no longer inwardly belongs. The millet system makes religious communities self-perpetuating whether they deserve to be or not, and irrespective of the consent of all who are within them.[2]

It may be hoped, however, that nationalism and other pressures will considerably modify the millet system in these matters. Elsewhere it is clearly in retreat. There is hope that an urge for some modification of the official religious attitude toward adherence and its legal sanctions will steadily grow and that the deterrents, direct and indirect, to the freedom of communal interchange will be diminished. Islam would be all the sounder for such developments, precisely because its allegiance would be less formal and so more real, less inevitable and so more spontaneous. And Christianity would have the greater opportunity to bear its witness and to express its allegiance to Christ in every realm. Only a timid or mistaken calculus could fear that Islam would be weakened. Whatever "secular" losses there might be numerically, its status religiously could not fail to be more validly based. Fear and timidity are, after all, poor and unworthy defenders of real faith.

We have insisted that the Christian's duty in this matter of Muslim religious toleration, legal and actual, is primarily to exalt and serve the ideal. Freedom of conscience has an absolute value which transcends all special pleading. We are not seeking such changes primarily for the benefit of potential converts. Nor should thinking Muslims resist them for the sake of deterring such converts. The matter is not one to be judged by particular consequences, for or against. We had rather say, it is to be judged for its absolute consequences in purer religion and more validly based allegiance—consequences which cannot be outweighed by numbers lost or gained.

It is clear, nonetheless, that such freedom in Islam would, in serving the quality of Muslim conviction, also lift a heavy incubus from Christian evangelism. Inquirers would no longer be intimidated by family consequences; the Muslim convert would no longer be under inappropriate difficulties as to marriage, nor would he have to face disinheritance. Considerations of legal status would not inhibit the free pursuit of religious inquiry. The ex-Muslim would not be worried or persecuted into mental instability nor become a rootless protégé of some alien friend.

If it be argued that such a hope is dim and distant and, therefore, impractical, our retort is that we have not advocated it on the grounds of expediency. There can be no doubt that the ultimate hope of the Christian mission is for just such a change in Muslim attitudes to toleration. It may be long, or longer, before particular areas begin to feel the liberating consequences of such a change, where now even to evince the least interest in Christianity is to invite personal tragedy in some form. If the reader tends to be skeptical of its possibility he may be reminded that we are writing about patience and that the principle here sought is one that can be argued from a valid extension of Quranic and traditional Muslim teaching. Also let it be remembered that the strong pressures of secularism, undesirable as in some respects they are, tend in the same direction. Anglo-Saxon freedoms owe much to those who defied Christian institutions in their passion for a fundamentally Christian thing. Could not patience in some senses be defined as expecting the unexpected? That at least we must learn to do.

IV

But patience is also not visionary. Assuming that such changes are our ultimate hope and that they are to be sought for their own sake, is there any evidence that Christ attracts and satisfies the Muslim heart? Is the record of Muslim response to Christianity convincing in quality, if scanty in extent? Is there not ground for suspicion that the Church in Muslim lands has been singularly unfruitful, despite decades of devotion as sacrificial as any achieved in other fields where sizable Churches now exist? Is there hope that, as and when the possibility of response becomes greater, and even before, the people of the mosque will have any ear for Christ?

The answer is "Yes." There is firm ground for the belief that many do and will reach out hands towards the Gospel, patiently and imaginatively presented, despite the antipathy towards it of much in the Muslim temper. Part of the evidence is the personal stature and fidelity of Muslim Christians through the years when disabilities and persecution have been unceasing. There is no space here for any detailed account of these examples. The largest Christian communities of former Muslims are in Indonesia and Iran.[3] Elsewhere in the Muslim world, Christian Churches are either ancient Churches of apostolic foundation and communal continuity, containing almost no former Muslims, or else Churches of Western planting, linked in some form with Rome or Protestantism and containing some members of Muslim origin but many more whose forebears have transferred from the ancient Churches. Arabic-speaking Christianity of Muslim background is a saga of the few.

Nevertheless, there has been a tenuous succession of notable as well as of obscure Muslims who have come into Christ. Their quality rebukes the fear that Islam is impervious to the meaning of the Gospel, while their fewness is at least in part explained by the mountainous obstacles that have confronted them and the crippling disabilities and inadequacies of the Christian mission. The source of amazement is not so much that there are few as that there are any. For the mission, though devoted, has often been clumsy, beset with handicaps of personnel, of language, of poverty in resources, of inexperience, as well as burdened with the associations of a disloyal "Christendom." He who contemplates the mission to Islam should remember to think before he starts to count.

A few names may perhaps be cited. One of the earliest pioneers of medical missions in India was a former Muslim shaikh, Sālih, master of the jewels at the Court of Oudh, who took the baptismal name of 'Abd al-Masīh and became a Christian minister. He was led to seek Christ through the preaching of Henry Martyn, whom he assisted in New Testament translation. He understood the implications of the Gospel and years before medical missions were known in India (indeed any organized missions, since Martyn and his successors were East India Company chaplains),[4] 'Abd al-Masīh established a dispensary for which he qualified himself and on which he spent his own personal resources. His pioneer example it was which stimulated English medical ministry in the sub-continent.

Another 'Abd al-Masīh, who died in 1953, became a fervent and effective minister of Christ. His story may perhaps be cited for the only reason that it embodies so many characteristic features of the Muslim encounter with Christ, its course and its costs. Born of uneducated parents in a village 150 miles south of Cairo, he was sent to the mosque school, where he became a memorizer of the Qur'ān and began at seven years the performance of the prayers. One day the young scholar found an Arabic Gospel of St. Matthew in the street. Picking it up, he read it aloud to friends until the blind schoolmaster intervened and after inquiry tore it in pieces. He ordered his two sons to burn the pieces, and washed his hands afterwards to cleanse the defilement at handling the Christian book. The boy's father took him later from the mosque school and sent him to a Christian one, for no special reason. Indelibly in the boy's mind was the belief that to touch St. Matthew's Gospel was to be defiled. He was horrified, therefore, to find there were copies of this book in the new school. He refused to attend the school until his father and some friends arranged with the headmaster that the boy would not have to handle St. Matthew's Gospel.

But morning and evening prayers were a further problem. The father was unwilling to seek exemption. "So I had to content myself with sitting on the last bench of the little Church and stuffing my fingers into my ears lest I should hear any word of the singing or prayers." Some time later in a friend's house he made acquaintance with the Psalms, and later, at a post-funeral visit, heard a Pastor read from St. Matthew's Gospel. The words gripped him and despite his earlier certainty that the book would defile him, he sought it out to read it. The reading went on in secret and extended to other parts of the Bible. There came a consequent search for forgiveness and a growing sense of need, which sent him to Muslim friends and teachers to learn more about Islam. The form of his questions roused these teachers to suspicion that he was "corrupted" by Christians. They assured him that to be a Muslim was to be secure and that God would pardon all who said the *Shahādah*. But a deepening restlessness possessed him, with a growing despair about any change of heart through a faith that did not recognize the nature of his need. Finally in great soul-concern he turned again to St. Matthew and found peace in the words: "Come unto Me all ye that labour and I will give you rest." He resolved to join himself to the Christian fellowship and to confess his trust in Christ as Saviour. "Then I begged the Lord to make me an evangelist that I might tell others of the love He had given to me."

The transaction of that solitary encounter with the forgiving Christ led to a confession like St. Thomas: "My Lord and my God." But it also entailed strong persecution. The boy's father put him in a dark store room for several weeks, on a ration of bread and water. He was beaten. When he was released he was ridiculed in the streets. "The children used to clap their hands on seeing me and chant 'Here comes the infidel.' Often they threw stones and dust at me, whilst men in the streets spat in my face and struck me on the head with their fists. These persecutions continued for about eighteen months." [5]

The sequel of the story tells of baptism two years after, of theological study and ordination. The name of Marcus 'Abd al-Masīh is loved throughout Egypt, Syria, and the Sudan as that of a devoted contemporary witness to the love of Christ. It must stand in our narrative here as representative of many more: Mikhā'īl Mansūr of Al-Azhar; Mirzā Ibrāhīm of Tabrīz; Chauduri Ināyat Ullāh of Qadiān; Sa'īd Kurdistānī of Teheran; John Subhān, author of *How a Sufi Found his Lord;* Dilawar Khān and Jehān Khān of the Pathan hills; Sima'ān Dibūnÿ of Palestine. Whatever else these names proclaim, they demonstrate that there are Muslim minds to open with gladness when Christ comes seeking. But great as are the stories of these men and their kind, the difficulties they encountered and the realization that there were many others, unknown to us, who never survived the mental or emotional strain of their desire to become Christ's compel us to face earnestly the question of baptismal concepts and policies.

v

The New Testament summons plainly involves the possibility of family antagonism and personal persecution. "A man's foes shall be they of his own household." "If any man will come after Me let him take up his cross and follow Me." We cannot seek either for ourselves or for others to facilitate the Christian life so as to be disloyal to its nature. The Church of the Apostolic generation became a church of the Catacombs. Costliness has always been a characteristic ingredient of Christian discipleship. The Christian Church is called to be so firm a fellowship that in its company nothing shall be too hard to undertake that may be required of us by the obedience of Christ. That the Gospel is set forth unto all nations for "the obedience of faith" is St. Paul's classic expression of the purpose of the witness of the Church. As in His earthly ministry, so when He is proclaimed throughout history, Christ is a Master and Saviour awaiting a verdict. The very name of the New Testament means a proffered relationship—a relationship which hinges upon the soul's response.

But the more insistently we recognize that Christianity is a confessed discipleship, the more urgently we must face the problems implicit in such confession in the Muslim world. We must also have regard to the corollaries for such discipleship of the way we administer the external forms of the confession. It would be wrong to administer baptism as a seal of individual confession, without regard to how the form was understood in the community we are also calling into discipleship. The baptism of the one cannot be in disconnection with the evangelizing of the many. On that point the mind of the Apostle is clear. "Christ," he said, "sent me not to baptise but to preach the Gospel." We cannot administer baptism in unconcern about the unity and quality of the Church into which we baptize and in whose strength of comradeship the individual alone can "come victor." We cannot administer baptism without patient relation to the potential misunderstandings of the watching, often apprehensive, community. There are some who have sought it as a kind of charm and others who have suspected it for the same reason. Arab mothers, for example, have kept their children from the hands of nurses who might wash them, in fear lest the latter should at the same time mumble over them some formula which would turn them inevitably into Christians.

346

For these and many other reasons there have been some within the Christian mission who have wondered whether in the Muslim context the familiar pattern of isolated individual baptism should not be reconsidered as perhaps being too "impatient" a way. The questions at issue are so real and go so deep, that, while no specific answer is offered here, it is well to state them briefly, as part of that travail in patience which is the Christian mission.

It should first be made indubitably clear that baptism after proper safeguards have been met, should never be positively and permanently withheld from one who has responsibly sought it in good faith and of his own volition. In such circumstances no policy has a right to impede the soul. The problem is not whether baptism should be withheld, but whether it should be encouraged or invariably sought on our part.

Those who suggest that perhaps it should not, have no desire to obscure the decisive quality of Christian discipleship or to obviate the cost and duty of witness. Nor is there any compromise on the theological question of the relation of baptism to faith. The purpose rather is to foster such witness and faith in a more promising way and in a more hopeful setting. It is clear that a Christian interest, a Christian seeking, cannot and should not be hid. But does baptism into Christ, as an individual step, have features which unnecessarily complicate and aggravate the task of Christian presentation? Perhaps.

In the first place Muslim society is not individualist but communal. Therefore is the individual the appropriate unit of baptism? Perhaps forms of new allegiance might be more meaningfully fulfilled in community. Official baptism may have in Muslim eyes an appearance of treason, because of strong communal and national ties attaching to Islam. In the New Testament days and in the modern West, baptism does not mean a rejection of particular citizenship. In the modern Muslim East it seems to mean that. The Muslim in the Arab world thinks of the Christian Church as a separate millet perhaps with a different language, certainly with a different "ethos" and different cohesion. What is a renunciation of sin looks to one's kin as denunciation of all that makes one "belong."

347

There is certainly an urgent need to militate strongly against this overwhelming Muslim concept of what baptism means and implies. The question is: Do we militate against it, by playing into its hands? Is there a way of demonstrating that to become a Christian is not to cease to be native, is not to become alien. Can we strive for that understanding of the institution of baptism on the part of Muslims? Has this, for a period at least, a priority over its unthinking application to particular people? It is argued that the more disposed we are to emphasize the ultimate indispensability of baptism to Christian discipleship the more concerned we should be that the relevance of the institution to the discipleship should not be misread by the multitudes for whom the Gospel is meant. Will such misreading be corrected unless we strenuously set out to do so?

Is it possible to familiarize the Muslim with the truth that to become a Christian is not a mere shift of communities, that it does not rob Muslim society, as such, of a potential servant and the local community, as such, of a loving son? How can we demonstrate that to become a Christian is to remain responsible in some sense for "Muslim" citizenship? If we are anxious, as we have argued above, to develop in at least some Muslims a less totalitarian view of the relation between dogma and society, shall we allow them to persist in a concept of baptism which is just as totalitarian? If we believe in a Church within a culture, shall we make the door into that Church, a door right out of the culture? "Let not thy good be evil spoken of," said the Apostle. He meant that we have a responsibility toward the concepts others form of our institutions in so far as we can affect and shape those concepts.

What, then, can be done to encourage in Islam the truth that becoming a Christian is not ceasing to belong with Muslim need, Muslim thought, and Muslim kin? Some have thought that the answer is to pioneer for a new status, in which those who respond, or desire to respond, to Christ might be encouraged to associate with fellow, or potentially fellow, Christians, without alienating their old context irrevocably by any formal step which that context will so interpret. Let it be clear that no sincere seeker will be hidden and unknown. The suggestion is not secret belief.

There will be issues like forms of prayer and fasting which will be invaded by new liberty and new meaning. But that newness of life will not be taken formally and officially out of the old context so as greatly to jeopardize the chances of that context understanding what it is.

It may be argued that this will be jeopardizing the disciple's own chances of growing in what he has found and of finding it further. In answer it is said that any such pioneer status, not yet baptized, should have the fullest fellowship and spiritual support of the Church. It will demand qualities no less tenacious than those which characterize the finally baptized. It is offered as something to which the Church must encourage new seekers and in which it must stand with them, as a creative venture. The Church must be ready to think out and sustain in prayer and fellowship all the implications of the new status. What is believed is that "Lovers of Jesus," or a fellowship under some other designation, may go further in preparing Christ's way among Muslims than would the same people promptly and singly baptized into a fellowship still largely alien, not of Muslim background, and set (by one initial transaction) out of reach of the Muslim mind.

When St. Paul argues about meats in the New Testament he suggests that what are duties (of distinction) in one context may be overridden in another and that there are liberties (of enjoying) which may rightly be self-denied. Can, then, an undoubted right and privilege be foregone *for the sake of the brethren for whom Christ died,* without jeopardizing its standing as a right and a privilege? It might have been argued that St. Paul was endangering a liberty by refraining from its use. But love was paramount and the liberty was safe in those hands. Baptism may well appear compromised in the proposal to hold back from it, until it is seen that brethren for whom Christ died have in love's reckoning a prior claim.

There are many facets of this approach which cannot here be further considered. Its advocates insist that full and loving provision must be made for the spiritual nurture of all "Lovers of Jesus" if baptism is left in abeyance. The only objective is to encourage the hope and ideal of larger and more viable units of baptism than the individual and to discourage Muslim misconception and antagonism. All the theological truth about the final place and necessity of baptism is recognized and upheld in a more patient effort to obey it.[6]

The ultimate question which has in any case to be faced is: To what quality of Christian life and witness are we to try to call the Muslim seeker? How should we encourage him to relate himself to his community of origin, since it cannot fail to remain in measure his community? Ultimately, there is no escaping these questions, since the quality and direction of soul of those who learn Christ from among our Muslim friends is the key to the Muslim world. No people of a community was ever yet won by aliens from it. As long as the mission is primarily "foreign" it will ultimately fail to be one. We must come, at all costs, by a creative loyalty to Christ, in all things.

Here, then, are the issues. The unit of Christianity is undoubtedly the person, but persons belong in communities and to cultures. We must preach so as to expect an answer to the offer of Christ. We cannot be accountable for all the motives of interest and response, though these depend in large measure upon the quality of the communication. Our institutional relationship to the Muslim seeker must be disarming and patient but always hopeful. Douglas Thornton of Cairo used to remark that he never knew which of his student friends might not prove a Saul of Tarsus. Nor must we have too Western an idea of what response to Christ is going to mean for those who hear us. If we have the right to say of the patriarchs: "They without us shall not be made perfect," surely Easterners have the right to say it to us. When their response comes we must "lay them on our shoulders rejoicing." This may well be the hardest part. If they have a cost to count, legal obstacles, economic difficulties, possible unemployment, so also have we, a cost of quiet nurture and of unstinting friendship that does not weaken the fibers of personal character.

VI

The responsibilities of success lead into another theme of great importance. It certainly belongs under "Patience." It is the spiritually welcoming quality that ought to belong to the local Church. Part of the problem of baptism is that the Church is as yet so imperfectly fitted to be a true home for the soul and mind of the Muslim. The newer Churches of Western planting, especially in the Arab world, are not spontaneously hospitable to the Muslim seeker. His good faith may be doubted, his presence mistrusted, and his interest questioned. Locally there is great reluctance to contemplate uninhibited friendship. Many Churches, moreover, operate under legal conditions which regard them as self-contained, not self-propagating, units. Their authority to worship, to solemnize marriages, to own property, and the like, is contingent on their observing a policy of "introversion." By a legacy of the millet concept, it is difficult for them to be at once communities of worship and communities of evangelism. This is a cruel dilemma, but a real one. The situation compels them to practice, if not also to feel, severe prudential reservations about baptism outside their own families. The legal difficulties tend to foster or excuse a certain spiritual lack of adventure in evangelism. The solutions call for long patience that strives for a steady deepening of the will to be hospitable and a removal of the legal deterrents.

But Christianity in the Eastern mind is not primarily represented by these new Churches. Through the Arab world, in Turkey, in South India, in Ethiopia, the ancient, Christian, Apostolic patriarchates of the Greek Orthodox, Coptic, Armenian, and other communions constitute by far the most important expression of Christian faith and worship. Books on these Churches have been included in the Bibliography, since a sympathetic knowledge of them is indispensable to the Western Christian and because there is no opportunity here even to begin to do justice to their significance. Missionary relationships with the Christian Churches of the East have often been difficult. Westerners have misunderstood, even despised, their traditions and have failed to enter into the riches of their long devotional continuity. They may have been repelled by features of doctrine or practice that offended their Protestant zeal. Or they have been unable to establish such positive relationships as might enable the mediation of the insights they had to bring, as well as to receive the wealth of fellowship they stood to gain.

The failures, of course, have not been all one-sided. The old traditions, in some of their representatives, were suspicious and apprehensive. They feared for their prestige or their communities—not always without reason, since many new Churches were recruited from their ranks. They were also unable to make the strenuous efforts required to understand the strange, activist, impatient forms of Western Christianity. In many directions, however, in late years there has been a steady growth of mutual desire for understanding and at least partial co-operation between the old and the new, the Eastern and the Western. The major Eastern communions have shared in the World Council of Churches and have discovered that they can trust and respect many of the Western Churches, while the latter have come to see more truly the genius of the orthodox East. In the area of mission, however, there remain serious problems of relationship. The missionary concept toward Islam makes only slow headway against the centuries of exclusiveness by which the Eastern Christian mind is still guided.

Nevertheless co-operative enterprises in the fields of theological education, social welfare, and Christian literature may become increasingly possible. There is great need for recruits to the Western mission who will make the understanding of the Eastern Churches their prime responsibility and who will seek to interpret differences and heal suspicions and articulate for the Muslim a clearer Christian call. An ambition on our part to be glad junior partners with an awakened and expressive Eastern Christianity would be the truest fulfillment of all the goals discussed here in the chapters in Part III, "Minaret and Christian."

As a postscript to this bare treatment of a great theme mention should be made of the distracting but increasing presence of sects on the wing of Western Christianity. These are quite unwilling to co-operate with older missions and certainly not with an Eastern Christianity they regard as apostate. They pay little attention to the comity of missions and efforts to work co-operatively meet with scant response and sometimes open rejection. Yet these groups exercise considerable influence and command large resources. They are liable to confuse the situation both for Christian and Muslim. Yet a staunchly Christian attitude towards them must be maintained at all costs by the "old-line" missions. They may serve perhaps to chasten complacency and deepen patience. They stimulate by contrast the need to preserve a well-rounded Gospel and to remember that there are very few single truths that will bear exclusive preaching. Extremism sometimes overreaches itself. The Apostle learned to rejoice every way. It is finally by the quality of our apprehension of Christ and devotion to Him that we may hope to deserve to succeed. In all our relationships "Let this mind be in us which was also in Christ Jesus."

VII

There remains here one final consideration. Christian discipleship, unto baptism, presupposes in its personal quality the continuity of the non-Christian context. This does not imply that the Church has no duty to that context other than baptizing people out of it. On the contrary, as a society within society it has searching responsibilities to the whole. Those who are gathered into the household of grace, by faith, should in virtue of their discipleship become the salt of their community. In proportion to their numbers they should influence the opinion that fashions behavior and the beliefs that inspire and govern institutions. The social and other corollaries of their discipleship will, in proportion to their strength and fidelity, steadily permeate and discipline the culture of their world. In this sense there are many things in Muslim society that are compatible with such Christian influence and can be served by it. Hospitality, cleanliness, moderation, simplicity, discipline, dignity, family affection, sensitivity to the poor, and many other traits which characterize Muslim attitudes at their best will be sustained and preserved. Doubtless there are other attitudes, or the reasons for holding them, which will be criticized and refused. Their basis in the concept of God and of man will be revised. The patterns which the changed beliefs unmake will be unmade, to the extent in which those beliefs penetrate. But there are others which will be confirmed and others again which only become

353

apparent in their quality when there are enough Christian-Muslims to recognize and make them actual. Perhaps the greatest contribution of all from the "disciples made" will be in the realm not of What? but of How? not of particular virtues but the means to them all, if it be true that the constraining love of Christ is the deepest wellspring of unselfish character and unwearied goodness.

Even, however, where personal allegiance is never won, nor the Church numerically enlarged, perhaps where these objectives, for any reason, are not even in view, there are endless services which the Christian witness can render. It will always be true, of course, that Christian quality belongs essentially in persons and only comes to attach derivatively to laws, or customs, or things. Nevertheless the Christ Who said "He that is not with Me is against Me," also declared: "He that is not against us is on our part," meaning that actions and attitudes could have place in His purpose even when their owners withheld themselves personally from His Kingdom. The Church that seeks to proclaim His ethic and to demonstrate His compassion may expect to see these make their way outside its membership. Moreover, we can never say at what point the soul of man awakes into the knowledge of Christ. Early discipleship is not always to the same features. In one sense the Christian mission is a cause that can never lose, even if it is also one that can rarely gain. If no Christians as such are gathered, this has not disarmed or immobilized the Gospel's criticism of men's lives, nor its measure of their recreation. The leaven works silently and unseen. There is nothing barren about the Gospel wherever it is active.

It may even be legitimate, in this connection, to turn to the supposition of absence and attempt to assess the consequences. If Christ did not exist, nor the Gospel, nor the Church, what of the form of the world's life and the fashion of its thinking? They would doubtless be unrecognizable. Though a mission to Islam would not be validated solely by the effect of its non-existence, it is important and legitimate sometimes to remember what the world around might not have been. Results, in other words, are more than those that are measurable. There is much ground for believing that modern versions of the Prophet Muhammad owe something to the parallel of Christ. When compared with those of the earliest historians, who were remarkably frank and unembarrassed, they show differences which are almost all Christward in their direction. This may be one form of the Gospel's impact. The same may be said of tendencies toward reconciliation and freedom. These unseen influences are not yet at an end. They may be part of the unpredictable consequences which the Christ-messenger sets under way when he intends the conversion of men. The Gospel is always bigger than the capacities and expectations even of those who take it. These truths, however, do not warrant the messenger in forbearing to seek what he is taught to seek, by his inward awareness of the nature of what he brings. He will not cease to preach for a verdict he can understand, in his knowledge that other verdicts are being slowly made before God. His is properly a person-to-person relationship, but its potentialities are not to be only personally measured. It has much to render even where it will never baptize.

It is important, therefore, to help the Muslim world to conceive of the Christian mission not as depredatory but as constructive. It is true that it seeks to make disciples, since discipleship is what Christ intends and claims. A Christian mission that renounces the making of Christians has forsaken both its genius and its duty. Christ did not serve the world with good advice and no more shall we. But such discipleship is not Western "aggression"; it is not religious competition. The faith that offers it is not truly seen as a rival. The truth is not rivalry but relevance. What Christ and what, therefore, the Christian mission hold in trust is profoundly meaningful to the whole life, aspiration, and humanity of the Muslim world. The herald wants only that it be available. The more he contemplates his duty the more surely he feels: "Woe is unto me if I preach not the Gospel." The call of the minaret is to every Muslim who understands its inclusiveness. But thereby the minaret is also a call to every Christian who understands his Christianity.

These, then, are some of our needs for patience: patience with our partners in the Christian fellowship; patience with monumental misunderstandings which must somehow be removed; patience with the massive external deterrents; patience with the inward spiritual unlikeness; patience with ourselves and our proneness to hasty ways and incomplete devotion; the patience of hope and resolve. What matters finally is the presentation of Christ in the full significance, for God and for man, of His ministry and His sorrows. The final urge to the Christian mission is what Christ is and what, because of Him, we know God to be. We must represent the Gospel of Christ in the spirit and fellowship of Him from Whom it derives.

VIII

Two of the most sacred mosques of the Islamic world look down from their sanctuaries eastward toward the trees of old Gethsemane. From its olive-covered slopes the Garden of the Agony looks westward to the domes and minarets of the ancient skyline. In the still dawn the muezzin can be heard calling to prayer across, the valley where Jesus communed with His spirit until midnight and went forth, the Christ of the Cross, the Saviour of the world. Through all their history, since the minarets were raised, the two faiths have been that near, that far. It is out of the meaning of the Garden that Christ's men have crossed into the world of the domes and the muezzin. We who, in our generation, listen to the call of the minaret may hear it most compellingly from the muezzin over Gethsemane. There we shall best understand wherewith we must answer—and how—and why.

NOTES *to Chapter XI*

1

On this theme see Khaddūrī, Majīd, *The Law of War and Peace in Islam,* Baltimore, 1955, and Zwemer, Samuel M., *The Law of Apostacy in Islam,* London, 1924.

2

A revolutionary step was taken in Egypt in 1955 when all court dealing with personal status, within all communities, were brough under the Government judicial system. Such changes, if established an extended elsewhere would completely transform the situation as hithert obtaining.

3

The reasons for this fact have often been conjectured but neve convincingly established. It may be agreed, however, that Arabic-speal ing Islam, for Quranic and other reasons, has always been the most tenacious.

4

It may be interesting to recall how inimical to the idea of missions was the attitude of the East India Company, for much is written about the supposed "collusion" between "empire" and faith. The Company's Committee passed the following Minute in 1793: "That the sending of missionaries into our Eastern possessions is the maddest, most extravagant and most unwarrantable project that was ever proposed by an enthusiastic lunatic."

5

Marcus 'Abd al-Masīh recounted his story in *The Muslim World*, July, 1945, Vol. 35, No. 3, pp. 211-15. From this account these extracts are taken with permission.

6

It is important to emphasize this intention. For the general position suggested here is often regarded with suspicion, cf., Neill, Stephen C., *Christian Faith Today*, Penguin Books Ltd., London, 1955, "The convert is cut off from all his past; he no longer has any access to his own people, and has no opportunity to bear any witness to them about his new-found faith. As an unbaptized Christian, he can move about among them freely and let character and conviction bear their own quiet witness." Having thus in part stated the argument of the text, Bishop Neill proceeds: "The argument is painfully plausible . . . Scarcely one of those who have started out, with whatever sincerity of conviction, on this course of inner Christian allegiance without overt Christian confession, has been able to resist the soothing influence of compromise: not one of them has ever succeeded in creating an unmistakably Christian movement among his own people." But are purely pragmatic and retrospective criteria necessarily the right ones in seeking to understand the mind of the Spirit? In any event, no avoidance of overt confession is here in mind: rather the form of legal status.

BOOK LIST

A selection of titles, mainly in English and not including works referred to in the footnotes. Works listed here under one Part may be relevant to another also.

PART I AND ALSO CHAPTER VII

'Abd al-Jalīl, J. M., and others, *Islam*, Studia Missionalia XI, Rome, 1961.

'Abdul-Latīf, Syed, *Towards a Re-Orientation of Islamic Thought*, Hyderabad, 1954.

Adams, C. C., *Islam and Modernism in Egypt*, London, 1933.

Alberuni, A. H., *Makers of Pakistan and Modern Muslim India*, Lahore, 1950.

'Alī, Muhammad, *Select Letters and Speeches*, edited by Afzal Iqbāl, Lahore, 1944.

'Alī, Zakī, *Islam in the World*, Lahore, 1938.

Allen, Henry E., *The Turkish Transformation*, Chicago, 1935.

Ambedkar, B. R., *Pakistan, or the Partition of India*, 3rd edition, Bombay, 1946.

Anderson, J. N. D., *Islamic Law in the Modern World*, New York, 1959.

Anshen, Ruth Nanda, editor, *Mid-East: World Center*, New York, 1956.

Antonius, George, *The Arab Awakening*, London, 1939.

Atiyeh, Edward, *An Arab Tells His Story*, London, 1946.

———, *The Arabs*, London, 1955.

Baljon, J. M. S., *The Reforms and Religious Ideas of Sir Sayyid Ahmad Khan*, Leiden, 1949.

Bennabi, Malek, *Vocation de l'Islam*, Paris, 1952.

Birge, J. Kingsley, *Guide to Turkish Area Study*, Washington, 1949.

Bisbee, Eleanor, *The New Turks*, Philadelphia, 1951.

Bolitho, Hector, *Jinnah, Creator of Pakistan*, New York, 1955.

Bukhsh, S. Khuda, *Essays: Indian and Islamic*, London, 1912.

——, *Studies: Indian and Islamic*, London, 1927.

Callard, Keith, *Pakistan: A Political Study*, London, 1957.

Caroe, Olaf, *Wells of Power*, London, 1951.

Crescent and Green: A Miscellany of Writings on Pakistan, New York, 1956.

Dodge, Bayard, editor, *The Colloquium on Islamic Culture and Its Relation to the Contemporary World*, Princeton, 1953.

Ettinghausen, Richard, editor, *A Selected and Annotated Bibliography of Books and Periodicals in Western Languages dealing with the Near and Middle East*, 2nd edition, Washington, 1954.

Fāris, Nabīh A., and Husayn, M. T., *Crescent in Crisis*, Lawrence, Kansas, 1955.

Fernau, F. W., *Moslems on the March*, trans. from German by E. W. Dickes, New York, 1954.

Fisher, Sidney N., editor, *Social Forces in the Middle East*, Ithaca, 1955.

Fyzee, A. A. A., *A Modern Approach to Islam*, Bombay, 1963.

Gibb, Hamilton A. R., *Studies in Contemporary Arabic Literature*, London, 1928-30.

——, editor, *Whither Islam?*, London, 1932.

——, *The Near East: Problems and Prospects*, Chicago, 1942.

——, *Modern Trends in Islam*, Chicago, 1947.

——, and Bowen, Harold, *Islamic Society and the West*, Vol. 1, London, 1950.

Grünebaum, G. E. von, *Islam: Essays in the Nature and Growth of a Cultural Tradition* (especially chap. xi: "Attempts at Self-Interpretation in Contemporary Islam"), Menasha, Wisconsin, 1955.

——, editor, *Unity and Variety in Muslim Civilization*, Chicago, 1955.

Hourani, Albert H., *Syria and Lebanon*, London, 1946.

Izzedin, Nejla, *The Arab World: Its Past, Present and Future*, Chicago, 1953.

Jäschke, G., *Der Islam in der Neuen Turkei*, Leiden, 1954.

Jinnah, Muhammad 'Alī, *Some Recent Speeches and Writings*, edited by Jamāl ud-Dīn Ahmad, Lahore, 1945.

Kahin, George McT., *Nationalism and Revolution in Indonesia*, Ithaca, 1952.

Khaddūrī, Majīd, *Independent Iraq*, London, 1951.

Khemiri, T., and Kampffmeyer, G., *Leaders in Contemporary Arabic Literature*, London, 1930.

Kirk, George E., *Short History of the Middle East*, Washington, 1949.

Landau, Jacob M., *Parliaments and Parties in Egypt*, New York, 1954.

Landau, Rom, and Arberry, A. J., editors, *Islam Today: A Survey*, London, 1943.

Laqueur, Walter Z., *The Middle East in Transition*, New York, 1958.

——, *Communism and Nationalism in the Middle East*, London, 1956.

Lenczowski, George, *The Middle East in World Affairs*, Ithaca, 1952.

Lewis, Geoffrey, *Turkey*, New York, 1955.

Le Tourneau, Roger, *L'Islam Contemporaine*, Paris, 1950.

Matthews, R. D., and Akrawi, Matta, *Education in the Arab Countries of the Near East*, Washington, 1949.

Morrison, S. A., *Middle East Tensions, Political, Social and Religious*, New York, 1954.

Orga, Irfan, *Portrait of a Turkish Family*, New York, 1950.

Price, Phillips, *A History of Turkey*, New York, 1956.

Rifā'at, Muhammad, *The Awakening of Modern Egypt*, London, 1947.

Rondot, Pierre, *L'Islam et les Musulmans d'aujourd'hui*, Paris, 1958-60.

Sadiq, Muhammad, *Urdu Literature in the 20th Century*, Baroda, 1947.

Smith, Wilfred Cantwell, *Islam in Modern History*, Princeton, 1957.

——, *Modern Islam in India*, Lahore, 1943.

Spear, T. G., *India, Pakistan and the West*, London, 1949.

Sutton, L. P. Elwell, *Modern Iran*, London, 1941.

Symonds, Richard, *The Making of Pakistan*, London, 1950.

Titus, Murray T., *Islam in India and Pakistan*, revised edition, Madras, 1959.

Toynbee, Arnold J., *The Islamic World since the Peace Settlement*, London, 1925.

——, *The World and the West*, New York, 1953.

Webster, Donald E., *The Turkey of Ataturk*, Philadelphia, 1939.

Woodman, Dorothy, *The Republic of Indonesia*, New York, 1955.

Young, T. Cuyler, editor, *Near East Culture and Society*, Princeton, 1951.

PART II

'Abd al-Jalīl, J. M., *Aspects Intérieures de l'Islam*, 2nd edition, Paris, 1949.

Abū-l-Fazl, Mirzā, *The Koran*, Bombay, 1955.

Ahmad, Mahmūd, *The Economics of Islam*, Lahore, 1947.

'Alī, 'Abdallāh Yūsuf, *The Holy Quran*, 2 vols., Lahore, 1937-8.

——, *The Message of Islam*, London, 1940.

——, *Fundamentals of Islam*, Geneva, 1929.

'Alī, Muhammād, *Manual of Hadith*, Lahore, n.d.

——, *The Living Thoughts of the Prophet Muhammad*, London, 1947.

Amīn, Osman, *Muhammad 'Abduh,* trans. into English, Washington, 1953.

Andrae, Tor, *Mohammed, the Man and His Faith,* trans. from the German, New York, 1936.

Arberry, Arthur J., *The Holy Koran: An Introduction with Selections,* London, 1953.

——, *The Koran Interpreted,* 2 vols., London, 1955.

——, *Revelation and Reason in Islam,* New York, 1957.

Archer, John C., *The Mystical Elements in Mohammed,* New Haven, 1924.

Arnold, Sir Thomas, *The Caliphate,* Oxford, 1924.

——, and Guillaume, Alfred, *The Legacy of Islam,* Oxford, 1931.

'Azād, Abū-l-Kalām, *Tarjumān al-Qur'ān,* Vol. 1: *Surat al-Fātihah,* trans. by Syed 'Abdul-Latīf, Bombay, 1962.

Bammate, Haidar, *Visages de l'Islam,* Lausanne, 1946.

Bell, Richard, *The Origin of Islam in Its Christian Environment,* London, 1926.

——, *The Qur'an,* 2 vols., Edinburgh, 1937-9.

Bennabi, Malek, *Lebbeik, Pèlerinage des Pauvres,* Algiers, 1948.

——, *Le Phénomine Coranique,* n.d.

Birge, J. Kingsley, *The Bektashi Order of Dervishes,* London, 1937.

Blachère, Regis, *Le Coran,* Paris, 1947.

——, *Le Problème de Mahomet,* Paris, 1952.

Bodley, Ronald V. C., *The Messenger,* New York, 1946.

Bousquet, Georges H., *La Morale de l'Islam et Son Ethique Sexuelle,* Paris, 1953.

Browne, E. G., *Literary History of Persia,* 4 vols., London and Cambridge, 1902-24.

Calverley, E. E., *Islam, An Introduction,* Cairo, 1958.

Cragg, Kenneth, *Sandals at the Mosque,* London, 1959.

——, *The Dome and the Rock,* London, 1964.

Dawood, N. J., *The Koran,* London, 1956.

De Boer, T. J., *The History of Philosophy in Islam,* trans. by E. R. Jones, London, 1903.

Depont, O., and Coppolani, X., *Les Confrèries Réligieuses Musulmanes,* Algiers, 1897.

Dermenghem, Emile, *Life of Mahomet,* trans. from the French, London, 1930.

——, *Muhammed and the Islamic Tradition,* trans. by Jean M. Watt, London, 1958.

Donaldson, Dwight M., *Studies in Muslim Ethics,* London, 1953.

——, *The Shi'ite Religion,* London, 1933.

Elder, Earl E., *Commentary on the Creed of Islam*, a trans. of Al-Taftāzānī, New York, 1950.

Fārūkī, Kemāl A., *Islamic Constitution*, Karachi, 1953.

Frye, Richard N., editor, *Islam and the West*, 's. Gravenhage, 1957.

Gardet, Louis, *Connaître l'Islam*, Paris, 1958.

———, *La Cité Musulmane: Vie Sociale et Politique*, Paris, 1954.

———, and Anawati, C. G., *Introduction à la Théologie Musulmane*, Paris, 1948.

Gaudefroy-Demombynes, Maurice, *Le Pèlerinage à la Mekke*, Paris, 1923.

———, *Mahomet*, Paris, 1957.

———, *Muslim Institutions*, trans. by John P. MacGregor, London, 1950.

Gibb, Hamilton A. R., Provençal, E. Levi, and Schacht, J., *The Encyclopaedia of Islam*, new edition, 1954-

Goldziher, Ignacz, *Etudes sur la Tradition Islamique*, trans. from Vol. 2 of above by Bercher, Leon, Paris, 1952.

———, *Le Dogme et La Loi*, Paris, 1920.

———, *Muhammedanische Studien*, 2 vols., Halle, 1890.

Grünebaum, G. E. von, *Modern Islam, The Search for Cultural Identity*, Berkeley, 1962.

Guillaume, Alfred, *Traditions of Islam*, Oxford, 1924.

———, *Islam*, London, 1954.

———, *The Life of Muhammad*, a translation of Ibn Ishāq's *Sīrat Rasūl Allāh*, Oxford, 1955.

Al-Hakīm, Tewfīg, *Maze of Justice*, trans. from the Arabic by A. S. Eban, London, 1947.

Hazard, Harry W., and Cook, H. L., *Atlas of Islamic History*, 3rd edition, Princeton, 1954.

Heyd, Uriel, *Foundations of Turkish Nationalism*, London, 1950.

Hitti, Philip K., *History of the Arabs*, 5th edition, London and New York, 1950.

Hurgronje, C. Snouck, *The Achenese*, 2 vols., Leiden, 1906.

———, *Selected Works*, edited in English and French by G. H. Bousquet and J. Schacht, Leiden, 1957.

Hussein, Mirzā Muhammad, *Islam and Socialism*, Lahore, 1946.

Jeffery, Arthur, *Islam, Muhammad and His Religion*, New York, 1958.

———, *Reader in Islam*, The Hague, 1962.

Jomier, Jacques, *Bible et Coran*, Paris, 1959.

———, *La Place du Coran dans la Vie Quotidienne en Egypte*, Tunis, 1952.

———, *Le Commentaire Coranique du Manar—Tendances Modernes de l'Exégèse Coranique en Egypte*, Paris, 1955.

Lammens, Henri, *Islam, Beliefs and Institutions*, trans. from the French by E. Denison Ross, London, 1929.

Lane-Poole, Stanley, *Studies in a Mosque*, London, 1893.

Laoust, Henri, *Le Califat dans la Doctrine de Rachid Rida*, Beirut, 1938.

Levy, Reuben, *The Social Structure of Islam*, London, 1957.

McCarthy, Richard J., *The Theology of Al-Ash'arī*, Beirut, 1953.

Macdonald, Duncan B., *Aspects of Islam*, New York, 1911.

——, *Religious Attitude and Life in Islam*, Chicago, 1909.

Margoliouth, David S., *Mohammed*, London, 1905.

——, *Early Development of Muhammadanism*, London, 1914.

Masson, D., *Le Coran et la Revelation Judéo-Chrétienne*, Paris, 1958.

Maudūdī, Abū-l-'Alā, *Towards Understanding Islam*, trans. from the Urdu, Lahore, 1940.

——, *Islamic Law and Constitution*, Karachi, 1955.

Merchant, Muhammad Valibhai, *Quranic Laws*, Lahore, n.d.

Michaud, Henri, *Jésus selon le Coran*, Paris, 1957.

Michel, B., and 'Abd al-Rāziq, Mustafā, *Risālat al-Tawhīd* (of Muhammad 'Abduh), trans. into French, with an introduction, Paris, 1925.

Morgan, Kenneth W., *Islam, The Straight Path*, London, 1958.

Muir, William, *Life of Mahomet*, 4 vols., London, 1858-61. New edition abridged, Edinburgh, 1923.

Nicholson, Reynold A., *Literary History of the Arabs*, 2nd edition, Cambridge, 1930.

Nöldeke, Theodor, *Geschichte des Qurans*, 2nd edition, Leipzig, 1909-38.

Padwick, Constance E., *Muslim Devotions*, London, 1961.

Pai, Yūsuf Ahmad, *Communism and Islam*, Delhi, 1935.

Parrinder, Geoffrey, *Religion in an African City*, London, 1953.

Qureishī, Anwār Iqbāl, *Islam and the Theory of Interest*, Lahore, n.d.

Rahbar, David, *God of Justice, Ethical Doctrine of the Quran*, Leiden, 1960.

Rahman, F., *Prophecy in Islam*, London, 1958.

Ramadān, Sa'īd, *Islamic Law*, London, 1961.

Roberts, Robert, *The Social Laws of the Quran*, London, 1925.

Sale, George, *The Koran*, introductory essay and translation. Many editions.

Sarwar, Hāfiz Ghulām, *The Holy Quran*, Singapore, 1929.

——, *The Philosophy of the Quran*, Lahore, 1938.

——, *Life of the Holy Prophet*, Lahore, 1937.

Schacht, Joseph, *The Origins of Muhammadan Jurisprudence*, Oxford, 1950.

Schroeder, Eric, *Muhammad's People*, Portland, Maine, 1955.

Schuon, Frithjof, *Comprendre l'Islam*, Paris, 1961.

Sell, Edward, *The Faith of Islam*, 4th edition, London, 1920.

——, *Studies in Islam,* Madras, 1928.

Sen, Ajit Kumar, *The Islamic State and other Political Essays,* Calcutta, 1950.

Siddīqī, Mazharuddīn, *Marxism or Islam?,* Hyderabad, 1951.

Stanton, H. U. Weilbrecht, *The Teaching of the Qur'ān,* London, 1919.

Subhān, John, *Sufism, Its Saints and Shrines,* Lucknow, 1938.

Sweetman, J. Windrow, *Islam and Christian Theology,* London, part I, vol. 1, 1945: part I, vol. 2, 1947: part II, vol. 1, 1955.

Tapiero, E., *Le Dogme et les Rites de l'Islam par les Textes,* Paris, 1957.

Tritton, Arthur S., *Islam, Belief and Practices,* London, 1951.

——, *Muslim Theology,* London, 1947.

Vaux, Carra da, *Gazali,* Paris, 1902.

——, *Les Penseurs de l'Islam,* 5 vols., Paris, 1926.

Waardenburg, Jean-Jacques, *L'Islam dans le Miroir de l'Occident,* The Hague, 1963.

Watt, W. Montgomery, *Free Will and Predestination in Early Islam,* London, 1948.

——, *Islamic Philosophy and Theology,* Edinburgh, 1962.

——, *Muhammad at Mecca,* Oxford, 1953.

——, *Muhammad at Medina,* London, 1956.

Wensinck, Arthur J., *The Muslim Creed,* Cambridge, 1932.

——, *A Handbook of Early Muhammadan Tradition,* Leiden, 1960.

——, *La Pensée de Ghazzali,* Paris, 1940.

Westermarck, E. A., *Pagan Survivals in Mohammedan Civilization,* London, 1933.

Williams, John A., *Islam,* London, 1961.

Ziadeh, Nicola A., *Sānūsīyah, A Study of a Revivalist Movement in Islam,* Leiden, 1958.

Zwemer, Samuel M., *Studies in Popular Islam,* London, 1939.

PART III

'Abd al-Jalīl, J. M., *Islam et Nous,* Paris, 1947.

——, *Marie et l'Islam,* Paris, 1950.

Addison, James T., *The Christian Approach to the Moslem,* New York, 1942.

Ammar, Hamid, *Growing up in an Egyptian Village,* New York, 1954.

Ashby, Philip H., *The Conflict of Religions,* New York, 1955.

Basetté-Sani, Giulio, *Muhammad et Saint Francis,* Ottawa, 1959.

Bates, M. Searle, *Religious Liberty,* New York, 1945.

Bethmann, Erich W., *Bridge to Islam,* Nashville, Tenn., 1950.

——, and Ziada M. Mustafā, editors, *Proceedings of the First Muslim-Christian Convocation* (Bhamdoun) , New York, 1956.

Bishop, Eric F. F., *Jesus of Palestine,* London, 1955.

Blanke, Fritz, *L'Islam, Problème Missionnaire*, Lausanne, 1946.

Bliss, Frederick J., *The Religions of Modern Syria and Palestine*, Edinburgh, 1912.

Brown, David A., *The Way of the Prophet*, London, 1962.

Browne, Laurence E., *The Prospects of Islam*, London, 1944.

——, *The Quickening Word*, Cambridge, 1955.

Bulgakov, Sergius, *The Orthodox Church*, London, 1935.

Burnaby, John, *Christian Words and Christian Meanings*, New York, 1955.

Cash, W. Wilson, *Christendom and Islam*, London, 1937.

Courtois, V., *Mary in Islam*, Calcutta, 1954.

Daniel, Norman, *Islam and the West, The Making of an Image*, Edinburgh, 1960.

Danielou, Jean, *Le Mystère du Salut des Nations*, Paris, 1948.

Dehqani-Tafti, Hassan, *Design of My World*, London, 1959.

De Lubac, Henri, *Le Fondement Théologique des Missions*, Paris, 1946.

Dib, Muhammad, *La Grande Maison*, Paris, 1952.

Dorman, H. G., Jr., *Towards Understanding Islam, Contemporary Apologetic of Islam and Missionary Policy*, New York, 1948.

Esin, Emil, *Mecca and Medina*, London, 1963.

Farūqi, Ismā'īl R. A. al, *On Arabism, 'Urūbah and Religion*, Amsterdam, 1962.

Fazlu-Rahmān, M., *Islam and Christianity in the Modern World*, Aligarh, 1943.

Fleming, Daniel J., *Living as Comrades*, New York, 1950.

——, *Each with His Own Brush*, New York, 1938.

French, R. M., *The Eastern Orthodox Church*, London, 1951.

Gairdner, W. H. Temple, *W.H.T.G. to His Friends*, London, 1930.

——, *God as Triune, Creator, Incarnate, Atoner*, Madras, 1916.

——, *The Gospel of Barnabas*, Cairo, 1907.

——, *The Muslim Idea of God*, 1909.

——, *Inspiration, A Dialogue*, Cairo, 1909.

——, *Inspiration, Christian and Islamic*, Cairo, 1913.

——, *Ecce Homo Arabicus*, Cairo, 1918.

——, and Eddy, W. H., "Christianity and Islam" in *The Christian Life and Message, in Relation to Non-Christian Systems*, being Vol. 1 of the Jerusalem Report, London, 1928, pp. 235-83.

Garlick, Phyllis L., *Man's Search for Health*, London, 1952.

Harries, Lyndon P., *Islam in East Africa*, London, 1954.

Hayek, Emile, *Le Christ de l'Islam*, Paris, 1959.

Hocking, William E., *Spirit of World Politics*, New York, 1932.

——, *Living Religions and a World Faith*, New York, 1940.

Husain, Taha, *An Egyptian Childhood,* trans. from the Arabic by E. H. Paxton, London, 1932, being Part 1 of *Al-Ayyām.*

——, *A Student at the Azhar,* trans. from the Arabic by Hilary Wayment, London, 1948, being Part 2 of *Al-Ayyām.*

Hussein, Kamel, *City of Wrong,* trans. Kenneth Cragg, Amsterdam, 1959.

Jones, L. Bevan, *The People of the Mosque,* London, 1932.

——, *Christianity Explained to Muslims,* Calcutta, 1938.

Jurji, Edward J., *The Christian Interpretation of Religion,* New York, 1952.

Khān, Sayyid Ahmad, *The Mohamedan Commentary on the Holy Bible,* Ghazipur, 1862.

Kraemer, Hendrick, *The Christian Message in a Non-Christian World,* London, 1938.

Leeuwen, A. T. van, *Christianity in World History,* London, 1964.

Levonian, Lootfi, *Studies in the Relationship between Christianity and Islam,* London, 1940.

Lings, Martin, *A Moslem Saint of the 20th Century, Shaikh Ahmad al-'Alāwī,* London, 1961.

Najafi, Najmeh, *Persia Is My Heart,* as told to Helen Hinckley, New York, 1953.

Neill, S. C., *Christian Faith and Other Faiths,* London, 1961.

Oldham, J. H., *Life Is Commitment,* London, 1953.

Padwick, Constance E., *Call to Istanbul,* London, 1958.

——, *Henry Martyn, Confessor of the Faith,* London, 1923.

——, *Temple Gairdner of Cairo,* London, 1928.

——, *With Him in His Temptations,* London, 1949.

Pannikar, K., *Asia and Western Dominance,* London, 1955.

Peake, A. S., and Parsons, R. G., *Outline of Christianity,* Vol. 5, see: Bukhsh, S. Khuda, "A Muslim View of Christianity," pp. 253 *seq.*

Peers, E. Allison, *Ramon Lull,* London, 1929.

Pennell, Alice M., *Pennell of the Afghan Frontier,* London, 1914.

Penrose, Stephen L. B., *That They May Have Life* (The Story of the American University of Beirut) , New York, 1941.

Perowne, Stewart, *The One Remains,* London, 1954.

Riggs, Alice S., *Shepard of Aintab,* New York, 1920.

Robson, James, *Christ in Islam,* London, 1930.

Rondot, Pierre, *Les Chrétiens d'Orient,* Paris, 1955.

Runciman, Steven, *History of the Crusades,* 3 vols., Cambridge, 1954.

Shah, Sirdar Iqbāl 'Alī, *Lights of Asia,* London, 1934.

Simon, Gottfried, *Die Welt des Islams und Ihre Berühringen, mit den Christenheit,* Gütersloer, 1948.

Slater, Robert L., *World Religions and World Community,* New York,

1963.

Smith, Henry P., *The Bible and Islam*, London, 1897.

Smith, Mary, *Baba of Karo*, London, 1954.

Suratgar, Olive, *I Sing in the Wilderness*, London, 1951.

Sweetman, J. Windrow, *The Bible in Islam*, London, 1953.

Trimingham, J. Spencer, *The Christian Approach to Islam in the Sudan*, London, 1948.

——, *The Christian Church and Islam in West Africa*, London, 1955.

Trotter, Lilias, *The Master of the Impossible*, arranged by Constance E. Padwick, London, 1938.

Tyndale-Biscoe of Kashmir, An Autobiography, London, 1956.

Ure, Ruth, *The Highway of Print*, New York, 1946.

Voillaume, R., *Seeds of the Desert*, London, 1958.

Warburton, Mabel C., *The Mind and Ways of Islam*, London, 1948.

Warren, Max A. C., *The Truth of Vision*, London, 1948.

——, *The Christian Imperative*, London, 1955.

——, *Caesar, The Beloved Enemy*, Chicago, 1955.

——, editor, *The Triumph of God*, London, 1949.

Wilson, J. Christy, *Apostle to Islam, A Biography of Samuel M. Zwemer*, Grand Rapids, 1952.

——, *The Christian Message to Islam*, New York, 1950.

Zwemer, Samuel M., *The Moslem Doctrine of God*, New York, 1905.

——, *The Moslem Christ*, London, 1912.

371